SCJA Sun® Certified Java™ Associate Study Guide

(Exam CX-310-019)

Robert Liguori
Edward Finegan

New York Chicago San Francisco Lisbon London Madrid
Mexico City Milan New Delhi San Juan Seoul Singapore Sydney Toronto

The McGraw·Hill Companies

Cataloging-in-Publication Data is on file with the Library of Congress

McGraw-Hill books are available at special quantity discounts to use as premiums and sales promotions, or for use in corporate training programs. To contact a representative, please e-mail us at bulksales@mcgraw-hill.com.

SCJA Sun® Certified Java™ Associate Study Guide (Exam CX-310-019)

1234567890   DOC DOC   019

ISBN: Book p/n 978-0-07149004-7 and CD p/n 978-0-07-149006-1
of set 978-0-07-149003-0

MHID: Book p/n 0-07-149004-3 and CD p/n 0-07-149006-X
of set 0-07-149003-5

Sponsoring Editor Timothy Green	**Technical Editor** Alistair Grieve	**Indexer** Karin Arrigoni	**Illustration** International Typesetting and Composition
Editorial Supervisor Jody McKenzie	**Acquisitions Coordinator** Meghan Riley	**Production Supervisor** James Kussow	**Art Director, Cover** Jeff Weeks
Project Manager Vipra Fauzdar, International Typesetting and Composition	**Copy Editor** Michael McGee **Proofreader** Paul Tyler	**Composition** International Typesetting and Composition	**Cover Series Design** Peter Grame

ABOUT THE AUTHORS

Robert Liguori is a Senior Software Engineer and has been developing, maintaining, and testing air traffic management systems since 1996. He is currently architecting, designing, developing, and maintaining Java EE E-business systems and Java-based air traffic management systems. Mr. Liguori is a Senior Software Engineer with MetaTec Group, Inc.

Mr. Liguori has a bachelor's degree in computer science and information technology from Richard Stockton College of New Jersey. He is the founder and president of the Atlantic City Java User Group (ACJUG) supporting the southern New Jersey area (http://acjug.dev.java.net). He is a Sun Certified Java Associate (SCJA) and Sun Certified Java Programmer (SCJP) and is currently pursuing various other Sun certifications.

For the better part of 2007, Mr. Liguori spent his free time with his wife co-authoring a handy Java reference guide: *Java Pocket Guide*, by Robert and Patricia Liguori (O'Reilly Media Inc., 2008). It succeeded in capturing Java's fundamentals in a companion-size book.

Mr. Liguori enjoys spending time with his family, as well as surf fishing for striped bass and red drum along the East Coast of the United States.

He can be contacted at robert@scjaexam.com.

Edward Finegan is a Senior Java Software Developer and is currently working in the casino gaming industry where he designs and implements software for gaming machines. He has previous experience in air traffic management systems and radar protocols.

Mr. Finegan has a bachelor's degree in computer science from Rowan University, and a master's degree in computer science from Virginia Commonwealth University. His thesis was entitled *Intelligent Autonomous Data Categorization*, which examined the possibility of using machine-learning algorithms to intelligently and autonomously categorize data. He is also a Sun Certified Java Professional.

Mr. Finegan is an avid Philadelphia sports fan. He enjoys outdoor activities and home-improvement projects, as well as tinkering with the latest technologies.

He can be contacted at edward@scjaexam.com.

About the Technical Editor

Alistair Grieve started his career as a Tandem NonStop COBOL programmer. Since then, he has worked for more than 20 years as a software developer and database administrator, primarily in the financial services sector, in the UK, the U.S.A., and New Zealand. He is also a freelance technical editor.

Mr. Grieve is an engineering science graduate of the University of Oxford. He is a Sun Certified Java Programmer (SCJP) and Web Component Developer (SCWCD), as well as an Oracle Certified Professional (OCP) database administrator.

He can be contacted at techedit@gmx.com.

About LearnKey

LearnKey provides self-paced learning content and multimedia delivery solutions to enhance personal skills and business productivity. LearnKey claims the largest library of rich streaming-media training content that engages learners in dynamic media-rich instruction, complete with video clips, audio, full motion graphics, and animated illustrations. LearnKey can be found on the Web at www.LearnKey.com.

CONTENTS AT A GLANCE

Part I
Fundamental Java Elements

1	Packaging, Compiling, and Interpreting Java Code	3
2	Programming with Java Statements	41
3	Programming with Java Operators and Strings	81

Part II
Object-Oriented Basic Concepts

4	Working with Basic Classes and Variables	129
5	Understanding Variable Scope and Class Construction	161
6	Working with Classes and Their Relationships	187
7	Understanding Class Inheritance	215
8	Understanding Polymorphism	259
9	Representing Object-Oriented Concepts with UML	289

Part III
Java-Related Platforms and Technologies

10	Understanding Java-Related Platforms and Integration Technologies	323
11	Understanding Client-Side Technologies	359
12	Understanding Server-Side Technologies	387

vii

Part IV
Appendixes

A   About the CD   419

B   Exam-Related Packages and Classes   425

C   Unicode Standard   429

D   Bracket Conventions   433

     Glossary   435

     Index   449

CONTENTS

Acknowledgments . . . . *xvii*

Preface . . . . *xix*

Introduction . . . . *xxv*

Part I
Fundamental Java Elements

1   Packaging, Compiling, and Interpreting Java Code **3**

Understanding Packages   4

    Package Design   5

    `package` and `import` Statements   6

    Exercise 1-1: Replacing Implicit `import` Statements
    with Explicit `import` Statements   9

Understanding Package-Derived Classes   11

    Java Utilities API   12

    Java Basic Input/Output API   14

    The Java Networking API   14

    Java Abstract Window Toolkit API   15

    Java Swing API   15

    Exercise 1-2: Understanding Extended Functionality
    of the Java Utilities API   17

Compiling and Interpreting Java Code   19

    Java Compiler   19

    Java Interpreter   22

    Exercise 1-3: Compiling and Interpreting
    Packaged Software   26

    ✓   Two-Minute Drill   29

Q&A   Self Test   31

    Self Test Answers   34

2   Programming with Java Statements **41**

Understanding Fundamental Statements 43

Assignment Statements 44

Conditional Statements 46

Iteration Statements 54

Exercise 2-1: Iterating Through an `ArrayList`
While Applying Conditions 58

Exercise 2-2: Performing Code Refactoring 60

Implementing Statement-Related Algorithms from Pseudo-code 61

Pseudo-code Algorithms 62

Exercise 2-3: Knowing Your Statement-Related
Keywords 63

Pseudo-code Algorithms and Java 65

Exercise 2-4: Implementing Pseudo-code Algorithm #1 66

Exercise 2-5: Implementing Pseudo-code Algorithm #2 66

Exercise 2-6: Implementing Pseudo-code Algorithm #3 67

✓ Two-Minute Drill 68

Q&A Self Test 70

Self Test Answers 74

3   Programming with Java Operators and Strings **81**

Understanding Fundamental Operators 82

Assignment Operators 84

Exercise 3-1: Using Compound Assignment Operators 85

Arithmetic Operators 87

Relational Operators 89

Logical Operators 92

Developing with String Objects and Their Methods 95

Strings 95

The String Concatenation Operator 97

Exercise 3-2: Uncovering Bugs that Your
Compiler May Not Find 100

Methods of the `String` Class 101

✓ Two-Minute Drill 109

Q&A Self Test 112

Self Test Answers 118

Part II
Object-Oriented Basic Concepts

4 **Working with Basic Classes and Variables** **129**

Understanding Primitives, Enumerations, and Objects 130
    Primitives 130
    Objects 134
    Exercise 4-1: Compile and Run an Object 137
    Arrays 138
    Enumerations 139
    Java Is Strongly Typed 140
    Naming Conventions 141
Practical Uses of Primitives, Enumerations, and Objects 142
    Literals 142
    Examples of Primitives, Enumerations, and Objects 143
   ✓ Two-Minute Drill 148
Q&A Self Test 149
    Self Test Answers 153

5 **Understanding Variable Scope and**
    Class Construction **161**

Understanding Variable Scope 162
    Local Variables 162
    Method Parameters 165
    Instance Variables 165
Constructing Methods 168
    Method Inputs 168
    Method Outputs 172
   ✓ Two-Minute Drill 175
Q&A Self Test 176
    Self Test Answers 180

6 **Working with Classes and Their Relationships** **187**

Understanding Class Compositions and Associations 188
    Class Compositions and Associations 188
    Class Relationships 190

Multiplicities 193
Association Navigation 195
Class Compositions and Associations in Practice 195
Examples of Class Association Relationships 196
Examples of Class Composition Relationships 199
Examples of Association Navigation 200
✓ Two-Minute Drill 203
Q&A Self Test 205
Self Test Answers 209

7 Understanding Class Inheritance **215**

Inheritance and Class Type 216
Inheritance 216
Overriding Methods 220
Abstract Classes 221
Interfaces 222
Advanced Concepts of Inheritance 224
Encapsulation 225
Good Design with Encapsulation 226
Access Modifiers 227
Setters and Getters 230
Advanced Examples of Classes with Inheritance and Encapsulation ... 231
Examples of Java Access Modifiers 232
Examples of Inheritance with Concrete Classes 233
Examples of Inheritance with Abstract Classes 235
Exercise 7-1: Add Functionality to the Plant Simulator 242
Examples of Interfaces 242
✓ Two-Minute Drill 246
Q&A Self Test 248
Self Test Answers 252

8 Understanding Polymorphism **259**

Polymorphism 260
Polymorphism 260
Programming to an Interface 264
Practical Examples of Polymorphism 265
Examples of Polymorphism 265

Exercise 8-1:   Add Functionality to
the Describable Example   272
Examples of Programming to an Interface   273
✓   Two-Minute Drill   278
Q&A   Self Test   279
Self Test Answers   283

**9   Representing Object-Oriented
Concepts with UML 289**
Recognizing Representations of Significant UML Elements   292
Classes, Abstract Classes, and Interface Diagrams   293
Attributes and Operations   295
Visibility Modifiers   298
Exercise 9-1:   Creating a Basic UML Diagram
with a UML Tool   299
Recognizing Representations of UML Associations   301
Graphic Paths   302
Exercise 9-2:   Hand-Drawing UML Diagrams from
the Java API Specification   304
Relationship Specifiers   305
✓   Two-Minute Drill   309
Q&A   Self Test   311
Self Test Answers   315

**Part III
Java-Related Platforms and Technologies**

**10   Understanding Java-Related Platforms
and Integration Technologies 323**
Understanding Java Platforms   326
Java Platform, Standard Edition   327
Java 2 Platform, Micro Edition   331
Java Platform, Enterprise Edition   333
Exercise 10-1:   Embracing Java Technology Forums as
Valuable Information Resources   336
Working with the Java Remote Method Invocation API   337
The Java Remote Method Invocation API   337

Working with Database Technologies 340
    Relational Database Management Systems 340
    Structured Query Language 341
    The Java Database Connectivity API 341
Working with Additional Java Integration APIs 342
    The Java Naming and Directory Interface API 342
    The Java Message Service API 344
   ✓ Two-Minute Drill 346
Q&A Self Test 348
    Self Test Answers 352

11 Understanding Client-Side Technologies **359**
Using Thin Clients with HTML and the JavaScript API 360
    HyperText Markup Language 361
    JavaScript API 362
    Thin Clients 363
    Thin-Client Disadvantages 363
    Thin-Client Deployment 364
Using J2ME MIDlets 364
    J2ME and MIDlets 365
    Configurations and Profiles 367
    J2ME Disadvantages 368
    J2ME Deployment 368
Using Java Applets as Fat Clients 369
    Java Applets 369
    Java Applet Disadvantages 370
    Java Applet Deployment 371
Using the Java Swing API as a Fat Client 371
    Java Swing API 372
    Java Swing API Disadvantages 373
    Java Swing API Deployment 373
   ✓ Two-Minute Drill 375
Q&A Self Test 377
    Self Test Answers 380

12 Understanding Server-Side Technologies **387**
Understanding Java EE–Related Tiers and Technologies 389
    Pros and Cons of the Server Side 389
    Enterprise Tiers 391

Understanding Server-Side Solutions 393

    Java Web Services 394

    SMTP and the JavaMail API 396

    Java API for XML-Based Remote Procedure Call 398

Understanding Dynamic Web Content Solutions 399

    Java Servlet API 400

    JavaServer Pages API 402

    Exercise 12-1: Creating Servlets, JSP Pages, and JSF Pages 402

Understanding Enterprise Business Logic Solutions 404

    Enterprise JavaBeans API 404

    ✓ Two-Minute Drill 407

Q&A Self Test 409

    Self Test Answers 412

Part IV
Appendixes

A About the CD **419**

B Exam-Related Packages and Classes **425**

C Unicode Standard **429**

D Bracket Conventions **433**

Glossary **435**

Index **449**

ACKNOWLEDGMENTS

The SCJA exam covers a significant amount of information detailing areas from basic object-oriented concepts to integration technologies. To complete a voluminous project like this book, covering all of the related objectives, the authors decided to take the divide-and-conquer approach by splitting up the chapters based on their individual expertise.

Mr. Liguori focused on three areas he had a heightened interest in: Java-related technologies, core Java fundamentals, and the Unified Modeling Language (UML). As such, he headed up Chapters 10 and 12 on Java-related technologies, the three Java-basics chapters in Part I, and Chapter 9 on UML.

Mr. Finegan specialized in object-oriented features while getting his master's. So heading up Part II on object-oriented basic concepts came naturally to him. Ed has also spent a lot of time on the client side building many diverse user-oriented applications. Therefore, writing Chapter 11 on client-side technologies was also a perfect fit.

Collectively, the authors would like to thank all of the people who have played technical roles in the development of this book, including:

- Timothy Green, McGraw-Hill Professional acquisitions editor
- Meghan Riley, McGraw-Hill Professional acquisitions coordinator
- Jody McKenzie, McGraw-Hill Professional editorial supervisor
- Jim Kussow, McGraw-Hill Professional production supervisor
- Alistair Grieve, technical editor
- Melinda Lytle, production consultant
- Vipra Fauzdar, ITC project manager
- The International Typesetting and Composition production team
- Shannon Reilly, informal reviewer
- Wayne Smith, informal reviewer
- Michael McGee, copy editor
- Paul Tyler, proofreader

This book project was made possible for us largely in part by the folks at Waterside Productions, Inc. (www.watersidesyndication.com/agency/). We would like to thank the Waterside team, specifically our agent for this book: Carole Jelen McClendon.

A critical piece related to the successful completion of any project is the source of inspiration and encouragement. Acknowledgment and thanks go out to those people who have provided emotional and spiritual support. As such, Mr. Liguori would like to acknowledge his parents and family as well as Edward Barski, Robert Cartier, Adrian Clunn, Edward Finegan, Brian Hartley, John Herouvis, Kenneth Johnson, Chris Loeb, James Michaelidis, John Michaelidis, Jayne Reinhard, Chad Sherwood, Jim Snyder, Martin Suech, Shelby and Petie. Mr. Finegan would like to acknowledge the following people for their support, patience, and inspiration: Ed J. Finegan and Denise Finegan (parents), Ben Lewitt (grandfather), Shannon Reilly (fiancée), Tim Reilly, Diane Reilly, Robert Liguori, Ed Busser, Geoff Gelay, David Primeaux, Ganesh Baliga, and Raven Finegan.

Finally, a special recognition goes out to Java, the Shearn family's Vizsla, for keeping everyone smiling.

PREFACE

The purpose of this study guide is to prepare you for the Sun Certified Java Associate exam. This preparation will be accomplished by familiarizing you with the necessary knowledge related to Java fundamentals, tools, and technologies that will be represented on the exam. The scope of this book is to help you pass the exam. As such, objective-specific areas are detailed throughout this book. Peripheral information, which is not needed to pass the exam, may not be included, or may be presented in a limited fashion. Since this book covers a lot of information on the fundamentals of Java and related technologies, you may also wish to use it as a general reference guide away from the certification process.

Achieving the SCJA Java certification will solidify your knowledge of the Java programming language, set the foundation for your evolvement through the related technologies, and mark you as a Java professional. We strongly recommend the SCJA certification to the following candidates:

- Entry-level and junior programmers wishing to start and/or continue down the path of using Java technologies

- Software developers and technical leads wishing to solidify their Java-related skillsets

- Project and program managers wishing to gain a true perspective of the work and challenge of their teams, complementary to their planning and direction

- Computer science and information system students wishing to complement their education

- IT job seekers looking for a well-deserved edge

- Certification seekers wishing to round out their resume or curriculum vitae

The Sun certification series for Java has various exams at different levels, as detailed in Table 1. Even though the SCJA exam is not required to take other

TABLE I   Java Certification Books

Exam Name and Abbreviation	Prerequisite	Level of Expertise	Directly Related Study and Reference Material
Sun Certified Java Associate (SCJA)	None	Entry-level	*Sun Certified Java Associate Study Guide*, by Robert Liguori and Edward Finegan (McGraw-Hill Professional, 2009)
Sun Certified Java Programmer (SCJP)	None	Foundational	*Sun Certified Programmer for Java 6 Study Guide*, by Kathy Sierra and Bert Bates (McGraw-Hill Professional, 2008)
Sun Certified Java Developer (SCJD)	SCJP	Specialty	*SCJD Exam with J2SE 5*, Second Edition, by Terry Camerlengo and Andrew Monkhouse (Apress, 2005)
Sun Certified Web Component Developer (SCWCD)	SCJP	Specialty	*Sun Certified Web Component Developer Study Guide*, by David Bridgewater (McGraw-Hill Professional, 2005)
Sun Certified Business Component Developer (SCBCD)	SCJP	Specialty	*Head First EJB*, by Kathy Sierra and Bert Bates (O'Reilly Media Inc., 2003)
Sun Certified Developer for Java Web Services (SCDJWS)	SCJP	Specialty	*J2EE Web Services: XML SOAP WSDL UDDI WS-I JAX-RPC JAXR SAAJ JAXP*, by Richard Monson-Haefel (Addison-Wesley Professional, 2003)
Sun Certified Mobile Application Developer (SCMAD)	SCJP	Specialty	*J2ME: The Complete Reference*, by James Edward Keogh (McGraw-Hill Professional, 2003)
Sun Certified Enterprise Architect (SCEA)	None	Advanced	*Sun Certified Enterprise Architect for Java EE Study Guide*, by Paul R. Allen and Joseph J. Bambara (McGraw-Hill Professional, 2007)

exams, it is the starting point in the series. Once you have acquired the certification, it provides a strong basis of knowledge with the Java language and supporting technologies.

Figure 1 shows Java certification books published by McGraw-Hill Professional in the same series as this book. These books provide strong learning materials directly geared towards the individual exams. The series also includes exams on many other certifications, including Sun's Solaris operating system in *Sun Certified System Administrator for Solaris 10 Study Guide* (Exams 310-200 and 310-202) by Paul Sanghera (McGraw-Hill Professional, 2005).

Additional
McGraw-Hill
Java certification
books

In This Book

The book is broken into four main parts. The first part covers Java fundamentals including development tools, basic constructs, operators, and strings. The second part dives right into object-oriented concepts, covering classes, class relationships, and object-oriented principles. UML modeling of these concepts is also covered. Part three discusses integration, client-side, and server-side technologies relative to their respective Java platforms. Part four wraps things up with notes on exam-related packages and classes, the Unicode standard, bracket conventions, and a useful glossary.

On the CD

The CD-ROM includes the CD exam, source code represented in the book, and the Enterprise Architect project file containing the UML diagrams that were rendered and used as draft images for the book (shown in Figure 2). For detailed information on the CD-ROM, please see Appendix A at the back of the book.

Exam Readiness Checklist

At the end of the Introduction you will find an Exam Readiness Checklist. This table has been constructed to allow you to cross-reference the official exam objectives with the objectives as they are presented and covered in this book. The checklist also lets you gauge your level of expertise on each objective at the outset of your studies. This should allow you to check your progress and make sure you spend the time you need on more difficult or unfamiliar sections. References have been provided for the objective exactly as the vendor presents it, the section of the study guide that covers that objective, and a chapter and page reference.

FIGURE 2 Enterprise Architect CASE tool

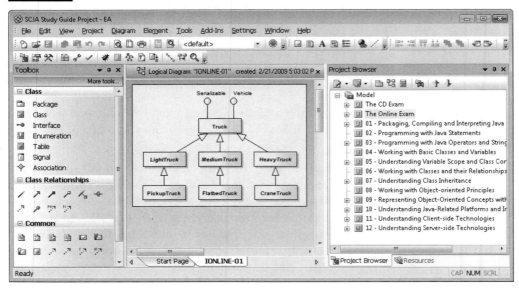

In Every Chapter

We've created a set of chapter components that call your attention to important items, reinforce important points, and provide helpful exam-taking hints. Take a look at what you'll find in every chapter:

- Every chapter begins with **Certification Objectives**—what you need to know in order to pass the section on the exam dealing with the chapter topic. The Objective headings identify the objectives within the chapter, so you'll always know an objective when you see it!

- **Exam Watch** notes call attention to information about, and potential pitfalls in, the exam. These helpful hints are written by authors who have taken the exams and received their certification (Who better to tell you what to worry about?). They know what you're about to go through!

- **Step-by-Step Exercises** are interspersed throughout the chapters. These are typically designed as hands-on exercises that allow you to get a feel for the real-world experience you need in order to pass the exams. They help you master skills that are likely to be an area of focus on the exam. Don't just read through the exercises—they are hands-on practice that you should be comfortable completing. Learning by doing is an effective way to increase your competency with a product.

- **On the Job** notes describe the issues that come up most often in real-world settings. They provide a valuable perspective on certification- and product-related topics. They point out common mistakes and address questions that have arisen from on-the-job discussions and experience.

- **Inside the Exam** sidebars highlight some of the most common and confusing problems that students encounter when taking a live exam. Designed to anticipate what the exam will emphasize, getting inside the exam will help ensure you know what you need to know to pass the exam. You can get a leg up on how to respond to those difficult-to-understand questions by focusing extra attention on these sidebars.

- **Scenario & Solution** sections lay out potential problems and solutions in a quick-to-read format.

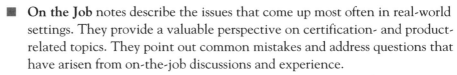

You wish to automate a business process using online forms and a relational database. Which Java editions would you use?	Java Platform, Standard Edition; and Java Platform, Enterprise Edition
You wish to develop an application to convert database records into XML files. Which Java edition would you use?	Java Platform, Standard Edition
You wish to develop a simple client-side text editor. Which Java edition would you use?	Java Platform, Standard Edition
You wish to develop a prize-fighting boxing game for use on a cell phone. Which Java edition would you use?	Java Platform, Micro Edition
You wish to develop a web-accessible application that also accesses a naming and directory service. Which Java editions would you use?	Java Platform, Standard Edition; and Java Platform, Enterprise Edition

- The **Certification Summary** is a succinct review of the chapter and a restatement of salient points regarding the exam.

- The **Two-Minute Drill** at the end of every chapter is a checklist of the main points of the chapter. It can be used for last-minute review.

- The **Self Test** offers questions similar to those found on the certification exams. The answers to these questions, as well as explanations of the answers, can be found at the end of each chapter. By taking the Self Test after completing each chapter, you'll reinforce what you've learned from that chapter while becoming familiar with the structure of the exam questions.

Some Pointers

Once you've finished reading this book, set aside some time to do a thorough review. You might want to return to the book several times and make use of all the methods it offers for reviewing the material:

- *Re-read all the Two-Minute Drills,* or have someone quiz you. You also can use the drills as a way to do a quick cram before the exam. You might want to make some flash cards out of 3×5 index cards that have the Two-Minute Drill material on them.

- *Re-read all the Exam Watch notes and Inside the Exam elements.* Remember that these notes are written by authors who have taken the exam and passed. They know what you should expect—and what you should be on the lookout for.

- *Review all the S&S sections* for quick problem solving.

- *Retake the Self Tests.* Taking the tests right after you've read the chapter is a good idea, because the questions help reinforce what you've just learned. However, it's an even better idea to go back later and do all the questions in the book in one sitting. Pretend that you're taking the live exam. When you go through the questions the first time, you should mark your answers on a separate piece of paper. That way, you can run through the questions as many times as you need to until you feel comfortable with the material.

- *Complete the Exercises.* Did you do the exercises when you read through each chapter? If not, do them! These exercises are designed to cover exam topics, and there's no better way to get to know this material than by practicing. Be sure you understand why you are performing each step in each exercise. If there is something you are not clear on, re-read that section in the chapter.

INTRODUCTION

This SCJA study guide has been designed to assist you in preparation of passing the Sun Certified Java Associate exam. The information in this book is presented through textual content, coding examples, exercises, and more. All code examples have been validated on Windows Vista and Macintosh OS X computers. Information is covered in detailed for all exam objectives. The main areas covered in this book are as listed:

- Java development and support tools
- Java fundamentals including statements, variables, method primitives, and operators
- Methods and functionality of the `String` class
- Basic Java elements including primitives, enumerations, and objects
- Classes and interfaces including class relationships
- Object-oriented principles
- The modeling of object-oriented concepts with the Unified Modeling Language
- Java platforms (Java SE, Java EE, Java ME)
- Basic tiers, including the client, middle, and EIS tiers
- Server-side and client-side technologies

Specifics about the SCJA Certification Exam

Specifics of the SCJA exam objectives are detailed on Sun's web site at www.sun .com/training/catalog/courses/CX-310-019.xml. Specifics about the exam process are supplied by Prometric when you enroll. However, we do detail in the following sections the important information you will need to know to enroll for and take the exam.

Dynamics of the SCJA Exam

The SCJA exam is geared towards entry-level Java programmers and program managers overseeing Java-rich efforts, who wish to achieve foundational Java certification. The prerequisite-free exam consists of 51 questions. A passing percentage of 68 percent is necessary—in other words, 35 of 51 questions. The designated time limit is one hour and fifty-five minutes. Multiple choice and a few drag-and-drop questions will be on the exam. The exam is given in English, German, Portuguese, Chinese (traditional and simplified), Japanese, Spanish, and Korean.

The current U.S. price to take the exam is $300. If you are employed by a technical organization, you can check to see if your company has an educational assistance policy. For education-related areas that do not return a "grade" such as an exam, the employers may require that you pass the exam with a certain percentage. You will receive your percentage immediately following the exam, plus you will be sent a detailed summary of how you did on the exam with an overall percentage, as well as percentages per objective. This information breakdown can be beneficial if you need to retake the exam or simply wish to restudy your weak areas. Sun allows you to publish your credentials through their certification manager web site at http://certmanager.net/sun/—thus, you should e-mail your certified results through their system to whomever you specify. It is important to note that this system only provides a pass or fail result, and not the actual percentage of how you scored.

Scheduling the SCJA Exam

You will need to perform two specific actions to schedule your exam. You will need to buy a voucher from Sun (www.sun.com/). More specifically, you can purchase the voucher from the Sun Education Services Office online at http://suned.sun.com/US/certification/register/. You will also need to sign up for the test with the purchased voucher through Prometric (www.prometric.com or http://www.2test.com/) since the exams are given by Prometric at Authorized Prometric Testing Centers.

Preparing for the SCJA Exam

Getting a good night's rest before the exam and eating a healthy breakfast will contribute to good test marks, but you should already know that. Don't cram for the exam the night before. If you find you need to cram, you should reschedule the exam since you are not ready for it.

You will need to bring a few things with you for the exam, *and* leave a few things behind. Let's take a look at some do's and don'ts.

Do's

- *Do* bring (at least) two forms of identification. Valid identification includes a valid passport, current driver's license, government-issued identification, credit cards, and check cashing cards. At least one item must include your photograph. Make sure you don't shorthand your signature when you sign in since it must match your identification.

- *Do* show up early, from fifteen minutes to a half hour before your exam's scheduled start time. You may find that the center needs to set up several people for exams. Getting in early may get you set up early, or at the least it will ensure that you don't start late.

- *Do* use the restroom ahead of time because the exam is close to two hours. Breaks are frowned upon and are most likely disallowed. In addition, you can't pause the time you have allocated if you take a break.

- *Do* print out directions to the test facility. Or get the address and punch it into your GPS navigator; if you have one.

Don'ts

- *Don't* bring writing supplies. This will be supplied at the facility. I have traditionally been given a small tabletop whiteboard with a dry erase marker for my exams. If for some reason you are not given this or something similar to use, just ask for it.

- *Don't* bring your laptop, cell phone, pager, or other similar device. You cannot phone a friend.

- *Don't* bring drinks or snacks since they are not allowed.

- *Don't* bring large items. Large storage may not be available for book bags and jackets. So the more items you can leave in your car, dorm, and so on, the less you'll have to worry about once you get to the testing facility. The testing facilities typically do have small securable lockers for your usage.

Taking the SCJA Exam

When you begin the exam, you may be presented with an optional computer-based survey. This survey will ask you about your technical background and other related information. A common misconception is that the answering of the questions may be related to which exam questions you will be presented with. Taking the survey is not related to the exam questions you will receive. The survey can take 20 to 30 minutes to complete. The information gathered is important for those developing and refining future exams, so answer the questions honestly.

After you have completed the exam, your results may or may not appear on the screen. In my case, I always had to wait for the testing personnel to retrieve my results from the printer before I knew what my results were. You will need to sign your results once completed. The point here is that *you should not leave* once you have completed the exam; stay and get your results.

Within a few weeks after your exam, you will receive a certificate, a pin, and a congratulation letter. If you should unfortunately somehow fail the exam, you will receive nothing, outside of the knowledge you gained. That's okay though, just sign up for the test again, study your weak areas, and give it another go.

Sun periodically runs a promotion where you get a free retake if you do happen to fail the exam. You may wish to look for or inquire about this promotion. However, if you do go through this book completely and thoroughly, you should do well enough on the exam to pass it with a high score. We would like to know how you did. You can send us an e-mail at results@scjaexam.com, or you can post your results on Java Ranch's Wall of Fame at http://faq.javaranch.com/java/ScjaWallOfFame.

Rescheduling the SCJA Exam

Rescheduling is easy. Just go to the Prometric site and follow the rescheduling prompts; it's an online process. It is not uncommon for work, school, personal events, and other priorities to delay your readiness for the exam. You may reschedule the exam as often as you like. Just make sure you reschedule your exam by 6:00 PM EST/EDT of the prior business day.

Additional SCJA Resources

Numerous resources can supplement this book in assisting you with your goal of SCJA certification. These resources include Java software utilities, Java community forums, language specifications and related documentation, SCJA-related books, online and purchasable mock exams, and UML modeling tools. While these peripheral tools and resources are highly beneficial and recommended, they are optional in regards to passing the SCJA exam since this book attempts to cover all of the necessary material.

The following sections detail the previously mentioned resources.

Java Software

- Java Development Kits, http://java.sun.com/products/archive/
- Java Enterprise Editions, http://java.sun.com/javaee/

Java Community Forums

- Java User Groups, http://java.sun.com/community/usergroups/
- Sun's Java developer forums, http://forums.sun.com/
- Java Ranch's Big Moose Saloon Java forums, including the SCJA forum, http://saloon.javaranch.com/

Java Tools and Technologies Specifications and Documentation

- Section 2.6 of the Java 2 Platform, Enterprise Edition Specification, v1.4 http://java.sun.com/j2ee/j2ee-1_4-fr-spec.pdf
- J2EE 1.4 Tutorial http://java.sun.com/j2ee/1.4/docs/tutorial/doc/
- Java 2 Platform, Micro Edition datasheet www.sun.com/aboutsun/media/presskits/ctia2004/J2ME.pdf
- Java Platform, Standard Edition 6 API Specification, http://java.sun.com/javase/6/docs/api/
- JDK 6 Documentation, http://java.sun.com/javase/6/docs/
- jDocs Java documentation repository, www.jdocs.com/
- UML specification, www.omg.org/spec/UML/Current/
- Java Language Specification, Third Edition, http://java.sun.com/docs/books/jls/

Books Covering Material Found on the SCJA Exam

While the book you are holding sufficiently covers everything you need to know to pass the exam, supplemental reading can only help. Consider reviewing the following books to refine your skills.

- *Java Pocket Guide*, by Robert and Patricia Liguori (O'Reilly Media Inc., 2008)
- *Java: The Complete Reference, Seventh Edition*, by Herbert Schildt (McGraw-Hill Professional, 2006)

- *Head First Java 2nd Edition*, by Kathy Sierra and Bert Bates (O'Reilly Media Inc., 2005)
- *SCJP Sun Certified Programmer for Java 6 Exam 310-065*, by Kathy Sierra and Bert Bates (McGraw-Hill Professional, 2008)
- *UML Distilled, 3rd Edition*, by Martin Fowler (Addison-Wesley, 2003)
- *SCJA Sun Certified Java Associate Study Guide for Test CX-310-019, 2nd Edition*, by Cameron W. McKenzie (PulpJava, 2007)
- *SCJA Sun Certified Java Associate Mock Exam Questions*, by Cameron W. McKenzie (PulpJava, 2007)

SCJA Mock Exams

In addition to the CD and online mock exams associated with this book, various other free and commercial SCJA mock exams exist. Various resources are listed here. As time goes by, this book cannot ensure the validity of these links.

- eJavaguru.com's online mock exam, www.ejavaguru.com/scjafreemockexam.php
- Enthuware's JAssPlus V1 mock exam software, www.enthuware.com/jassplus/
- SCJA.de e-book and online mock exam questions, http://scja.de/
- Sun's ePractice mock exam questions, www.sun.com/training/catalog/courses/ WGS-PREX-J019C.xml
- uCertify PrepKit and downloadable mock exam questions, www.ucertify .com/exams/SUN/CX310-019.html
- Whizlabs SCJA Preparation Kit, www.whizlabs.com/scja/scja.html

Tools with UML Modeling Features

Dozens of tools and IDEs have UML modeling features. A few are listed here.

- Enterprise Architect CASE tool
- Visual Paradigm for UML (provides plug-ins for the popular IDEs)
- Sun Java Studio Enterprise IDE
- NetBeans IDE

If you wish to get a rough idea of your current SCJA knowledge base, a good place to start is with Sun's SCJA proficiency assessment at www.sun.com/training/ certification/assessment/.

Sun's Certification Program in Java Technology

This section maps the exam's objectives to specific coverage in the study guide.

Exam Readiness Checklist						
Official Objective	**Study Guide Coverage**	**Ch #**	**Pg #**	**Beginner**	**Intermediate**	**Expert**
Fundamental Java Elements						
5.1 Describe the purpose of packages in the Java language.	Understanding Packages	1	4			
5.2 Describe the purpose and types of classes for the following Java packages: java.awt.	Understanding Package-Derived Classes	1	11			
5.3 Demonstrate the proper use of the "javac" command (including the command-line options: -d and –classpath).	Compiling and Interpreting Java Code	1	19			
4.1 Describe, compare, and contrast these three fundamental types of statements: assignment, conditional, and iteration, and given a description of an algorithm, select the appropriate type of statement to design the algorithm.	Understanding Fundamental Statements	2	43			
4.3 Given an algorithm as pseudo-code, develop method code that implements the algorithm using conditional statements (if and switch), iteration statements (for, for-each, while, and do-while), assignment statements, and break and continue statements to control the flow within switch and iteration statements.	Implementing Statement-Related Algorithms from Pseudo-code	2	61			
4.5 Given an algorithm as pseudo-code, develop code that correctly applies the appropriate operators, including assignment operators (limited to: =, +=, -=), arithmetic operators (limited to: +, -, *, /, %, ++, --), relational operators (limited to: <, <=, >, >=, ==, !=), logical operators (limited to: !, &&, ||) to produce a desired result. Also, write code that determines the equality of two objects or two primitives.	Understanding Fundamental Operators	3	82			
4.6 Develop code that uses the concatenation operator (+), and the following methods from the String class: charAt, indexOf, trim, substring, replace, length, startsWith, and endsWith.	Developing with String Objects and Their Methods	3	95			

Exam Readiness Checklist

Official Objective	Study Guide Coverage	Ch #	Pg #	Beginner	Intermediate	Expert
Object-Oriented Basic Concepts						
1.1 Describe, compare, and contrast primitives (integer, floating point, boolean, and character), enumeration types, and objects.	Understanding Primitives, Enumerations, and Objects	4	130			
3.1 Develop code that uses primitives, enumeration types, and object references, and recognize literals of these types.	Practical Uses of Primitives, Enumerations, and Objects	4	142			
4.2 Given an algorithm as pseudo-code, determine the correct scope for a variable used in the algorithm, and develop code to declare variables in any of the following scopes: instance variable, method parameter, and local variable.	Understanding Variable Scope	5	162			
4.4 Given an algorithm with multiple inputs and an output, develop method code that implements the algorithm using method parameters, a return type, and the return statement, and recognize the effects when object references and primitives are passed into methods that modify them.	Constructing Methods	5	168			
1.3 Describe, compare, and contrast class compositions, associations (including multiplicity—one-to-one, one-to-many, and many-to-many), and association navigation.	Understanding Class Compositions and Associations	6	188			
3.3 Develop code that implements simple class associations, code that implements multiplicity using arrays, and recognize code that implements compositions as opposed to simple associations, and code that correctly implements association navigation.	Class Compositions and Associations in Practice	6	195			
1.2 Describe, compare, and contrast concrete classes, abstract classes, and interfaces, and how inheritance applies to them.	Inheritance and Class Type	7	216			
1.4 Describe information hiding (using private attributes and methods), encapsulation, and exposing object functionality using public methods; and describe the JavaBeans conventions for setter and getter methods.	Encapsulation	7	225			

Exam Readiness Checklist

Official Objective	Study Guide Coverage	Ch #	Pg #	Beginner	Intermediate	Expert
3.2 Develop code that declares concrete classes, abstract classes, and interfaces, code that supports implementation and interface inheritance, code that declares instance attributes and methods, and code that uses the Java access modifiers: private and public.	Advanced Examples of Classes with Inheritance and Encapsulation	7	231			
1.5 Describe polymorphism as it applies to classes and interfaces, and describe and apply the "program to an interface" principle.	Polymorphism	8	260			
3.4 Develop code that uses polymorphism for both classes and interfaces, and recognize code that uses the "program to an interface" principle.	Practical Examples of Polymorphism	8	265			
2.1 Recognize the UML representation of classes (including attributes and operations, abstract classes, and interfaces), the UML representation of inheritance (both implementation and interface), and the UML representation of class member visibility modifiers (−/private and +/public).	Recognizing Representations of Significant UML Elements	9	292			
2.2 Recognize the UML representation of class associations, compositions, association multiplicity indicators, and association navigation indicators.	Recognizing Representations of UML Associations	9	301			
Object-Oriented Basic Concepts						
6.1 Distinguish the basic characteristics of the three Java platforms—J2SE, J2ME, and J2EE—and given a high-level architectural goal, select the appropriate Java platform or platforms.	Understanding Java Platforms	10	326			
6.2 Describe at a high level the benefits and basic characteristics of RMI.	Working with the Java Remote Method Invocation API	10	337			
6.3 Describe at a high level the benefits and basic characteristics of JDBC, SQL, and RDBMS technologies.	Working with Database Technologies	10	340			
6.4 Describe at a high level the benefits and basic characteristics of JNDI, messaging, and JMS technologies.	Working with Additional Java Integration APIs	10	342			

Exam Readiness Checklist

Official Objective	Study Guide Coverage	Ch #	Pg #	Beginner	Intermediate	Expert
7.1 Describe at a high level the basic characteristics, benefits, and drawbacks of creating thin clients using HTML and JavaScript and the related deployment issues and solutions.	Using Thin Clients with HTML and the JavaScript API	11	360			
7.2 Describe at a high level the basic characteristics, benefits, drawbacks, and deployment issues related to creating clients using J2ME MIDlets.	Using J2ME MIDlets.	11	364			
7.3 Describe at a high level the basic characteristics, benefits, drawbacks, and deployment issues related to creating fat clients using Applets.	Using Java Applets as Fat Clients	11	369			
7.4 Describe at a high level the basic characteristics, benefits, drawbacks, and deployment issues related to creating fat clients using Swing.	Using the Java Swing API as a Fat Client	11	371			
8.4 Describe at a high level the fundamental benefits and drawbacks of using J2EE server-side technologies, and describe and compare the basic characteristics of the web-tier, business-tier, and EIS tier.	Understanding Java EE–Related Tiers and Technologies	12	389			
8.1 Describe at a high level the basic characteristics of EJB, servlets, JSP, JMS, JNDI, SMTP, JAX-RPC, Web Services (including SOAP, UDDI, WSDL, and XML), and JavaMail.	Understanding Server-Side Solutions	12	393			
8.2 Describe at a high level the basic characteristics of servlet and JSP support for HTML thin clients.	Understanding Dynamic Web Content Solutions	12	399			
8.3 Describe at a high level the use and basic characteristics of EJB session, entity, and message-driven beans.	Understanding Enterprise Business Logic Solutions	12	404			

Part I

Fundamental Java Elements

CHAPTERS

1   Packaging, Compiling, and Interpreting
      Java Code

2   Programming with Java Statements

3   Programming with Java Operators and Strings

1

Packaging, Compiling, and Interpreting Java Code

CERTIFICATION OBJECTIVES

- Understanding Packages

- Understanding Package-Derived Classes

- Compiling and Interpreting Java Code

 Two-Minute Drill

Q&A Self Test

Since you are holding this book or reading an electronic version of it, you must have an affinity for Java. You must also have the desire to let everyone know through the Sun Certified Java Associate certification process that you are truly Java savvy. As such, you should either be—or have the desire to be—a Java programmer, and in the long term, a true Java developer. You may be or plan to be a project manager heading up a team of Java programmers and/or developers. In this case, you will need to acquire a basic understanding of the Java language and its technologies. In either case, this book is for you.

To start, you may be wondering about the core functional elements provided by the basic Java Standard Edition platform in regards to libraries and utilities, and how these elements are organized. This chapter answers these questions by discussing Java packages and classes, along with their packaging, compilation, and interpretation processes.

When you have finished this chapter, you will have a firm understanding of packaging Java classes, high-level details of common Java SE packages, and the fundamentals of Java's compilation and interpretation tools.

CERTIFICATION OBJECTIVE

Understanding Packages

Exam Objective 5.1   Describe the purpose of packages in the Java language, and recognize the proper use of import and package statements.

Packaging is a common approach used to organize related classes and interfaces. Most reusable code is packaged. Unpackaged classes are commonly found in books and online tutorials, as well as software applications with a narrow focus. This section will show you how and when to package your Java classes and how to import external classes from your Java packages. The following topics will be covered:

- Package design
- Package and import statements

Package Design

Packages are thought of as containers for classes, but actually they define where classes will be located in the hierarchical directory structure. Packaging is encouraged by Java coding standards to decrease the likelihood of classes colliding. Packaging your classes also promotes code reuse, maintainability, and the object-oriented principle of encapsulation and modularity.

When you design Java packages, such as the grouping of classes, the following key areas (shown in Table 1-1) should be considered.

Let's take a look at a real-world example. As program manager you need two sets of classes with unique functionality that will be used by the same end product. You task Developer A to build the first set and Developer B to build the second. You do not define the names of the classes, but you do define the purpose of the package and what it must contain. Developer A is to create several geometry-based classes including a point class, a polygon class, and a plane class. Developer B is to build classes that will be included for simulation purposes, including objects such as hot air balloons, helicopters, and airplanes. You send them off to build their classes (without having them package their classes). Come delivery time, they both give you a class named `Plane.java`—that is, one for the geometry plane class and one for the airplane class. Now you have a problem because both of these source files (class files, too) cannot coexist in the same directory since they have the same name. The solution is packaging. If you had designated package names to the developers, this conflict never would have happened (as shown in Figure 1-1). The lessoned learned is: Always package your code, unless your coding project is trivial in nature.

TABLE 1-1	Package Attribute	Benefits of Applying the Package Attribute
Package Attributes Considerations	Class Coupling	Package dependencies are reduced with class coupling.
	System Coupling	Package dependencies are reduced with system coupling.
	Package Size	Typically, larger packages support reusability, whereas smaller packages support maintainability.
	Maintainability	Often, software changes can be limited to a single package when the package houses focused functionality.
	Naming	Consider conventions when naming your packages. Use reverse domain name for the package structure. Use lowercase characters delimited with underscores to separate words in package names.

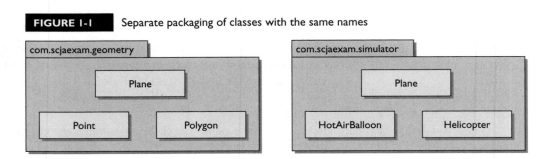

FIGURE 1-1   Separate packaging of classes with the same names

package and import **Statements**

You should now have a general idea of when and why to package your source files. Now you need to know exactly how. To place a source file into a package, use the package statement at the beginning of that file. You may use zero or one package statements per source file. To import classes from other packages into your source file, use the import statement. The java.lang package that houses the core language classes is imported by default.

The following code listing shows usage of the package and import statements. You can continue to come back to this listing as we discuss the package and import statements in further detail throughout the chapter.

```
package com.scjaexam.tutorial; // Package statement
/* Imports class ArrayList from the java.util package */
import java.util.ArrayList;
/* Imports all classes from the java.io package */
import java.io.*;
public class MainClass {
  public static void main(String[] args) {
    /* Creates console from java.io package */
    Console console = System.console();
    String planet = console.readLine("\nEnter your favorite
    planet: ");
    /* Creates list for planets */
    ArrayList planetList = new ArrayList();
    planetList.add(planet); // Adds users input to the list
    planetList.add("Gliese 581 c"); // Adds a string to the list
    System.out.println("\nTwo cool planets: " + planetList);
  }
}
$ Enter your favorite planet: Jupiter
$ Two cool planets: [Jupiter, Gliese 581 c]
```

The `package` Statement

The `package` statement includes the `package` keyword, followed by the package path delimited with periods. Table 1-2 shows valid examples of `package` statements. Package statements have the following attributes:

- Package statements are optional.
- Package statements are limited to one per source file.
- Standard coding convention for package statements reverses the domain name of the organization or group creating the package. For example, the owners of the domain name `scjaexam.com` may use the following package name for a utilities package: `com.scjaexam.utilities`.
- Package names equate to directory structures. The package name `com.scjaexam.utils` would equate to the directory *com/scjaexam/utils*.
- The package names beginning with `java.*` and `javax.*` are reserved for use by JavaSoft, the business unit of Sun Microsystems that is responsible for Java technologies.
- Package names should be lowercase. Individual words within the package name should be separated by underscores.

The Java SE API contains several packages. These packages are detailed in Sun's Online JavaDoc documentation at http://java.sun.com/javase/6/docs/api.

Common packages you will see on the exam are packages for the Java Abstract Window Toolkit API, the Java Swing API, the Java Basic Input/Output API, the Java Networking API, the Java Utilities API, and the core Java Language API. You will need to know the basic functionality that each package/API contains.

The `import` Statement

An `import` statement allows you to include source code from other classes into a source file at compile time. In J2SE 1.4, the `import` statement includes the

TABLE 1-2	`package` Statement	Related Directory Structure
Valid `package` Statements	`package java.net;`	*[directory_path]\java\net*
	`package com.scjaexam.utilities;`	*[directory_path]\com\scjaexam\utilities*
	`package package_name;`	*[directory_path]\package_name*

SCENARIO & SOLUTION

To paint basic graphics and images, which package should you use?	You will need to use the Java AWT API package.
To create lightweight components for GUI, which package should you use?	You will need to use the Java Swing API package.
To utilize data streams, which package should you use?	You will need to use the Java Basic I/O package.
To develop a networking application, which package should you use?	You will need to use the Java Networking API package.
To work with the collections framework, event model, and date/time facilities, which package should you use?	You will need to use the Java Utilities API package.
To utilize the core Java classes and interfaces, which package should you use?	You will need to use the core Java Language package.

import keyword followed by the package path delimited with periods and ending with a class name or an asterisk, as shown in Table 1-3. These import statements occur after the optional package statement and before the class definition. Each import statement can only relate to one package.

TABLE I-3 Valid import Statements	import **Statement**	**Definition**
	import java.net.*;	Imports all of the classes from the package java.net.
	import java.net.URL;	Imports only the URL class from the package java.net.
	import static java.awt.Color.*;	Imports all static members of the Color class of the package java.awt (J2SE 5.0 onward only).
	import static java.awt.color.ColorSpace .CS_GRAY;	Imports the static member CS_GRAY of the Color class of the package java.awt (J2SE 5.0 onward only).

on the **job**

For maintenance purposes, it is better to explicitly import your classes. This will allow the programmer to quickly determine which external classes are used throughout the class. As an example, rather than using `import java .util.*,` *use* `import java.util.Vector.` *In this real-world example, the coder would quickly see (with the latter approach) that the class only imports one class and it is a collection type. In this case, it is a legacy type and the determination to update the class with a newer collection type could be done quickly.*

C and C++ programmers will see some look-and-feel similarities between Java's `import` statement and C/C++'s `#include` statement, even though there isn't a direct mapping in functionality.

exam
watch

Static imports are a new feature to Java SE 5.0. Static imports allow you to import static members. The following example statements would be valid in Java SE 5.0, but would be invalid for J2SE 1.4.

```
/* Import static member ITALY */
import static java.util.Locale.ITALY;
/* Imports all static members in class Locale */
import static java.util.Locale.*;
```

EXERCISE 1-1

Replacing Implicit `import` Statements with Explicit `import` Statements

Consider the following sample application:

```
import java.io.*;
import java.text.*;
import java.util.*;
import java.util.logging.*;

public class TestClass {
  public static void main(String[] args) throws IOException {
```

```
      /* Ensure directory has been created */
      new File("logs").mkdir();
      /* Get the date to be used in the filename */
      DateFormat df = new SimpleDateFormat("yyyyMMddhhmmss");
      Date now = new Date();
      String date = df.format(now);
      /* Set up the filename in the logs directory */
      String logFileName = "logs\\testlog-" + date + ".txt";
      /* Set up Logger */
      FileHandler myFileHandler = new FileHandler(logFileName);
      myFileHandler.setFormatter(new SimpleFormatter());
      Logger scjaLogger = Logger.getLogger("SCJA Logger");
      scjaLogger.setLevel(Level.ALL);
      scjaLogger.addHandler(myFileHandler);
      /* Log Message */
      scjaLogger.info("\nThis is a logged information message.");
      /* Close the file */
      myFileHandler.close();
    }
}
```

There can be implicit imports that allow all necessary classes of a package to be imported.

```
import java.io.*; // Implicit import example
```

There can be explicit imports that only allow the designated class or interface of a package to be imported.

```
import java.io.File; // Explicit import example
```

This exercise will have you using explicit import statements in lieu of the implicit import statements for all of the necessary classes of the sample application. If you are unfamiliar with compiling and interpreting Java programs, complete this chapter and then come back to this exercise. Otherwise, let's begin.

1. Type the sample application into a new file and name it *TestClass.java*. Save the file.

2. Compile and run the application to ensure that you have created the file contents without error; javac TestClass.java to compile, java TestClass to run. Verify that the log message prints to the screen. Also verify that a file has been created in the *logs* subdirectory with the same message in it.

3. Comment out all of the `import` statements.

```
//import java.io.*;
//import java.text.*;
//import java.util.*;
//import java.util.logging.*;
```

4. Compile the application; `javac TestClass.java`. You will be presented with several compiler errors related to the missing class imports. As an example, the following illustration demonstrates the errors seen when only the `java.io` package has been commented out.

```
Command Prompt                                        _ □ X
c:\code>javac TestClass.java
TestClass.java:7: cannot find symbol
symbol  : class IOException
location: class TestClass
  public static void main(String[] args) throws IOException {
                                                      ^
TestClass.java:9: cannot find symbol
symbol  : class File
location: class TestClass
    new File("logs").mkdir();
        ^
2 errors

c:\code>_
```

5. For each class that cannot be found, use the online Java Specification API to determine which package it belongs to and then update the source file with the necessary explicit `import` statement. Once completed, you will have replaced the four *implicit* `import` statements with nine *explicit* `import` statements.

6. Run the application again to ensure the application works the same with the explicit imports as it did with the implicit import.

CERTIFICATION OBJECTIVE

Understanding Package-Derived Classes

Exam Objective 5.3   Describe the purpose and types of classes for the following Java packages: java.awt, javax.swing, java.io, java.net, java.util.

Sun includes over 100 packages in the core Java SE API. Each package has a specific focus. Fortunately, you only need to be familiar with a few of them for the SCJA exam. These include packages for Java utilities, basic input/output, networking, AWT and Swing.

- Java Utilities API
- Java Basic Input/Output API
- Java Networking API
- Java Abstract Window Toolkit API
- Java Swing API

Java Utilities API

The Java Utilities API is contained in the package `java.util`. This API provides functionality for a variety of utility classes. The API's key classes and interfaces can be divided into several categories. Categories of classes that may be seen on the exam include the Java Collections Framework, date and time facilities, internationalization, and some miscellaneous utility classes.

Of these categories, the Java Collections Framework pulls the most weight since it is frequently used and provides the fundamental data structures necessary to build valuable Java applications. Table 1-4 details the classes and interfaces of the Collections API that you may see referenced on the exam.

To assist collections in sorting where the ordering is not natural, the Collections API provides the `Comparator` interface. Similarly, the `Comparable` interface that resides in the `java.lang` package is used to sort objects by their natural ordering.

TABLE 1-4	Interface	Implementations	Description
Various Classes of the Java Collections Framework	List	`ArrayList, LinkedList, Vector`	Data structures based on positional access.
	Map	`HashMap, Hashtable, LinkedHashMap, TreeMap`	Data structures that map keys to values.
	Set	`HashSet, LinkedHashSet, TreeSet`	Data structures based on element uniqueness.
	Queue	`PriorityQueue`	Queues typically order elements in a FIFO manner. Priority queues order elements according to a supplied comparator.

Various other classes and interfaces reside in the `java.util` package. Date and time facilities are represented by the `Date`, `Calendar`, and `TimeZone` classes. Geographical regions are represented by the `Locale` class. The `Currency` class represents currencies per the ISO 4217 standard. A random number generator is provided by the `Random` class. And `StringTokenizer` breaks strings into tokens. Several other classes exist within `java.util`, but these (and the collection interfaces and classes) are the ones most likely to be seen on the exam. The initially discussed classes are represented in Figure 1-2.

on the
Job

Many packages have related classes and interfaces that have unique functionality, so they are included in their own subpackages. For example, regular expressions are stored in a subpackage of the Java utilities (`java.util`) package. The subpackage is named `java.util.regex` and houses the `Matcher` and `Pattern` classes. Where needed, consider creating subpackages for your own projects.

FIGURE 1-2   Various utility classes

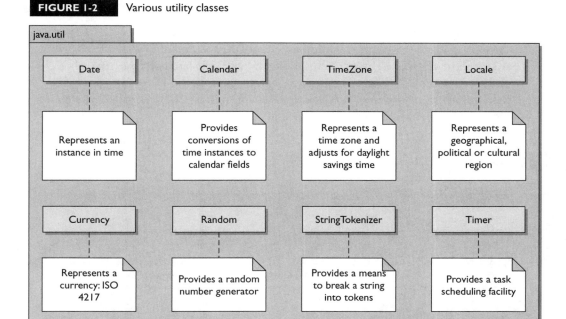

Java Basic Input/Output API

The Java Basic Input/Output API is contained in the package `java.io`. This API provides functionality for general system input and output in relationships to data streams, serialization, and the file system. Data stream classes include byte-stream subclasses of the `InputStream` and `OutputStream` classes. Data stream classes also include character-stream subclasses of the `Reader` and `Writer` classes. Figure 1-3 depicts part of the class hierarchy for the `Reader` and `Writer` abstract classes.

Other important `java.io` classes and interfaces include `File`, `FileDescriptor`, `FilenameFilter`, and `RandomAccessFile`. The `File` class provides a representation of file and directory pathnames. The `FileDescriptor` class provides a means to function as a handle for opening files and sockets. The `FilenameFilter` interface, as its name implies, defines the functionality to filter filenames. The `RandomAccessFile` class allows for the reading and writing of files to specified locations.

The Java Networking API

The Java Networking API is contained in the package `java.net`. This API provides functionality in support of creating network applications. The API's key classes and interfaces are represented in Figure 1-4. You probably will not see few, if any, of these classes on the exam but the figure will help you conceptualize what's in the `java.net` package. The improved performance New I/O API (`java.nio`) package, which provides for nonblocking networking and the socket factory support package (`javax.net`), is not on the exam.

| FIGURE 1-3 | **Reader** and **Writer** class hierarchy |

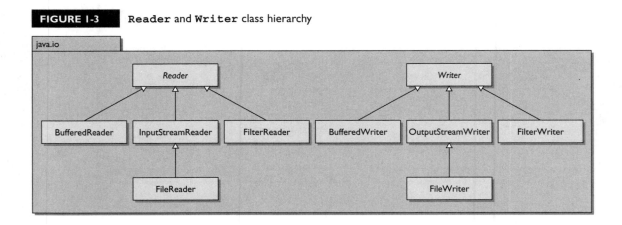

[Oracle certified Java Associate SE8

① By Khalid MUGAL

② By

_____

[   ]

① By Jeanne Boyarsky, Scott Selikoff
② By Edward Finegan, Robert Liguori
③ "   Malu Gupta

FIGURE 1-4   Various classes of the Networking API

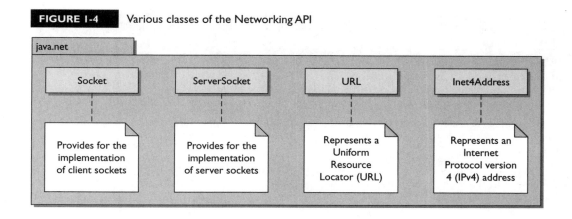

Java Abstract Window Toolkit API

The Java Abstract Window Toolkit API is contained in the package `java.awt`. This API provides functionality for creating heavyweight components in regards to creating user interfaces and painting associated graphics and images. The AWT API was Java's original GUI API and has been superseded by the Swing API. Where Swing is now recommended, certain pieces of the AWT API still remain commonly used, such as the AWT Focus subsystem that was reworked in J2SE 1.4. The AWT Focus subsystem provides for navigation control between components. Figure 1-5 depicts these major AWT elements.

Java Swing API

The Java Swing API is contained in the package `javax.swing`. This API provides functionality for creating lightweight (pure-Java) containers and components. The Swing API superseded the AWT API. Many of the new classes were simply prefaced with the addition of "J" in contrast to the legacy AWT component equivalent.

FIGURE 1-5

AWT major
elements

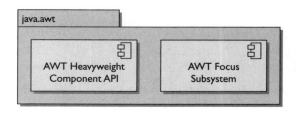

SCENARIO & SOLUTION

You need to create basic Java Swing components such as buttons, panes, and dialog boxes. Provide the code to import the necessary classes of a package.	```// Java Swing API package
import javax.swing.*;```
You need to support text-related aspects of your Swing components. Provide the code to import the necessary classes of a package.	```// Java Swing API text subpackage
import javax.swing.text.*;```
You need to implement and configure basic pluggable look-and-feel support. Provide the code to import the necessary classes of a package.	```// Java Swing API plaf subpackage
import javax.swing.plaf.*;```
You need to use Swing event listeners and adapters. Provide the code to import the necessary classes of a package.	```// Java Swing API event subpackage
import javax.swing.event.*;```

For example, Swing uses the class `JButton` to represent a button container, whereas AWT uses the class `Button`.

Swing also provides look-and-feel support, allowing for universal style changes of the GUI's components. Other features include tooltips, accessibility functionality, an event model, and enhanced components such as tables, trees, text components, sliders, and progress bars. Some of the Swing API's key classes are represented in Figure 1-6. See Chapter 11 for more information on the Swing API as a client-side user-interface solution.

FIGURE 1-6 Various classes of the Swing API

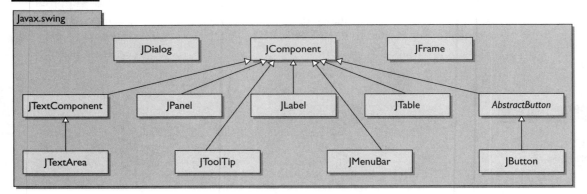

The Swing API makes excellent use of subpackages, with 16 of them total in Java SE 6. As mentioned earlier, when common classes are separated into their own packages, code usability and maintainability is enhanced.

Swing takes advantage of the model-view-controller architecture (MVC). The model represents the current state of each component. The view is the representation of the components on the screen. The controller is the functionality that ties the UI components to events. While understanding the underlying architecture of Swing is important, it's not necessary for the exam. For comprehensive information on the Swing API, look to the book *Swing: A Beginner's Guide*, by Herbert Schildt (McGraw-Hill Professional, 2007).

---

exam

ⓦatch

Be familiar with the package prefixes `java` and `javax`. The prefix `java` is commonly used for the core packages. The prefix `javax` is commonly used for packages comprised of Java standard extensions. Take special notice of the prefix usage in the AWT and Swing APIs: `java.awt` and `javax.swing`.

EXERCISE 1-2

Understanding Extended Functionality of the Java Utilities API

In Java SE 6, a total of ten packages are in direct relationship to the Java Utilities API, with the base package being named `java.util`. J2SE 5.0 has only nine packages; J2SE 1.4, just six. This exercise will have you exploring the details of the Java Utilities API subpackages that were added in subsequent releases of the Java SE 1.4 platform.

1. Go to the online J2SE 1.4.2 API specification: http://java.sun.com/j2se/1.4.2/docs/api/.

2. Use the web browser's scroll bar to scroll down to the Java Utilities API packages.

3. Click the link for each related package. Explore the details of the classes and interfaces within each package.

4. Go to the online J2SE 5.0 API specification: http://java.sun.com/j2se/1.5.0/ docs/api/. This is the API specification you should be referencing for the exam. It is shown in the following illustration.

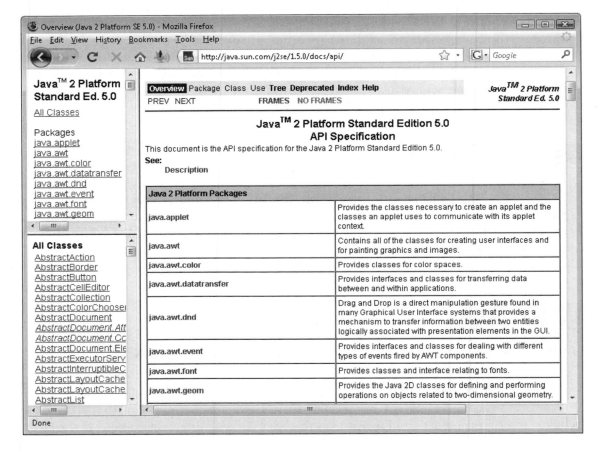

5. Use the web browser's scroll bar to scroll down to the Java Utilities API packages.

6. Determine which three new subpackages were added to the Java Utilities API. Click the link for each of these new packages. Explore the details of the classes and interfaces within each package.

7. Go to the online Java SE 6 API specification: http://java.sun.com/javase/6/ docs/api/.

8. Use the web browser's scroll bar to scroll down to the Java Utilities API packages.

9. Determine which new subpackage was added to the Java Utilities API. Click the link for the new package. Explore the details of the classes within the package.

Compiling and Interpreting Java Code

Exam Objective 5.2   Demonstrate the proper use of the "javac" command (including the command-line options: -d and –classpath) and demonstrate the proper use of the "java" command (including the command-line options: -classpath, -D and –version).

The Java Development Kit includes several utilities for compiling, debugging, and running Java applications. This section details two utilities from the kit: the Java compiler and the Java interpreter. For more information on the JDK and its other utilities, see Chapter 10.

Java Compiler

We will need a sample application to use for our Java compiler and interpreter exercises. We shall employ the simple *GreetingsUniverse.java* source file, shown here in the following listing, throughout the section.

```
public class GreetingsUniverse {
  public static void main(String[] args) {
    System.out.println("Greetings, Universe!");
  }
}
```

Let's take a look at compiling and interpreting simple Java programs along with their most basic command-line options.

Compiling Your Source Code

The Java compiler is only one of several tools in the JDK. When you have time, inspect the other tools resident in the JDK's bin folder, as shown in Figure 1-7. For the scope of the SCJA exam, you will only need to know the details surrounding the compiler and interpreter.

The Java compiler simply converts Java source files into bytecode. The Java compiler's usage is as follows:

```
javac [options] [source files]
```

The most straightforward way to compile a Java class is to preface the Java source files with the compiler utility from the command line: `javac.exe FileName.java`. The `.exe` is the standard executable file extension on Windows machines and is optional. The `.exe` extension is not present on executables on Unix-like systems.

```
javac GreetingsUniverse.java
```

This will result in a bytecode file being produced with the same preface, such as *GreetingsUniverse.class*. This bytecode file will be placed into the same folder as the source code, unless the code is packaged and/or it's been told via a command-line option to be placed somewhere else.

FIGURE 1-7

Java Development
Kit utilities

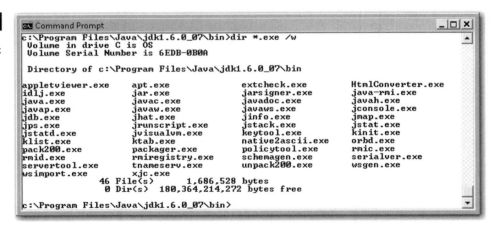

INSIDE THE EXAM

Command-Line Tools

Most projects use Integrated Development Environments (IDEs) to compile and execute code. The clear benefit in using IDEs is that building and running code can be as easy as stepping through a couple of menu buttons or even just hitting a hot key. The disadvantage is that even though you may establish your settings through a configuration dialog box and see the commands and subsequent arguments in one of the workspace windows, you are not getting direct experience in repeatedly creating the complete structure of

the commands and associated arguments by hand. The exam is structured to validate that you have experience in scripting compiler and interpreter invocations. Do not take this prerequisite lightly. Take the exam only after you have mastered when and how to use the tools, switches, and associated arguments. At a later time, you can consider taking advantage of the "shortcut" features of popular IDEs such as those provided by NetBeans, Eclipse, IntelliJ IDEA, and JDeveloper.

Compiling Your Source Code with the `-d` Option

You may wish to explicitly specify where you would like the compiled bytecode class files to go. You can accomplish this using the `-d` option.

```
javac -d classes GreetingsUniverse.java
```

This command-line structure will place the class file into the `classes` directory, and since the source code was packaged (that is, the source file included a `package` statement), the bytecode will be placed into the relative subdirectories.

```
[present working directory]\classes\com\scjaexam\tutorial\
    GreetingsUniverse.class
```

Compiling Your Code with the `-classpath` Option

If you wish to compile your application with user-defined classes and packages, you may need to tell the JVM where to look by specifying them in the classpath. This classpath inclusion is accomplished by telling the compiler where the desired classes and packages are with the `-cp` or `-classpath` command-line option. In the following compiler invocation, the compiler includes in its compilation any source files that are located under the *3rdPartyCode\classes* directory, as well as any classes located in the present working directory (the period). The -d option (again) will place the compiled bytecode into the *classes* directory.

```
javac -d classes -cp 3rdPartyCode\classes\;. GreetingsUniverse
    .java
```

Note that you do not need to include the classpath option if the classpath is defined with the CLASSPATH environment variable, or if the desired files are in the present working directory.

On Windows systems, classpath directories are delimited with backward slashes, and paths are delimited with semicolons:

```
-classpath .;\dir_a\classes_a\;\dir_b\classes_b\
```

On POSIX-based systems, classpath directories are delimited with forward slashes and paths are delimited with colons:

```
-classpath .:/dir_a/classes_a/:/dir_b/classes_b/
```

Again, the period represents the present (or current) working directory.

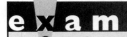

Java Interpreter

Interpreting the Java files is the basis for creating the Java application, as shown in Figure 1-8. Let's examine how to invoke the interpreter and its command-line options.

```
java [-options] class [args...]
```

| FIGURE 1-8 | Bytecode conversion |

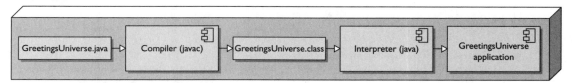

Interpreting Your Bytecode

The Java interpreter is invoked with the `java[.exe]` command. It is used to interpret bytecode and execute your program.

You can easily invoke the interpreter on a class that's not packaged as follows:

```
java MainClass
```

You can optionally start the program with the `javaw` command on Microsoft Windows to exclude the command window. This is a nice feature with GUI-based applications since the console window is often not necessary.

```
javaw.exe MainClass
```

Similarly, on POSIX-based systems, you can use the ampersand to run the application as a background process.

```
java MainClass &
```

Interpreting Your Code with the `-classpath` Option

When interpreting your code, you may need to define where certain classes and packages are located. You can find your classes at runtime when you include the `-cp` or `-classpath` option with the interpreter. If the classes you wish to include are packaged, then you can start your application by pointing the full path of the application to the base directory of classes, as in the following interpreter invocation:

```
java -cp classes com.scjaexam.tutorial.MainClass
```

The delimitation syntax is the same for the `-cp` and `-classpath` options, as defined earlier in the "Compiling Your Code with the `-classpath` Option" section.

Interpreting Your Bytecode with the -D Option

The -D command-line option allows for the setting of new property values. The usage is as follows:

```
java -D<name>=<value> class
```

The following single-file application comprised of the PropertiesManager class prints out all of the system properties.

```java
import java.util.Properties;
public class PropertiesManager {
  public static void main(String[] args) {
    Properties props = System.getProperties();
      /* New property example */
      props.setProperty("new_property2", "new_value2");
      if (args[0].equals("-list_all")) {
        props.list(System.out); // Lists all properties
      } else if (args[0].equals("-list_prop")) {
        /* Lists value */
        System.out.println(props.getProperty(args[1]));
      } else {
        System.out.println("Usage: java PropertiesManager
        [-list_all]");
        System.out.println("       java PropertiesManager
        [-list_prop [property]]");
      }
  }
}
```

Let's run this application while setting a new system property called "new_property1" to the value of "new_value1".

```
java -Dnew_property1=new_value1 PropertiesManager -list_all
```

You'll see in the standard output that the listing of the system properties includes the new property that we set and its value.

```
...
new_property1=new_value1
java.specification.name=Java Platform API Specification
...
```

Optionally, you can set a value by instantiating the Properties class, and then setting a property and its value with the setProperty method.

To help you conceptualize system properties a little better, Table 1-5 details a subset of the standard system properties.

Retrieving the Version of the Interpreter with the `-version` Option

The `-version` command-line option is used with the Java interpreter to return the version of the JVM and exit. Don't take the simplicity of the command for granted, as the designers of the exam may try to trick you by including additional arguments after the command. Take the time to toy with the command by adding arguments and placing the `-version` option in various places. Do not make any assumptions about how you think the application will respond. Figure 1-9 demonstrates varying results based on where the `-version` option is used.

TABLE 1-5   Subset of System Properties

System Property	Property Description
`file.separator`	The platform specific file separator ('/' for POSIX, '\' for Windows)
`java.class.path`	The classpath as defined for the system's environment variable
`java.class.version`	The Java class version number
`java.home`	The directory of the Java installation
`java.vendor`	The vendor supplying the Java platform
`java.vendor.url`	The vendor's Uniform Resource Locator
`java.version`	The version of the Java Interpreter/JVM
`line.separator`	The platform-specific line separator ("\r" on Mac OS 9, "\n" for POSIX, "\r\n" for Microsoft Windows)
`os.arch`	The architecture of the operating system
`os.name`	The name of the operating system
`os.version`	The version of the operating system
`path.separator`	The platform-specific path separator (":" for POSIX, ";" for Windows)
`user.dir`	The current working directory of the user
`user.home`	The home directory of the user
`user.language`	The language code of the default locale
`user.name`	The username for the current user
`user.timezone`	The system's default time zone

The -version
command-line
option

```
Command Prompt                                              _ □ ✗
c:\code>java -version
java version "1.6.0_07"
Java(TM) SE Runtime Environment (build 1.6.0_07-b06)
Java HotSpot(TM) Client VM (build 10.0-b23, mixed mode, sharing)

c:\code>java -version INVALID_ARGUMENT
java version "1.6.0_07"
Java(TM) SE Runtime Environment (build 1.6.0_07-b06)
Java HotSpot(TM) Client VM (build 10.0-b23, mixed mode, sharing)

c:\code>java HelloWorld -version
Hello, World!
```

on the Job

Check out the other JDK utilities at your disposal. You can find them in the bin directory of your JDK. JConsole in particular is a valuable GUI-based tool that is used to monitor and manage Java applications. Among the many features, JConsole allows for viewing memory and thread usages. JConsole was released with J2SE 5.0.

EXERCISE 1-3

Compiling and Interpreting Packaged Software

When you compile and run packaged software from an IDE, it can be as easy as clicking a run icon as IDE's support, setting the necessary paths that will be used by the compiler and interpreters. However, when you try to compile and interpret the code yourself from the command line, you will need to know exactly how to path your files. Consider our sample application that is now placed in the com.scjaexam.tutorial package.

```
package com.scjaexam.tutorial;
public class GreetingsUniverse {
  public static void main(String[] args) {
    System.out.println("Greetings, Universe!");
  }
}
```

This exercise will have you compiling and running the application with new classes created in a separate package.

1. Compile the program.

```
javac -d . GreetingsUniverse.java
```

2. Run the program to ensure it is error-free.

```
java -cp . com.scjaexam.tutorial.GreetingsUniverse.
```

3. Create three classes named `Earth`, `Mars`, and `Venus` and place them in the `com.scja.exam.tutorial.planets` package. Create constructors that will print the names of the planets to standard out. Note that the details for the `Earth` class are given here as an example of what you will need to do.

```
package com.scja.exam.tutorial.planets;
public class Earth {
  public Earth {
    System.out.println("Hello from Earth!");
  }
}
```

4. Instantiate each class from the main program, by adding the necessary code to the `GreetingsUniverse` class.

```
Earth e = new Earth();
```

5. Ensure that all of the source code is in the paths *src/com/scjaexam/tutorial/* and *src/com/scjaexam/tutorial/planets/*, respectively.

6. Determine the command-line arguments needed to compile the complete program. Compile the program, and debug where necessary.

7. Determine the command-line arguments needed to interpret the program. Run the program.

The standard output will read:

```
$ Greetings, Universe!
Hello from Earth!
Hello from Mars!
Hello from Venus!
```

CERTIFICATION SUMMARY

This chapter discussed packaging, compiling, and interpreting Java code. The chapter started with a discussion on the importance of organizing your classes into packages as well as using the `package` and `import` statements to define and include different pieces of source code. Through the middle of the chapter, we discussed the key features of the most commonly used Java packages: `java.awt`, `javax.swing`, `java.net`, `java.io`, and `java.util`. We concluded the chapter by providing detailed information on how to compile and interpret Java source and class files and how to work with their command-line options. At this point, you should be able to independently (outside of an IDE) package, build, and run basic Java programs.

✓ TWO-MINUTE DRILL

Understanding Packages

- ❏ Packages are containers for classes.
- ❏ A `package` statement defines the directory path where files are stored.
- ❏ A `package` statement uses periods for delimitation.
- ❏ Package names should be lowercase and separated with underscores between words.
- ❏ Package names beginning with `java.*` and `javax.*` are reserved for use by JavaSoft.
- ❏ There can be zero or one `package` statement per source file.
- ❏ An `import` statement is used to include source code from external classes.
- ❏ An `import` statement occurs after the optional `package` statement and before the class definition.
- ❏ An `import` statement can define a specific class name to import.
- ❏ An `import` statement can use an asterisk to include all classes within a given package.

Understanding Package-Derived Classes

- ❏ The Java Abstract Window Toolkit API is included in the `java.awt` package and subpackages.
- ❏ The `java.awt` package includes GUI creation and painting graphics and images functionality.
- ❏ The Java Swing API is included in the `javax.swing` package and subpackages.
- ❏ The `javax.swing` package includes classes and interfaces that support lightweight GUI component functionality.
- ❏ The Java Basic Input/Output-related classes are contained in the `java.io` package.
- ❏ The `java.io` package includes classes and interfaces that support input/output functionality of the file system, data streams, and serialization.

❑ Java networking classes are included in the `java.net` package.

❑ The `java.net` package includes classes and interfaces that support basic networking functionality that is also extended by the `javax.net` package.

❑ Fundamental Java utilities are included in the `java.util` package.

❑ The `java.util` package and subpackages includes classes and interfaces that support the Java Collections Framework, legacy collection classes, event model, date and time facilities, and internationalization functionality.

Compiling and Interpreting Java Code

❑ The Java compiler is invoked with the `javac[.exe]` command.

❑ The `.exe` extension is optional on Microsoft Windows machines and is not present on UNIX-like systems.

❑ The compiler's `-d` command-line option defines where compiled class files should be placed.

❑ The compiler's `-d` command-line option will include the package location if the class has been declared with a `package` statement.

❑ The compiler's `-classpath` command-line option defines directory paths in search of classes.

❑ The Java interpreter is invoked with the `java[.exe]` command.

❑ The interpreter's `-classpath` switch defines directory paths to use at runtime.

❑ The interpreter's `-D` command-line option allows for the setting of system property values.

❑ The interpreter's syntax for the `-D` command-line option is `-Dproperty=value`.

❑ The interpreter's `-version` command-line option is used to return the version of the JVM and exit.

SELF TEST

Understanding Packages

1. Which two `import` statements will allow for the import of the `HashMap` class?

   A. `import java.util.HashMap;`

   B. `import java.util.*;`

   C. `import java.util.HashMap.*;`

   D. `import java.util.hashMap;`

2. Which statement would designate that your file belongs in the package `com.scjaexam.utilities`?

   A. `pack com.scjaexam.utilities;`

   B. `package com.scjaexam.utilities.*`

   C. `package com.scjaexam.utilities.*;`

   D. `package com.scjaexam.utilities;`

3. Which of the following is the only Java package that is imported by default?

   A. `java.awt`

   B. `java.lang`

   C. `java.util`

   D. `java.io`

4. What Java-related features are new to J2SE 5.0?

   A. Static imports

   B. `package` and `import` statements

   C. Autoboxing and unboxing

   D. The enhanced for-loop

Understanding Package-Derived Classes

5. The `JCheckBox` and `JComboBox` classes belong to which package?

   A. `java.awt`

   B. `javax.awt`

   C. `java.swing`

   D. `javax.swing`

6. Which package contains the Java Collections Framework?

   A. `java.io`

   B. `java.net`

   C. `java.util`

   D. `java.utils`

7. The Java Basic I/O API contains what types of classes and interfaces?

   A. Internationalization

   B. RMI, JDBC, and JNDI

   C. Data streams, serialization, and file system

   D. Collection API and data streams

8. Which API provides a lightweight solution for GUI components?

   A. AWT

   B. Abstract Window Toolkit

   C. Swing

   D. AWT and Swing

9. Consider the following illustration. What problem exists with the packaging? You may wish to reference Chapter 9 for assistance with UML.

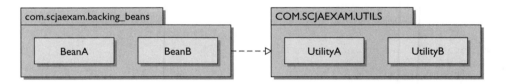

   A. You can only have one class per package.

   B. Packages cannot have associations between them.

   C. Package `com.scjaexam.backing_beans` fails to meet the appropriate packaging naming conventions.

   D. Package `COM.SCJAEXAM.UTILS` fails to meet the appropriate packaging naming conventions.

Compiling and Interpreting Java Code

10. Which usage represents a valid way of compiling a Java class?

A. `java MainClass.class`

B. `javac MainClass`

C. `javac MainClass.source`

D. `javac MainClass.java`

11. Which two command-line invocations of the Java interpreter return the version of the interpreter?

A. `java -version`

B. `java --version`

C. `java -version ProgramName`

D. `java ProgramName -version`

12. Which two command-line usages appropriately identify the classpath?

A. `javac -cp /project/classes/ MainClass.java`

B. `javac -sp /project/classes/ MainClass.java`

C. `javac -classpath /project/classes/ MainClass.java`

D. `javac -classpaths /project/classes/ MainClass.java`

13. Which command-line usages appropriately set a system property value?

A. `java -Dcom.scjaexam.propertyValue=003 MainClass`

B. `java -d com.scjaexam.propertyValue=003 MainClass`

C. `java -prop com.scjaexam.propertyValue=003 MainClass`

D. `java -D:com.scjaexam.propertyValue=003 MainClass`

SELF TEST ANSWERS

Understanding Packages

1. Which two import statements will allow for the import of the HashMap class?

   A. `import java.util.HashMap;`

   B. `import java.util.*;`

   C. `import java.util.HashMap.*;`

   D. `import java.util.hashMap;`

   Answer:

   ☑ **A** and **B.** The HashMap class can be imported directly via `import java.util.HashMap` or with a wild card via `import java.util.*;`.

   ☒ **C** and **D** are incorrect. **C** is incorrect because the answer is a static import statement that imports static members of the HashMap class, and not the class itself. **D** is incorrect because class names are case-sensitive, so the class name hashMap does not equate to HashMap.

2. Which statement would designate that your file belongs in the package com.scjaexam .utilities?

   A. `pack com.scjaexam.utilities;`

   B. `package com.scjaexam.utilities.*`

   C. `package com.scjaexam.utilities.*;`

   D. `package com.scjaexam.utilities;`

   Answer:

   ☑ **D.** The keyword package is appropriately used, followed by the package name delimited with periods and followed by a semicolon.

   ☒ **A, B,** and **C** are incorrect answers. **A** is incorrect because the word pack is not a valid keyword. **B** is incorrect because a package statement must end with a semicolon. **C** is incorrect because you cannot use asterisks in package statements.

3. Which of the following is the only Java package that is imported by default?

A. `java.awt`

B. `java.lang`

C. `java.util`

D. `java.io`

Answer:

☑ **B.** The `java.lang` package is the only package that has all of its classes imported by default.

☒ **A, C,** and **D** are incorrect. The classes of packages `java.awt`, `java.util`, and `java.io` are not imported by default.

4. What Java-related features are new to J2SE 5.0?

A. Static imports

B. `Package` and `import` statements

C. Autoboxing and unboxing

D. The enhanced for-loop

Answer:

☑ **A, C,** and **D.** Static imports, autoboxing/unboxing, and the enhanced `for`-loop are all new features of J2SE 5.0.

☒ **B** is incorrect because basic `package` and `import` statements are not new to J2SE 5.0.

Understanding Package-Derived Classes

5. The `JCheckBox` and `JComboBox` classes belong to which package?

A. `java.awt`

B. `javax.awt`

C. `java.swing`

D. `javax.swing`

Answer:

☑ **D.** Components belonging to the Swing API are generally prefaced with a capital J. Therefore, `JCheckBox` and `JComboBox` would be part of the Java Swing API and not the Java AWT API. The Java Swing API base package is `javax.swing`.

☒ **A, B,** and **C** are incorrect. **A** is incorrect because the package `java.awt` does not include the `JCheckBox` and `JComboBox` classes since they belong to the Java Swing API. Note that the package `java.awt` includes the `CheckBox` class, as opposed to the `JCheckBox` class. **B** and **C** are incorrect because the package names `javax.awt` and `java.swing` do not exist.

6. Which package contains the Java Collections Framework?

A. `java.io`

B. `java.net`

C. `java.util`

D. `java.utils`

Answer:

☑ **C.** The Java Collections Framework is part of the Java Utilities API in the `java.util` package.

☒ **A, B,** and **D** are incorrect. **A** is incorrect because the Java Basic I/O API's base package is named `java.io` and does not contain the Java Collections Framework. **B** is incorrect because the Java Networking API's base package is named `java.net` and also does not contain the Collections Framework. **D** is incorrect because there is no package named `java.utils`.

7. The Java Basic I/O API contains what types of classes and interfaces?

A. Internationalization

B. RMI, JDBC, and JNDI

C. Data streams, serialization, and file system

D. Collection API and data streams

Answer:

☑ **C.** The Java Basic I/O API contains classes and interfaces for data streams, serialization, and the file system.

☒ **A, B,** and **D** are incorrect because internationalization (i18n), RMI, JDBC, JNDI, and the Collections Framework are not included in the Basic I/O API.

8. Which API provides a lightweight solution for GUI components?

A. AWT

B. Abstract Window Toolkit

C. Swing

D. AWT and Swing

Answer:

☑ **C.** The Swing API provides a lightweight solution for GUI components, meaning that the Swing API's classes are built from pure Java code.

☒ **A, B,** and **D** are incorrect. AWT and the Abstract Window Toolkit are one and the same and provide a heavyweight solution for GUI components.

9. Consider the following illustration. What problem exists with the packaging? You may wish to reference Chapter 9 for assistance with UML.

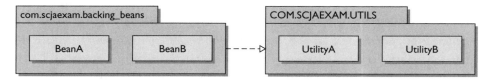

A. You can only have one class per package.

B. Packages cannot have associations between them.

C. Package `com.scjaexam.backing_beans` fails to meet the appropriate packaging naming conventions.

D. Package `COM.SCJAEXAM.UTILS` fails to meet the appropriate packaging naming conventions.

Answer:

☑   **D.** COM.SCJAEXAM.UTILS fails to meet the appropriate packaging naming conventions. Package names should be lowercase. Note that package names should also have an underscore between words; however, the words in "scjaexam" are joined in the URL, therefore excluding the underscore here is acceptable. The package name should read com.scjaexam.utils.

☒   **A, B,** and **C** are incorrect. **A** is incorrect because being restricted to having one class in a package is ludicrous. There is no limit. **B** is incorrect because packages can and frequently do have associations with other packages. **C** is incorrect because com.scjaexam.backing_beans meets appropriate packaging naming conventions.

Compiling and Interpreting Java Code

10.   Which usage represents a valid way of compiling a Java class?

A.   `java MainClass.class`

B.   `javac MainClass`

C.   `javac MainClass.source`

D.   `javac MainClass.java`

Answer:

☑   **D.** The compiler is invoked by the `javac` command. When compiling a java class, you must include the filename, which houses the main classes including the `.java` extension.

☒   **A, B,** and **C** are incorrect. **A** is incorrect because `MainClass.class` is bytecode that is already compiled. **B** is incorrect because `MainClass` is missing the `.java` extension. **C** is incorrect because `MainClass.source` is not a valid name for any type of Java file.

11.   Which two command-line invocations of the Java interpreter return the version of the interpreter?

A.   `java -version`

B.   `java --version`

C.   `java -version ProgramName`

D.   `java ProgramName -version`

Answer:

☑ **A** and **C**. The `-version` flag should be used as the first argument. The application will return the appropriate strings to standard output with the version information and then immediately exit. The second argument is ignored.

☒ **B** and **D** are incorrect. **B** is incorrect because the version flag does not allow double dashes. You may see double dashes for flags in utilities, especially those following the GNU license. However, the double dashes do not apply to the version flag of the Java interpreter. **D** is incorrect because the version flag must be used as the first argument or its functionality will be ignored.

12. Which two command-line usages appropriately identify the class path?

   A. `javac -cp /project/classes/ MainClass.java`

   B. `javac -sp /project/classes/ MainClass.java`

   C. `javac -classpath /project/classes/ MainClass.java`

   D. `javac -classpaths /project/classes/ MainClass.java`

Answer:

☑ **A** and **C**. The option flag that is used to specify the classpath is `-cp` or `-classpath`.

☒ **B** and **D** are incorrect because the option flags `-sp` and `-classpaths` are invalid.

13. Which command-line usages appropriately set a system property value?

   A. `java -Dcom.scjaexam.propertyValue=003 MainClass`

   B. `java -d com.scjaexam.propertyValue=003 MainClass`

   C. `java -prop com.scjaexam.propertyValue=003 MainClass`

   D. `java -D:com.scjaexam.propertyValue=003 MainClass`

Answer:

☑ **A.** The property setting is used with the interpreter, not the compiler. The property name must be sandwiched between the `-D` flag and the equal sign. The desired value should immediately follow the equal sign.

☒ **B, C,** and **D** are incorrect because `-d`, `-prop`, and "`-D:`" are invalid ways to designate a system property.

2

Programming with Java Statements

CERTIFICATION OBJECTIVES

- Understanding Fundamental Statements

- Implementing Statement-Related Algorithms from Pseudo-code

✓   Two-Minute Drill

Q&A   Self Test

S oftware applications are composed of various statements. It is these language statements that allow for the proper sequence of execution and associated functionality to occur. The more statement types a software language has, the more effective the language can be. Table 2-1 provides short definitions of the Java statement types defined in the *Java Language Specification, Third Edition*, by James Gosling, Bill Joy, Guy Steele, and Gilad Bracha (Addison Wesley, June 2005). Those covered on the exam and in this chapter are accompanied by a checkmark. You can refer to the language specification for more details on the statements that are not on the exam.

TABLE 2-1   Java Statements

Statement Name	Definition	On the Exam
The `assert` statement	Used to determine if code is functioning as expected. When its expression is evaluated to false, an exception is thrown.	
The `break` statement	Used to exit the body of a `switch` statement or loop.	✓
The `case` statement	Used as part of the `switch` statement to execute statements when its value matches the `switch` statement's conditional value.	✓
The `continue` statement	Used to terminate the current iteration of a `do-while`, `while`, or `for` loop and continue with the next iteration.	✓
The `while` statement	Used for iteration based on a condition.	✓
The `do-while` statement	Used for iteration based on a condition. The body of the `do-while` statement is executed at least once.	✓
The `empty` statement	Used for trivial purposes where no functionality is needed. It is represented by a single semicolon.	
The expression statements	Used to evaluate expressions. See Table 2-2.	✓
The `for` loop statement	Used for iteration. Main components are an initialization part, an expression part, and an update part.	✓
The enhanced `for` loop statement	Used for iteration through an iterable object or array.	✓
The `if` statement	Used for the conditional execution of statements.	✓
The `if-then` statement	Used for the conditional execution of statements by providing multiple conditions.	✓

TABLE 2-1	Java Statements (*Continued*)	
Statement Name	**Definition**	**On the Exam**
The `if-then-else` statement	Used for the conditional execution of statements by providing multiple conditions and fall-through when no conditions are met.	✓
The *labeled* statement	Used to give a statement a prefixed label.	
The `return` statement	Used to exit a method and return a specified value.	✓
The `switch` statement	Used for branching code based on conditions.	✓
The `synchronized` statement	Used for access control of threads.	
The `throw` statement	Used to throw an exception.	
The `try-catch-finally` statement	Used for exception handling.	

To be an effective Java programmer, you must master the basic statements. Sun knows this so they have included complete coverage of the basic statements on the exam. In addition, it is common practice for developers to work out detailed algorithms in pseudo-code before coding them up. As such, the exam contains questions to validate your ability to match implemented Java code with pseudo-code algorithms. This chapter will teach you how to recognize and code Java statements, as well as implement and recognize code produced from pseudo-code algorithms.

CERTIFICATION OBJECTIVE

Understanding Fundamental Statements

Exam Objective 4.1   Describe, compare, and contrast these three fundamental types of statements: assignment, conditional, and iteration, and given a description of an algorithm, select the appropriate type of statement to design the algorithm.

The Java programming language contains a variety of statement types. Even though the various statement types serve different purposes, the ones covered against this objective can be grouped into four main categories: expression statements, conditional statements, iteration statements, and transfer of control statements.

Expression statements are used for the evaluation of expressions. The only expression statement required for this objective is the assignment statement. Assignment statements allow for the ability to perform assignments on variables. Conditional statements, also known as decision statements, assist in directing the flow of control when a decision needs to be made. Conditional statements include the `if`, `if-then`, `if-then-else`, and `switch` statements. Iteration statements provide support in looping through blocks of code. Iteration statements include the `for` loop, the enhanced `for` loop, the `while` and the `do-while` statements. Transfer of control statements provide a means to stop or interrupt the normal flow of control. Transfer of control statements include the `continue`, `break`, and `return` statements. Transfer of control statements are always seen within other types of statements. The goal of this chapter is for you to gain the knowledge of when and how to use all of the necessary types of Java statements that will be seen on the SCJA exam. In the upcoming sections, we will examine the following statements:

- Assignment statements
- Conditional statements
- Iteration statements

Assignment Statements

An assignment statement is considered an expression statement. Let's briefly discuss expression statements first. Expression statements essentially work with expressions. Expressions in Java are considered to be anything that has a value or is reduced to a value. Typically, expressions evaluate to primitive types, such as in the case of adding two numbers [for example, `(1+2)`]. Concatenating strings together with the concatenation (+) operator results in a string, and is also considered an expression. All expressions can be used as statements; the only requirement is that they end with a semicolon. Of the Java expression statements represented in Table 2-2, the only expression statement covered on the exam via the objectives in this chapter is the assignment expression statement.

The Assignment Expression Statement

Assignment expression statements, commonly known as just assignment statements, are designed to assign values to variables. All assignment statements must be terminated with a semicolon. Having this ability to store information in variables provides the main characteristic of usefulness to computer applications.

	TABLE 2-2	Expression Statements

Expression Statement	Expression Statement Example	Coverage
Assignment	`variableName = 7;`	This chapter
Pre-increment	`++variableName;`	Chapter 4
Pre-decrement	`--variableName;`	Chapter 4
Post-increment	`variableName++;`	Chapter 4
Post-decrement	`variableName--;`	Chapter 4
Method invocation	`performMethod();`	Chapter 5
Object creation	`new ClassName();`	Chapter 4

The general usage of the assignment statement:

variable = *value*;

Given the declaration of an integer primitive, let's look at an assignment in its most basic form. There are three key elements. On the left you will find the variable that will be associated with the memory and type necessary to store the value. On the right is a literal value. If an expression is on the right, such as (1+2), it must be evaluated down to its literal value before it can be assigned. Lastly, an equal sign will reside between the variable and value of an assignment statement.

```
int variableName; // Declaration of an integer
variableName = 100; // Assignment expression statement
```

For as long as the application is running and the object in which the variable exists is still alive, the value for `variableName` will remain the assigned value, unless it is explicitly changed with another expression statement. The statement, illustrated in Figure 2-1, combines a declaration, an expression, and an assignment statement. In addition, it uses the values stored from previous assignment statements.

```
int fishInTank = 100; int fishInCooler = 50;
int totalFish = fishInTank + fishInCooler;
```

FIGURE 2-I	
Combined statements	

Trying to save an invalid literal to a declared primitive type variable will result in a compiler error. For more information about working with primitives, see Chapter 4.

Conditional Statements

Conditional statements are used when there is a need for determining the direction of flow based on conditions. Conditional statements include the `if`, `if-then`, `if-then-else`, and `switch` statements. The conditional statements represented in Table 2-3 will be seen on the exam.

The `if` Conditional Statement

The `if` statement is designed to conditionally execute a statement or conditionally decide between a choice of statements. The `if` statement will execute only one statement upon the condition, unless braces are supplied. Braces, also known as curly brackets, allow for multiple enclosed statements to be executed. This group of statements is also known as a block. The expression that is evaluated within `if` statements must evaluate to a `boolean` value, or the application will not compile. The `else` clause is optional and may be omitted.

TABLE 2-3   Conditional Statements

Formal Name	Keywords	Expression Types	Example
`if`	`if`, `else` (optional)	`boolean`	`if (value == 0) {}`

`if-then`	`if`,
	`else if`,
	`else if` (optional)
		`boolean`	`if (value == 0) {}`
			`else if (value == 1) {}`
			`else if (value >= 2) {}`

`if-then-else`	`if`,
	`else if`,
	`else if` (optional),
	`else`
		`boolean`	`if (value == 0) {}`
			`else if (value >=1) {}`
			`else {}`

`switch`	`switch`,
	`case`,
	`default` (optional),
	`break`
	(optional)
		`char`, `byte`, `short`,
		`int`, `Character`,
		`Byte`, `Short`,
		`Integer`,
		enumeration types
			`switch (100) {`
			`    case 100: break;`
			`    case 200: break;`
			`    case 300: break;`
			`    default: break;`
			`}`

INSIDE THE EXAM

Peculiarities with *if-related* Statements

The distinction between the `if`, `if-then`, and `if-then-else` statements may seem blurred. This is partially because the `then` keyword used in some other programming languages is not used in Java, even though the Java constructs are formally known as `if-then` and `if-then-else`. Let's clarify some confusing points about the `if`-related statements by providing some facts.

The `if` statement allows for the optional use of the `else` branch. This may be a little confusing since you may expect the `if` statement to stand alone without any branches, but it is what it is.

The `if-then` statement must have at least one `else if` branch. Optionally, an unlimited amount of `else if` branches may be included. You cannot use an `else` statement in an `if-then` statement, or the statement would be considered an `if-then-else` statement.

The `if-then-else` statement must have at least one `else if` branch. The `else if` branch is not optional, because if it was not present, the statement would be considered to be an `if` statement that includes the optional `else` branch.

The general usage of the `if` statement:

```
if (expression)
    statementA;
else
    statementB;
```

In the following example, we look at the most basic structure of an `if` statement. Here, we check to see if a person (`isFisherman`) is a fisherman, and if so, the expression associated with the `if` statement would evaluate to `true`. Because it is `true`, the example's fishing trip value (`isFishingTrip`) is modified to `true`. No action would have been taken if the `isFisherman` expression evaluated to `false`.

```java
boolean isFisherman = true;
boolean isFishingTrip = false;
if (isFisherman)
    isFishingTrip = true;
```

Let's change the code up a little bit. Here, you will see that a fishing trip will only occur if there are one or more fishermen as the expression reads (`fishermen >= 1`). See Chapter 3 for more details on relationship operators (for example, `<`, `<=`, `>`, `>=`, `==`, `!=`). We also see that when "one or more fishermen" evaluates to `true`, a block of statements will be executed.

```
int fishermen = 2;
boolean isFishingTrip = false;
if (fishermen >= 1) {
    isFishingTrip = true;
    System.out.print("Going Fishing!");
}
$ Going Fishing!
```

Executing statements in relationship to `false` conditions is also common in programming. In the following example, when the expression evaluates to `false`, the statement associated with the `else` part of the `if` statement is executed:

```
boolean isFisherman = false;
if (isFisherman) System.out.println("Going fishing!");
else System.out.println("I'm doing anything but fishing!");
$ I'm doing anything but fishing!
```

The `if-then` Conditional Statement

The `if-then` conditional statement—also known as the `if else if` statement—is used when multiple conditions need to flow through a decision-based scenario.

The general usage of the `if-then` statement:

if (*expressionA*)
   statementA;
else if (*expressionB*)
   statementB;

The expressions must evaluate to `boolean` values. Each statement may optionally be a group of statements enclosed in braces.

Let's look at an example. For those not familiar with surf-fishing, when fishing off the beach, a lead pyramid-shaped sinker is used to keep the line on the bottom

INSIDE THE EXAM

The most important thing to remember about the expression in the `if` statement is that it can accept any expression that returns a `boolean` value. Even though relational operators (for example, >=) are commonly used, assignment statements are allowed. Review and understand the following code examples:

```
boolean b;
boolean bValue = (b = true); // Evaluates to true
if (bValue) System.out.println("TRUE");
else System.out.println("FALSE");
if (bValue = false) System.out.println("TRUE");
else System.out.println("FALSE");
if (bValue == false) System.out.println("TRUE");
else System.out.println("FALSE");
$ TRUE
$ FALSE
$ TRUE
```

You also need to be aware that the assignment statements of all primitives will return their primitive values. So, if it's not an assignment of a `boolean` type, then the return value will not be `boolean`.

As such, the following code will not compile:

```
int i; // Valid declaration
int iValue = (i=1); // Valid evaluation to int
/* Fails here as boolean value is expected in the expression */
if (iValue) {};
```

Similarly, this code will not compile:

```
/* Fails here as boolean value is expected in the expression */
if (i=1) {};
```

The compile error will look like this:

```
Error: incompatible types; found: int, required: boolean
```

of the ocean. In the following code segment, conditions are evaluated matching the appropriate pyramidSinker by weight against the necessary tide:

```
int pyramidSinker = 3;
System.out.print("A pyramid sinker that weighs " + pyramidSinker
  + "ounces is ");
if (pyramidSinker == 2)
  System.out.print("used for a slow moving tide. ");
else if (pyramidSinker == 3)
  System.out.print("used for a moderate moving tide. ");
else if (pyramidSinker == 4)
  System.out.print("used for a fast moving tide. ");
$ A pyramid sinker that weighs 3 ounces is used for a moderate
  moving tide.
```

We used the string concatenation (+) operator in this example. While the functionality is straightforward, you will want to see Chapter 3 for more information on its behavior.

exam
watch

The if *family of statements evaluate expressions that must result in a* boolean *type where the value is* true *or* false. *Be aware that an object from the* Boolean *wrapper class is also allowed because it will go through unboxing in order to return the expected type. Unboxing is the automatic production of its primitive value in cases where it is needed. The following code demonstrates the use of a* Boolean *wrapper class object within the expression of an* if *statement:*

```
Boolean wrapperBoolean = new Boolean ("true");
/* Valid */
boolean primitiveBoolean1 = wrapperBoolean.booleanValue();
/* Valid because of unboxing */
boolean primitiveBoolean2 = wrapperBoolean;
if (wrapperBoolean)
System.out.println("Works because of unboxing");
```

For more information on autoboxing and unboxing, see Chapter 4.

The `if-then-else` Conditional Statement

As with the `if` and `if-then` statements, all expressions must evaluate to `true` or `false` as the expected primitive type is `boolean`. The main difference in the `if-then-else` statement is that the code will fall through to the final stand-alone `else` when the expression fails to return `true` for any condition. Each statement may optionally be a group of statements enclosed in braces. There is no limit to the number of `else if` clauses.

The general usage of the `if-then-else` statement:

if (*expressionA*)
   statementA;
else if (*expressionB*)
   statementB;
else if (*expressionC*)
   statementC;
...
else
   statementZZ;

In the following code listing, the method `getCastResult()` represents the efforts of a fisherman casting his line out into the ocean. The return value will be a `String` of value "fish," "shark," or "skate" and in this application the value is stored into the `resultOfCast` variable. This `String` value is evaluated against the stipulated string passed into the `equals` method. If the criteria are met for any `if` or `else if` condition, the associated block of code is executed, otherwise the code related to the final `else` is executed. This code clearly demonstrates a complete `if-then-else` scenario.

```
...
private FishingSession fishingSession = new FishingSession();
...
public void castForFish() {
  fishingSession.setCatch();
  String resultOfCast = fishingSession.getCastResult();
  if (resultOfCast.equals("fish")) {
    Fish keeperFish = new Fish();
    keeperFish = fishingSession.getFishResult();
    String type = keeperFish.getTypeOfFish();
    System.out.println("Wahoo! Keeper fish: " + type);
  } else if (resultOfCast.equals("shark")) {
```

```
      System.out.println("Need to throw this one back!");
    } else if (resultOfCast.equals("skate")) {
      System.out.println("Yuck, Leo can take this one off the
        hook!");
    } else {
      System.out.println("Darn, no catch!");
    }
  }
  ...


$ Wahoo! Keeper fish: Striped Bass
```

Note that the Fish class and associated methods were deliberately not shown since the scope of this example was the if-then-else scenario only.

If abrupt termination occurs during the evaluation of the conditional expression within an if statement, then all subsequent if-then (that is, else if) and if-then-else (that is, else) statements will end abruptly as well.

The switch Conditional Statement

The switch conditional statement is used to match the value from a switch statement expression against a value associated with a case keyword. Once matched, the enclosed statement(s) associated with the matching case value are executed and subsequent case statements are executed, unless a break statement is encountered. The break statements are optional and will cause the immediate termination of the switch conditional statement.

When two case statements within the same switch statement have the same value, a compiler error will be thrown.

```
switch (intValue){
  case 200: System.out.println("Case 1");
  /* Compiler error, Error: duplicate case label */
  case 200: System.out.println("Case 2");
}
```

The expression of the switch statement must evaluate to byte, short, int, or char. Wrapper classes of type Byte, Short, Int, and Character are also allowed since they are automatically unboxed to primitive types. Enumerated types are permitted as well.

The general usage of the switch statement:

```
switch (expression) {
    case valueA:
        // Sequences of statements
        break;
    case valueB:
        // Sequences of statements
        break;
    default:
        // Sequences of statements
    ...
}
```

Let's take a look at a complete switch conditional statement example. In the following generateRandomFish method, we use a random number generator to produce a value that will be used in the switch expression. The number generated will either be a 0, 1, 2, or 3. The switch statement will use the value to match it to the value of a case statement. In the example, a String with the name randomFish will be set depending on the case matched. In this example, the only possible value that does not have a matching case statement is the number 3. Therefore, this condition will be handled by the default statement. Whenever a break statement is hit, it will cause immediate termination of the switch statement.

```
public String generateRandomFish() {
    String randomFish;
    Random randomObject = new Random();
    int randomNumber = randomObject.nextInt(4);
    switch (randomNumber) {
        case 0:
            randomFish = "Blue Fish";
            break;
        case 1:
            randomFish = "Red Drum";
            break;
```

```
      case 2:
        randomFish = "Striped Bass";
        break;
      default:
        randomFish = "Unknown Fish Type";
        break;
    }
    return randomFish;
  }
```

The case statements can be organized in any manner. The default case is often listed last for code readability. Remember that without break statements, the switch block will continue with its fall-through, from the point that the condition has been met. The following code is a valid switch conditional statement that uses an enumeration type for its expression value:

```
private enum ClamBait {FRESH,SALTED,ARTIFICIAL}
...
ClamBait bait = ClamBait.SALTED;
switch (bait) {
default:
  System.out.println("No bait");
  break;
 case FRESH:
  System.out.println("Fresh clams");
  break;
 case SALTED:
  System.out.println("Salted clams");
  break;
 case ARTIFICIAL:
  System.out.println("Artificial clams");
  break;
 }
```

Knowing what you can and cannot do with switch statements will help expedite your development efforts.

Iteration Statements

Iteration statements are used when there is a need to iterate through pieces of code. Iteration statements include the for loop, enhanced for loop, the while and the do-while statements. The break statement is used to exit the body of any

SCENARIO & SOLUTION

To ensure your statement is bug free, which type of statements should you include within the switch?	Both `break` statements and the `default` statement are commonly used in the switch. Forgetting these statements can lead to improper fall-throughs or unhandled conditions. Note that many bug-finding tools will flag missing `default` statements.
You wish to use a range in a `case` statement (for instance, `case 7-35`). Is this a valid feature in Java, as it is with other languages?	Ranges in `case` statements are *not* allowed. Consider setting up a condition in an `if` statement. For example: `if (x >=7 && x <=35){}`
You wish to use the `switch` statement, using `String` values where the expression is expected, as is possible with other languages. Is this a valid feature in Java?	Strings are not valid at the decision point for `switch` statements. Consider using an `if` statement instead. For example: `if (strValue.equals("S1")){}`

iteration statement. The `continue` statement is used to terminate the current iteration and continue with the next iteration. The iteration statements detailed in Table 2-4 will be seen on the exam.

TABLE 2-4   Iteration Statements

Formal Name	Keywords	Main Expression Components	Example
`for` loop	`for`, `break` (optional), `continue` (optional)	Initializer, expression, update mechanism	`for (i=0; i<j; i++) {}`
Enhanced `for` loop	`for`, `break` (optional), `continue` (optional)	Element, array, or collection	`for (Fish f : listOfFish) {};`
`while`	`while`, `break` (optional), `continue` (optional)	Boolean expression	`while (value == 1) {` `}`
`do-while`	`do, while`, `break` (optional), `continue` (optional)	Boolean expression	`do {` `} while (value == 1);`

The `for` Loop Iteration Statement

The `for` loop statement is designed to iterate through code. It has main parts that include an initialization part, an expression part and an iteration part. The initialization does not need to declare a variable as long as the variable is declared before the `for` statement. So, "int x = 0;" and "x=0;" are both acceptable in the initialization part. Be aware though that the scope of the variable declared within the initialization part of the `for` loop ends once the `for` loop terminates. The expression within the `for` loop statement must evaluate to a boolean value. The iteration, also known as the update part, provides the mechanism that will allow the iteration to occur. A basic update part is represented as "i++;".

The general usage of the `for` statement:

```
for ( initialization; expression; iteration) {
   // Sequence of statements
}
```

The following is an example of a basic `for` loop where the initialization variable is declared outside the `for` loop statement:

```
int m;
for (m = 1; m < 5; m++) {
   System.out.print("Marker " + m + ", ");
}
System.out.print("Last Marker " + m + "\n");
$ Marker 0, Marker 1, Marker 2, Marker 3, Marker 4, Last Marker 5
```

The following is a similar example, but with the variable declared in the `for` loop:

```
for (int m = 1; m < 5; m++) {
   System.out.print("Marker " + m + ", ");
}
```

Declaring the initialize variable in the `for` loop is allowed and is the common approach. However, you can't use the variable once you have exited the loop. The following will result in a compilation error:

```
for (int m = 1; m < 5; m++) {
   System.out.print("Marker " + m + ", ");
}
System.out.print("Last Marker " + m + "\n"); // m is out of scope
# Error: variable m not found in class [ClassName].
```

INSIDE THE EXAM

Exposing Corner Cases with Your Compiler

The exam designers were not satisfied with just validating your knowledge of the fundamental Java material. They took the time to work in corner cases as well as modify the structure of the code in such a slight manner that it appears to be correct but is not. When you work through the examples in this book, take the time to modify things a bit, intentionally introducing errors, to see how the compiler reacts. Being able to think like the compiler will help you score higher on the exam.

Third-party developers of Java development kits can define their own text for compiler error messages. Where they will likely try to model the messages provided by Sun's JDK, sometimes care will be taken to make the messages more precise. Consider invoking compiler errors with the latest Sun JDK compiler, as well as a compiler providing an IDE such as the Eclipse SDK. Compare the similarities and differences.

The Enhanced `for` Loop Iteration Statement

The enhanced `for` loop is used to iterate through an array, a collection, or an object that implements the interface iterable. The enhanced `for` loop is also commonly known as the "for each" loop and the "for in" loop. Iteration occurs for each element in the array or iterable class. Remember that the loop can be terminated at any time by the inclusion of a `break` statement. And as with the other iteration statements, the `continue` statement will terminate the current iteration and start with the next iteration.

The general usage of the `for` statement:

for (type variable : collection) statement-sequence

The following code segment demonstrates how a `for` loop can easily dump out the contents of an array. Here, the enhanced `for` loop iterates over each `hook` integer in the array `hookSizes`. For each iteration, the hook size is printed out.

```
int hookSizes[] = { 1, 1, 1, 2, 2, 4, 5, 5, 5, 6, 7, 8, 8, 9 };
for (int hook: hookSizes) System.out.print(hook + " ");
$ 1 1 1 2 2 4 5 5 5 6 7 8 8 9
```

The enhanced `for` loop is frequently used for searching through items in a collection. Here, the enhanced `for` loop iterates over each `hook` `Integer` in the collection `hookSizesList`. For each iteration, the `hook` size is printed out. This example demonstrates the use of collections and generics.

```
Integer hookSizeList;
ArrayList<Integer> hookSizesList = new ArrayList<Integer>();
hookSizesList.add(1);
hookSizesList.add(4);
hookSizesList.add(5);
for (Integer hook : hookSizesList) System.out.print(hook + " ");
$ 1 4 5
```

See *Java Generics and Collections* by Maurice Naftalin and Philip Wadler (O'Reilly, October 2006) for comprehensive coverage of the Generics and Collections frameworks.

EXERCISE 2-1

Iterating Through an `ArrayList` While Applying Conditions

This exercise will have you iterating through an `ArrayList` of floats. Specifically, this exercise will have you printing out only the legal sizes of keeper fish.

1. Create an `ArrayList` of floats called `fishLengthList`. This list will represent the sizes of a few striped bass.

2. Add the following floats to the list: 10.0, 15.5, 18.0, 29.5, 45.5. These numbers represent the length in inches of the bass.

3. Iterate through the list, printing out only the numbers larger than the required length. Assume the required length is 28 inches.

The `while` Iteration Statement

The `while` statement is designed to iterate through code. The `while` loop statement evaluates an expression and only executes the `while` loop body if the expression evaluates to true. There is typically an expression within the body that will affect the result of the expression.

The general usage of the `while` statement:

```
while (expression) {
    // Sequences of statements
}
```

The following code example demonstrates the use of the `while` statement. Here, a fisherman will continue fishing until his fish limit has been reached. Specifically, when the `fishLimit` variable within the body of the `while` statement reaches `10`, the fisherman's `session` will be set to inactive. Since the `while` statement demands that the `session` be active, its loop will terminate upon the change.

```
fishingSession.setSession("active");
/* WHILE STATEMENT */
while (fishingSession.getSession().equals("active")) {
 castForFish(); // Updates fishLimit instance variable
 if (fishLimit == 10) {
   fishingSession.setSession("inactive");
 }
}
```

on the **job**

Various formatting styles can be followed when formatting your code. Formatting considerations include indentation, white space usage, line wrapping, code separation, and braces handling. You should select a style and maintain it throughout your code. For demonstration purposes, here are two distinct ways that braces are handled:

K&R style braces handling:

```
while (x==y) {
  performSomeMethod();
}
```

Allman style brace handling:

```
while (x==y)
{
  performSomeMethod();
}
```

Most IDEs support customizable formatting that can often be applied by selecting a format option from a menu. Using an IDE to ensure formatting is properly and consistently applied is a good idea. A popular Java code beautifier that is available as a plug-in to many tools is Jalopy: http://jalopy .sourceforge.net/jalopy/manual.html.

The `do-while` Iteration Statement

The `do-while` statement is designed to iterate through code. It is very similar to the `while` loop statement except that it always executes the body at least once. The `do-while` loop evaluates an expression and only continues to execute the body if it evaluates to true. There is typically an expression within the body that will affect the result of the expression.

The general usage of the `do-while` statement:

```
do {
    // Sequence of statements
} while (expression)
```

EXERCISE 2-2

Performing Code Refactoring

In the following code example, we want to make sure the fisherman gets at least one cast in. While this appears to make logical sense, you always need to think about corner cases. What if a fox steals the fisherman's bait before he gets a chance to cast? In this case, the `piecesOfBait` variable would equal zero, but the fisherman would still cast as the body of the `do-while` loop is guaranteed at least one iteration. See if you can refactor this code with a `while` statement to avoid the possible condition of casting with no bait.

```java
fishingSession.setSession("active");
int piecesOfBait = 5;
piecesOfBait = 0; // Fox steals the bait!
 do {
   castForFish();
   /* Check to see if bait is available */
   if (fishingSession.isBaitAvailable() == false) {
     /* Place a new piece of bait on the hook */
     fishingSession.setBaitAvailable(true);
     piecesOfBait--;
   }
 } while (piecesOfBait != 0);
```

SCENARIO & SOLUTION

You wish to iterate though a collection. Which iteration statement would be the best choice?	You will need to use the enhanced `for` loop statement.
You wish to execute a statement based on the result of a boolean expression. Which conditional statement would be the best choice?	You will need to use the `if` statement.
You wish to provide conditional cases in relationship to enumeration values. What conditional statement would be your only choice?	You will need to use the `switch` statement.
You wish to execute a block of statements and then iterate through the block based on a condition. What iteration statement would be your only choice?	You will need to use the `do-while` statement.
You wish to permanently exit a case statement. What transfer of control statement would you choose?	You will need to use the `break` statement.

Selecting the right statement types during development can make coding your algorithms easier. Proper statement selection will also promote the ease of software maintenance efforts if the code ever needs to be modified. It's important to realize that statements are used for different purposes and one particular type of statement cannot solve all development needs. You will find it not uncommon to use a combination of statement types to implement the code for many algorithms. Having a strong foundation of what the main purposes are of the different types of statements will assist you when you need to use them together.

CERTIFICATION OBJECTIVE

Implementing Statement-Related Algorithms from Pseudo-code

Exam Objective 4.3   Given an algorithm as pseudo-code, develop method code that implements the algorithm using conditional statements (if and switch), iteration statements (for, for-each, while, and do-while), assignment statements, and break and continue statements to control the flow within switch and iteration statements.

Pseudo-code is a structured means to allow algorithm designers to express computer programming algorithms in a human-readable format. Pseudo-code is informally written and has the characteristics of being very compact and high-level in nature. Even though pseudo-code does not need to be tied to any specific software language, the designer will typically script the pseudo-code algorithms based on the structural conventions of their target software language. You may be thinking, "Hey, pseudo-code sound great! Where do I get started writing high-quality algorithms in pseudo-code!" Well, don't get too excited. No standards exist for writing pseudo-code, since its main purpose is to help designers build algorithms in their own language. With so many different languages having varying structural differences and paradigms, creating a pseudo-code standard that applies to them all would be impossible. Essentially, writing pseudo-code allows for the quick and focused production of algorithms based on logic, not language syntax. The following topics presented in the next sections will discuss working with basic pseudo-code and converting pseudo-code algorithms into Java code with an emphasis on statements:

- Pseudo-code algorithms
- Pseudo-code algorithms and Java

Pseudo-code Algorithms

The exam will present pseudo-code algorithms to you. In turn, you will have options to decide which Java code segment correctly implements the algorithms. This can be tricky since the pseudo-code algorithms do not need to represent Java syntax in any way, but the Java code segments must be structurally and syntactically accurate to be correct.

Let's take a look at a pseudo-code algorithm.

```
value := 20
IF value >= 1
  print the value
ELSEIF value = 0
  print the value
ELSE
  print "less than zero"
ENDIF
```

When converting this algorithm to Java, you may naturally want to use "ELSEIF", "ELSE", and "ENDIF". This is a gotcha... because they are not keywords. Let's do an exercise to review valid keywords that may be seen on the exam.

EXERCISE 2-3

Knowing Your Statement-Related Keywords

Table 2-5 represents all of the valid Java keywords. This exercise will allow you to use the table to assist you in deducing the keywords you may see while using the various types of statements.

On a tangent, the following bullets are included here to remove confusion about some of the keywords:

- Keywords `const` and `goto` are reserved Java keywords but are not functionally used. Since they are commonly used C++ keywords, the Java language designers felt that providing them as keywords would allow the IDEs and compilers to provide better error messages when these keywords are encountered.

- The `assert` keyword was added with J2SE 1.4.

- The enum keyword was added with J2SE 5.0.

- Reserved literals named `true`, `false`, and `null` are not keywords.

- Java keywords cannot be used as identifiers.

TABLE 2-5	Java Keywords				
Java EE 5 Keywords	abstract	continue	for	new	switch
	assert	default	goto	package	synchronized
	boolean	do	if	private	this
	break	double	implements	protected	throw
	byte	else	import	public	throws
	case	enum	instanceof	return	transient
	catch	extends	int	short	try
	char	final	interface	static	void
	class	finally	long	strictfp	volatile
	const	float	native	super	while

Let's start the exercise.

1. List the primary keywords you may see in conditional statements.
2. List the primary keywords you may see in iteration statements.
3. List the primary keywords you may see in transfer of control statements.
4. Bonus: List the primary keywords you may see in exception handling statements.

While surfing the Internet, you'll find there is no universally accepted convention for pseudo-code. However, Table 2-6 gives you a general idea as to what you may expect on the exam. This information was reduced from the

TABLE 2-6   Pseudo-code Conventions

Pseudo-code Element	Pseudo-code Convention	Java Example
Assignment	`variable := value`	`wreckYear = 1511;`

if statement	`IF condition THEN`
	`    //statement sequence`
	`ELSEIF`
	`    //statement sequence`
	`ELSE`
	`    //statement sequence`
	`ENDIF`
		`if (wreckYear == 1502)`
		`    wreck = "Santa Ana";`
		`elseif (wreckYear == 1503)`
		`    wreck = "Magdalena";`
		`else`
		`    wreck = "Unknown";`

switch statement	`CASE expression OF`
	`    Condition A: statement sequence`
	`    Condition B:`
	`statement sequence`
	`    Default: sequence of statements`
	`ENDCASE`
		`switch (wreckYear) {`
		`    case 1502:`
		`        wreck = "Santa Ana";`
		`        break;`
		`    case 1503:`
		`        wreck = "Magdalena";`
		`        break;`
		`    default:`
		`        wreck = "Unknown"`
		`}`

while statement	`WHILE condition`
	`    //statement sequence`
	`ENDWHILE`
		`while (n < 4) {`
		`    System.out.println(i);`
		`    n++;`
		`}`

for statement	`FOR iteration bounds`
	`    //statement sequence`
	`ENDFOR`
		`for (int i=0; i<j; i++) {`
		`    System.out.println(i);`
		`}`

"PSEUDOCODE STANDARD" page of the Cal Poly State University web site. The authors did a pretty good job proposing a standard.

Pseudo-code Algorithms and Java

The exam will give you a piece of pseudo-code and ask you to select the correct Java source code conversion. The code will likely be a fragment of a complete source file and while it is okay that some primitive declarations may be missing, conditional and iteration statements are always represented completely. Let's take a look at an example: Given:

```
fishingRods := 5
fishingReels := 4
IF fishingRods does not equal fishingReels THEN
   print "We are missing fishing equipment"
ELSE
   print "The fishing equipment is all here"
ENDIF
```

Answer:

```
int fishingRods = 5;
int fishingReels = 4;
if (fishingRods != fishingReels)
   System.out.print("We are missing fishing equipment");
else
   System.out.print("The fishing equipment is all here");
```

e x a m
ⓦ a t c h
> *Three objectives on the exam have to do with producing Java code from pseudo-code algorithms. These objectives cover statement-related (objective 4.3), operator-related (objective 4.5), and variable scope–related (objective 4.2) pseudo-code algorithms.*

The following three exercises will assist you in preparing for the pseudo-code-related questions on the exam.

EXERCISE 2-4

Implementing Pseudo-code Algorithm #1

Given:

```
location := Corson's Inlet
IF location != NULL THEN
  print "Fishing spot: " + location
ENDIF
```

1. Convert the pseudo-code to Java.
2. Compile the Java source code and debug any errors and warnings.
3. Interpret the compiled bytecode.

EXERCISE 2-5

Implementing Pseudo-code Algorithm #2

Given:

```
IF waterTemperature greater than or equal to 69 THEN
   isStripersMostActive := false // Stripers are less active
ELSEIF waterTemperature less than 69 but greater than 47 THEN
   isStripersMostActive := true // Stripers are most active
ELSEIF waterTemperature less than or equal to 47 THEN
   isStripersMostActive := false // Stripers are less active
ENDIF
```

1. Convert the pseudo-code to Java.
2. Compile the Java source code and debug any errors and warnings.
3. Interpret the compiled bytecode.

EXERCISE 2-6

Implementing Pseudo-code Algorithm #3

Given:

```
fishingList = rods, reels, bait, lunch
FOR EACH variable in fishingList
  print variable

ENDFOR
```

1. Convert the pseudo-code to Java.
2. Compile the Java source code and debug any errors and warnings.
3. Interpret the compiled bytecode.

CERTIFICATION SUMMARY

This chapter on fundamental statements discussed details related to the fundamental statement types. By studying this chapter, you should now be able to recognize and develop the following types of statements:

- Expression statements, with a focus on the assignment statement
- Conditional statements (`if`, `if-then`, `if-then-else`, and `switch`)
- Iteration statements (`for`, enhanced `for`, `while`, and `do-while`)
- Transfer of control statements (`continue`, `break`, and `return`)

The types of pseudo-code-related questions you can expect to see on the exam were covered in this chapter. To prepare you, we explored the basics of pseudo-code in detail and discussed how to convert statement-related pseudo-code algorithms to pure Java code.

At this point, you should be well prepared for exam questions covering Java statements and relative pseudo-code being converted to Java.

✓ # TWO-MINUTE DRILL

Understanding Fundamental Statements

❏ Assignment statements assign values to variables.

❏ Assignment statements that do not return `boolean` types will cause the compiler to report an error when used as the expression in an `if` statement.

❏ Trying to save an invalid literal to a declared primitive type variable will result in a compiler error.

❏ Conditional statements are used for determining the direction of flow based on conditions.

❏ Types of conditional statements include the `if`, `if-then`, `if-then-else`, and `switch` statements.

❏ The `default` case statement can be placed anywhere in the body of the `switch` statement.

❏ The expressions used in `if` statements must evaluate to `boolean` values, or the application will fail to compile.

❏ `Boolean` wrapper classes are allowed as expressions in `if` statements since they are unboxed. Remember that unboxing is the automatic production of primitive values from their related wrapper classes when the primitive value is required.

❏ Iteration statements are designed for iterating through pieces of code.

❏ Iteration statements include the `for` loop, enhanced `for` loop, and the `while` and `do-while` statements.

❏ The `for` loop statement has main components that include an initialization part, an expression part, and an update part.

❏ The enhanced `for` loop statement is used for iteration through an iterable object or array.

❏ The `while` loop statement is used for iteration based on a condition.

❏ The `do-while` statement is used for iteration based on a condition. The body of this statement is always executed at least once.

❏ Transfer of control statements interrupt or stop the flow of execution.

❏ The transfer of control statements include the `continue`, `break`, and `return` statements.

❑ The `continue` statement is used to terminate the current iteration of a `do-while`, `while`, or `for` loop, and then continue with the next iteration.

❑ The `break` statement is used to exit the body of a `switch` statement or loop.

❑ The `return` statement is used to exit a method and return a specified value.

❑ A block is a sequence of statements within braces—for example, { `int x=0; int y=1` }.

Implementing Statement-Related Algorithms from Pseudo-code

❑ Pseudo-code allows algorithm designers to express computer programming algorithms in a human-readable format.

❑ Writing pseudo-code allows for the quick and focused production of algorithms based on logic, not language syntax.

❑ Java keywords and statement usage structures are used when implementing pseudo-code algorithms.

❑ There are no universally accepted standards for writing pseudo-code.

SELF TEST

Understanding Fundamental Statements

1. Given x is declared with a valid integer, which conditional statement will not compile?

   A. `if (x == 0) {System.out.println("True Statement");}`

   B. `if (x == 0) {System.out.println("False Statement");}`

   C. `if (x == 0) {;} elseif (x == 1) {System.out.println("Valid Statement");}`

   D. `if (x == 0) ; else if (x == 1){} else {;}`

2. Which is not a type of statement?

   A. Conditional statement

   B. Assignment statement

   C. Iteration statement

   D. Propagation statement

3. What type of statement would be used to code the following equation: y = (m*x) + b?

   A. Conditional statement

   B. Assignment statement

   C. Assertion statement

   D. Transfer of control statement

4. You need to update a value of a hash table (that is, HashMap) where the primary key must equal a specified string. Which statements would you need to use in the implementation of this algorithm?

   A. Iteration statement

   B. Expression statement

   C. Conditional statement

   D. Transfer of control statement

5. Which keyword is part of a transfer of control statement?

   A. `if`

   B. `return`

   C. do

   D. assert

6. A switch statement works with which wrapper class/reference type?

   A. Character

   B. Byte

   C. Short

   D. Int

7. Which statements correctly declare boolean variables?

   A. Boolean isValid = true;

   B. boolean isValid = TRUE;

   C. boolean isValid = new Boolean (true);

   D. boolean isValid = 1;

8. Which of the following statements will not compile?

   A. if (true) ;

   B. if (true) {}

   C. if (true) {:}

   D. if (true) {;}

9. Given:

```
public class Dinner {
  public static void main (String[] args)
  {
    boolean isKeeperFish = false;
    if (isKeeperFish = true) {
      System.out.println("Fish for dinner");
    } else {
      System.out.println("Take out for dinner");
    }
  }
}
```

What will be the result of the application's execution?

   A. Fish for dinner will be printed.

   B. Take out for dinner will be printed.

   C. A compilation error will occur.

10. The `for` loop has been enhanced in Java 5.0. Which is NOT a common term for the improved *for* loop.

    A. The "for in" loop

    B. The specialized *for* loop

    C. The "*for each*" loop

    D. The enhanced `for` loop

Implementing Statement-Related Algorithms from Pseudo-code

11. Given:

```
COUNTER := 1
WHILE COUNTER LESS THAN 10
  PRINT COUNTER AND A NEW LINE
  COUNTER := COUNTER + 1
ENDWHILE
```

    Which Java code segment implements the pseudo-code algorithm?

    A.
    ```
    INT counter = 1;
    WHILE (counter < 10) {
      System.out.print(counter + "\n");
      counter++;
    }
    ```

    B.
    ```
    int counter = 1;
    while {counter < 10} {
      System.out.print(counter + "\n");
      counter++;
    }
    ```

    C.
    ```
    int counter = 1;
    while (counter < 10) {
      System.out.println(counter);
      counter++;
    }
    ```

    D.
    ```
    int counter = 1;
    while (counter < 10) {
      System.out.println(counter + "\n");
      counter++;
    }
    ```

12. Given:

```
ISRECORD := FALSE
FLOAT RECORD := 78.8
IF WEIGHT > RECORD
THEN ISRECORD := TRUE
ELSE ISRECORD := FALSE
ENDIF
```

Which Java code segment implements the pseudo-code algorithm?

A.
```
boolean isRecord = false
float record = 78.8f
if (weight > record) isRecord = true
else isRecord = false
```

B.
```
boolean isRecord = false;
float record = 78.8f;
if (weight > record) isRecord = true;
else isRecord = false;
endif
```

C.
```
boolean isRecord = FALSE;
float record = 78.8f;
if (weight > record) isRecord = true;
else isRecord = false;
```

D.
```
boolean isRecord = false;
float record = 78.8f;
if (weight > record) isRecord = true;
else isRecord = false;
```

SELF TEST ANSWERS

Understanding Fundamental Statements

1. Given x is declared with a valid integer, which conditional statement will not compile?

    A. `if (x == 0) {System.out.println("True Statement");}`

    B. `if (x == 0) {System.out.println("False Statement");}`

    C. `if (x == 0) {;} elseif (x == 1) {System.out.println("Valid Statement");}`

    D. `if (x == 0) ; else if (x == 1){} else {;}`

    > Answer:
    >
    > ☑ **C.** The statement will not compile. Without a space between the `else` and `if` keywords, the compiler will be thrown an error similar to "Error: method elseif (boolean) not found…"
    >
    > ☒ **A, B,** and **D** are incorrect. All of these conditional statements will compile successfully.

2. Which is not a type of statement?

    A. Conditional statement

    B. Assignment statement

    C. Iteration statement

    D. Propagation statement

    > Answer:
    >
    > ☑ **D.** There is no such thing as a propagation statement.
    >
    > ☒ **A, B,** and **C** are incorrect. Conditional, assignment, and iteration are all types of statements.

3. What type of statement would be used to code the following equation: $y = (m*x) + b$?

    A. Conditional statement

    B. Assignment statement

C. Assertion statement

D. Transfer of control statement

Answer:

☑ **B.** An assignment statement would be used to code the given example of y = (m*x) + b.

☒ **A, C,**and **D** are incorrect. The conditional, assertion, and transfer of control statements are not used to perform assignments.

4. You need to update a value of a hash table (that is, HashMap) where the primary key must equal a specified string. Which statements would you need to use in the implementation of this algorithm?

A. Iteration statement

B. Expression statement

C. Conditional statement

D. Transfer of control statement

Answer:

☑ **A, B,**and **C.** An Iteration, expression, and conditional statements would be used to implement the algorithm. The following code segment demonstrates the use of these statements by programmatically replacing the ring on the little finger of a person's left hand. The statements are prefaced by comments that identify their types.

```
import java.util.HashMap;
public class HashMapExample {
  public static void main(String[] args) {
    HashMap<String,String> leftHand = new HashMap<String,String>();
    leftHand.put("Thumb", null);
    leftHand.put("Index finger", "Puzzle Ring");
    leftHand.put("Middle finger", null);
    leftHand.put("Ring finger", "Engagement Ring");
    leftHand.put("Little finger", "Pinky Ring");
    // Iteration statement
    for (String s : leftHand.keySet()) {
      // Conditional statement
      if (s.equals("Little finger")) {
        System.out.println(s + " had a " + leftHand.get(s));
        // Expression Statement
        leftHand.put("Little finger", "Engineer's Ring");
```

```
            System.out.println(s + " has an " + leftHand.get(s));
         }
      }
    }
  }
$ Little finger had a Pinky Ring
$ Little finger has an Engineer's Ring
```

☒ **D** is incorrect. There is no transfer of control statement in the algorithm.

5. Which keyword is part of a transfer of control statement?

A. `if`

B. `return`

C. `do`

D. `assert`

Answer:

☑ **B.** The keyword `return` is used as part of a transfer of control statement.

☒ **A, C,** and **D** are incorrect. The keywords `if`, `do`, and `assert` are not part of any transfer of control statements.

6. A `switch` statement works with which wrapper class/reference type?

A. `Character`

B. `Byte`

C. `Short`

D. `Int`

Answer:

☑ **A, B,** and **C.** The `switch` statements work with `Character`, `Byte`, and `Short` wrapper classes as well as the `Integer` wrapper class.

☒ **D** is incorrect. There is no such thing as an `Int` wrapper type. This was a trick question. The `switch` statement works with either the `int` primitive or the `Integer` wrapper type.

7. Which statements correctly declare `boolean` variables?

 A. `Boolean isValid = true;`

 B. `boolean isValid = TRUE;`

 C. `boolean isValid = new Boolean (true);`

 D. `boolean isValid = 1;`

Answer:

 ☑ **A** and **C.** These statements properly declare `boolean` variables. Remember, the only valid literal values for the `boolean` primitives are `true` and `false`.

 ☒ **B** and **D** are incorrect. **B** is incorrect because TRUE is not a valid literal value. **D** is incorrect because you cannot assign the value 1 to a `boolean` variable.

8. Which of the following statements will not compile?

 A. `if (true) ;`

 B. `if (true) {}`

 C. `if (true) {:}`

 D. `if (true) {;}`

Answer:

 ☑ **C.** A colon is invalid by itself.

 ☒ **A, B,** and **D** are incorrect. All of the statements represent compilable code.

9. Given:

```
public class Dinner {
  public static void main (String[] args)
  {
    boolean isKeeperFish = false;
    if (isKeeperFish = true) {
      System.out.println("Fish for dinner");
    } else {
      System.out.println("Take out for dinner");
    }
  }
}
```

What will be the result of the application's execution?

A. `Fish for dinner` will be printed.

B. `Take out for dinner` will be printed.

C. A compilation error will occur.

Answer:

☑ **A.** Since only one equals sign (that is, assignment statement) was used in the `if` statement, the `isKeeperFish` variable was assigned the value of `true`.

☒ **B** and **C** are incorrect.

10. The `for` loop has been enhanced in Java 5.0. Which is NOT a common term for the improved for loop.

A. The "for in" loop

B. The specialized for loop

C. The "for each" loop

D. The enhanced `for` loop

Answer:

☑ **B.** The enhanced `for` loop is not commonly referenced as a specialized *for* loop.

☒ **A, C,** and **D** are incorrect. The enhanced `for` loop is also commonly referenced as the *for in* loop and the *for each* loop.

Implementing Statement-Related Algorithms from Pseudo-code

11. Given:

```
COUNTER := 1
WHILE COUNTER LESS THAN 10
   PRINT COUNTER AND A NEW LINE
   COUNTER := COUNTER + 1
ENDWHILE
```

Which Java code segment implements the pseudo-code algorithm?

A.
```
INT counter = 1;
WHILE (counter < 10) {
   System.out.print(counter + "\n");
   counter++;
}
```

B.
```
int counter = 1;
while {counter < 10} {
   System.out.print(counter + "\n");
   counter++;
}
```

C.
```
int counter = 1;
while (counter < 10) {
   System.out.println(counter);
   counter++;
}
```

D.
```
int counter = 1;
while (counter < 10) {
   System.out.println(counter + "\n");
   counter++;
}
```

Answer:

☑ **C.** The answer implements the pseudo-code algorithm correctly.

☒ **A, B,** and **D** are incorrect. Answer **A** is incorrect because INT and WHILE are not Java keywords. **B** is incorrect because the expression for the `while` statement is enclosed in braces where parentheses are expected. **D** is incorrect because two new lines are printed, one with (\n) and one with the `println` method.

12. Given:

```
ISRECORD := FALSE
FLOAT RECORD := 78.8
IF WEIGHT > RECORD
THEN ISRECORD := TRUE
ELSE ISRECORD := FALSE
ENDIF
```

Which Java code segment implements the pseudo-code algorithm?

A.
```
boolean isRecord = false
float record = 78.8f
if (weight > record) isRecord = true
else isRecord = false
```

B.
```
boolean isRecord = false;
float record = 78.8f;
if (weight > record) isRecord = true;
else isRecord = false;
endif
```

C.
```
boolean isRecord = FALSE;
float record = 78.8f;
if (weight > record) isRecord = true;
else isRecord = false;
```

D.
```
boolean isRecord = false;
float record = 78.8f;
if (weight > record) isRecord = true;
else isRecord = false;
```

Answer:

☑ **D.** The answer implements the pseudo-code algorithm correctly.

☒ **A, B,**and **C** are incorrect. **A** is incorrect because all of the required semicolons are missing. **B** is incorrect because the answer uses `endif`, which is not a Java keyword. Answer **C** is incorrect because the answer incorrectly uses FALSE. The only valid Java boolean literals are `true` and `false`.

3

Programming with Java Operators and Strings

CERTIFICATION OBJECTIVES

- Understanding Fundamental Operators

- Developing with String Objects and Their Methods

✓   Two-Minute Drill

Q&A   Self Test

T wo of the most fundamental elements of the Java programming language are Java operators and strings. This chapter discusses Java operators and how they manipulate their operands. You will need a full understanding of the different types and groupings of operators to score well on the exam. This chapter provides you with all of the operator-related information you need to know.

Strings are commonly used in Java, therefore they will also be present throughout the exam. This chapter details the String class and its related functionality. Topics include the string concatenation operator and the toString method, as well as a discussion of valuable methods straight from the String class.

After completing this chapter, you will have all the knowledge necessary to score well on the operator- and string-related questions on the exam.

CERTIFICATION OBJECTIVE

Understanding Fundamental Operators

Exam Objective 4.5   Given an algorithm as pseudo-code, develop code that correctly applies the appropriate operators, including assignment operators (limited to: =, +=, -=), arithmetic operators (limited to: +, -, *, /, %, ++, --), relational operators (limited to: <, <=, >, >=, ==, !=), logical operators (limited to: !, &&, | |), to produce a desired result. Also, write code that determines the equality of two objects or two primitives.

Java operators are used to return a result from an expression using one, two, or three operands. Operands are the values placed to the right or left side of the operators. Prefix/postfix-increment/decrement operators use one operand. The conditional ternary operator (? :) uses three operands. All other operators use two operands. Examples of "operand use" are shown in Figure 3-1. Note that the result of evaluating operands is typically a primitive value.

Table 3-1 represents all of the operators you may see on the exam. The precedence defines the order of which operator will be evaluated when several are included in an expression. The association defines which operand will be used (or evaluated) first. The Java operators that are not on the exam are the bitwise complement (~), left shift (<<), right shift (>>), unsigned right shift (>>>), boolean AND (&), bitwise AND (&), boolean exclusive OR (^), bitwise OR(^), boolean OR (|), bitwise OR(|), conditional ternary operator (? :), and the following compound assignment operators (*=, /=, %=, &=, ^=, | =, <<=, >>=, >>>=).

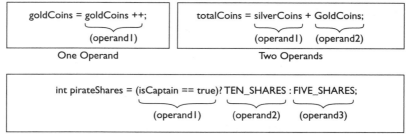

FIGURE 3-1

Operands

goldCoins = goldCoins ++;

(operand1)

One Operand

totalCoins = silverCoins + GoldCoins;

(operand1) (operand2)

Two Operands

int pirateShares = (isCaptain == true)? TEN_SHARES : FIVE_SHARES;

(operand1) (operand2) (operand3)

Three Operands

The following topics will be covered in these pages:

- Assignment operators
- Arithmetic operators
- Relational operators
- Logical operators

TABLE 3-1   Java Operators on the SCJA Exam

Relative Precedence	Operator	Description	Operator Type	Association
1	++,--	Postfix increment, postfix decrement	Arithmetic	Right to left
2	++,--	Prefix increment, prefix decrement	Arithmetic	Right to left
2	!	Boolean NOT	Logical	Right to left
3	*,/,%	Multiplication, division, remainder (modulus)	Arithmetic	Left to right
4	+,-	Addition, subtraction	Arithmetic	Left to right
5	<, <=, >, >=	Less than, less than or equal to, greater than, greater than or equal to	Relational	Left to right
6	==, !=	Value equality and inequality	Relational	Left to right
6	==, !=	Reference equality and inequality	Relational	Left to right
7	&&	Conditional AND	Logical	Left to right
8	||	Conditional OR	Logical	Left to right
9	=, +=, -=	Assignment and compound assignments (addition and subtraction)	Assignment	Right to left

Assignment Operators

Assignment operators are used to assign values to variables.

- ■ =   assignment operator

The assignment operator by itself is the equal sign (=). Chapter 2 discusses assignment statements, and Chapter 4 discusses the assignment of literals into primitive data types and the creation of reference type variables. At its simplest, the assignment operators move valid literals into variables or cause compiler errors when the literals are not valid. The following are valid assignment statements using the assignment operator.

```
boolean hasTreasureChestKey = true;
byte shipmates = 20;
PirateShip ship = new PirateShip();
```

The following are invalid assignments and will cause compiler errors:

```
/* Invalid literal, TRUE must be lower case */
boolean hasTreasureChestKey = TRUE;
/* Invalid literal, byte value cannot exceed 127 */
byte shipmates = 500;
/*  Invalid constructor */
PirateShip ship = new PirateShip(UNEXPECTED_ARG);
```

Compound Assignment Operators

A variety of compound assignment operators exist. The exam only covers the addition and subtraction compound assignment operators.

- ■ +=   assignment by addition operator
- ■ -=   assignment by subtraction operator

Consider the following two assignment statements:

```
goldCoins = goldCoins + 99;
pirateShips = pirateShips - 1;
```

The following two statements (with the same meaning and results as earlier) are written with compound assignment operators.

```
goldCoins += 99;
pirateShips -= 1;
```

on the **Job** *While the use of compound assignment operators cuts down on keystrokes, it is generally good practice to use the former "longhand" approach since the code is clearly more readable.*

watch *It is common to represent assignments in pseudo-code with the colon and equal sign characters (for example, A := 20). Notice that := looks strikingly familiar to +=, -=, and other Java assignment operators such as *=, /=, and %=. Be aware though that the pseudo-code assignment representation (:=) is not a Java assignment operator, and if you see it in any Java code, it will not compile.*

EXERCISE 3-1

Using Compound Assignment Operators

This exercise will clear up any confusion about compound assignment operators. The following application will be used for the exercise. Don't run it until after step 3.

```
public class Main {
  public static void main(String[] args) {
    byte a;
    a = 10;
    System.out.println(a += 3);
    a = 15;
    System.out.println(a -= 3);
    a = 20;
    System.out.println(a *= 3);
    a = 25;
    System.out.println(a /= 3);
    a = 30;
    System.out.println(a %= 3);
    /* Optional as outside of scope of exam */
    a = 35;
    System.out.println(a &= 3);
    a = 40;
    System.out.println(a ^= 3);
    a = 45;
```

```
        System.out.println(a |= 3);
        a = 50;
        System.out.println(a <<= 3);
        a = 55;
        System.out.println(a >>= 3);
        a = 60;
        System.out.println(a >>>= 3);
        /* End optional */
    }
}
```

1. Grab a pencil and a piece of paper. Optionally, you can use Table 3-2 as your worksheet.

2. For each statement that has a compound assignment operator, rewrite the statement without the compound assignment operator and replace the variable with its associated value. For example, let's take the assignment statement with the addition compound assignment operator:

```
a = 5;
System.out.println(a += 3);
```

It would be rewritten as (a = a + 3), specifically (a = 5 + 3);

TABLE 3-2	Assigned Value of a	Compound Assignment	Refactored Statement	New Value of a
Refactoring Compound Assignment Statements	a = 10;	a += 3;	a = 10 + 3;	13
	a = 15;	a -= 3;		
	a = 20;	a *= 3;		
	a = 25;	a /= 3;		
	a = 30;	a %= 3;		
	a = 35;	a &= 3;		
	a = 40;	a ^= 3;		
	a = 45;	a |= 3;		
	a = 50;	a <<= 3;		
	a = 55;	a >>= 3;		
	a = 60;	a >>>= 3;		

3. Evaluate the expressions, without using a computer.

4. Compile and run the given application. Compare your results.

   Note that many of these operators do not appear on the exam. The point of the exercise is getting you properly acquainted with compound assignment operators, by repetition.

Arithmetic Operators

The exam will include nine arithmetic operators. Five of these operators are used for basic operations (addition, subtraction, multiplication, division, and modulus). The other four operators are used for incrementing and decrementing a value. We'll examine the five operators used for basic operations first.

Basic Arithmetic Operators

The five basic arithmetic operators are

- + addition (sum) operator
- – subtraction (difference) operator
- * multiplication (product) operator
- / division (quotient) operator
- % modulus (remainder) operator

Adding, subtracting, multiplying, dividing, and producing remainders with operators is straightforward. The following examples demonstrate this.

```
/* Addition (+) operator example */
int greyCannonBalls = 50;
int blackCannonBalls = 50;
int totalCannonBalls = greyCannonBalls + blackCannonBalls; // 100

/* Subtraction (-) operator example */
int firedCannonBalls = 10;
totalCannonBalls = totalCannonBalls - firedCannonBalls; // 90

/* Multiplication (*) operator example */
int matches = 20;
```

```
int matchboxes = 20;
int totalMatches = matches * matchboxes; // 400

/* Division (/) operator example */
int pirates = 104;
int pirateShips = 3;
int assignedPiratesPerShip = pirates / pirateShips; // 34

/* Remainder (modulus) (%) operator example */
(left operand is divided by right operand and the remainder is
produced)
int pirateRemainder = pirates % pirateShips; // 2
```

Prefix Increment, Postfix Increment, Prefix Decrement, and Postfix Decrement Operators

Four operators allow decrementing or incrementing of variables:

- ++x   prefix increment operator
- --x   prefix decrement operator
- x++   postfix increment operator
- x--   postfix decrement operator

Prefix increment and prefix decrement operators provide a shorthand way of incrementing the value of a variable by 1. Rather than creating an expression as y=x+1, you could write y=++x. Similarly, you could replace the expression y=x-1 with y=--x. This works because the execution of the prefix operators occurs on the operand prior to the evaluation of the whole expression. Postfix increment and postfix decrement characters execute the postfix operators after the expression has been evaluated. Therefore y = x++ would equate to y=x followed by x=x+1. And y = x-- would equate to y=x, followed by x=x-1.

It's important to note that y=++x is not exactly equivalent to y=x+1 because the value of x changes in the former but not in the latter. This is the same for y=--x and y=x-1.

The prefix increment operator increments a value by 1 before an expression has been evaluated.

```
int x = 10;
int y = ++x ;
System.out.println("x=" + x + ", y=" + y); // x= 11, y= 11
```

The postfix increment operator increments a value by 1 after an expression has been evaluated.

```
int x = 10;
int y = x++ ;
System.out.println("x=" + x + ", y=" + y); // x= 11, y= 10
```

The prefix decrement operator decrements a value by 1 before an expression has been evaluated.

```
int x = 10;
int y = --x ;
System.out.println("x=" + x + ", y=" + y); // x= 9, y= 9
```

The postfix decrement operator decrements a value by 1 after an expression has been evaluated.

```
int x = 10;
int y = x-- ;
System.out.println("x=" + x + ", y=" + y); // x= 9, y= 10
```

Relational Operators

Relational operators return Boolean values in relationship to the evaluation of their left and right operands. The six most common relational operators are on the exam. Four of them equate to the greater than and less than comparisons. Two are strictly related to equality as we will discuss at the end of this section.

Basic Relational Operators

- < "less than" operator
- <= "less than or equal to" operator
- > "greater than" operator
- >= "greater than or equal to" operator

The "less than," "less than or equal to," "greater than," and "greater than or equal to" operators are used to compare integers, floating points, and characters. When the expression used with the relational operators is true, the Boolean value of true is returned; otherwise, false is returned.

```
/* returns true as 1 is less than 2 */
boolean b1 = 1 < 2;
/* returns false as 3 is not less than 2 */
boolean b2 = 3 < 2;
```

```
/* returns true as 3 is greater than 2 */
boolean b3 = 3 > 2;
/* returns false as 1 is not greater than 2 */
boolean b4 = 1 > 2;
/* returns true as 2 is less than or equal to 2 */
boolean b5 = 2 <= 2;
/* returns false as 3 is not less than or equal to 2 */
boolean b6 = 3 <= 2;
/* returns true as 3 is greater than or equal to 3 */
boolean b7 = 3 >= 3;
/* returns false as 2 is not greater than or equal to 3 */
boolean b8 = 2 >= 3;
```

So far we've only examined the relationship of int primitives. Let's take a look at the various ways char primitives can be evaluated with relational operators, specifically the "less than" operator for these examples. Remember that characters (that is, char primitives) accept integers (within the valid 16-bit unsigned range), hexadecimal, octal, and character literals. Each literal in the following examples represents the letters "A" and "B." The left operands are character "A" and the right operands are character "B." Since each expression is essentially the same, they all evaluate to true.

```
boolean b1 = 'A' < 'B'; // Character literals
boolean b2 = '\u0041' < '\u0042'; // Unicode literals
boolean b3 = 0x0041 < 0x0042; // Hexadecimal literals
boolean b4 = 65 < 66; // Integer literals that fit in a char
boolean b5 = 0101 < 0102; //Octal literals
boolean b6 = '\101' < '\102'; //Octal literals with escape
sequences
boolean b7 = 'A' < 0102; // Character and Octal literals
```

As mentioned, you can also test the relationship between floating points. The following are a few examples.

```
boolean b1 = 9.00D < 9.50D; // Floating points with D postfixes
boolean b2 = 9.00d < 9.50d; // Floating points with d postfixes
boolean b3 = 9.00F < 9.50F; // Floating points with F postfixes
boolean b4 = 9.0f < 9.50f; // Floating points with f postfixes
boolean b5 = (double)9 < (double)10; // Integers with explicit
casts
boolean b6 = (float)9 < (float)10; // Integers with explicit casts
boolean b7 = 9 < 10; // Integers that fit into floating points
boolean b8 = (9d < 10f);
boolean b9 = (float)11 < 12;
```

Equality Operators

Relational operators that directly compare the equality of primitives (numbers, characters, Booleans) and object reference variables are considered equality operators.

- ■ `==` "equal to" operator
- ■ `!=` "not equal to" operator

Comparing primitives of the same type is straightforward. If the right and left operands of the "equal to" operator are equal, the Boolean value of true is returned, otherwise false is returned. If the right and left operands of the "not equal to" operator are not equal, the Boolean value of true is returned, otherwise false is returned. The following code has examples that compare all eight primitives to values of the same type.

```
int value = 12;
/* boolean comparison, prints true */
System.out.println(true == true);
/* char comparison, prints false */
System.out.println('a' != 'a');
/* byte comparison, prints true */
System.out.println((byte)value == (byte)value);
/* short comparison, prints false */
System.out.println((short)value != (short)value);
/* integer comparison, prints true */
System.out.println(value == value);
/* float comparison, prints true */
System.out.println(12F == 12f);
/* double comparison, prints false */
System.out.println(12D != 12d);
```

Reference values of objects can also be compared. Consider the following code:

```
Object a = new Object();
Object b = new Object();
Object c = b;
```

The reference variables are a, b, and c. As shown, reference variables a and b are unique. Reference variable c refers to reference variable b, so for equality purposes, they are the same.

```
/* Prints false, different references */
System.out.println(a == b);
/* Prints false, different references */
System.out.println(a == c);
/* Prints true, same references */
System.out.println(b == c);
```

The following are similar statements, but using the "not equal to" operator.

```
System.out.println(a != b); // Prints true, different references
System.out.println(a != c); // Prints true, different references
System.out.println(b != c); // Prints false, same references
```

Numeric Promotion of Binary Values   By this point, you may be wondering what the compiler does with the operands when they are of different primitive types. Numeric promotion rules are applied on binary values for the additive (+, -), multiplicative (*, /, %), comparison (<, <=, >, >=), equality (==, !=), bitwise (&, ^, |), and conditional (? :) operators. See Table 3-3.

Logical Operators

Logical operators return Boolean values. Three are logical operators on the exam: logical AND, logical OR, and logical negation.

Logical (Conditional) Operators

Logical (conditional) operators evaluate a pair of Boolean operands. Understanding their short-circuit principle is necessary for the exam.

- ■ && logical AND (conditional-AND) operator
- ■ || logical OR (conditional-OR) operator

The logical AND operator evaluates the left and right operands. If both values of the operands have a value of true, then a value of true is returned. The logical AND is considered a short-circuit operator. If the left operand returns false, then there is no

TABLE 3-3		**Binary Numeric Promotion**
Numeric Promotion of Binary Values	Check 1	Check if one and only one operand is a double primitive. If so, convert the non-double primitive to a double, and stop checks.
	Check 2	Check if one and only one operand is a float primitive. If so, convert the non-float primitive to a float, and stop checks.
	Check 3	Check if one and only one operand is a long primitive. If so, convert the non-long primitive to a long, and stop checks.
	Check 4	Convert both operands to int.

need to check the right operator since both would need to be true to return true; thus, it short-circuits. Therefore, whenever the left operand returns false, the expression terminates and returns a value of false.

```
/* Assigns true */
boolean and1 = true && true;
/* Assigns false */
boolean and2 = true && false;
/* Assigns false, right operand not evaluated */
boolean and3 = false && true;
/* Assigns false, right operand not evaluated */
boolean and4 = false && false;
```

The logical OR operator evaluates the left and right operands. If either value of the operands has a value of true, then a value of true is returned. The logical AND is considered a short-circuit operator. If the left operand returns true, there is no need to check the right operator, since either needs to be true to return true; thus, it short-circuits. Again, whenever the left operand returns true, the expression terminates and returns a value of true.

```
/* Assigns true, right operand not evaluated */
boolean or1 = true || true;
/* Assigns true, right operand not evaluated */
boolean or2 = true || false;
/* Assigns true */
boolean or3 = false || true;
/* Assigns false */
boolean or4 = false || false;
```

Logical Negation Operator

The logical negation operator is also known as the inversion operator or Boolean invert operator. This is a simple operator, but don't take it lightly… you may see it quite often on the exam.

■   !   logical negation (inversion) operator

The logical negation operator returns the opposite of a Boolean value.

```
System.out.println(!false); // Prints true
System.out.println(!true); // Prints false
System.out.println(!!true); // Prints true
System.out.println(!!!true); // Prints false
System.out.println(!!!!true); // Prints true
```

Expect to see the logical negation operator used in conjunction with any method or expression that returns a Boolean value. The following list details some of these expressions that return Boolean values:

- Expressions with relational operators return Boolean values.
- Expressions with logical (conditional) operators return Boolean values.
- The `equals` method of the `Object` class returns Boolean values.
- The `String` methods `startsWith` and `endsWith` return Boolean values.

The following are some examples of statements that include the logical negation operator.

```
/* Example with relational expression */
iVar1 = 0;
iVar2 = 1;
if (!(iVar1 <= iVar2)) {};

/* Example with logical expressions */
boolean bVar1 = false; boolean bVar2 = true;
if ((bVar1 && bVar2) || (!(bVar1 && bVar2))){}

/* Example with equals method */
if (!"NAME".equals("NAME")) {}

/* Example with the String class's startsWith method */
String s = "Captain Jack";
System.out.println(!s.startsWith("Captain"));
```

The logical inversion operator cannot be used on a non-Boolean value. The following code will not compile:

```
!10; // compiler error, '!' must be used with a boolean value
not an integer
!"STRING"; // compiler error, '!' must be used with a boolean
value, not a string
```

Logical AND and logical OR are on the exam. Boolean AND and Boolean OR, along with bitwise AND and bitwise OR, are not on the exam. A reason why you may wish to use the nonlogical expressions associated with the right operand is if a change occurs to a variable where the new result is used later in your code. The following Scenario & Solution details the specifics of this scenario.

SCENARIO & SOLUTION

You wish to use an AND operator that evaluates the second operand whether the first operand evaluates to true or false. Which would you use?	Boolean AND (&)
You wish to use an OR operator that evaluates the second operand whether the first operand evaluates to true or false. Which would you use?	Boolean OR (|)
You wish to use an AND operator that evaluates the second operand only when the first operand evaluates to true. Which would you use?	Logical AND (&&)
You wish to use an OR operator that evaluates the second operand only when the first operand evaluates to false. Which would you use?	Logical OR (||)

CERTIFICATION OBJECTIVE

Developing with String Objects and Their Methods

Exam Objective 4.6   Develop code that uses the concatenation operator (+), and the following methods from class String: charAt, indexOf, trim, substring, replace, length, startsWith, and endsWith.

Strings are commonly used in the Java programming language. This section discusses what strings are, how to concatenate separate strings, and then details the methods of the `String` class. When you have completed this section, which covers the following topics, you should fully understand what strings are and how to use them.

■ Strings
■ String concatenation operator
■ Methods of the `String` class

Strings

String objects are used to represent 16-bit Unicode character strings. Consider the 16 bits `000001011001` followed by `000001101111`. These bits in Unicode are represented as `\u0059` and `\u006F`. `\u0059` is mapped to the character "Y", and

\u006F is mapped to the character "o". An easy way of adding 16-bit Unicode character strings together in a reusable element is by declarating the data within a string.

```
String exclamation = "Yo"; // 000001011001 and 000001101111
```

See Appendix C for more information on the Unicode standard.

Strings are immutable objects, meaning their values never change. For example, the following text, "Dead Men Tell No Tales", can be created as a string.

```
String quote = "Dead Men Tell No Tales";
```

In the following example, the value of the string does not change after a String method returns a modified value. Remember that strings are immutable. Here, we invoke the replace method on the string. Again, the new string is returned, but will not change the value.

```
quote.replace("No Tales", "Tales"); // Returns new value
System.out.println(quote); // Prints the original value
$ Dead Men Tell No Tales
```

We can create strings in several ways. As with instantiating any object, you need to construct an object and assign it to a reference variable. As a reminder, a reference variable holds the value's address. Let's look at some of the things you can do with strings.

You can create a string without an assigned string object. Make sure you eventually give it a value, or you'll get a compiler error.

```
String quote1; // quote1 is a reference variable with no
assigned string object
quote1 = "Ahoy matey"; // Assigns string object to the reference
variable
```

You can use a couple of basic approaches to create a string object with an empty string representation.

```
String quote2a = new String(); // quote2a is a reference variable
String quote2b = new String(""); // Equivalent statement
```

You can create a string object without using a constructor.

```
String quote3 = "The existence of the sea means the existence
of Pirates! -- Malayan proverb";
```

SCENARIO & SOLUTION

You wish to use an object that represents an immutable character string. Which class will you use to create the object?	The `String` class
You wish to use an object that represents a thread-safe mutable character string. Which class will you use to create the object?	The `StringBuffer` class
You wish to use an object that represents a mutable character string. Which class will you use to create the object?	The `StringBuilder` class

You can create a string object while using a constructor.

```
/* quote4 is a reference variable to the new string object */
String quote4 = new String("Yo ho ho!");
```

You can create a reference variable that refers to a separate reference variable of a string object.

```
String quote5 = "You're welcome to my gold -- William Kidd.";
String quote6 = quote5; // quote6 refers to the quote5 reference
variable of a string
```

You can assign a new string object to an existing string reference variable.

```
String quote7 = "The treasure is in the sand. "; // Assigns
string object to the reference variable
quote7 = "The treasure is between the rails."; // Assigns new
string to the same reference variable
```

If you wish to use a mutable character string, consider `StringBuffer` or `StringBuilder` as represented in the preceding Scenario & Solution.

The String Concatenation Operator

The string concatenation operator concatenates (joins) strings together. The operator is denoted with the + sign.

■ + String concatenation operator

If you have been programming for at least six months, odds are you have glued two strings together at some time. Java's string concatenation operator makes the act of joining two strings very easy. For example, "doub" + "loon" equates to "doubloon". Let's look at some more complete code.

```
String item = "doubloon";
String question = "What is a " + item + "? ";
System.out.println ("Question: " + question);
```

Line 2 replaces the item variable with its contents, "doubloon", and so the question string becomes:

```
What is a doubloon?
```

Notice that the question mark was appended as well.

Line 3 replaces the question variable with its contents and so the following string is returned:

```
$ Question: What is a doubloon?
```

It is that simple.

The toString Method

The Object class has a method that returns a string representation of objects. This method is appropriately named the toString method. All classes in Java extend the Object class by default, so therefore every class inherits this method. When creating classes, it is common practice to override the toString method to return the data that best represents the state of the object. The toString method makes common use of the string concatenation operator.

Let's take a look at a TreasureMap class with the toString method overridden.

```
public class TreasureMap {
  private String owner = "Blackbeard";
  private String location = "Outer Banks";
  public String toString () {
    return "Map Owner: " + this.owner + ", treasure location: "
    + this.location;
  }
}
```

Here, the `toString` method returns the contents of the class's instance variables. Let's print out the representation of a `TreasureMap` object.

```
TreasureMap t = new TreasureMap();
System.out.println(t);
$ Map Owner: Blackbeard, treasure location: Outer Banks
```

Concatenation results may be unexpected if you are including variables that are not initially strings.

Consider a string and two integers:

```
String title1 = " shovels.";
String title2 = "Shovels: ";
int flatShovels = 5;
int roundPointShovels = 6;
```

The compiler performs left-to-right association for the additive and string concatenation operators. For the following two statements, the first two integers are added together. Next, the concatenation operator takes the `toString` representation of the result and concatenates it with the other string.

```
/* Prints '11 shovels' */
System.out.println(flatShovels + roundPointShovels + title1);

/* Prints '11 shovels' */
System.out.println((flatShovels + roundPointShovels) + title1);
```

Moving from left to right, the compiler takes the `title2` string and joins it with the string representation of the `flatShovels` integer variable. The result is a string. Now this result string is joined to the string representation of the `roundPointShovels` variable. Note that the `toString` method is used to return the string.

```
/* Prints 'Shovels: 56' */
System.out.println(title2 + flatShovels + roundPointShovels);
```

Parentheses take precedence, so you can join the sum of the integer values with the string if you code it as follows:

```
/* Prints 'Shovels: 11' */
System.out.println(title2 + (flatShovels + roundPointShovels));
```

EXERCISE 3-2

Uncovering Bugs that Your Compiler May Not Find

Consider the strings in the following application:

```
public class StringTest {
  public static void main(String[] args) {
    String s1 = new String ("String one");
    String s2 = "String two";
    String s3 = "String " + "three";
  }
}
```

One of the strings is constructed in an inefficient manner. Do you know which one? Let's find out using the FindBugs application from the University of Maryland.

1. Create a directory named "code" somewhere on your PC (for example, c:\code).

2. Create the StringTest.java source file.

3. Compile the StringTest.java source file; javac StringTest.java.

4. Download the FindBugs software from http://findbugs .sourceforge.net/.

5. Extract, install, and run the FindBugs application. Note that the Eclipse and NetBeans IDEs have plug-ins for the FindBugs tool as well as other "software quality" tools such as PMD and Checkstyle.

6. Create a new project in FindBugs by choosing File and then New Project...

7. Add the project name (for instance, SCJA String Test).

8. Click the Add button for the text area associated with the "Class archives and directories to analyze." Find and select the StringTest.class file under the C:\code directory and click Choose.

9. Click the Add button for the text area associated with the "Source Directories." Find and select the C:\code directory (not the source file) and then click Choose.

10. The New Project dialog box will look similar to the following Illustration with the exception of your personal directory locations. Click Finish.

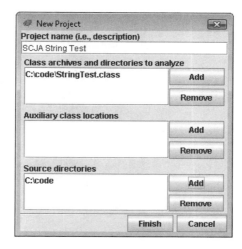

11. You will see that two bugs are returned. We are concerned with the first one. Drill down in the window that shows the bugs (Bugs | Performance | [...]). The application will detail the warning and show you the source code with the line in error highlighted.

12. Fix the bug.

Methods of the `String` Class

Several methods of the `String` class are commonly used. The common methods, `charAt`, `indexOf`, `length`, `replace`, `startsWith`, `endsWith`, `substring`, and `trim` were chosen by Sun to be included on the exam. These methods are detailed in Figure 3-2 and in the following section.

Coming up, we will be providing a description of each method, followed by the method declarations and associated examples.

First, consider the following string:

```
String pirateMessage = "  Buried Treasure Chest! ";
```

The string has two leading blank spaces and one trailing blank space. This is important in relationship to the upcoming examples. The string is shown again in Figure 3-3 with the index values shown in relationship to the individual characters.

FIGURE 3-2

Commonly used
methods of the
`String` class

```
                           String
  + charAt(int) : char
  + endsWith(String) : boolean
  + indexOf(int) : int
  + indexOf(int, int) : int
  + indexOf(String) : int
  + indexOf(String, int) : int
  + length() : int
  + replace(char, char) : String
  + replace(CharSequence, CharSequence) : String
  + startsWith(String, int) : boolean
  + startsWith(String) : boolean
  + substring(int) : String
  + substring(int, int) : String
  + trim() : String
```

Let's use each method to perform some action with the string `pirateMessage`.

The `charAt` Method

The `String` class's `charAt` method returns a primitive `char` value from a specified `int` index value in relationship to the referenced string object.

There is one `charAt` method declaration:

```
public char charAt(int index) {...}
```

Examples:

```
/* Returns the 'blank space' character from location 0 */
char c1 = pirateMessage.charAt(0);
/* Returns the character 'B' from location 2 */
char c2 = pirateMessage.charAt(2);
/* Returns the character '!' from location 23 */
char c3 = pirateMessage.charAt(23);
/* Returns the 'blank space' character from location 24 */
char c4 = pirateMessage.charAt(24);
```

FIGURE 3-3   SCJA string detailing blanks

	B	u	r	i	e	d		T	r	e	a	s	u	r	e		C	h	e	s	t	!	
0	1	2	3	4	5	6	7	8	9	10	11	12	13	14	15	16	17	18	19	20	21	22	23	24

The `indexOf` Method

The `String` class's `indexOf` methods return primitive `int` values representing the index of a character or string in relationship to the referenced string object.

Four `indexOf` method declarations exist:

```
public int indexOf(int ch) {...}
public int indexOf(int ch, int fromIndex) {...}
public int indexOf(String str) {...}
public int indexOf(String str, int fromIndex) {...}
```

Examples:

```
/* Returns the integer 3 as it is the first 'u' in the string. */
int i1 = pirateMessage.indexOf('u'); // 3
/* Returns the integer 14 as it is the first 'u' in the string
past location 9. */
int i2 = pirateMessage.indexOf('u', 9); // 14
/* Returns the integer 13 as it starts at location 13 in the
string. */
int i3 = pirateMessage.indexOf("sure"); // 13
/* Returns the integer -1 as there is no Treasure string on or
past location 10 */
int i4 = pirateMessage.indexOf("Treasure", 10); // -1!
/* Returns the integer -1 as there is no character u on or past
location 100 */
int i5 = pirateMessage.indexOf("u", 100); // -1!
```

The `length` Method

The `String` class's `length` method returns a primitive `int` value representing the length of the referenced string object.

There is one `length` method declaration:

```
public int length() {...}
```

Examples:

```
/* Returns the string's length of 25 */
int i = pirateMessage.length(); // 25
```

e x a m

The `String` **class uses the length method (for example,** `string` `.length()`**). Arrays reference an instance variable in their state (for example,** `array` `.length`**). Therefore, the string methods use the set of parentheses to return their length, and arrays do not. This is a gotcha that you will want to look for on the exam.**

```
// Use of String's length method
String string = "box";
string.length(); // 3
// Use of array's length attribute
String[] stringArray = new String[3];
stringArray.length; // 3
```

The `replace` Method

The `String` class's `replace` method returns strings, replacing all characters or strings in relationship to the referenced string object. The `CharSequence` interface allows for the use of either a `String`, `StringBuffer`, or `StringBuilder` object.

Two `replace` method declarations can be used:

```
public String replace(char oldChar, char newChar) {…}
public String replace(CharSequence target, CharSequence
replacement) {…}
```

Examples:

```
/* Returns the string with all characters 'B' replaced with 'J'.
*/
String s1 = pirateMessage.replace('B', 'J'); // Juried Treasure
Chest!
/* Returns the string with all blank characters ' ' replaced
with 'X'. */
String s2 = pirateMessage.replace(' ', 'X'); // XXBuriedXTreasur
eXChest!X
/* Returns the string with all strings 'Chest' replaced with
'Coins'. */
String s3 = pirateMessage.replace("Chest", "Coins"); // Buried
Treasure Coins!
```

The startWith Method

The String class's startsWith method returns a primitive boolean value representing the results of a test to see if the supplied prefix starts the referenced String object.

Two startsWith method declarations can be used:

```
public boolean startsWith(String prefix, int toffset) {…}
public boolean startsWith(String prefix) {…}
```

Examples:

```
/* Returns true as the referenced string starts with the
compared string. */
boolean b1 = pirateMessage.startsWith(" Buried Treasure"); //
true
/* Returns false as the referenced string does not start with
the compared string. */
boolean b2 = pirateMessage.startsWith(" Discovered"); // false
/* Returns false as the referenced string does not start with
the compared string at location 8. */
boolean b3 = pirateMessage.startsWith("Treasure", 8); // false
/* Returns true as the referenced string does start with the
compared string at location 9. */
boolean b4 = pirateMessage.startsWith("Treasure", 9); // true
```

The endsWith Method

The String class's endsWith method returns a primitive boolean value representing the results of a test to see if the supplied suffix ends the referenced string object.

There is one endsWith method declaration:

```
public boolean endsWith(String suffix) {…}
```

Examples:

```
/* Returns true as the referenced string ends with the compared
string. */
boolean b1 = pirateMessage.endsWith("Treasure Chest! "); // true
/* Returns false as the referenced string does not end with the
compared string. */
boolean b2 = pirateMessage.endsWith("Treasure Chest "); // false
```

The substring Method

The String class's substring methods return new strings that are substrings of the referenced string object.

Two substring method declarations exist:

```
public String substring(int beginIndex) {…}
public String substring(int beginIndex, int endIndex) {
```

Examples:

```
/* Returns the entire string starting at index 9. */
String s1 = pirateMessage.substring(9); // Treasure Chest!
/* Returns the string at index 9. */
String s2 = pirateMessage.substring(9, 10); // T
/* Returns the string at index 9 and ending at index 23. */
String s3 = pirateMessage.substring(9, 23); // Treasure Chest
/* Produces runtime error. */
String s4 = pirateMessage.substring(9, 8); // String index out
of range: -1
/* Returns a blank */
String s5 = pirateMessage.substring(9, 9); // Blank
```

The trim Method

The String class's trim method returns the entire string minus leading and trailing whitespace characters in relationship to the referenced string object. The whitespace character corresponds to the Unicode character \u0020.

The sole trim method declaration is

```
public String trim() {…}
```

Examples:

```
/* "Buried Treasure Chest!" with no leading or trailing white
spaces */
String s = pirateMessage.trim();
```

on the Job

To view the source of the Java SE source files directly, either download the source code off the Internet or visit JDocs at `http://www.jdocs.com/`*. JDocs provides an interface to the source code of several Java-based projects, including the Java platform, Standard Edition.*

INSIDE THE EXAM

Chaining

Java allows for methods to be chained together. Consider the following message from the captain of a pirate ship:

```
String msg = "  Maroon the First Mate with a flagon of water and a
pistol!  ";
```

We wish to change the message to read, "`Maroon the Quartermaster with a flagon of water.`"

Three changes need to be made to adjust the string as desired:

1. Trim the leading and trailing whitespace.
2. Replace the substring "`First Mate`" with "`Quartermaster`".
3. Remove "`and a pistol!`"
4. Add a period at the end of the sentence.

A variety of methods and utilities can be used to make these changes. We will use the `trim`, `replace`, and `substring` methods, in this order.

```
msg = msg.trim(); // Trims whitespace
msg = msg.replace("First Mate", "Quartermaster");// Replaces text
msg = msg.substring(0,47);  // Returns first 48 characters.
```

Rather than writing these assignments individually, we can have one assignment statement with all of the methods chained. For simplicity, we also add the period with the string concatenation operator.

```
msg = msg.trim().replace("First Mate", "Quartermaster").substring(0,47) +
".";
```

Whether methods are invoked separately or chained together, the end result is the same.

```
System.out.println (msg);
$  Maroon the Quartermaster with a flagon of water.
```

Look for chaining on the exam.

CERTIFICATION SUMMARY

This chapter discussed everything you need to know about operators and strings for the exam.

Operators of type assignment, arithmetic, relational, and logical were all presented in detail. Assignment operators included the general assignment, assignment by addition, and assignment by subtraction operators. Arithmetic operators included the addition, subtraction, multiplication, division, and remainder (modulus) operators, as well as the prefix increment, prefix decrement, postfix increment, and postfix decrement operators. Relational operators included the "less than," "less than or equal to," "greater than," "greater than or equal to," "equal to," and "not equal to" operators. Logical operators included the logical negation, logical AND, and logical OR operators.

Strings were discussed in three main areas: creating strings, the string concatenation operator, and methods of the `String` class. The following methods of the `String` class were covered: `charAt`, `indexOf`, `length`, `replace`, `startsWith`, `endsWith`, `substring`, and `trim`.

Knowing the fine details of these core areas related to operators and strings is necessary for the exam.

✓ TWO-MINUTE DRILL

Understanding Fundamental Operators

❑ The exam covers the following assignment and compound assignment operators: =, +=, and -=.

❑ The assignment operator (=) assigns values to variables.

❑ The additional compound assignment operator is used for shorthand. As such, a=a+b is written a+=b.

❑ The subtraction compound assignment operator is used for shorthand. As such, a=a-b is written a-=b.

❑ The exam covers the following arithmetic operators: +, -, *, /, %, ++, and --.

❑ The addition operation (+) is used to add two operands together.

❑ The subtraction operator (-) is used to subtract the right operand from the left operand.

❑ The multiplication operator (*) is used to multiply two operands together.

❑ The divisor operator (/) is used to divide the right operand into the left operand.

❑ The modulus operator (%) returns the remainder of a division.

❑ The prefix increment (++) and prefix decrement (--) operators are used to increment or decrement a value before it is used in an expression.

❑ The postfix increment (++) and postfix decrement (--) operators are used to increment or decrement a value after it is used in an expression.

❑ The exam covers the following relational operators: <, <=, >, >=, ==, and !=.

❑ The "less than" operator (<) returns true if the left operand is less than the right operand.

❑ The "less than or equal to" operator (<=) returns true if the left operand is less than or equal to the right operand.

❑ The "greater than" operator (>) returns true if the right operand is less than the left operand.

❑ The "greater than or equal to" operator (>=) returns true if the right operand is less than or equal to the left operand.

❏ The "equal to" equality operator (==) returns true if the left operand is equal to the right operand.

❏ The "not equal to" equality operator (!=) returns true if the left operand is not equal to the right operand.

❏ Equality operators can test numbers, characters, Booleans, and reference variables.

❏ The exam covers the following logical operators: !, &&, and ||.

❏ The logical negation (inversion) operator (!) negates the value of the boolean operand.

❏ The logical AND (conditional AND) operator (&&) returns true if both operands are true.

❏ The logical AND operator is known as a short-circuit operator because it does not evaluate the right operand if the left operand is false.

❏ The logical OR (conditional OR) operator (||) returns true if either operand is true.

❏ The conditional OR operator is known as a short-circuit operator because it does not evaluate the right operand if the left operand is true.

Developing with String Objects and Their Methods

❏ An object of the String class represents an immutable character string.

❏ An object of the StringBuilder class represents a mutable character string.

❏ An object of the StringBuffer class represents a thread-safe mutable character string.

❏ Mutable means "changeable." Note that Java variables such as primitives are mutable by default and can be made immutable by using the final keyword.

❏ The CharSequence interface is implemented by the String, StringBuilder, and StringBuffer classes. It can be used as an argument in the String class's replace method.

❏ The string concatenation operator (+) joins two strings together.

❏ The string concatenation operator will join two operands together, as long as one or both of them are strings.

❏ The String class's charAt method returns a primitive char value from a specified int index value in relationship to the referenced string.

❑ The `String` class's `indexOf` methods returns a primitive `int` value representing the index of a character or string in relationship to the referenced string.

❑ The `String` class's `length` method returns a primitive `int` value representing the length of the referenced string.

❑ The `String` class's `replace` methods return strings replacing all characters or strings in relationship to the referenced string.

❑ The `String` class's `startsWith` method returns a primitive `boolean` value representing the results of a test to see if the supplied prefix starts the referenced string.

❑ The `String` class's `endsWith` method returns a primitive `boolean` value representing the results of a test to see if the supplied suffix ends the referenced string.

❑ The `String` class's `substring` methods return new strings that are substrings of the referenced string.

❑ The `String` class's `trim` method returns the entire string minus leading and trailing whitespace characters in relationship to the referenced string.

SELF TEST

Understanding Fundamental Operators

1. Given:

```
public class ArithmeticResultsOutput {
    public static void main (String[] args) {
        int i = 0;
        int j = 0;
        if (i++ == ++j) {
            System.out.println("True: i=" + i + ", j=" + j);
        } else {
            System.out.println("False: i=" + i + ", j=" + j);
        }
    }
}
```

What will be printed to standard out?

A. `True: i=0, j=1`

B. `True: i=1, j=1`

C. `False: i=0, j=1`

D. `False: i=1, j=1`

2. Which set of operators represents the complete set of valid Java assignment operators?

A. `%=, &=, *=, $=, :=, /=, ^=, |=, +=, <<=, =, -=, >>=, >>>=`

B. `%=, &=, *=, /=, ^=, |=, +=, <<=, <<<=, =, -=, >>=, >>>=`

C. `%=, &=, *=, /=, ^=, |=, +=, <<=, =, -=, >>=, >>>=`

D. `%=, &=, *=, $=, /=, ^=, |=, +=, <<=, <<<=, =, -=, >>=, >>>=`

3. Given the following Java code segment, what will be printed, considering the usage of the modulus operators?

```
System.out.print(49 % 26 % 5 % 1);
```

A. 23

B. 3

C. 1

D. 0

4. Given:

```java
public class BooleanResultsOutput {
  public static void main (String[] args) {
    boolean booleanValue1 = true;
    boolean booleanValue2 = false;
    System.out.print(!(booleanValue1 & !booleanValue2) + ", ");
    System.out.print(!(booleanValue1 | !booleanValue2)+ ", ");
    System.out.print(!(booleanValue1 ^ !booleanValue2));
  }
}
```

What will be printed, considering the usage of the logical Boolean operators?

A. false, false, true

B. false, true, true

C. true, false, true

D. true, true, true

5. Given:

```java
public class ArithmeticResultsOutput {
  public static void main (String[] args) {
    int i1 = 100; int j1 = 200;
    if ((i1 == 99) & (--j1 == 199)) {
      System.out.print("Value1: " + (i1 + j1) + " ");
    } else {
      System.out.print("Value2: " + (i1 + j1) + " ");
    }
    int i2 = 100; int j2 = 200;
    if ((i2 == 99) && (--j2 == 199)) {
      System.out.print("Value1: " + (i2 + j2) + " ");
    } else {
      System.out.print("Value2: " + (i2 + j2) + " ");
    }
    int i3 = 100; int j3 = 200;
    if ((i3 == 100) | (--j3 == 200)) {
      System.out.print("Value1: " + (i3 + j3) + " ");
    } else {
      System.out.print("Value2: " + (i3 + j3) + " ");
    }
    int i4 = 100; int j4 = 200;
    if ((i4 == 100) || (--j4 == 200)) {
      System.out.print("Value1: " + (i4 + j4) + " ");
```

```
    } else {
     System.out.print("Value2: " + (i4 + j4) + " ");
    }

   }

}
```

What will be printed to standard out?

A. `Value2: 300 Value2: 300 Value1: 300 Value1: 300`

B. `Value2: 299 Value2: 300 Value1: 299 Value1: 300`

C. `Value1: 299 Value1: 300 Value2: 299 Value2: 300`

D. `Value1: 300 Value1: 299 Value2: 300 Value2: 299`

6. Given the following code segment:

```
public void validatePrime() {
   long p = 17496; // 'prime number' candidate
   Double primeSquareRoot = Math.sqrt(p);
   boolean isPrime = true;
   for (long j = 2; j <= primeSquareRoot.longValue(); j++) {
     if (p % j == 0) {
       // Print divisors
       System.out.println(j + "x" + p / j);
       isPrime = false;
     }
   }
   System.out.println("Prime number: " + isPrime);
}
```

Which of the following is true? Hint: 17496 is not a prime number.

A. The code will not compile due to a syntactical error somewhere in the code.

B. The code will not compile since the expression (p % j == 0) should be written as
   ((p % j) == 0).

C. Divisors will be printed to standard out (for example, 2x8478, and so on), along with
   "Prime number: false" as the final output.

D. Divisors will be printed to standard out (for example, 2x8478, and so on), along with
   "Prime number: 0" as the final output.

7. Given:

```
public class EqualityTests {
  public static void main (String[] args) {
    Integer value1 = new Integer("312");
    Integer value2 = new Integer("312");
    Object object1 = new Object();
    Object object2 = new Object();
    Object object3 = value1;
  }
}
```

Which expressions evaluate to `true`?

A. `value1.equals(value2)`

B. `value1.equals(object1)`

C. `value1.equals(object3)`

D. `object1.equals(object2)`

Developing with String Objects and Their Methods

8. Given:

```
System.out.print(3 + 3 + "3");
System.out.print(" and ");
System.out.println("3" + 3 + 3);
```

What will be printed to standard out?

A. `333 and 333`

B. `63 and 63`

C. `333 and 63`

D. `63 and 333`

9. Consider the interface `CharSequence` that is a required argument in one of the `replace` method declarations:

```
public String replace(CharSequence target, CharSequence
replacement) {
    ...
}
```

This `CharSequence` interface is a super interface to which concrete classes?

A. `String`

B. `StringBoxer`

C. `StringBuffer`

D. `StringBuilder`

10. Which statement is false about the `toString` method?

A. The `toString` method is a method of the `Object` class.

B. The `toString` method returns a string representation of the object.

C. The `toString` method must return the object's state information in the form of a string.

D. The `toString` method is commonly overridden.

11. Which `indexOf` method declaration is invalid?

A. `indexOf(int ch)`

B. `indexOf(int ch, int fromIndex)`

C. `indexOf(String str, int fromIndex)`

D. `indexOf(CharSequence str, int fromIndex)`

12. Given:

```
String tenCharString = "AAAAAAAAAA";
System.out.println(tenCharString.replace("AAA", "LLL"));
```

What is printed to the standard out?

A. `AAAAAAAAAA`

B. `LLLAAAAAAA`

C. `LLLLLLLLLA`

D. `LLLLLLLLLL`

13. Consider the following illustration. Which statements, also represented in the illustration, are true?

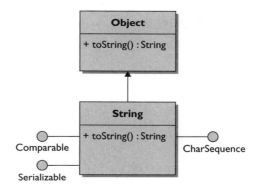

A. The String class implements the Object interface.

B. The String class implements the Comparable, Serializable, and CharSequence interfaces.

C. The toString method overrides the toString method of the Object class, allowing the String object to return its own string.

D. The toString method is publicly accessible.

SELF TEST ANSWERS

Understanding Fundamental Operators

1. Given:

```java
public class ArithmeticResultsOutput {
  public static void main (String[] args) {
      int i = 0;
      int j = 0;
      if (i++ == ++j) {
        System.out.println("True: i=" + i + ", j=" + j);
      } else {
        System.out.println("False: i=" + i + ", j=" + j);
      }
  }
}
```

What will be printed to standard out?

A. `True: i=0, j=1`

B. `True: i=1, j=1`

C. `False: i=0, j=1`

D. `False: i=1, j=1`

Answer:

☑ **D.** The value of `j` is prefix incremented before the evaluation; however, the value of `i` is not. Therefore, the expression is evaluated with a `boolean` value of `false` as a result since 0 does not equal 1 (that is, i=0 and j=1). After the expression has been evaluated, but before the associated print statement is executed, the value of `i` is postfix incremented (that is, (i=1)). Therefore, the correct answer is False: i=1, j=1).

☒ **A, B,** and **C** are incorrect answers as justified by the correct answer's explanation.

2. Which set of operators represents the complete set of valid Java assignment operators?

A. `%=, &=, *=, $=, :=, /=, ^=, |=, +=, <<=, =, -=, >>=, >>>=`

B. `%=, &=, *=, /=, ^=, |=, +=, <<=, <<<=, =, -=, >>=, >>>=`

C. `%=, &=, *=, /=, ^=, |=, +=, <<=, =, -=, >>=, >>>=`

D. `%=, &=, *=, $=, /=, ^=, |=, +=, <<=, <<<=, =, -=, >>=, >>>=`

Answer:

☑ **C.** The complete set of valid Java assignment operators is represented.

☒ **A, B,** and **D** are incorrect answers. **A** is incorrect since $= and : = are not valid Java assignment operators. **B** is incorrect because <<<= is not a valid Java assignment operator. **D** is incorrect because $= and <<<= are not valid Java assignment operators.

3. Given the following Java code segment, what will be printed, considering the usage of the modulus operators?

```
System.out.print(49 % 26 % 5 % 1);
```

A. 23

B. 3

C. 1

D. 0

Answer:

☑ **D.** The remainder of 49/26 is 23. The remainder of 23/5 is 3. The remainder of 3/1 is 0. The answer is 0.

☒ **A, B,** and **C** are incorrect answers as justified by the correct answer's explanation.

4. Given:

```
public class BooleanResultsOutput {
  public static void main (String[] args) {
    boolean booleanValue1 = true;
    boolean booleanValue2 = false;
    System.out.print(!(booleanValue1 & !booleanValue2) + ", ");
    System.out.print(!(booleanValue1 | !booleanValue2)+ ", ");
    System.out.print(!(booleanValue1 ^ !booleanValue2));
  }
}
```

What will be printed, considering the usage of the logical Boolean operators?

A. false, false, true

B. false, true, true

C. true, false, true

D. true, true, true

Answer:

☑ **A.** The first expression statement (`!(true & !(false))`) evaluates to `false`. Here, the right operand is negated to `true` by the (Boolean invert) operator, the Boolean AND operator equates the expression of the two operands to `true`, and the (Boolean invert) operator equates the resultant value to `false`. The second expression statement (`!(true | !(false))`) evaluates to `false`. Here, the right operand is negated to `true` by the (Boolean invert) operator, the Boolean OR operator equates the expression of the two operands to `true`, and the (Boolean invert) operator equates the resultant value to `false`. The third expression statement (`!(true ^ !(false))`) evaluates to `true`. Here, the right operand is negated to `true` by the (Boolean invert) operator, the Boolean XOR operator equates the expression of the two operands to `false`, and the (Boolean invert) operator equates the resultant value to `true`.

☒ **B, C,** and **D** are incorrect answers as justified by the correct answer's explanation.

5. Given:

```java
public class ArithmeticResultsOutput {
  public static void main (String[] args) {
    int i1 = 100; int j1 = 200;
    if ((i1 == 99) & (--j1 == 199)) {
      System.out.print("Value1: " + (i1 + j1) + " ");
    } else {
      System.out.print("Value2: " + (i1 + j1) + " ");
    }
    int i2 = 100; int j2 = 200;
    if ((i2 == 99) && (--j2 == 199)) {
      System.out.print("Value1: " + (i2 + j2) + " ");
    } else {
      System.out.print("Value2: " + (i2 + j2) + " ");
    }
    int i3 = 100; int j3 = 200;
    if ((i3 == 100) | (--j3 == 200)) {
      System.out.print("Value1: " + (i3 + j3) + " ");
    } else {
      System.out.print("Value2: " + (i3 + j3) + " ");
    }
    int i4 = 100; int j4 = 200;
    if ((i4 == 100) || (--j4 == 200)) {
      System.out.print("Value1: " + (i4 + j4) + " ");
     } else {
      System.out.print("Value2: " + (i4 + j4) + " ");
    }
  }
}
```

What will be printed to standard out?

A. `Value2: 300 Value2: 300 Value1: 300 Value1: 300`

B. `Value2: 299 Value2: 300 Value1: 299 Value1: 300`

C. `Value1: 299 Value1: 300 Value2: 299 Value2: 300`

D. `Value1: 300 Value1: 299 Value2: 300 Value2: 299`

Answer:

☑ **B** is the correct because `Value2: 299 Value2: 300 Value1: 299 Value1: 300` will be printed to the standard out. Note that `&&` and `||` are short-circuit operators. So... When the first operand of a conditional AND (`&&`) expression evaluates to `false`, the second operand is not evaluated. When the first operand of a conditional OR (`||`) expression evaluates to `true`, the second operand is not evaluated. Thus, for the second and fourth `if` statements, the second operand isn't evaluated. Therefore, the prefix increment operators are never executed and do not affect the values of the j[x] variables.

☒ **A, C,** and **D** are incorrect answers as justified by the correct answer's explanation.

6. Given the following code segment:

```
public void validatePrime() {
   long p = 17496; // 'prime number' candidate
   Double primeSquareRoot = Math.sqrt(p);
   boolean isPrime = true;
   for (long j = 2; j <= primeSquareRoot.longValue(); j++) {
     if (p % j == 0) {
        // Print divisors
        System.out.println(j + "x" + p / j);
        isPrime = false;
     }
   }
   System.out.println("Prime number: " + isPrime);
}
```

Which of the following is true? Hint: 17496 is not a prime number.

A. The code will not compile due to a syntactical error somewhere in the code.

B. The code will not compile since the expression (`p % j == 0`) should be written as (`(p % j) == 0`).

C. Divisors will be printed to standard out (for example, `2x8478`, and so on), along with "`Prime number: false`" as the final output.

D. Divisors will be printed to standard out (for example, `2x8478`, and so on), along with "`Prime number: 0`" as the final output.

Answer:

☑ **C.** Divisors will be printed to standard out followed by "`Prime number: false`". For those curious, the complete list of divisors printed are 2x8748, 3x5832, 4x4374, 6x2916, 8x2187, 9x1944, 12x1458, 18x972, 24x729, 27x648, 36x486, 54x324, 72x243, 81x216, and 108x162.

☒ **A, B,** and **D** are incorrect answers. **A** is incorrect because there are no syntactical errors in the code. **B** is incorrect because a set of parentheses around "`p % j`" is not required. Answer **D** is incorrect because the code does not print out the character 0, it prints out the `boolean` literal value `false`.

7. Given:

```
public class EqualityTests {
  public static void main (String[] args) {
    Integer value1 = new Integer("312");
    Integer value2 = new Integer("312");
    Object object1 = new Object();
    Object object2 = new Object();
    Object object3 = value1;
  }
}
```

Which expressions evaluate to `true`?

A. `value1.equals(value2)`

B. `value1.equals(object1)`

C. `value1.equals(object3)`

D. `object1.equals(object2)`

Answer:

☑ **A** and **C.** **A** is correct because the class Integer implements the Comparable interface, allowing use of the `equals` method. **C** is correct because the `Integer` object was used to create the `Object` reference.

☒ **B** and **D** are incorrect because the code cannot equate two objects with different references.

Developing with String Objects and Their Methods

8. Given:

```
System.out.print(3 + 3 + "3");
System.out.print(" and ");
System.out.println("3" + 3 + 3);
```

What will be printed to standard out?

A. `333 and 333`

B. `63 and 63`

C. `333 and 63`

D. `63 and 333`

> Answer:
>
> ☑   **D.**The (+) operators have left-to-right association. The first two operands of the first
> statement are numeric, so the addition (+) operator is used. Therefore, 3 + 3 = 6.
> Since `6 + "3"` uses a string as an operand, the string concatenation (+) operator is
> used. Therefore, concatenating the strings "6" and "3" renders the string "63". The last
> statement is handled a little differently. The first operand is a `String`, therefore the string
> concatenation operator is used with the other operands. Thus, concatenating strings "3" +
> "3" + "3" renders the string "333". The correct answer is "63 and 333".
>
> ☒   **A, B,**and **C** incorrect. Note that changing `("3" + 3 + 3)` to `("3" + (3 + 3))`
> would have rendered "36".

9. Consider the interface `CharSequence` that is a required argument in one of the `replace`
method declarations:

```
public String replace(CharSequence target, CharSequence replacement) {
    ...
}
```

This `CharSequence` interface is a super interface to which concrete classes?

A. `String`

B. `StringBoxer`

C. `StringBuffer`

D. `StringBuilder`

Answer:

☑ **A, C,** and **D.** The concrete classes `String`, `StringBuffer`, and `StringBuilder` all implement the interface `CharSequence`. These classes can all be used in a polymorphic manner in regards to CharSequence being an expected argument in one of the `String` class's `replace` methods.

☒ **B** is incorrect. There is no such thing as a `StringBoxer` class.

10. Which statement is false about the `toString` method?

A. The `toString` method is a method of the `Object` class.

B. The `toString` method returns a string representation of the object.

C. The `toString` method must return the object's state information in the form of a string.

D. The `toString` method is commonly overridden.

Answer:

☑ **C.** While the `toString` method is commonly used to return the object's state information, any information that can be gathered may be returned in the string.

☒ **A, B,** and **D** are incorrect answers since they all represent true statements. **A** is incorrect because the `toString` method is a method of the `Object` class. **B** is incorrect because the `toString` method returns a string representation of the object. **D** is incorrect because the `toString` method is also commonly overridden.

11. Which `indexOf` method declaration is invalid?

A. `indexOf(int ch)`

B. `indexOf(int ch, int fromIndex)`

C. `indexOf(String str, int fromIndex)`

D. `indexOf(CharSequence str, int fromIndex)`

Answer:

☑ **D.** The method declaration including `indexOf(CharSequence str, int fromIndex)` is invalid. `CharSequence` is not used as an argument in any `indexOf` method. Note that `String`, `StringBuffer`, and `StringBuilder` all declare their own `indexOf` methods.

☒ **A, B,** and **C** are incorrect because they are all valid method declarations.

12. Given:

```
String tenCharString = "AAAAAAAAAA";
System.out.println(tenCharString.replace("AAA", "LLL"));
```

What is printed to the standard out?

A. AAAAAAAAAA

B. LLLAAAAAAA

C. LLLLLLLLLA

D. LLLLLLLLLL

> Answer:
>
> ☑ **C.** The `replace` method of the `String` class replaces all instances of the specified string. The first three instances of AAA are replaced by LLL, making LLLLLLLLLA.
>
> ☒ **A, B,** and **D** are incorrect answers as justified by the correct answer's explanation.

13. Consider the following illustration. Which statements, also represented in the illustration, are true?

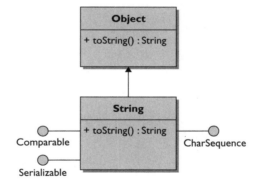

A. The `String` class implements the `Object` interface.

B. The `String` class implements the `Comparable`, `Serializable`, and `CharSequence` interfaces.

C. The `toString` method overrides the `toString` method of the `Object` class, allowing the `String` object to return its own string.

D. The `toString` method is publicly accessible.

Answer:

☑ **B, C,** and **D** are all correct because they represent true statements. **B** is correct because the `String` class implements the `Comparable`, `Serializable`, and `CharSequence` interfaces. **C** is correct because the `toString` method overrides the `toString` method of the `Object` class, allowing the `String` object to return its own string. **D** is correct because the `toString` method is also publicly accessible.

☒ **A** is incorrect. The `Object` class is a concrete class. Therefore, the `String` class does not implement an `Object` interface since there is no such thing as an `Object` interface. The `String` class actually extends an `Object` concrete class.

Part II

Object-Oriented Basic Concepts

CHAPTERS

4   Working with Basic Classes and Variables

5   Understanding Variable Scope and Class
    Construction

6   Working with Classes and Their Relationships

7   Understanding Class Inheritance

8   Understanding Polymorphism

9   Representing Object-Oriented Concepts
    with UML

4

Working with Basic Classes and Variables

CERTIFICATION OBJECTIVES

- Understanding Primitives,
  Enumerations, and Objects

- Practical Uses of Primitives,
  Enumerations, and Objects

✓   Two-Minute Drill

 Q&A   Self Test

CERTIFICATION OBJECTIVE

Understanding Primitives, Enumerations, and Objects

Exam Objective 1.1   Describe, compare, and contrast primitives (integer, floating point, boolean, and character), enumeration types, and objects.

An application is made up of variables that store data and code that manipulates the data. Java uses primitives to store its most basic data types. These primitives are then used to create more advanced data types called objects. This is what makes Java an object-oriented language. It allows the developer to store related code and data together in discrete objects.

This is a very important and fundamental concept that must be understood to truly understand how the Java language works. This chapter will cover the basics of primitive variables and objects. The SCJA will have questions that will require the testtaker to understand the difference between primitives and objects and how each is used. The next few chapters will build off this foundation. The following topics will be covered in this chapter:

- Primitives
- Objects
- Arrays
- Enumerations
- Java's strongly typed nature
- Naming conventions

Primitives

This section examines Java primitives. Primitives are a special subset of Java data types. They are the foundation of storing data in a program. It is important to understand what a primitive is and what it is not for the SCJA exam. The Java language has eight primitives. Luckily, only four are required for the SCJA exam. The important thing to remember about each primitive is what kind of value you would store in it. The size in memory and minimum/maximum value sizes are good to know, but you won't be required to memorize them for the exam.

What Is a Primitive?

A primitive is the most basic form of data in a Java program, hence the name primitive. In fact, all advanced data types such as objects can be broken down into their primitive parts. When a primitive is declared, it reserves a certain number of bits in memory. The size of the memory allocation is dependent on the type of primitive. Each primitive data type has a set size that it will always occupy in memory. The four primitive data types that will be on the SCJA exam are `int` (integer), `float` (floating point), `boolean` (boolean), and `char` (character). It is important to remember that something represented in code as an `Integer` (this refers to an object) is different than an `int` (which refers to a primitive containing an integer).

While working with a primitive variable, you may only set it or read it. Calculations performed with primitives are much faster than calculations performed with similar objects. The following code shows a primitive `int` being declared:

```
int inchesOfRain;
```

The `inchesOfRain` variable is now declared as an `int`. This variable can only store an integer and cannot be broken down into any smaller elements. Now that the variable is declared, it can only be set or read, that is all. No methods can be called using this variable because it is a primitive. This will be discussed in more depth later when objects are explored. This code uses the new integer:

```
inchesOfRain = 2;
totalInchesOfRain += inchesOfRain;
```

ints

An `int` is the most commonly used Java primitive. Once declared, it has a default value of 0. An `int` occupies 32 bits in memory and can store a 32-bit signed two's complement non-floating point number. It has a maximum value of 2,147,483,647 and a minimum value of –2,147,483,648 inclusive. The following code segments demonstrate the uses of `int`:

```
int x;
x = 3;
int y = x;
int z = 5 + x;
```

floats

A `float` is a primitive that is used to store decimal values. It has a default value of 0.0f. This value is equal to zero, but the "f" or "F" appended to the end indicates that this value is a float, not a double. They require 32 bits in memory and may contain a 32-bit value with a maximum of $3.4e^{+38}$ and a minimum positive nonzero value of $1.4e^{-45}$ inclusive. These values are rounded for simplicity. The exact size of a float is a formula that can be found in section 4.2.3 of the official Java Language Specification. This is beyond the scope of this book and the SCJA exam. The following code segments demonstrate the uses of float (note the use of f or F to denote that the number is a float):

```
float a = 0.2f;
float b = a;
a = 5.0f;
a = 10.5F;
/* An integer literal fits in a float and does not need to be
casted */
a = 1118;
```

booleans

A boolean primitive is used to store a value of true or false. They store a one-bit value and will default to false. Although they represent only one bit of information, their exact size is not defined in the Java standard and may occupy more space on different platforms.

```
boolean isWorking = true;
isWorking = false;
```

chars

The char primitive is used to store a single 16-bit Unicode character and requires 16 bits of memory. The range of a char corresponds to the minimum and maximum as defined by the Unicode specification '\u0000' (or 0) and '\uffff' (or 65,535 inclusive), respectively. When a char is set with a character in code, single quotes should be used—'Y', for example. A char has a default value of '\u0000' or 0. This is the only Java primitive that is unsigned. The following code segments demonstrate the uses of char (note that '\u0046' is Unicode that corresponds to the F character):

```
char c = 'X';
char upperCaseF = '\u0046';
c = upperCaseF;
```

The following Scenario & Solution details each of the primitives that will be on the SCJA exam. It is important to understand this content.

SCENARIO & SOLUTION

What primitive would you use to store a value that will be true or false?	`boolean`
What primitive would you use to store a value that will be a whole number?	`int`
What primitive would you use to store a Unicode value?	`char`
What primitive would you use to store a value that may not be a whole number?	`float`

Primitives vs. Their Wrapper Class

We have discussed what a primitive type is in the previous section. Primitives are the basic building blocks in Java and are one of the few things that are not objects. Java has a built-in wrapper class for each primitive that can convert a primitive to an object. The wrapper classes are `Integer`, `Float`, `Boolean`, and `Character`. Note that each of these classes starts with a capital letter, whereas the primitive begins with a lowercase letter. If you see a data type `Float`, it is referring to the object, while the data type `float` refers to the primitive. As of J2SE 5.0, a primitive will automatically be converted in either direction between its wrapper class and associated primitive. This feature is called autoboxing and unboxing. The following is an example of an `Integer` object being initialized:

```
// An Integer is created and initialized to 5
Integer valueA = new Integer(5);
/* A primitive int is set to the int value stored in the Integer
object */
int num = number.intValue();
// Autoboxing is used to convert an int to an Integer
Integer valueB = num;
```

Primitives and their equivalent objects can, in most cases, be used interchangeably. However, this is bad practice. When performing math operations, using primitives will result in much faster calculations. Primitives also consume a smaller memory footprint.

INSIDE THE EXAM

The Other Four Java Primitives

Java has a total of eight primitives. We have discussed `boolean`, `char`, `float`, and `int`. These are the four primitives on the SCJA exam. Four more exist in Java but are not on the exam. While they are not required, it is beneficial to understand them in order to have a fuller understanding of the language. The remaining four are `byte`, `short`, `long`, and `double`.

The `byte` primitive is like an `int`, but smaller. It stores eight-bit signed integers ranging from −128 to 127 inclusive. A `short` is also like an `int`. It is bigger than a `byte` but smaller than an `int`. It stores a 16-bit integer ranging from −32768 to 32767 inclusive. The `long` primitive is also like an `int`, but twice

the size. It stores a 64-bit integer ranging from -2^{63} to $2^{63}-1$ inclusive. The last primitive is the `double`. It is like a `float` and stores up to a 64-bit floating-point number. It holds a value in the range of $5e^{-324}$ to a minimum positive non-zero value of $1.8e^{+308}$, inclusive. Like the `float`, this range is rounded and the exact formula can be found in the Java Language Specification.

These primitives are not as frequently used as the four on the SCJA. They tend to be used when either a larger value needs to be handled or the code must be optimized for a smaller memory footprint.

Reviewing All Primitives

Table 4-1 details all eight Java primitives. For the SCJA exam, it is most important to remember what data type you would use for the data you are storing. The size and range is nice to know but not required for the exam.

Objects

This section will discuss Java objects. Java is an object-oriented language, and as the name implies, understanding what they are and how they work is a fundamental and very important concept. Almost everything you work with in Java is an object. Primitives are one of the few exceptions to this rule. This chapter will discuss what is stored in objects and how they help keep code organized.

	Data Type	Used For	Size	Range	On SCJA
TABLE 4-1	`boolean`	true or false	1 bit	NA	Yes
Java Primitive Data Types	`char`	Unicode character	16 bits	\u0000 to \uFFFF (0 to 65,535)	Yes
	`byte`	integer	8 bits	−128 to 127	No
	`short`	integer	16 bits	−32768 to 32767	No
	`int`	integer	32 bits	−2,147,483,648 to 2,147,483,647	Yes
	`long`	integer	64 bits	-2^{63} to $2^{63}-1$	No
	`float`	floating point	32 bits	positive $1.4e^{-45}$ to $3.4e^{+38}$	Yes
	`double`	floating point	64 bits	positive $5e^{-324}$ to $1.8e^{+308}$	No

Understanding Objects

Objects are a more advanced data type than primitives. They internally use primitives and other objects to store their data and contain related code. The data is used to maintain the state of the object, while the code is organized into methods that perform actions on this data. A well-designed class should be clearly defined and easily reused in different applications. This is the fundamental philosophy of an object-oriented language.

Objects vs. Classes and the New Operator

The distinction between objects and classes is important to understand. When a developer writes code, they are creating or modifying a class. A class is the file containing the code that the developer writes. It is a tangible item. A class is like a blueprint to tell the Java Virtual Machine how to create an object at runtime. The new operator tells the Java Virtual Machine to create a new instance of this class, the result of which is an object. Many objects can be built from one class. The following is an example of a class. This class is employed to create an object used to represent a car.

```
public class Car {
  int topSpeed;
  boolean running;
  Car(int topSpeed, boolean running){
    this.running = running;
    this.topSpeed = topSpeed;
```

```
  }
  boolean isRunning(){
    return running;
  }
}
```

The preceding class can be used to represent a `Car` object. The class can store a `boolean` value that represents whether the car is running and an `int` value that represents the top speed. From this class, the Java Virtual Machine can create one or many instances of the `Car` class. Each instance will become its own `Car` object. In the following code segment, two car objects are created:

```
Car fastCar = new Car(200,true);

Car slowCar = new Car(100,true);
```

Both `fastCar` and `slowCar` are instances of the `Car` class. The new operator is used to tell the Java Virtual Machine that it needs to create a `Car` object with the arguments given to the constructor. The new operator will always return a new and independent instance of the class.

Using Objects

In the section about primitives, we learned how each primitive could be initialized and how they have a finite predetermined size. Unlike primitives, the size of an object is not clearly defined. An object's size depends on the size of all the primitives and objects that it stores. Since objects store other objects, their size must also be considered. When an object is declared, the Java Virtual Machine makes a reference in memory to the location of the object. Objects also have the ability to change in size as the objects they store grow or shrink. An object is declared in the same manner as a primitive, but cannot be used until it has been initialized with the new operator or set equal to an existing object. In the following example, we will use the `Car` class again.

```
/* This is legal. You can use the method isRunning because
the object has been initialized. */
Car bigCar;
bigCar = new Car(125,true);
boolean running = bigCar.isRunning();

/* This is legal. You can use the method isRunning because
the object smallCar has been set to the same initialized
```

```
object as bigCar. This will make smallCar and bigCar the same
object. */
Car smallCar;
smallCar = bigCar;
boolean running = smallCar.isRunning();

/* This is an illegal example. You cannot use a method on an
uninitialized object. */
Car oldCar;
boolean running = oldCar.isRunning();
```

It is important to notice that, unlike a primitive, an object must be initialized. Before initialization, an object is set to null by default. If a null object is used, it will throw a null pointer exception.

When to Use Objects

Primitives are used to store simple values. Integers or floating point numbers within the bounds of a primitive data type are easy to store. Unfortunately, not all applications deal with values that fit neatly in the bounds of a primitive. For example, if an integer value is very large and has the potential to become even larger, the primitive int or long may not be appropriate. Instead, the developer may have to use one of the classes from the built-in Java packages for handling large numbers. Remember that a class is the blueprint on how to build an object.

Objects can and should be created to store data that is similar. Remember, it is good object-oriented design to group together like code and data in a distinct class. Objects should be used to store complex related data.

EXERCISE 4-1

Compile and Run an Object

This exercise will get you more familiar with objects. You will use the Car class and then add more functionality to it.

1. Copy the Car class into a text file and save it as **Car.java**.

2. Create a new text file and call it **Main.java**. This will be your main class. Copy the following code into this file:

```
public class Main {
  public static void main(String[] args) {
```

```
        // Your code goes here
    }
}
```

3. Use the following code to create a `Car` object:

```
Car yourCar = new Car(230,true);
```

4. Use the following code to display to the user if the car is running or not:

```
System.out.println(yourCar.isRunning());
```

5. Go back to the `Car` class and add a method to get the car's top speed.

6. Add a line to your Main.java file that will display the car's top speed.

Arrays

An array is a series of variables of the same type that can be accessed by an index. Arrays are useful when you have a set of data that will all be used in a similar way. Arrays can be made from primitive data types or objects. Even if an array is made of a primitive data type, the new operator must be used. The following is an example of an array made up of the `int` data type:

```
int[] testScore = new int[3];
```

In this example, we declare a variable named `testScore` to be an integer array. This is done by adding box brackets to the end of the data type: `int []` is the result. The `[]` after the data type means it will be an array. The box brackets should follow the data type, but it is valid for them to follow the variable name instead. Standard Java coding conventions suggest they should only be used with the data type. Regardless of whether the new array is of primitives or objects, it must be initialized with new and then the data type. The number in brackets indicates the size of the array. In this example, the array has three items. Each item is of type `int`. Individual elements in the array can be accessed or modified; they can also be placed in another `int`. The index for an array is zero-based. This means that the first element has an index of zero. The example that follows demonstrates how an array can be used.

```
int[] testScore = new int[3];
testScore[0] = 98;
testScore[1] = 100;
testScore[2] = 72;
int shannonsTestScore = testScore[1];
```

FIGURE 4-1

Array declaration

```
int[] intArray = new int[4]
```
| int[0] | int[1] | int[2] | int[3] |

Arrays are useful in loops. It is very common to access an array in a loop with a variable as the index. This variable would be incremented each time through the loop until the end of the array. The developer must take caution not to use an index that is out of bounds. An out of bounds index will cause the Java Virtual Machine to throw an exception at runtime. Once the size of an array is set, it cannot be changed. This makes arrays less useful in situations where the data set may grow. Figure 4-1 shows a basic array declaration.

Enumerations

Enumerations are a special data type in Java that allows for a variable to be set to predefined constants. The variable must equal one of the values that have been predefined for it. An enumeration is useful when there is a limited set of options that a variable can equal and it is restricted to these known values. For example, a deck of playing cards will always have four suits: clubs, diamonds, hearts, and spades. If a developer wanted to represent a card, an enumeration could be used to represent the suit.

```
enum Suit { CLUBS, DIAMONDS, HEARTS, SPADES }
```

The preceding is an example of an enumeration that would be used to store the suit of a playing card. It is defined with the keyword enum. The enum keyword is used in the same manner as the class keyword. It can be defined in its own Java file, or embedded in a class.

```
Suit cardSuit;
cardSuit = Suit.CLUBS;
if(cardSuit == Suit.CLUBS){
  System.out.println("The suit of this card is clubs.");
}
```

The preceding example demonstrates an enumeration being used. The variable card is declared as a `Suit`. `Suit` was defined earlier as an enumeration. The `cardSuit` variable can now be used to store one of the four predefined suit values.

Benefits of Using Enumerations

An object can be created to work in the same manner as enumerations. In fact, enumerations were not even in the Java language until version 5.0. However, enumerations make code more readable and provide less room for programmer error.

Java Is Strongly Typed

Java is a strongly typed programming language. Java requires that a developer declare the data type of each variable they use. Once a variable is declared as one type, all data stored in it must be compatible with that type. Think back to the primitive data types we reviewed previously. For example, once a variable is declared as an `int`, only `int` data can be stored within it. Data can be converted from one type to another. This will be discussed later in this section.

Understanding Strongly Typed Variables

Strongly typed variables help to create more reliable code. In most cases, the Java compiler will not allow the developer to inadvertently store mismatched data types. Only variables with the same data type are compatible with each other. For example, a `float` cannot be stored in any other data type other than a `float`. The same is true for all primitives and objects. The Java Virtual Machine will do some automatic conversions for the developer. It is important to understand that the types are not compatible and that the code will only work because of the conversion that is happening. An example of a conversion would be going from an `int` to a `float`. The Java Virtual Machine will allow for an `int` to be placed into a `float` because it can convert an `int` to a `float` without losing precision. The converse is not true. A `float` cannot be converted to an `int` without the loss of precision.

Casting Variables to Different Types

Java does allow a variable to be cast to a different type. To cast a variable, place the new data type in parentheses in front of the data, or variable. Data can only be cast to types it is compatible with. If data is illegally cast, the program will throw an exception at runtime. An object can be cast to any parent or child object if the object was initialized as that child object. This is an advanced concept of object-oriented languages. This will be discussed in more detail in later chapters. Primitives can also be cast to other primitives or compatible objects. For example, a `float` can be cast to an `int`. In this scenario, the cast would truncate the `float` to a whole number. The following are some examples of casting variables and data:

```
float floatNum = 1.5f;
int wasFloat = (int) floatNum;
```

The variable `wasFloat` would be equal to 1 since the .5 would be truncated to make the data compatible.

on the **Job**

Casting variables is something that a developer should use lightly. There are times that variables must be cast, and even advanced programming techniques that rely on it. However, casting variables just adds unneeded complexity to the code when there are better ways to convert that data.

Naming Conventions

Using the correct naming conventions while creating a Java application is a critical step in creating easy reading and maintainable code. Java does not have many restrictions on how classes and objects can be named. However, nearly every experienced Java developer uses a single naming convention suggested by Sun Microsystems.

When creating a class, the class name should be a noun. The first letter should be capitalized along with each internal word after the first. They should be short yet descriptive. Shown next are some examples of good class names following the naming convention.

```
class SportCar {…}
class BaseballPlayer {…}
class Channel {…}
```

Variables should also have short but meaningful names. However, it is okay to use one-letter names for temporary variables. Their name should give an outside observer some insight as to what the variable is used for. A variable's name should start with a lowercase letter, but each sequential internal word should be capitalized. Shown next is a sample of some variables named following the convention.

```
int milesPerGallon;
float price;
int i;
Car raceCar;
```

CERTIFICATION OBJECTIVE

Practical Uses of Primitives, Enumerations, and Objects

Exam Objective 3.1   Develop code that uses primitives, enumeration types, and object references, and recognize literals of these types.

This section will build on the fundamental concepts that were discussed in the previous sections. The SCJA exam will not require code to be written from scratch. However, the exam creators have decided to present scenarios where the candidate will need to determine the best-suited code from a list of segments. The exam will also present segments of code and ask varying questions about its elements. This section specifically covers literals and practical examples of primitives, enumerations, and objects.

Literals

A literal is a term used for a hardcoded value used within code. The following example demonstrates the use of literals:

```
int daysInMay = 31;
int daysInJune;
daysInJune = 30;
char y  = 'Y';
```

As used here, 31, 30, and 'Y' are examples of using a literal. A literal is any value that is not a variable. Valid literal value formats for all primitives except the `boolean` type include character, decimal, hexadecimal, octal and Unicode. Literals values for `boolean`s must be 'true' or 'false'.

Examples of Primitives, Enumerations, and Objects

This section will provide a few examples of all the topics we have covered in this chapter so far. Each example will be accompanied by an explanation. These examples will mimic the types of scenarios likely found on the SCJA exam.

Primitives in Action

Primitives are the most basic data types in Java. As stated before, they can only be set or read. The following sample program uses each primitive that will be on the SCJA. This program calculates a baseball pitcher's earned run average.

```java
public class EraCalculator{
  public static void main(String[] args) {
    int earnedRuns = 3;
    int inningsPitched = 6;
    int inningsInAGame = 9;
    float leagueAverageEra = 4.25f;
    float era = ((float)earnedRuns / (float)inningsPitched) *
      inningsInAGame;
    boolean betterThanAverage;
    if (era < leagueAverageEra) {
      betterThanAverage = true;
    } else {
      betterThanAverage = false;
    }
    char yesNo;
    if (betterThanAverage) {
      yesNo = 'Y';
    } else {
      yesNo = 'N';
    }
    System.out.println("Earned Runs\t\t" + earnedRuns);
    System.out.println("Innings Pitched\t\t" + inningsPitched);
    System.out.println("ERA\t\t\t" + era);
    System.out.println("League Average ERA\t"+leagueAverageEra);
    System.out.println("Is player better than league average "+
      yesNo);
  }
}
```

Note that on the line where the variable era is calculated, the two int variables, earnedRuns and inningsPitched, are cast to a float. The cast to a float is needed so the division will be performed on variables of type float instead of their original type of int. The variables earnedRuns, inningsPitched, inningsInAGame, and leagueAverageEra are all set by literals. The preceding program shows how primitives are used. When the code is executed, it will produce the following output:

```
Earned Runs                      3
Innings Pitched                  6
ERA                              4.5
League Average ERA               4.25
Is player better than league average      N
```

Primitives and Their Wrapper Class

The code segment that follows shows four variables being declared. Of the four, two are primitives and two are objects. The objects are instances of primitive wrapper classes. On the exam, pay close attention to how the variables are declared. There will likely be a segment where the question will ask how many of the variables are primitives.

```
Integer numberOfCats;
Float averageWeightOfCats;
int numberOfDogs;
float averageWeightOfDogs;
```

In the preceding example, int and float are primitives and Integer and Float are objects. Note that the capital F in Float signifies an object.

Enumerations

Questions about enumerations will typically be related to picking the correct line of code for a given scenario. The following example demonstrates a small class. This class has an enumeration defined that contains three different shoe types. The createRunningShoes() method below is used to set the shoe varible to the enumerated type of a running shoe:

```
public class EnumExample {
    enum TypeOfShoe { RUNNING, BASKETBALL, CROSS_TRAINING }
    TypeOfShoe shoe;
    void createRunningShoes(){
```

```
    shoe = TypeOfShoe.RUNNING;
  }
}
```

Objects

The SCJA exam does not require the development of your own objects. But it is important to understand the content of one and be able to recognize it in code. It is also important to understand how to use methods that an object contains. In the following example, a class is defined. This class is the Heater class. As its name suggests, it would be used to represent a heater. This is a very basic class because it only has two methods and one instance variable. A more useful class would have many more of both.

```
class Heater{
  int temperatureTrigger;
  int getTemperatureTrigger() {
    return temperatureTrigger;
  }
  void setTemperatureTrigger(int temperatureTrigger) {
    this.temperatureTrigger = temperatureTrigger;
  }
}
```

The preceding Heater class stores the temperature that will trigger the system to turn on in the variable named temperatureTrigger. The two methods are used to get the value and set the value. These are called getters and setters and will be discussed in a later chapter. The following code segments will use the Heater class to create an object:

```
Heater houseHeater = new Heater();
houseHeater.setTemperatureTrigger(68);
System.out.println(houseHeater.getTemperatureTrigger());
```

This code segment declares a new variable as a Heater object. The object is then initialized with the new keyword. The next line uses the setTemperatureTrigger method to modify the state of the object. The final line uses the getTemperatureTrigger method to read this value and display it to the user. For the SCJA exam, it is important to be familiar with this syntax and understand how the methods are used.

on the **ob**

Creating a dozen getter and setter methods by hand could take a while to complete. Fortunately, most modern IDEs have an automated way of creating getters and setters methods. Using this automated feature produces the methods with just a few mouse clicks.

For example, in the Eclipse IDE, highlight the desired instance variable you wish to produce getters and setters for, followed by a right-click of the mouse. A popup menu will be displayed. Select "Source" followed by "Generate Getters and Setters..." Another dialog box will be displayed with additional options that are not needed for this example. Finally, selecting the "Ok" pushbutton will generate the methods for you. See Chapter 7 for more information on getter and setter methods.

CERTIFICATION SUMMARY

In this chapter, some of the most fundamental concepts of Java were discussed in relationship to basic classes and variables. Even though the SCJA exam only has two objectives covering these concepts, many advanced concepts and objectives are built upon the content of this chapter. A good understanding of this chapter will result in a better understanding of the next few chapters.

Java primitives were examined first. Primitives are the basic building blocks of a Java program. The four primitive variable data types that will appear on the SCJA are int, float, boolean, and char. It is important to remember these primitives and what type of data they are designed to store.

Objects were then discussed. Objects are a very important concept to understand for the SCJA exam. Objects are an advanced Java data type that can be custom created or found in the many Java packages that are included with the Java Virtual Machine. Objects are the pieces that interact to make up an application. Java is an object-oriented language, which means that nearly every aspect of the program is represented as objects, and the interaction between the objects is what gives an application its functionality.

Arrays were then discussed. Arrays are good for keeping like data together. They use a zero-based index to access the individual elements of the array. Arrays can be of objects or primitives and must be initialized.

Enumerations were the last group of data types discussed. Enumerations are special objects that are used to denote a value among a pre-known set of values.

Although regular objects can be used to achieve the same results, enumerations provide a way to limit the data set without implementing a lot of custom code.

Next, the details of what makes Java a strongly typed language were examined. In general, the Java language only allows for variables to change data type by explicitly casting them to a new data type. If a variable is cast to a data type that it is not compatible with, an exception will be generated.

The final Java concept covered was Java naming conventions. Even though there are very few limitations on how variables and classes can be named, it is good coding practice to follow the conventions used by nearly every Java developer. Not following these conventions is a quick way to test the patience of your fellow developers.

The chapter concluded with a group of examples and explanations. These examples are important to understand. The SCJA will not ask you to write large sections of code, but you must be able to understand code segments and determine what the output will be or if there are any errors present in the code.

✔ TWO-MINUTE DRILL

- ❑ Primitives are the fundamental data type in Java.
- ❑ `int` is a primitive data type that is used to store integer values.
- ❑ `float` is a primitive data type that is used to store floating-point values.
- ❑ `boolean` is a primitive data type that is used to store true or false values.
- ❑ `char` is a primitive data type that is used to store a single Unicode character.
- ❑ Primitive data types all start with a lowercase letter, while classes start with a capital letter.
- ❑ Each primitive data type has a corresponding wrapper class: `Integer`, `Float`, `Boolean`, and `Character`. Note the capital letters.
- ❑ Objects are more advanced data types. They may be defined by a developer or found in a built-in Java package.
- ❑ Objects must be initialized by using the new keyword.
- ❑ Arrays are objects and allow you to store multiple variables together that can be accessed by an index.
- ❑ Enumerations are special objects that allow a developer to create a predefined set of constants. A variable can then be set to only one of the predefined values.
- ❑ Java is a strongly typed language. Variables must be declared as a type, and any value that is stored must be compatible with this type.
- ❑ It is possible to cast a variable to a different data type. If incompatible types are cast, an exception will be thrown.
- ❑ A literal is a value that is hardcoded in code as the value itself.
- ❑ Java naming conventions dictate that a class should be named with the first letter capitalized, along with each sequential word in the name.
- ❑ Java naming conventions dictate that a variable should be named with the first letter being lowercase, and with each sequential word in the name beginning with a capital.

SELF TEST

Understanding Primitives, Enumerations, and Objects

1. You need to create an application that is used to calculate the attendance at a baseball game. What data type would be most appropriate for storing the attendance?

    A. `boolean`

    B. `char`

    C. `float`

    D. `int`

2. What is the best data type to use if you are required to perform many addition, subtraction, and multiplication calculations on a whole number?

    A. `float`

    B. `Float`

    C. `int`

    D. `Integer`

3. You are writing a class that will store the status of an on/off switch. Which data type is most appropriate to store this value?

    A. `boolean`

    B. `char`

    C. `float`

    D. `int`

4. You have decided on the data type for a variable that will store the information about the on/off switch. Now you must determine a name for it. Which of the following names follows the Java naming conventions?

    A. `LIGHTSWITCHENABLED`

    B. `LightSwitchEnabled`

    C. `lightSwitchEnabled`

    D. `x`

5. What is the best data type to use when storing a status code that may have one of the following values: success, failed, success with errors, undetermined?

A. `Object`

B. `Class`

C. `boolean`

D. `enum`

E. `int`

6. A system has three sensors attached to it. You need a way to represent this system in your program. What would be the best data type to use to model this system and sensors?

A. `Object`

B. `boolean`

C. `enum`

D. `int`

7. The new keyword is used to initialize which of the following data types? (Choose all that apply.)

A. `Object`

B. `boolean`

C. `Boolean`

D. `Float`

E. `float`

F. `float[]`

8. In the following line of code, what does the `(int)` represent:

```
number = (int)sensorReading;
```

A. Rounding the `sensorReading` variable to the nearest `int`.

B. Casting the `sensorReading` variable to the `int` data type.

C. Nothing, it is there as a comment.

9. Given the following line of code, which of the lines of code listed are INCORRECT? (Choose all that apply.)

```
char c;
```

A. `c = new char();`

B. `c = 'Y';`

C. `c = '\u0056';`

D. `c = "Yes";`

Practical Uses of Primitives, Enumerations, and Objects

10. Which of the following variables are being set with the use of a literal? (Choose all that apply.)

   A. `int tvChannel = 4;`

   B. `char c = '5';`

   C. `char d = '\u0123';`

   D. `char e = c;`

   E. `int oldChannel = tvChannel;`

11. Given the following line of code, what lines below are valid? (Choose all that apply.)

   `enum Sports { FOOTBALL, BASKETBALL, BASEBALL, TRACK }`

   A. `Sports sport = FOOTBALL;`

   B. `Sports sport = Sports.FOOTBALL;`

   C. `Sports sport = Sports.HOCKEY;`

   D. `Sports sport = 'TRACK'`

12. How many objects are referenced in this code segment?

   `int numberOfTrees = 5;`

   `Integer ageOfFarm = 14;`

   `float averageHeightOfTrees = 124.2f`

   `Tree treeType;`

   `int[] heightOfEachTree;`

   A. 0

   B. 1

   C. 2

   D. 3

   E. 4

   F. 5

13. What is the correct way to create an array with five `int` data types? (Choose all that apply.)

   A. `int intArray = new int[5];`

   B. `int intArray = new int(5);`

   C. `int[] intArray = new int[5];`

   D. `int intArray[] = new int[5];`

14. What is the correct way to initialize a variable declared with the data type of `Book`, as a new `Book` object?

   A. `Book b;`

   B. `Book b = new Book();`

   C. `Book b = new Book[];`

   D. `Book b = Book();`

15. What is the difference between an `int` and an `Integer`?

   A. Nothing. They are both fully interchangeable.

   B. An `int` is an object and `Integer` is a primitive. An `int` is fastest when performing calculations.

   C. An `int` is a primitive and `Integer` is an object. An `int` is fastest when performing calculations.

   D. This is a trick question. There is no such thing as an `Integer`.

   E. This is a trick question. An `Integer` can be defined to be anything a developer wants it to be.

SELF TEST ANSWERS

Understanding Primitives, Enumerations, and Objects

1. You need to create an application that is used to calculate the attendance at a baseball game. What data type would be most appropriate for storing the attendance?

A. `boolean`

B. `char`

C. `float`

D. `int`

Answer:

☑ **D.** The attendance of a baseball game is going to be a whole number within the range of an `int`.

☒ **A, B,** and **C** are incorrect. **A** is incorrect because `boolean` variables are used to store literals with values of `true` or `false`. **B** is incorrect because the `char` data type is used to store a single Unicode character. **C** is incorrect because `float` is used to store floating-point numbers.

2. What is the best data type to use if you are required to perform many addition, subtraction, and multiplication calculations on a whole number?

A. `float`

B. `Float`

C. `int`

D. `Integer`

Answer:

☑ **C.** An `int` is used to store whole numbers and is a primitive. Primitive variables are faster to perform calculations than their associated wrapper class.

☒ **A, B,** and **D** are incorrect. **A** is incorrect because a `float` is used for floating-point numbers. **B** is incorrect because `Float` is a primitive wrapper class used for floating-point numbers. **D** is incorrect because the `Integer` data type is the wrapper class for an `int`. You can tell that it is not a primitive because the first letter is capitalized like all class names. Performing calculations with an `Integer` would be much slower than the primitive `int`.

3. You are writing a class that will store the status of an on/off switch. Which data type is most appropriate to store this value?

   A. `boolean`

   B. `char`

   C. `float`

   D. `int`

   Answer:

   ☑ **A.** A `boolean` primitive is used to store true or false which can be applied to a switch.

   ☒ **B, C,** and **D** are incorrect. They are all primitives used for different types of data.

4. You have decided on the data type for a variable that will store the information about the on/off switch. Now you must determine a name for it. Which of the following names follows the Java naming conventions?

   A. `LIGHTSWITCHENABLED`

   B. `LightSwitchEnabled`

   C. `lightSwitchEnabled`

   D. `x`

   Answer:

   ☑ **C.** A variable should begin with a lowercase letter, with each sequential word capitalized. The name should also be descriptive of what the variable is used for.

   ☒ **A, B,** and **D** are incorrect.

5. What is the best data type to use when storing a status code that may have one of the following values: success, failed, success with errors, undetermined?

   A. `Object`

   B. `Class`

   C. `boolean`

   D. `enum`

   E. `int`

Answer:

☑ **D.** An enum or enumeration is used to store data that has the possibility to be one of a few predefined data types.

☒ **A, B, C,** and **E** are incorrect. **A** is incorrect because objects are used to store complex data structures. **B** is incorrect because classes are used to create objects. **C** and **E** are incorrect because both are primitives and not suitable for this specific application.

6. A system has three sensors attached to it. You need a way to represent this system in your program. What would be the best data type to use to model this system and sensors?

A. `Object`

B. `boolean`

C. `enum`

D. `int`

Answer:

☑ **A.** An `Object` data type is one that the developer can define to represent the system and its state in the application's code.

☒ **B, C,** and **D** are all incorrect because they are primitive types and cannot be defined to hold complex data structures.

7. The new keyword is used to initialize which of the following data types? (Choose all that apply.)

A. `Object`

B. `boolean`

C. `Boolean`

D. `Float`

E. `float`

F. `float[]`

Answer:

☑ **A, C, D** and **F** are correct. New is used to initialize any variable that is not a primitive.

☒ **B** and **E** are incorrect because `float` and `boolean` are both primitive data types.

8. In the following line of code, what does the `(int)` represent:

```
number = (int)sensorReading;
```

A. Rounding the `sensorReading` variable to the nearest `int`.

B. Casting the `sensorReading` variable to the `int` data type.

C. Nothing, it is there as a comment.

Answer:

☑ **B.** It is casting the variable `sensorReading` to an `int`.

☒ A and C are incorrect.

9. Given the following line of code, which of the lines of code listed are INCORRECT? (Choose all that apply.)

```
char c;
```

A. `c = new char();`

B. `c = 'Y';`

C. `c = '\u0056';`

D. `c = "Yes";`

Answer:

☑ **A and D. A** is a correct answer because the `new` keyword cannot be used with the primitive `char`. **D** is a correct answer because `char` cannot store a string.

☒ **B and C** are incorrect answers because both lines are valid lines of code.

Practical Uses of Primitives, Enumerations, and Objects

10. Which of the following variables are being set with the use of a literal? (Choose all that apply.)

A. `int tvChannel = 4;`

B. `char c = '5';`

C. `char d = '\u0123';`

D. `char e = c;`

E. `int oldChannel = tvChannel;`

> Answer:
>
> ☑ **A, B,** and **C** are correct. A literal is a value that is not a variable. **A** has the literal 4. **B** has the literal '5'. **C** has the literal '\u0123'.
>
> ☒ **D** and **E** are incorrect. **D** is incorrect because the variable c is used to set this char. **E** is incorrect since tvChannel is a variable.

11. Given the following line of code, what lines below are valid? (Choose all that apply.)

```
enum Sports { FOOTBALL, BASKETBALL, BASEBALL, TRACK }
```

A. `Sports sport = FOOTBALL;`

B. `Sports sport = Sports.FOOTBALL;`

C. `Sports sport = Sports.HOCKEY;`

D. `Sports sport = 'TRACK'`

> Answer:
>
> ☑ **B.** This is the only line that uses a sport that is in the enumeration, and which uses the correct syntax.
>
> ☒ **A, C,** and **D** are incorrect. **A** is incorrect because it uses incorrect syntax. **C** is incorrect because HOCKEY is not defined as a sport type. **D** is incorrect because the syntax is incorrect.

12. How many objects are referenced in this code segment?

```
int numberOfTrees = 5;
Integer ageOfFarm = 14;
float averageHeightOfTrees = 124.2f
Tree treeType;
int[] heightOfEachTree;
```

A. 0

B. 1

C. 2

D. 3

E. 4

F. 5

Answer:

☑ **D.** `Integer`, `Tree`, and `int[]` are all references to objects. Remember an array is an object.

☒ **A, B, C, E,** and **F** are incorrect.

13. What is the correct way to create an array with five `int` data types? (Choose all that apply.)

A. `int intArray = new int[5];`

B. `int intArray = new int(5);`

C. `int[] intArray = new int[5];`

D. `int intArray[] = new int[5];`

Answer:

☑ **C** and **D. C** is the preferred way to declare an array. **D** is correct but does not follow standard conventions.

☒ **A** and **B** are incorrect.

14. What is the correct way to initialize a variable declared with the data type of `Book`, as a new `Book` object?

A. `Book b;`

B. `Book b = new Book();`

C. `Book b = new Book[];`

D. `Book b = Book();`

Answer:

☑ **B.** The correct way to declare an object is to use new and then the object name followed by parentheses. The parentheses are used to pass arguments to the constructor if needed.

☒ **A, C,** and **D** are incorrect. **A** is incorrect because it does not initialize a new `Book` object. **C** is incorrect because the square brackets are used instead of parentheses. **D** is incorrect because the new keyword is missing.

15. What is the difference between an `int` and an `Integer`?

A. Nothing. They are both fully interchangeable.

B. An `int` is an object and `Integer` is a primitive. An `int` is fastest when performing calculations.

C. An `int` is a primitive and `Integer` is an object. An `int` is fastest when performing calculations.

D. This is a trick question. There is no such thing as an `Integer`.

E. This is a trick question. `AnInteger` can be defined to be anything a developer wants it to be.

Answer:

☑ **C.** An `int` is a primitive, and primitives are faster when performing calculations. An `Integer` is an object. The capital letter 'I' should help you distinguish objects from primitives.

☒ **A, B, D,** and **E** are incorrect.

5

Understanding Variable Scope and Class Construction

CERTIFICATION OBJECTIVES

- Understanding Variable Scope
- Constructing Methods

✓ Two-Minute Drill

Q&A Self Test

Understanding Variable Scope

Exam Objective 4.2   Given an algorithm as pseudo-code, determine the correct scope for a variable used in the algorithm and develop code to declare variables in any of the following scopes: instance variable, method parameter, and local variable.

The last chapter discussed what a variable is and how it is declared to store different values. This section will explore the way variables are organized in your code. As you can imagine, any nontrivial application will have countless variables. If variables could be accessed anywhere in the code, it would be hard to find unique names that still conveyed a meaning. This scenario would also promote bad coding practices. A programmer may try to access a variable that is in a completely different part of the program. To solve these problems, Java has variable scope. Scope refers to the section of code that has access to a declared variable. The scope may be as small as a few lines, or may include the entire class.

In this section, we will cover the following topics:

■ Local variables

■ Method parameters

■ Instance variables

Local Variables

The first variable scope that will be discussed is local variable scope. Local variables are the variables that are declared inside of methods. As the name implies, they are used locally in code. They are commonly declared at the start of a method and in loops but can be declared anywhere in code. A local variable may be a temporary variable that is used just once, or one that is used throughout a method. The block of code that a variable is declared in determines the scope of the local variable. A block of code is determined by braces, { }. For example, if the variable is declared at the start of a method after the left brace "{", it would remain in scope until the method is closed with the right brace "}". Once a variable goes out of scope, it can no longer be used and its value is lost. The Java Virtual Machine may reallocate the memory that it occupies at any time. A block of code can be created anywhere. They can also be nested inside each other. A variable is in scope for the code block in which it is declared and all code blocks that exist inside it. The most common blocks are for `if` statements and `for` or `while` loops. The following example will demonstrate the use of local variables in code blocks:

```
void sampleMethod() { // Start of code block A
  int totalCount = 0;
    for (int i = 0; i < 3; i++) { // Start of code block B
      int forCount = 0;
      totalCount++;
      forCount++;
      { // Start of code block C
        int block1Count = 0;
        totalCount++;
        forCount++;
        block1Count++;
      } // End of code block C
      { // Start of code block D
        int block2Count = 0;
        totalCount++;
        forCount++;
        block2Count++;
      } // End of code block D
  /* These two variables have no relation to the above ones of
     the same name */
  int block1Count;
  int block2Count;
  }  // End of code block B
}  // End of code block A
```

Code block A is the method. Any variable that is declared in this block is in scope for the entire method. The variable `totalCount` is declared in block A, therefore it can be accessed from anywhere else in the example method.

Code block B starts with the `for` loop. The variable `i` is declared in this block. Even though it is not between the brackets, since it was declared in the `for` statement it is considered to be in code block B. The variable `forCount` is also declared in block B. Since both of these variables are declared in block B, they are only in scope for block B and any blocks contained within B. They are out of scope for block A, and a compiler error would be generated if they were accessed from this block.

Contained in block B is code block C. This block is started arbitrarily. In Java, it is valid to start a block of code at any time, although this is not done often in practice. The variable `block1Count` is declared in this block. In the preceding example, it is only in scope for block C. However, any code in this block also has access to the variables that have been declared in blocks A and B. Block C is closed and block D is created in block B. Block D contains the variable `block2Count`. This variable is only in scope for this block. Like block C, block D can also access variables that have been declared in blocks A and B. It is important to understand that the variables in block C are not in scope for block D, and variables in D are not in scope for C.

In block B, the line after the closure of block D, two new variables are declared. The variables are given the name `block1Count` and `block2Count`. These variables happen to have the same names as the variables that were declared in blocks C and D. Since the variables in blocks C and D are now out of scope, these two new variables have no relationship with them. Giving variables the same name as ones that are out of scope is valid in Java; however, it is not a good coding practice since it can create hard-to-read code.

Figure 5-1 represents another way to visualize this code example. Each code block represents scope. This figure shows each variable as it is declared in the code example. A variable is in scope from where it is declared till the end of its block; nested code blocks are included. These blocks correspond to the braces in the code example.

FIGURE 5-1

Code blocks
visualized

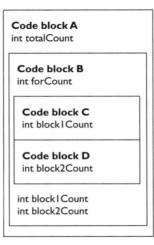

Code block A
int totalCount

Code block B
int forCount

Code block C
int block1Count

Code block D
int block2Count

int block1Count
int block2Count

All of the variables in the examples are considered local variables. The SCJA exam will focus mainly on questions that ask what appropriate type of variable to use in a given situation. A local variable is used when that data only needs to be accessed in a certain part, or locally, in your code. It is not good coding practice to use variables with a larger scope than is needed. This can create hard-to-maintain code. For example, a variable used as a counter should be a local variable. Oftentimes, a variable that you want to return will start as a local variable. Understanding variable scope is important. It is likely that at least one question on the test will require the determination of a variable's scope.

on the **Job**

When developing Java source code, variables should be declared with the most limited scope possible. This is a coding practice that helps reduce programming mistakes and improves code readability.

Method Parameters

Method parameters are the variables that are passed to the method from the calling segment of code. They are passed as arguments to the method. Method parameters may be primitives or objects. A method can have as many parameters as the developer defines. These variables are in scope for the entire method block. Method parameters are defined in the declaration for the method. The following example contains two method parameters:

```
float findMilesPerHour(float milesTraveled, float hoursTraveled)
{
  return milesTraveled / hoursTraveled;
}
```

In this example, `milesTraveled` and `hoursTraveled` are both method parameters. They are declared in the method's declaration. In this example, they are declared as `float`s. When this method is called, two `float`s must be passed to the method as arguments. These two variables may be accessed anywhere in this method.

Instance Variables

Instance variables are the variables that are declared in the class. They are called instance variables because they are created and remain in memory for as long as the instance of the class exists. Instance variables store the state of the object. They are not within the scope of any one particular method, instead they are in scope for the entire class. They exist and retain their value from the time a class is initialized until that class is either reinitialized or no longer referenced. The following example demonstrates two instance variables:

```
public class Television {
   int channel = 0;
   boolean on = false;
   void setChannel(int channelValue) {
     this.channel = channelValue;
   }
   int getChannel() {
     return this.channel;
   }
   void setOn(boolean on) {
     this.on = on;
   }
   boolean isOn() {
     return this.on;
     }
}
```

In this example, channel is declared as an int, and on is declared as a boolean. These are both instance variables. It is important to understand that instance variables must be declared in the class, not in a method. The four methods in this class each access one of the instance variables. The setChannel method is used to set the instance variable channel to the value of the int that was passed to it as an argument. The getChannel and isOn methods return the values that are stored in the two instance variables, respectively. Notice that the setOn method has a parameter that is the same name as an instance variable. This is valid code. In a method that has these conditions, if the variable is referenced, it will be the method argument. To reference the instance variable, use the this keyword. The following code segment demonstrates the Television class in use:

```
Television tv1 = new Television();
Television tv2 = new Television();
tv1.setChannel(2);
```

FIGURE 5-2

Two instances
of the tv class

```
tv2.setChannel(7);
System.out.println("Television channel for tv1: " + tv1.getChannel());
System.out.println("Television channel for tv2: " + tv2.getChannel());
```

The first two lines of this example create two unique instances of the `Television` class. When the instance of the class is created, each object gets an instance variable that will store a channel. The next two lines use the `setChannel` method to set the channel to 2 and 7, respectively.

Figure 5-2 represents the two objects that have been created and the value of both of their instance variables. The last two lines of code use the `getChannel` method to retrieve the value stored in the channel instance variable.

```
Television channel for tv1: 2
Television channel for tv2: 7
```

If the code were executed, the preceding would be the output. It is important to remember that each `tv` object has a unique set of instance variables. The following Scenario & Solution covers each type of variable scope and a likely use for it.

SCENARIO & SOLUTION

What variable scope would be best suited for a counter in a loop?	Local variable
What variable scope must be used to store information about the state of an object?	Instance variable
What variable scope must be used to pass information to a method?	Method parameter

Constructing Methods

Exam Objective 4.4   Given an algorithm with multiple inputs and an output, develop method code that implements the algorithm using method parameters, a return type, and the return statement, and recognize the effects when object references and primitives are passed into methods that modify them.

This section will explore the construction of methods. Methods are able to accept many different arguments or none at all. They are able to return one variable, but may also not return any data. The SCJA exam will ask questions that expect the test taker to understand how the input and output of a method works. Scenarios for a method will be presented with a list of code segments. The correct code segment must be matched to the given scenario. The following topics are covered in this section:

- Method inputs
- Method outputs

Method Inputs

Arguments are passed to methods as parameters and are used to input data into a method. These arguments can be primitives, objects, or both. A method may have many or zero parameters. Passing data to a method has different characteristics depending on whether the data is a primitive or an object. This section will review how method parameters are used and defined. The difference between passing primitives by value, and objects by reference, will also be covered.

Method Parameters

Method parameters represent the arguments that were used when the method was called. A method may have many parameters or none at all. A developer defines the parameters for a method in the method declaration. A method's declaration consists of the following parts: modifiers such as public or private, a return type, the method name, a list enclosed in parentheses of parameters that are comma-delimited and are preceded by their data type, an exception list, and the code of the method enclosed in braces. At this time, disregard the modifier and exception list; they will be covered later in this book. The following is an example of a method declaration:

```
void initializeLoanDetails(int months, float amount, float rate) {...}
```

In this example, void is the return type. Return types and returning data will be discussed later. The name of the method is initializeLoanDetails. The next item is the parameter list, which is enclosed in parentheses. This may be empty or contain the list of parameters. The parentheses must always be present even if they are empty, which would represent an empty parameter list. The parameter list must declare the data type and then the name of the variable. A comma is used to delimit the items in the list. Finally, the code of the method is enclosed in braces. The following is an example of a code segment that invokes this method:

```
int numMonths = 12;
float amountBorrowed = 12000.00;
initializeLoanDetails(numMonths, amountBorrowed, 6.99);
```

In this example, two variables are declared and literal values are assigned to them. Next, the initializeLoanDetails method is called. This method is given three arguments. Since the initializeLoanDetails method is defined with three parameters, the code that invokes it must pass three arguments. The calling code must match the data types defined in the method declaration. The arguments may be variables or literals as long as they match the data types of the method's parameters.

When a parameter is defined in the parameter list, it is similar to declaring a variable in the method body. The data type that is given determines what data this parameter contains and the name given is the name of the variable. This parameter becomes a variable that can be used in code just as any other variable would be used. However, this variable comes preset to the value of the argument used to call the method. It is valid to set this variable to a different value if needed.

Passing Primitives by Value to Methods

When a primitive is used as an argument, a copy of the value is made and given to the method. If the method sets the value of the parameter to a different value, it has no effect on the variable that was passed to the method. The following is an example of a method that adds two to the int that is passed to it:

```
void addTwo(int value) {
  System.out.println("Parameter: value = " + value);
  value = value + 2;
  System.out.println("Leaving method: value = " + value);
}
```

Since primitives are passed by value, a copy of the variable value is passed to the method. Even though the method modifies the parameter (since it is just a copy of the original argument used to invoke the method), the original argument remains unchanged from the perspective of the calling code. The following is a code segment that could be used to call this method:

```
int value = 1;
System.out.println("Argument: value = " + value);
addTwo(value);
System.out.println("After method call: value = " + value);
```

If this code segment was executed, it would produce the following results. Read the output that follows and walk through the code.

```
Argument: value = 1
Parameter: value = 1
Leaving method: value = 3
After method call: value = 1
```

Passing Objects by Reference to Methods

Objects are passed by reference to a method. This means that instead of making a copy of the object and passing it, a reference to the original object is passed to the method. A reference is basically an internal index that represents the object. This can start a very technical conversation, which is beyond the scope of this book. The SCJA is not going to drill into the details of how an object is passed internally. In short, for the SCJA exam it is important to understand that any object is passed by reference. This means that the object passed to a method as an argument is the same as the object that the method receives as a parameter. Any actions that are performed on the parameter will be reflected in the variable that was used as an argument.

The following example is similar to the one that demonstrated how primitives were passed by value. Instead of passing an `int` this time, it will pass a custom `Number` object. The following is the `Number` class:

```
public class Number {
  int number;
  public Number(int number) {
    this.number = number;
  }
  int getNumber() {
    return this.number;
  }
```

```
    void setNumber(int number) {
      this.number = number;
    }
  }
```

The following is the method that will be called. This time it will add three to the value passed to it.

```
void addThree(Number value) {
  System.out.println("Parameter: value = " + value.getNumber());
  value.setNumber(value.getNumber() + 3);
  System.out.println("Leaving method: value = " + value.getNumber());
}
```

Finally, we have the code segment used to call this method.

```
Number value = new Number(1);
System.out.println("Argument: value = " + value.getNumber());
addThree(value);
System.out.println("After method call: value = " + value.getNumber());
```

This example is almost identical to the earlier one. The only difference is that now an object is passed by reference and the method adds three instead of two. If this code segment were executed, the following would be the output. Notice that this time when the method returns to the calling code, the object has been modified.

```
Argument: value = 1
Parameter: value = 1
Leaving method: value = 4
After method call: value = 4
```

Method Outputs

Methods are able to return data to the code that has called them. A method can return either one variable or none at all. The returned variable may be an object or primitive. A method must declare if it will return a value and what type this value must be.

Declaring a Return Type

Earlier in this chapter, we examined a method declaration. This section will look at the declaration again, but this time it will focus on the return type. The following is another example of a method declaration. Assume that the running variable has been declared as an instance variable of type boolean.

```
boolean isRunning(){
   return running;
}
```

In this example, the method is declaring that it will return a boolean variable. Once a method declares it will return a variable, it must include a return statement to pass the data back to the calling code. A return statement must be the keyword return followed by a variable or a literal of the declared return type. Once the return statement is executed, the method is finished. No code will execute after the return statement. In the preceding example, the variable running is returned to the calling code. This method could be declared to return any other primitive or object by changing its return type declaration. If the data type in the declaration is changed, the code must also be updated to return a variable that is of the new data type. It is also possible for a method to return no data. To declare a method that does not return any data, the void keyword should be used in place of a data type. The following is an example of a method declaration that does not return any data:

```
void changeStateOfObject() {
   /* Code that changes the state of the object would go here */
}
```

In the preceding example, the method changeStateOfObject does not return a variable. If the declaration void is used to declare that the method will not return data, a return statement is not needed in the method. If return is used, it must be used alone without a variable. Once the return is executed, the method is done and the flow of execution returns to the code that invoked the method.

Using Methods that Return Variables

When the code invokes a method that returns a variable, that method call can be used in place of the variable. The following is a method and a code segment that invokes the method. The method returns an int. The code segment will use the method to set an int equal to the variable that is returned.

```
int winsInASeason() {
  return 92;
}
/* Code Segment */
int wins = winsInASeason();
System.out.println("Wins = " + wins);
```

In the preceding example, the method winsInASeason returns an int. The code in the method is trivial and just returns a literal value. The code segment is an example of how to use a method that returns a value. In the code segment, a variable is declared as an int. The variable wins is set to the value that the method winsInASeason returns. A method that returns a value can be used interchangeably with a literal or where a variable of the same data type is being accessed.

CERTIFICATION SUMMARY

This chapter was about the organization of variables inside of a class. Mastering the scope of variables is important in designing and reading large Java applications. First, local variables were discussed. These are the variables that should be used when the data only needs to be stored for a short amount of time and accessed from only one place in a class. The scope of these variables is the block of code in which they are declared.

The next variable scope covered was method parameters. These are the variables passed to the method. These variables will only be used when the method needs outside input from the code that is calling it. They are declared in the method's signature and have a scope of the entire method.

The final scope is instance variables. These variables are declared inside of a class, but outside of a method. These variables are accessible throughout the entire class. These variables provide the state of an object and retain their value through the life of the object. Different methods may access them to read or modify the instance variables data.

The difference between passing objects to methods and passing primitives was also examined in this chapter. When a primitive is passed as an argument, a copy is made and the original will remain unchanged. However, when an object is passed as an argument, a reference of it is passed to the method and any changes made to the object in the method will be present in the original calling object.

Finally, returning data from a method was covered. The `return` statement is used to return a variable. Only one variable can be returned from a method. It may either be a primitive or an object. A method may return no data if the `void` keyword is used in the method signature.

✓ TWO-MINUTE DRILL

- ❏ A variable's scope defines what parts of the code have access to that variable.
- ❏ An instance variable is declared in the class, not inside of any method. It is in scope for the entire method and remains in memory for as long as the instance of the class it was declared in remains in memory.
- ❏ Method parameters are declared in the method declaration; they are in scope for the entire method.
- ❏ Local variables may be declared anywhere in code. They remain in scope as long as the execution of code does not leave the block they were declared in.
- ❏ Code that invokes a method may pass arguments to it for input.
- ❏ Methods receive arguments as method parameters.
- ❏ Primitives are passed by value.
- ❏ Objects are passed by reference.
- ❏ Methods may return one variable or none at all. It can be a primitive or an object.
- ❏ A method must declare the data type of any variable it returns.
- ❏ If a method does not return any data, it must use `void` as its return type.

SELF TEST

Understanding Variable Scope

1. What variable scope is best suited for a temporary variable?

   A. Local variable

   B. Static variable

   C. Global variable

   D. Method parameter

   E. Instance variable

2. You need to create a class to store information about books contained in a library. What variable scope is best suited for the variable that will store the title of a book?

   A. Local variable

   B. Static variable

   C. Global variable

   D. Method parameter

   E. Instance variable

3. You need to create a method that has two parameters to perform many complex steps and then return a result. What variable scope is best suited to store the value to be returned while calculations are carried out upon it?

   A. Local variable

   B. Static variable

   C. Global variable

   D. Method parameter

   E. Instance variable

4. What is the scope of a variable that is passed to a method?

   A. Local variable

   B. Static variable

   C. Global variable

    D. Method parameter

    E. Instance variable

5. Two variables can have the same name in a method if the second is declared when the first is out of scope.

    A. True

    B. False

6. When a variable goes out of scope, it can never go back into scope.

    A. True

    B. False

7. When a variable is referenced with the `this` keyword, it is referring to the method parameter.

    A. True

    B. False

Constructing Methods

8. You need to create a method called `findTotal`. This method should take three arguments that are of type `int`. This method will return an `int`. Which of the following is the correct method declaration for this scenario?

    A. `int findTotal(int, int, int){…}`

    B. `findTotal(int num1, int num2, int num3) return int{…}`

    C. `int findTotal(int num1, int num2, int num3) return int{…}`

    D. `int findTotal(int num1, int num2, int num3) {…}`

9. A method needs to be created that accepts an array of `floats` as an argument and does not return any variables. The method should be called `setPoints`. Which of the following method declarations is correct?

    A. `setPoints(float[] points) {…}`

    B. `void setPoints(float points) {…}`

    C. `void setPoints(float[] points) {…}`

    D. `float setPoints(float[] points) {…}`

10. Objects are passed by _____.

   A. Value

   B. Reference

11. Primitives are passed by _____.

   A. Value

   B. Reference

12. When a method uses `void` to indicate it does not return a value, then a `return` statement is not required.

   A. True

   B. False

13. Given the following class—`FloatNumber`—and method—`addHalf`—what is the output if the code segment is executed?

```
public class FloatNumber {
  float number;
  public FloatNumber(float number) {
    this.number = number;
  }
  float getNumber() {
    return number;
  }
  void setNumber(float number) {
    this.number = number;
  }
}

void addHalf(FloatNumber value) {
  value.setNumber(value.getNumber() + (value.getNumber()/2f));
}

/* CODE SEGMENT */
FloatNumber value = new FloatNumber(1f);
addHalf(value);
System.out.println("value = " + value.getNumber());
```

   A. value = 1

   B. value = 1.5

C. `value = 2`

D. `value = 0`

14. Code that is after a `return` statement will be executed but cannot change the variable that is being returned.

A. True

B. False

15. Passing objects to a method is a good coding practice to use when you need to return more than one variable.

A. True

B. False

SELF TEST ANSWERS

Understanding Variable Scope

1. What variable scope is best suited for a temporary variable?

   A. Local variable

   B. Static variable

   C. Global variable

   D. Method parameter

   E. Instance variable

   Answer:

   ☑ **A.** A variable should also be declared using the least amount of scope. Since a temporary variable will normally only be used for a few lines of code, it should be declared as a local variable.

   ☒ **B, C, D,** and **E** are incorrect.

2. You need to create a class to store information about books contained in a library. What variable scope is best suited for the variable that will store the title of a book?

   A. Local variable

   B. Static variable

   C. Global variable

   D. Method parameter

   E. Instance variable

   Answer:

   ☑ **E.** In a class that stores information about books, you would want to store the title of the book in a variable that will remain in scope for the life of the object.

   ☒ **A, B, C,** and **D** are incorrect.

3. You need to create a method that has two parameters to perform many complex steps and then return a result. What variable scope is best suited to store the value to be returned while calculations are carried out upon it?

A. Local variable

B. Static variable

C. Global variable

D. Method parameter

E. Instance variable

Answer:

☑ **A.** As calculations are performed on a variable, it should be stored as a local variable. In this scenario, the variable is only needed for this one method.

☒ **B, C, D,** and **E** are incorrect.

4. What is the scope of a variable that is passed to a method?

A. Local variable

B. Static variable

C. Global variable

D. Method parameter

E. Instance variable

Answer:

☑ **D.** Any variable that is passed to a method is a method parameter.

☒ **A, B, C,** and **E** are incorrect.

5. Two variables can have the same name in a method if the second is declared when the first is out of scope.

A. True

B. False

Answer:

☑ **A.** Once a variable is out of scope, another variable can be declared with the same name.

6. When a variable goes out of scope, it can never go back into scope.

A. True

B. False

Answer:

☑   **A.** Once a variable is out of scope, it can never come back into scope. Its value is lost and the Java Virtual Machine may reallocate the memory the variable occupies.

7. When a variable is referenced with the `this` keyword, it is referring to the method parameter.

A. True

B. False

Answer:

☑   **B.** The `this` keyword will reference the instance variable.

Constructing Methods

8. You need to create a method called `findTotal`. This method should take three arguments that are of type `int`. This method will return an `int`. Which of the following is the correct method declaration for this scenario?

A. `int findTotal(int, int, int){…}`

B. `findTotal(int num1, int num2, int num3) return int{…}`

C. `int findTotal(int num1, int num2, int num3) return int{…}`

D. `int findTotal(int num1, int num2, int num3) {…}`

Answer:

☑   **D.** A method declaration should be an optional modifier followed by the return data type, and then the method's name with a list of parameters. The parameters must be comma delimited and contain both their data type and name.

☒   **A, B,** and **C** are incorrect. **A** is incorrect because it is missing the names of the parameters. **B** is incorrect because it is missing the return type and places an incorrect return after the parameter list. **C** is incorrect because it has an incorrect return after the parameter list.

9. A method needs to be created that accepts an array of `float`s as an argument and does not return any variables. The method should be called `setPoints`. Which of the following method declarations is correct?

A. `setPoints(float[] points) {…}`

B. `void setPoints(float points) {…}`

C. `void setPoints(float[] points) {…}`

D. `float setPoints(float[] points) {…}`

> **Answer:**
>
> ☑ **C.** `void` must be used for methods that do not return any data.
>
> ☒ **A, B,** and **D** are incorrect. **A** is incorrect because it is missing the return type. If the method is not going to return a variable, it still must use `void`. **B** is incorrect because it does not have an array of `float`s as a parameter. **D** is incorrect because it uses the incorrect return type.

10. Objects are passed by _____.

A. Value

B. Reference

> **Answer:**
>
> ☑ **B.** Objects are always passed to methods by reference. This means changes made to the object in the method will be reflected in the object in the code that invoked the method.
>
> ☒ **A** is incorrect.

11. Primitives are passed by _____.

A. Value

B. Reference

> **Answer:**
>
> ☑ **A.** Primitives are always passed to methods by value. This means that a copy is made and then given to the method. Changes made in the method will not affect the variable that was passed to the method.
>
> ☒ **B** is incorrect.

12. When a method uses `void` to indicate it does not return a value, then a `return` statement is not required.

A. True

B. False

Answer:

☑ **A.** A `return` statement is not needed if the method does not return a variable. However, one can be used.

13. Given the following class—FloatNumber—and method—addHalf—what is the output if the code segment is executed?

```
public class FloatNumber {
  float number;
  public FloatNumber(float number) {
    this.number = number;
  }
  float getNumber() {
    return number;
  }
  void setNumber(float number) {
    this.number = number;
  }
}

void addHalf(FloatNumber value) {
  value.setNumber(value.getNumber() + (value.getNumber()/2f));
}

/* CODE SEGMENT */
FloatNumber value = new FloatNumber(1f);
addHalf(value);
System.out.println("value = " + value.getNumber());
```

A. value = 1

B. value = 1.5

C. value = 2

D. value = 0

Answer:

☑ **B.** The `FloatNumber` object is passed by reference. Therefore, when the method changes its value, this change is still present when the code returns to the original calling code segment.

☒ **A, C,** and **D** are incorrect.

14. Code that is after a `return` statement will be executed but cannot change the variable that is being returned.

A. True

B. False

Answer:

☑ **B.** Once a `return` statement is executed, the flow of execution returns to the code that invoked the method.

15. Passing objects to a method is a good coding practice to use when you need to return more than one variable.

A. True

B. False

Answer:

☑ **B.** Even though it would be possible to return data back from a method by using this practice, it is not considered a good coding practice.

6

Working with Classes and Their Relationships

- Understanding Class Compositions and Associations

- Class Compositions and Associations in Practice

✓ Two-Minute Drill

Q&A Self Test

Understanding Class Compositions and Associations

Exam Objective 1.3   Describe, compare, and contrast class compositions, and associations (including multiplicity: one-to-one, one-to-many, and many-to-many), and association navigation.

Composition and association are two general descriptions for object relationships. The SCJA exam will ask about the relationship between objects and require the test taker to distinguish between a composition or just an association relationship. Composition and association can be further broken down into four more specific types of relationship descriptors. Each descriptor will be covered in this chapter. The four specific relationship types are not directly on the SCJA, but by studying them you will have a greater understanding of the difference between composition and association. These concepts will also be present in the UML section of the SCJA exam. Finally, multiplicities will be discussed. Every object relationship has a multiplicity. The SCJA exam will require you to determine the multiplicity based on a given scenario or code segment.

The following topics will be covered in this chapter:

- Class compositions and associations
- Class relationships
- Multiplicities
- Association navigation

Class Compositions and Associations

Composition and association are the general terms used to describe a class relationship. An association or composition relationship is formed between two objects when one contains a reference to the other. The reference is often stored as an instance variable. The reference may be in one direction or bidirectional.

An association relationship is a relationship of two objects where neither one directly depends on the other for their logical meaning. For example, object A has an association relationship with object B. If this relationship was lost, both objects would still retain the same meaning they previously had. These relationships are considered weak. Objects in an association relationship have no dependence on each other for the management of their life cycle. In other words, the existence of an object is not tied to the existence of the other object in the relationship. Another example would be a `CarFactory` object and a `CarFrame` object. The `CarFactory` object and `CarFrame` object have an association relationship. If this relationship no longer existed, each object could continue to logically make sense and retain its original meaning on its own.

A composition relationship is stronger than an association relationship. Composition means that one object is composed of another. An object may be composed of one or multiple objects. If object A is composed of object B, it depends on object B. This statement does not imply that object A is only composed of object B. Object A may also be composed of other objects. If the relationship were lost between object A and object B, the logical meaning of the objects would be lost or significantly altered. In this example, object B—the inner object that object A is composed-of—would depend on object A to manage its life cycle. The existence of object B is directly tied to the existence of object A. When object A no longer exists, object B would also no longer exist. Object B would also become nonexistent if the relationship between the two objects were lost. Examples of objects that have a composition relationship tend to be more abstract than association relationships. A `Car` object and `CarStatus` object would be an example of a composition relationship. The `Car` object is composed-of the `CarStatus` object. Both objects depend on this relationship to define their meanings. The `CarStatus` object also depends on the `Car` object to maintain its life cycle. When the `Car` object no longer exists, the `CarStatus` object would also no longer exist.

SCENARIO & SOLUTION

You have an object that controls the life cycle of another object. What term can be used to describe it?	Composition
You have an object that has a weak relationship with another object. What term can be used to describe it?	Association
You have an object that has a strong relationship with another object. What term can be used to describe it?	Composition

In many cases, it is not as clear as the preceding examples regarding what type of relationship two objects possess. Some interpretation is needed to determine the relationship. A composition will always be responsible for an object's life cycle. Composition relationships also represent a stronger relationship compared to an association. Objects belonging to an association make more sense by themselves than objects of composition.

Class Relationships

This section will break down the specific class relationships that are possible. Each one represents a different way objects can have relationships. In total, there are four detailed types of relationships: direct association, composition association, aggregation association, and temporary association. The objective on the SCJA exam presents association and composition as if they were mutually exclusive. In fact, composition association is just one of the detailed relationship types. This relationship is referred to as composition on the SCJA exam. The other three detailed relationship types are referred to as just association. The SCJA exam will contain questions that require the highest-level knowledge of these relationships. The questions on the exam will only require the determination of association versus composition. However, it would be unwise to ignore this section since the understanding of these topics will help make the determination of the relationship much easier.

Composition and association are general terms used to describe object relationships. The SCJA exam will give a code segment or scenario that will require the determination of what general type of relationship is present. Association relationships can be broken down into more specific terms. Composition is a special type of association, but on the SCJA exam it will only be referred to as composition. The next section will discuss the four specific types of object relationships. It is important to remember that you are only required to determine if a relationship is a composition or an association on the exam.

The following topics will be covered in the next few sections:

- Direct association
- Composition association
- Aggregation association
- Temporary association

Direct Association

Direct association describes a "has-a" relationship. This is a basic association that represents navigability. Direct association is a weak relationship and therefore can be generalized to an association. There is no life cycle responsibility and each object in the relationship can conceptually be independent. This tends to be the default association when nothing else can accurately describe the relationship.

If a truck was modeled as an object to create a `Truck` object, it may have a `Trailer` object that it has a direct association with. The `Truck` object and `Trailer` object are weakly associated because each could be used without the other and still maintain their intended purpose. A `Truck` object does not need to have a `Trailer` object, and a `Trailer` object is not required for the construction of the `Truck` object.

This direct association relationship is depicted in the UML diagram in Figure 6-1.

Composition Association

Composition associations are used to describe an object's relationship where one object is composed of one or more objects. A composition association is a strong relationship and will be generalized as composition on the SCJA exam. The internal object only makes conceptual sense while stored in the containing object. This relationship represents ownership. A composition association can be described as object A is "composed-of" object B. For example, a `Tire` object would be composed-of a `TireAirPressure` object. The `Tire` object requires a `TireAirPressure` object; the `TireAirPressure` object is not very useful by itself.

The containing object also has the responsibility of managing the life cycle of the internal object. It is possible for this object to pass the life cycle management to another object. Life cycle management means that the object composed of the

FIGURE 6-1

Direct association

FIGURE 6-2

Composition
association

second object, or the containing object, must maintain a reference to the inner
object, otherwise the Java Virtual Machine will destroy it. If the containing object is
destroyed, any objects that compose it will also be destroyed.

This composition association relationship is depicted in the UML diagram in
Figure 6-2.

Aggregation Association

An aggregation association is a relationship that represents one object being part-
of another object. An aggregation association represents a "part-of" the whole
relationship. In this relationship, even though one object is a part-of the other,
each object can maintain its own meaning independently if the relationship is lost.
Neither object depends on the other for its existence. The aggregation relationship
does not require the object to perform life cycle management for the object that it
references. Aggregation association is a weak relationship. It can be generalized as an
association.

A `Motorcycle` object would have a `Windshield` object that it has an
aggregation association with. The `Motorcycle` object and `Windshield` object are
weakly associated because each could be used without the other and still maintain
their intended purpose. A `Windshield` object has a part-of relationship with the
`Motorcycle` object.

This aggregation association relationship is depicted in the UML diagram in
Figure 6-3.

Temporary Association

Temporary association is also known as a dependency. Typically, a temporary
association will be an object used as a local variable, return value, or method
parameter. It is considered a dependency because object A depends on object B as

FIGURE 6-3

Aggregation
association

FIGURE 6-4

Temporary
association

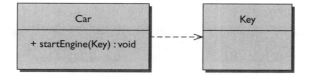

either an argument, return value, or at some point a local variable. A temporary association is the weakest form of association. This relationship will not persist for the entire life cycle of the object.

For example, a `Car` object may have a method called `startEngine` that has a `Key` object as a parameter. The `Key` object as a parameter would represent a temporary association.

This temporary association relationship is depicted in the UML diagram in Figure 6-4.

Multiplicities

Every relationship has a multiplicity. Multiplicity refers to the number of objects that are part of a relationship. The three general classifications of multiplicity you should know for the SCJA exam are one-to-one, one-to-many, and many-to-many.

The following topics will be covered in the next few sections:

- One-to-one multiplicity
- One-to-many multiplicity
- Many-to-many multiplicity

INSIDE THE EXAM

Composition vs. Association

The SCJA exam requires you to thoroughly know the differences between composition and association. Be sure to understand how each of the four specific relationship types relates to these terms, as detailed in Table 6-1.

TABLE 6-1	Object Relationship Characteristics			
	Composition Association	**Aggregation Association**	**Direct Association**	**Temporary Association**
General term is association		✓	✓	✓
General term is composition	✓			
Strong relationship	✓			
Weak relationship		✓	✓	✓
Has life cycle responsibility	✓			
Persists for most of the object's lifetime	✓	✓	✓	
Is used as a critical part of an object	✓	✓		
Is often a local variable, return variable, or method parameter				✓

One-to-One Multiplicity

A one-to-one association is a basic relationship where one object contains a reference to another object. All four relationship types may have a one-to-one multiplicity. An example of a one-to-one relationship would be the Motorcycle object that has a relationship with a single Engine object.

One-to-Many Multiplicity

One-to-many relationships are created when one object contains a reference to a group of like objects. The multiple object references are normally stored in an array or a collection. All four relationship types may be one-to-many. The Car object can contain four Tire objects. This would be an aggregation association since the Car and Tire objects have a part-of association between each other. The Tire objects can be stored in an array or collection. As the name implies, a one-to-many relationship may have many more than four objects. A many-to-one relationship is also possible.

Many-to-Many Multiplicity

Many-to-many relationships are only possible for aggregation associations, direct associations, and temporary associations. Composition association is a strong relationship that implies a life cycle responsibility for the object that composes it. If many objects have a relationship with an object, it is impossible for any individual object to control the life cycle of the other object in the relationship. If the car example were broadened to a traffic simulator application, it would include many other Car objects. Each of these Car objects contains references to many other TrafficLight objects. This represents a direct association since a single Car object does not maintain the life cycle of the TrafficLight objects. Each car object has-a TrafficLight object. The relationship between a Car object and the TrafficLight object is weak. The TrafficLight objects are all shared between all of the Car objects. A many-to-many association does not have to include an equal number of objects on each side of the relationship.

on the
j o b

Relationships (for example, aggregation and composition) and multiplicities can be easily depicted with the Unified Modeling Language (UML). Drawing out class relationships can help convey design concepts to your fellow employees. UML diagrams are covered in Chapter 9.

Association Navigation

Association navigation is a term used to describe the direction in which a relationship can be traveled. An object that is contained within another object is said to be navigable if the containing object has methods for accessing the inner object. Most relationships are navigable in one direction, but if both objects contain references to the other, it is possible to have a bidirectional navigable relationship. Oftentimes, the methods for accessing inner objects are called getters and setters. A getter is a simple method that just returns an instance variable. A setter is a method that accepts an argument and uses it to set an instance variable.

CERTIFICATION OBJECTIVE

Class Compositions and Associations in Practice

Exam Objective 3.3   Develop code that implements simple class associations, code that implements multiplicity using arrays, and recognize code that implements compositions as opposed to simple associations, and code that correctly implements association navigation.

This section will review practical examples of association and composition relationships. It will also demonstrate how different multiplicities are represented in code. The SCJA exam will not require code to be produced. However, you may have to determine a type of association by examining a code segment. The following examples and explanations should help provide a solid understanding of these concepts.

The topics listed next will be covered in the following sections:

- Examples of class association relationships
- Examples of class composition relationships
- Examples of association navigation

Examples of Class Association Relationships

This section will examine associations. The following three examples will demonstrate possible multiplicities of an aggregation association. An explanation will follow highlighting the important points from the example.

The topics covered include:

- One-to-one class association
- One-to-many class association
- Many-to-many class association

One-to-One Class Association

The following example is of a `Truck` object and `Trailer` object. This is an example of a one-to-one direct association.

```
public class Truck {
/* This is an example of a one-to-one
direct association */
    Trailer trailer;
    void setTrailer(Trailer t){
        trailer = t;
    }
    /*
     * Remainder of Truck class would be here
     */
}
```

In this example of a one-to-one association, the `Truck` object contains a reference to the `Trailer` object. This is a one-to-one association because the variable trailer is a single variable. It is not part of an array or collection. This example is a direct association because the Truck object is not responsible for the life cycle of the trailer variable. Another indication that it is a direct association is that logically the Truck object has-a Trailer object. In this example, and in most real-world situations, it is not always easy or even possible to determine if one object controls the life cycle of another. Oftentimes, you must make the best determination based on the information that is available. In this example, the trailer variable is being set by the method setTrailer. Since this method is used to set the variable, it can be assumed that other objects contain a reference to the trailer object and therefore there is no sole object responsible for the life cycle of the object. Finally, since this was determined to be a direct association, the relationship can be generalized to just an association relationship.

One-to-Many Class Association

The next example will demonstrate an aggregation association. This example will have a relationship that is one-to-many. Wheel objects will be part-of a Car object.

```
public class Car {
  Wheel[] wheel = new Wheel[4];
  void setWheels(Wheel w) {
    wheel[0] = w;
    wheel[1] = w;
    wheel[2] = w;
    wheel[3] = w;
  }
  // Remainder of Car class would be here
}
```

This example has an array of four Wheel objects. Since there is one Car object that contains four Wheel objects, this relationship is one-to-many. With a one-to-many relationship the multiple objects will normally be stored in an array or collection such as a Vector. This example is an aggregation association since the Wheel object is part-of the Car object. Because this is a weak relationship and there are no life cycle responsibilities, this can be generalized as an association.

Many-to-Many Class Association

The many-to-many relationship is more complex than the previous one-to-one and one-to-many relationships. This relationship is between a group of Car objects and a group of `TrafficLight` objects. The following is the code segment for the two objects:

```
// TrafficLight class
public class TrafficLight {
    int lightID;
      TrafficLight(int ID) {
         lightID = ID;
      }
}

// Car class
public class Car {
  TrafficLight[] allTrafficLights;
  Car(TrafficLight[] trafficLights) {
    allTrafficLights=trafficLights;
  }
}
```

This next segment is the code that creates both objects. This segment is important because it shows how the relationships are formed between the objects.

```
public class TrafficSimulator {
  Car[] cars = new Car[3];
  TrafficLight[] trafficLights = new TrafficLight[8];
  public static void main(String[] args) {
    new TrafficSimulator();
  }

  TrafficSimulator() {
    for (int i = 0; i < trafficLights.length; i++) {
      trafficLights[i] = new TrafficLight(i);
    }
    cars[0] = new Car(trafficLights);
    cars[1] = new Car(trafficLights);
    cars[2] = new Car(trafficLights);
  }
}
```

This segment contains a `main` method. The sole job of `main` is to create a new `TrafficSimulator` object. The `TrafficSimulator` object contains an array of `Car` objects and an array of `TrafficLight` objects. First, the `TrafficLight` objects are created. Each `TrafficLight` object stores a unique ID. Next, the `Car` objects are created. Each `Car` object contains an array of all the `TrafficLight` objects. This example is many-to-many because each `Car` object contains the same group of multiple `TrafficLight` objects. This relationship can be classified as a direct association because the `Car` objects has-an array of `TrafficLight` objects.

e**x**a**m**

w a t c h   *An array or collection should be a dead giveaway that you are looking at a *-to-many relationship. If there is only one object and an array or collection, it will be a one-to-many relationship. If there are two arrays or collections with references to each other, it will be a many-to-many relationship.*

Examples of Class Composition Relationships

This section will be similar to the last section except that composition associations will be demonstrated. Composition associations only have two possible multiplicities. This section will have an example of each followed by an explanation.

One-to-One Class Composition

This example will demonstrate a one-to-one composition relationship. This will be a composition association since that is the only type of association that can create a composition relationship.

```
public class Tire {
    TireAirPressure tireAirPressure;
        Tire(){
            tireAirPressure = new TireAirPressure();
    }
}
```

In the preceding example, the `Tire` object and the `TireAirPressure` object have a one-to-one relationship. The `Tire` object is composed-of the `TireAirPressure` object. This represents a composition association. The relationship between the two objects is strong. The `Tire` object has life cycle management responsibilities to the `TireAirPressure` object. If the `Tire` object was destroyed, the `TireAirPressure` object would also be destroyed.

One-to-Many Class Composition

This final example will demonstrate a composition relationship with a one-to-many multiplicity. The following code segment is of a `SensorStatus` class:

```
public class SensorStatus {
  int status;
  public SensorStatus(int newStatus) {
    status = newStatus;
  }
}
```

The next segment demonstrates a `CarComputer` object that is composed-of an array of five `SensorStatus` objects.

```
public class CarComputer {
  SensorStatus[] sensorStatus = new SensorStatus[5];
  public CarComputer() {
    sensorStatus[0] = new SensorStatus(1);
    sensorStatus[1] = new SensorStatus(1);
    sensorStatus[2] = new SensorStatus(1);
    sensorStatus[3] = new SensorStatus(1);
    sensorStatus[4] = new SensorStatus(1);
  }
}
```

Since there is one `CarComputer` object and five `SensorStatus` objects, this represents a one-to-many relationship. The relationship is composition association. Again, notice how the relationship is strong, and that the `SensorStatus` array depends on the `CarComputer` object to manage its life cycle.

Examples of Association Navigation

Association navigation is the ability to navigate a relationship. The following example will demonstrate a `PinStripe` object that is composed-of a `Color` object:

```
public class PinStripe {
  Color color = new Color(Color.blue);
```

```
Color getColor(){
  return color;
}
}
```

In this example, any object that had access to the PinStripe object could use its getColor method, which is considered a getter, to navigate to the Color object. In this example, the navigation is only in a single direction.

CERTIFICATION SUMMARY

This chapter has discussed the different relationships that are possible between objects. Association and composition were the general description of relationships that will be directly on the SCJA exam. Both concepts are important to understand as a developer as well as for the SCJA exam.

Association is used to describe an object-to-object reference. This type of reference means that object A has a reference to object B and can access its public methods and member variables. Object B may or may not have a reference back to object A. A relationship of association means that both objects are independent and neither one relies on the other to maintain its existence. Direct association, aggregation association, and temporary association are all more detailed forms of association.

Composition relationships are a stronger form of association relationships. A composition relationship is a type of association where an object that is composed of another object is also responsible for the life cycle management of that object. A composition relationship may have one-to-one or one-to-many multiplicities. Composition association is an example of composition.

Next, this chapter covered each of the four possible relationships in detail. Direct association, aggregation association, and temporary association are three of the four relationship types. Each of these belongs in the general category of association. They imply no responsibility of life cycle management. Composition association belongs to the category of general composition. Composition association has a life cycle responsibility.

There may be three different multiplicities of relationships. A one-to-one relationship has one object that contains a reference to another object of a particular type. A one-to-many relationship has an object that contains an array of object references, or a collection such as an ArrayList or Vector. The final relationship is many-to-many. This relationship has many objects that contain a reference to the same collection or array of objects. The many-to-many relationship is unique for association and cannot exist for a composition relationship.

This chapter concludes with examples of each multiplicity for association and composition relationships. These examples are important to understand. In Chapter 9 of this book, these relationships will be revisited when UML modeling is discussed.

TWO-MINUTE DRILL

Understanding Class Compositions and Associations

- ❏ Composition and association are both general descriptions for object-to-object relationships.
- ❏ A relationship is created when an object contains a reference to another object, often through an instance variable.
- ❏ Direct association is a "has-a" relationship.
- ❏ Direct association is a weak relationship.
- ❏ Direct association has no life cycle responsibilities.
- ❏ Direct association tends to be the default relationship if no other relationship seems to fit.
- ❏ Two objects that have a direct association will logically make sense if the relationship is lost.
- ❏ Composition association is a "composed-of" relationship.
- ❏ Composition association is a strong association.
- ❏ Composition association has life cycle responsibilities.
- ❏ Composition association represents possession and ownership.
- ❏ Two objects that have a composition association will not logically make sense if the association is lost.
- ❏ When two objects have a composition association, the containing object often requires the inner object.
- ❏ Aggregation association is a "part-of" relationship.
- ❏ Aggregation association is a weak relationship.
- ❏ Aggregation association has no life cycle responsibilities.
- ❏ Two objects that have an aggregation association will logically make sense if the relationship is lost.
- ❏ Temporary association is also known as a dependency.
- ❏ Temporary association is a weak relationship.
- ❏ Temporary association has no life cycle responsibilities.
- ❏ A temporary association relationship is created when a return value, method parameter, or local variable is used.

❑ One-to-one relationships are possible with both composition and association.

❑ One-to-one relationships have one object that contains a reference to another object.

❑ One-to-many relationships are possible with both composition and association.

❑ One-to-many relationships are one object that contains a reference to an array or collection of similar objects.

❑ Many-to-many relationships are possible only with association.

❑ Many-to-many relationships have many similar objects that contain a reference to the same array or collection of objects.

❑ Association navigation is a term used to describe the ability to access an object that is contained in another object.

❑ Relationships may be able to navigate bidirectional or unidirectional.

❑ Getter methods are often used to navigate an inner object.

Class Compositions and Associations in Practice

❑ In an association, the inner object normally is not created in the containing object but is instead passed to it as a method argument.

❑ In a composition, the inner object is normally created in the containing object.

❑ In a one-to-many relationship, the inner object is stored in an array or collection.

❑ A many-to-many relationship is when objects in an array or collection each contain a reference to another array or collection.

❑ A many-to-many relationship can only exist for associations.

SELF TEST

Understanding Class Compositions and Associations

1. What associations are considered weak relationships? (Choose all that apply.)

   A. Direct association

   B. Temporary association

   C. Composition association

   D. Aggregation association

2. What associations are considered strong relationships? (Choose all that apply.)

   A. Direct association

   B. Temporary association

   C. Composition association

   D. Aggregation association

3. Which association can be said as object A has-an object B?

   A. Direct association

   B. Temporary association

   C. Composition association

   D. Aggregation association

4. Which association can be said as object A is part-of object B?

   A. Direct association

   B. Temporary association

   C. Composition association

   D. Aggregation association

5. Which association can be said as object A is composed-of object B?

   A. Direct association

   B. Temporary association

   C. Composition association

   D. Aggregation association

6. Which association has a life cycle responsibility for the object it contains?

   A. Direct association

   B. Temporary association

   C. Composition association

   D. Aggregation association

7. Association navigation is best described as which of the following?

   A. The ability to navigate, or access, an object that is contained in another object.

   B. The ability to search for and find an object that is contained in another object.

   C. The possibility of passing an object to another object via a method.

   D. The ability to invoke methods of an object that will then change the path of code execution.

   E. The ability to invoke methods of an object to determine the current path of execution.

8. What would the multiplicity be in the following relationship? A `Lamp` object has-a `LightBulb` object.

   A. One-to-one

   B. One-to-many

   C. Many-to-many

9. A composition association cannot exist in what multiplicity?

   A. One-to-one

   B. One-to-many

   C. Many-to-many

10. What would the multiplicity be in the following relationship? A `BookShelf` object has-a reference to an array made up of `Book` objects.

   A. One-to-one

   B. One-to-many

   C. Many-to-many

Class Compositions and Associations in Practice

Use the following code example for the next four questions:

```
public class Client {
   Address address;
```

```
AccountNum[] accountNums;
void setAddress(Address newAddress) {
  address = newAddress;
}
public Client() {
  accountNums = new AccountNum[2];
  accountNums[0] = new AccountNum();
  accountNums[1] = new AccountNum();
}
}
```

11. In the preceding code segment, what is the relationship of the `Client` object and the `address` variable?

A. Direct association

B. Temporary association

C. Composition association

D. Aggregation association

12. In the preceding code segment, what is the relationship of the `Client` object and the `accountNums` variable?

A. Direct association

B. Temporary association

C. Composition association

D. Aggregation association

13. In the preceding code segment, what is the multiplicity between the `Client` object and the `address` variable?

A. One-to-one

B. One-to-many

C. Many-to-many

14. In the preceding code segment, what is the multiplicity between the `Client` object and the `accountNums` variable?

A. One-to-one

B. One-to-many

C. Many-to-many

15. Which of the following statements are true? (Choose all that apply.)

A. Association navigation can be quad-directional.

B. Association navigation can be bidirectional.

C. Association navigation can have no direction.

D. Association navigation can be unidirectional.

SELF TEST ANSWERS

Understanding Class Compositions and Associations

1. What associations are considered weak relationships? (Choose all that apply.)

A. Direct association

B. Temporary association

C. Composition association

D. Aggregation association

Answer:

☑ **A, B** and **D.** Each of these associations is considered weak. This means that they do not have any life cycle responsibility and that if the relationship was lost, each object would still maintain its meaning.

☒ **B** is incorrect. This is an example of composition and has a strong relationship.

2. What associations are considered strong relationships? (Choose all that apply.)

A. Direct association

B. Temporary association

C. Composition association

D. Aggregation association

Answer:

☑ **C.** This association is considered strong. It does have a life cycle responsibility and if the relationship was lost, each object would lose some or all of its meaning.

☒ **A, B,** and **D** are incorrect. They are examples of associations that have weak relationships.

3. Which association can be said as object A has-an object B?

A. Direct association

B. Temporary association

C. Composition association

D. Aggregation association

Answer:

☑ **A.** Direct association is a has-a relationship.

☒ **B, C,** and **D** are incorrect.

4. Which association can be said as object A is part-of object B?

A. Direct association

B. Temporary association

C. Composition association

D. Aggregation association

Answer:

☑ **D.** Aggregation association is a part-of relationship. One object will be used to make up another object. However, neither object depends on the other for its existence and meaning.

☒ **A, B,** and **C** are incorrect.

5. Which association can be said as object A is composed-of object B?

A. Direct association

B. Temporary association

C. Composition association

D. Aggregation association

Answer:

☑ **C.** Composition association is a composed-of relationship. One object will be used to make up another object. If this relationship was lost, the meaning of the objects would also change. This is a strong relationship and has a life cycle responsibility for the inner object.

☒ **A, B,** and **D** are incorrect.

6. Which association has a life cycle responsibility for the object it contains?

A. Direct association

B. Temporary association

C. Composition association

D. Aggregation association

Answer:

☑ **C.** Composition association has the responsibility to maintain the life cycle of the object that it is composed-of.

☒ **A, B,** and **D** are incorrect. They are all weak relationships that have no life cycle responsibility.

7. Association navigation is best described as which of the following?

   A. The ability to navigate, or access, an object that is contained in another object.

   B. The ability to search for and find an object that is contained in another object.

   C. The possibility of passing an object to another object via a method.

   D. The ability to invoke methods of an object that will then change the path of code execution.

   E. The ability to invoke methods of an object to determine the current path of execution.

Answer:

☑ **A.** Association navigation is the ability to access an object that is contained in another.

8. What would the multiplicity be in the following relationship? A `Lamp` object has-a `LightBulb` object.

   A. One-to-one

   B. One-to-many

   C. Many-to-many

Answer:

☑ **A.** There is one `Lamp` object and one `LightBulb` object, therefore this is one-to-one.

9. A composition association cannot exist in what multiplicity?

   A. One-to-one

   B. One-to-many

   C. Many-to-many

Answer:

☑ **C** is the correct answer. Composition association requires that it have responsibility for the life cycle of the objects it is composed-of. It is impossible to have this responsibility in a many-to-many relationship because many objects would contain references to all of the objects.

☒ **A** and **B** are incorrect.

10. What would the multiplicity be in the following relationship? A `BookShelf` object has-a reference to an array made up of `Book` objects.

A. One-to-one

B. One-to-many

C. Many-to-many

Answer:

☑ **B.** `BookShelf` is a single object and contains a reference to an array of `Book` objects. The key to this question is the fact that you are dealing with an array. This means there are many `Book` objects; therefore it is a one-to-many relationship.

☒ **A** and **C** are incorrect.

Class Compositions and Associations in Practice

Use the following code example for the next four questions:

```
public class Client {
  Address address;
  AccountNum[] accountNums;
  void setAddress(Address newAddress) {
    address = newAddress;
  }
  public Client() {
    accountNums = new AccountNum[2];
    accountNums[0] = new AccountNum();
    accountNums[1] = new AccountNum();
  }
}
```

11. In the preceding code segment, what is the relationship of the `Client` object and the `address` variable?

   A. Direct association

   B. Temporary association

   C. Composition association

   D. Aggregation association

   Answer:

   ☑ **A.** Direct association is the best answer, because logically a `Client` object has-an `Address` object.

   ☒ **B, C,** and **D** are incorrect.

12. In the preceding code segment, what is the relationship of the `Client` object and the `accountNums` variable?

   A. Direct association

   B. Temporary association

   C. Composition association

   D. Aggregation association

   Answer:

   ☑ **C.** This is a composition association because the `Client` object is composed-of the `AccountNum` objects. This is a strong relationship since the `Client` object maintains the life cycle of the `AccountNum` objects.

   ☒ **A, B,** and **D** are incorrect.

13. In the preceding code segment, what is the multiplicity between the `Client` object and the `address` variable?

   A. One-to-one

   B. One-to-many

   C. Many-to-many

Answer:

☑ **A** is the correct answer. Since there are no arrays or collections involved with either the `Client` object or `Address` object, this must be one-to-one.

☒ **B** and **C** are incorrect.

14. In the preceding code segment, what is the multiplicity between the `Client` object and the `accountNums` variable?

A. One-to-one

B. One-to-many

C. Many-to-many

Answer:

☑ **B.** The array of `AccountNum` objects should be a giveaway that this is one-to-many.

☒ **A** and **C** are incorrect.

15. Which of the following statements are true? (Choose all that apply.)

A. Association navigation can be quad-directional.

B. Association navigation can be bidirectional.

C. Association navigation can have no direction.

D. Association navigation can be unidirectional.

Answer:

☑ **B** and **D.** A relationship can only be unidirectional or bidirectional.

☒ **A** and **C** are incorrect.

7

Understanding Class Inheritance

CERTIFICATION OBJECTIVES

- Inheritance and Class Type

- Encapsulation

- Advanced Examples of Classes with Inheritance and Encapsulation

✓   Two-Minute Drill

Q&A   Self Test

CERTIFICATION OBJECTIVE

Inheritance and Class Type

Exam Objective 1.2   Describe, compare, and contrast concrete classes, abstract classes, and interfaces, and how inheritance applies to them.

Inheritance is a fundamental concept of the Java language. It allows specific classes to inherit the methods and instance variables of more general classes. This creates code that is maintainable and emphasizes code reuse. The SCJA exam will require a thorough understanding of these topics.

This section will also examine the differences between concrete classes and abstract classes. Concrete classes are the standard class, but abstract classes are tied to inheritance. The SCJA exam will surely have a few questions where it will be important to understand what type of class is being used.

Finally, interfaces will be discussed. In short, an interface allows the developer to specify an external public interface to a class. Any class that implements or uses this interface must abide by the specifications the interface outlines.

This section is about inheritance and the details of how inheritance works. This concept will not only be a major part of the SCJA exam, but is also a very important concept to understand as a developer. The following topics will be covered over the next few pages:

- Inheritance
- Overriding methods
- Abstract classes
- Interfaces
- Advanced concepts of inheritance

Inheritance

Inheritance allows a developer to create general classes that can then be used as the foundation for multiple specific classes. For example, a program may be required to have classes that represent animals. The animals that must be represented are dogs, cats, and horses. All of these animal classes share some common elements. In this simple example, each animal would have a `weight`, `age`, and `color` instance variable.

Each animal class would also have methods that allow it to do such things as eat, rest, and move. These methods could be called eat(), rest(), and move(int direction).

This can be implemented without inheritance by creating a class for each animal type and then defining each of the previously mentioned methods. This implementation approach will work but has a few drawbacks. Since each type of animal eats, rests, and moves very similarly, there will be a lot of duplicated code between each class. Duplicated code makes a program hard to maintain. If a bug is found in one class, the developer must remember to go find it in every other class that has a copy of that code. The same problem exists for adding features to the duplicated code. It becomes very easy for code that *should* perform the same to slowly start performing differently as the code goes through the development and maintenance process. Another disadvantage of this approach is that polymorphism cannot be used. Polymorphism is a technique that allows a specific object, like a dog object, to be referred to in code as its more general parent animal. Polymorphism will be covered in detail in Chapter 8. Since this approach does not use inheritance, polymorphism is not possible. The following is an example of each animal class implemented in this approach. The details of the class are represented as comments to explain what functionality would be present if implemented.

```
public class Dog1 {
   int weight;
   int age;
   String hairColor;

   public void eat(){ /* Eat food by chewing */ }

   public void rest(){ /* Rest */ }

   public void move(int direction)
      { /* Walk in the direction given as a parameter */ }

   public void bark() { /* Bark */ }
}

public class Cat1 {
   int weight;
   int age;
   String hairColor;

   public void eat(){ /* Eat food by chewing */ }
```

```
    public void rest(){ /* Rest */ }

    public void move(int direction)
        { /* Walk in the direction given as a parameter */ }

    public void meow() { /* Meow */ }
}

public class Horse1 {

    int weight;
    int age;
    String hairColor;

    public void eat(){ /* Eat food by chewing */ }

    public void rest(){ /* rest */ }

    public void move(int direction)
        { /* Walk in the direction given as a parameter */ }

    public void neigh() { /* Neigh */ }
}
```

The first implementation of these animals is to create a unique class for each one. Each of the preceding classes has no relationship to the other. It is easy to see that the classes are all very similar and there is duplicated code between them. In fact, all the methods are the same except the bark(), meow(), and neigh() methods. Although there is no explicit relationship defined in the code, it is easy to infer that all three classes are related.

The same example can be better implemented by using inheritance. In this simple example, three of the four methods that need to be implemented are common to each different animal. A dog, cat, and horse all eat, rest, and move in similar fashion. This common functionality can be placed in a general Animal class. This class defines all the general methods and instance variables that make up an animal. When the developer creates more specific types of animals such as dogs, cats, or horses, they can use the Animal class as a base, or superclass. The more specific classes will inherit all of the nonprivate methods and instance variables from the base Animal class. A class is inherited when it is extended. It is important to remember that a class can only extend one class. It is invalid to inherit multiple classes. The extends keyword is used in the class signature line.

The following is an example of the same animals being implemented using inheritance:

```
public class Animal {
   int weight;
   int age;
   String hairColor;

   public void eat(){ /* Eat food by chewing */ }

   public void rest(){ /* Rest */ }

   public void move(int direction)
      { /* Walk in the direction given as a parameter */ }
}
public class Dog2 extends Animal{
   public void bark() { /* Bark */ }
}

public class Cat2 extends Animal{
   public void meow() { /* Meow */ }
}

public class Horse2 extends Animal{
   public void neigh() { /* Neigh */ }
}
```

This example creates dog2, cat2, and horse2 classes that are functionally the same as the first example. Each one of these classes extends, or inherits, the Animal class. The Animal class is used as their base, or superclass. The specific classes inherit all of the methods and instance variables from the Animal class, and are then permitted to add specific methods and variables that the particular class may need. In this example, each class added a method to make the noise of the animal. The classes may add as many instance variables or methods as needed, or only use the ones provided from the superclass.

When a class extends another class, any nonprivate methods that are contained in the superclass are accessible from the subclass. They can be invoked in the same manner as the methods implemented in the subclass. The following example demonstrates how the Dog2 class can be used:

```
Dog2 dog = new Dog2();
dog.bark();
dog.eat();
```

In the preceding example, a Dog2 object named dog is created. Then, the bark() and eat() methods are called. Notice that both methods can be called in the same manner, even though only the bark() method is implemented in the Dog2 class. This is because any Dog2 object inherits all of the nonprivate methods in the Animal class.

Overriding Methods

Inheriting, or extending, a class is a very good approach for factoring out common functionality between classes. Specific classes extending more general classes allow code to be reused in a project. As stated before, this helps keep the project more maintainable and less prone to bugs as the development cycle progresses.

The problem with this approach is that the subclass that inherits the methods of the superclass is sometimes slightly different. For example, if a Fish class extends the Animal class, the move() method would not work since it is implemented by code that walks—and a fish would need to swim. A class that extends another class may override any inherited method. This is done by defining another method called move() with the same arguments. When the move() method is invoked, the one that is implemented in the Fish class will be used. A class may override all, none, or just some of the methods it inherits from a parent class. The following is an example of the Fish class extending the Animal class and then overriding the move() method:

```
public class Fish extends Animal {
  public void move(int direction)
      { /* Swim in the direction given as a parameter */ }
}
```

Note in the preceding example of the Fish class that the move() method signature is the same as in the Animal class. The move() method in the Fish class is overriding the move() method in the Animal class. When a Fish object is created and the move() method is called, it will execute the code that is located in the Fish class. To override a method, the method signatures must be identical.

When a subclass overrides a method, it has the option of calling the method that is being overridden. This can be achieved by using the super keyword. The super keyword works just like the this keyword, but instead of referring to the current class, super refers to the superclass. When super is used, it must pass the correct arguments to the parent method. The following is an example of super being used in the Horse3 class. Since horses normally rest standing, the Horse2 class from earlier can be further modified to put the horse in a standing position before it performs the rest() method.

```
public class Horse3 extends Animal{
  public void rest(){
    /* Stand before rest */
    super.rest();
  }

  public void neigh() { /* Neigh */ }
}
```

When a Horse3 object has its rest() method called, it will execute the code inside the rest() method of the Horse3 class. This is because the rest() method overrides the rest() method in the Animal class. The Horse3's rest() method makes the horse stand and then uses super to call the rest() method in the Animal class.

Abstract Classes

So far, all the examples presented use concrete classes. A concrete class is a regular class that can be instantiated. Java has another class type called an abstract class. An abstract class is different from a concrete class because it cannot be instantiated and must be extended. An abstract class may contain abstract methods. Abstract methods are methods that are not implemented. They have a valid method signature but must be overridden and implemented in the class that extends the abstract class. The following is an example of an abstract class:

```
public abstract class MusicPlayer {
  public abstract void play();

  public abstract void stop();

  public void changeVolume(int volumeLevel)
      { /* Set volume to volumeLevel */}
}
```

The preceding example is an abstract class for a music player. This is intended to be the base class for different music-playing devices such as MP3 players or CD players. Notice how the class is defined; the keyword `abstract` is used to indicate that this is an abstract class. This class provides some functionality with the `changeVolume()` method. It also contains two abstract methods. An abstract method can only exist in an abstract class. The `abstract` keyword is used to mark a method as such. Every abstract method must be implemented in the subclass that extends it. The purpose of an abstract method is to define the required functionality that any subclass must have. In this case, any music player must be able to play and stop. The functionality cannot be implemented in the `MusicPlayer` class because it is different from player to player. The following example is of two classes extending the `MusicPlayer` class:

```
public class MP3Player extends MusicPlayer{
  public void play() { /* Start decoding and playing MP3 */ }

  public void stop() { /* Stop decoding and playing MP3 */ }
}

public class CDPlayer extends MusicPlayer {
  public void play() { /* Start reading and playing disc */ }

  public void stop() { /* Stop reading disc */ }
}
```

The `MP3Player` and `CDPlayer` classes are both types of music players. By extending the `MusicPlayer` class, they are required to implement the `play()` and `stop()` methods by overriding the abstract classes in the base class.

Interfaces

Interfaces are used in the Java language to define a required set of functionalities from the classes that implement the interface. Unlike extending base classes, a class is free to implement as many interfaces as needed. An interface can be thought of as an abstract class with all abstract methods.

When a class implements an interface, it is required to implement all of the methods defined in the interface. Interfaces are used to create a standard public interface for similar items. This enables code to be more modular. The `interface` keyword is used to create an interface in the next example.

```
public interface Phone {
  public void dialNumber(int number);

  public boolean isCallInProgress();
}
```

The preceding example is a very basic interface for a phone. The next example demonstrates this interface being implemented by a cell phone class and a landline phone. The keyword implements is used to implement an interface.

```
public class LandlinePhone implements Phone{
  private boolean callInProgress;

  public void dialNumber(int number)
     { /* Dial number via wired network */}

  public boolean isCallInProgress() { return callInProgress; }
}

public class CellPhone implements Phone{
  private boolean callInProgress;

  public void dialNumber(int number)
     { /* Dial number via cell network */ }

  public boolean isCallInProgress() { return callInProgress; }
}
```

When an interface is implemented, all of its methods must then be implemented in that class. It is possible to implement multiple interfaces. When more than one interface is being used they are separated in a comma-delimited list. When multiple interfaces are used, all of the methods defined in each one must be implemented. Any unimplemented methods will cause the compiler to generate errors. The following is an example of a class implementing two interfaces:

```
public class VideoPhone implements Phone, VideoPlayer{
     ...
}
```

The big advantage of using interfaces is that any class that uses the same interface will have the same public methods, as shown in Figure 7-1. This means that the CellPhone class shown earlier could be used instead of LandlinePhone. Changing between these classes should not require any code change other than the type declared. This gets close to the idea of polymorphism, and will be covered in detail in Chapter 8.

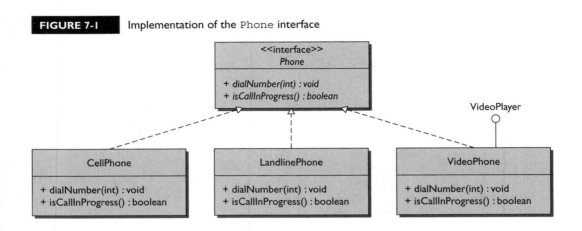

FIGURE 7-1   Implementation of the Phone interface

Advanced Concepts of Inheritance

The last few sections discussed the basic cases of inheritance—one concrete class extending another concrete class, abstract class, or implementing interfaces. However, it is possible and common to have many levels of inheritance. In fact, every class in the Java language inherits from the base class Object. This includes the classes built by developers. The use of Object as a base class is implied and does not have to be explicitly extended with the extends keyword. This means that in the preceding examples where a class was inherited, there were really two levels of inheritance. Looking back at the animal example, the Dog2 class extended the Animal class, and the Animal class extended the Object class. This means that the Dog2 class gains all of the functionality of both classes. If a class overrides the methods of another, the new method is then passed down the inheritance chain. The inheritance chain can continue as long as it is applicable to the application, meaning class A can extend class B that extends C that extends D and so forth. The classes can be a mixture of abstract and concrete. The classes are also able to implement any interfaces required.

Interfaces may also extend other interfaces. When an interface extends another interface, it gains all of the defined methods of the extended interface. Unlike a class, an interface may extend multiple interfaces. This is achieved by using the extends keyword, followed by a comma-delimited list of interfaces.

The diagram in Figure 7-2 represents a possible inheritance tree. At the bottom of this tree is the concrete class SportsCar. This class extends the abstract class Car. The Car class extends the PassengerVehicle class, which extends the base

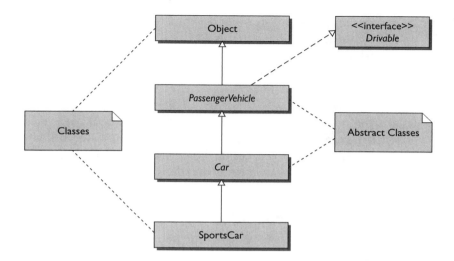

FIGURE 7-2

An example of an inheritance tree

`Object` class. The `PassengerVehicle` class also implements the `Drivable` interface.

In an example like this, the `SportsCar` class has access to all the visible methods and instance variables in both the `PassengerVehicle` class and the `Car` class. The `SportsCar` class must also implement any methods that were unimplemented, including the ones required by the `Drivable` interface.

CERTIFICATION OBJECTIVE

Encapsulation

Exam Objective 1.4   Describe information hiding (using private attributes and methods), encapsulation, and exposing object functionality using public methods; and describe the JavaBeans conventions for setter and getter methods.

Encapsulation is the concept of storing data together with methods that operate on that data. Objects are used as the container for the data and code. This section discusses the principles of encapsulation and how it should be applied as a developer.

Encapsulation allows for data and method hiding. This concept is called information hiding. Information hiding makes it possible to expose a public interface while hiding the implementation details. Finally, this section will explore the JavaBean conventions for creating getter and setter methods. These are the methods used to read and modify properties of a Java object.

This section will expose the reader to some good basic design principles that should be used with the Java language. The SCJA exam will require an understanding of these principles. These conventions will be used on the exam even when the question is not directly related to it. Understanding them thoroughly will help in understanding many questions.

Good Design with Encapsulation

The fundamental theory of an object-oriented language is that software is designed by creating discrete objects that interact to make up the functionality of the application. Encapsulation is the concept of storing similar data and methods together in discrete classes. In many nonobject-oriented languages there is no association between where the data is and where the code is. This can increase the complexity of maintaining the code because oftentimes the variables that the code is using are spread apart over the code base. Bugs in the code can be hard to find and resolve due to different remote procedures using the same variables.

Encapsulation tries to solve these problems. It creates easier to read and maintainable code by grouping related variables and methods together in classes. Object-oriented software is very modular, and encapsulation is the term used for creating these modules. Encapsulation allows for information hiding. Information hiding will be covered in detail in the next section.

A well-encapsulated class is one that has a single clear purpose. This class should only contain the methods and variables that are needed to fulfill its purpose. For example, if a class was intended to represent a television, it should contain variables such as `currentChannel`, `volume`, and `isPoweredOn`. A `Television` class would also have methods such as `setChannel(int channel)` or `setVolume(int volume)`. These variables and methods are all related. They are specific to the properties and actions needed to create a `Television` class. The `Television` class would not contain methods such as `playDVD()`; this should be contained in a separate `DVD` class.

Encapsulation is about creating well-defined classes that have a clear purpose. These classes contain all the data and methods needed to perform their intended functions.

Encapsulation is defined slightly different depending on the source. Sometimes the definition is that encapsulation is solely about storing related data and methods together in a class. Other places will define encapsulation to also include information hiding of the implementation details.

Access Modifiers

Access modifiers are the keywords that define what can access methods and instance variables. The three access modifiers are `private`, `protected`, and `public`. These all change the default level of access. The default access level does not use a keyword and is assigned to a method or instance variable when neither `private`, `protected`, nor `public` is used, and the area is left blank. Access modifiers are an important concept in object-oriented languages. They allow the implementation details to be hidden in a class. The developer can choose specifically what parts of a class are accessible to other objects. Most of the code examples in the book use the default access level. This was done for clarity in the examples. The SCJA exam will focus on the different effects that the `public` and `private` modifiers have. The topics listed next will be covered in the following subsections:

- The access modifiers
- Information hiding
- Exposing object functionality

The Access Modifiers

Java has three access modifiers: `private`, `protected`, and `public`. There is also the default access level, which is known as *package-private*. Each access level has different restrictions that allow or deny classes access to methods or instance variables. Access modifiers are also used when defining a class. This is beyond the scope of the SCJA, so just assume all classes are `public`. The Java compiler will produce errors if a restricted method or instance variable is accessed by code that is unauthorized.

The `private` access modifier is the most restrictive and most commonly used access modifier. Any method or instance variable that is marked as `private` can only be accessed by other methods in the same class. Subclasses cannot access instance variables or methods that are `private`. The following is an example of the `private` keyword in use:

```
private int numberOfPoints;
private int calculateAverage() { … }
```

The default access level is the second most restrictive. It is often referred to as *package-private*. This access level allows access to its methods and instance variables from code that is in the same package. The default access level does not have a keyword to indicate it is in use. A method or instance variable is set to default when an access modifier is omitted. The following is an example of this access level in use:

```
int maxSpeed;
float calculateAcceleration() { … }
```

The `protected` access modifier is the third most restrictive. It is the same as the default access level but adds the ability of subclasses outside of the package to access its methods or instance variables. This means the methods that can access this data must either be in the same package (same as default) or be in a subclass of the class that contains the `protected` data. Remember that a subclass is a class that extends another class. The following is an example of the use of the `protected` access modifier:

```
protected boolean active;
protected char getFirstChar() { … }
```

The final access modifier is `public`. This is the least restrictive and second most common access modifier. The `public` access modifier provides no restriction to what can access its methods and instance variables. Any method can access a `public` method or instance variable regardless of which package it is contained in or which superclass it extends. An item marked as public is accessible to the world. The following is an example of using the `public` access modifier:

```
public int streetAddress;
public int findZipCode(){ … };
```

Information Hiding

Information hiding is the concept of hiding the implementation details of a class. Information hiding is achieved by using restrictive access modifiers. The advantage of hiding data is so the developer can control how the data is accessed.

Instance variables are used to store the state of an object. If outside objects were able to access an object's entire set of instance variables, the risk of introducing bugs would be increased. A developer may create a new class that incorrectly tries to use the internal features of another class. Even if this approach works at first, it requires that the class's internal data structure not change. This concept also applies to methods. Not all methods need to be accessible by external classes. Oftentimes,

SCENARIO & SOLUTION

You need to make an instance variable available only to the class it is declared in. What access modifier would you use?	The `private` access modifier should be used.
You need to make a method only available to other methods in the same package or a subclass of the class it is defined in. What access modifier would you use?	The `protected` access modifier should be used.
You need to make a method that is available to any other method in the application. What access modifier would you use?	The `public` access modifier should be used.
You need to make an instance variable that is available only to other objects in the same package. What access modifier would you use?	*Package-private* (default) should be used.

a class will be composed of more methods used internally to perform tasks rather than methods designed for external objects.

A benefit of hiding data can be seen in this scenario. A class contains an instance variable that must be between a certain range. An outside object may set this variable and disregard the proper range. To prevent this, the variable can be marked `private` and a `public` method can be used to set it. This method would contain code that would only change its value if the new value were valid. A general rule is that every method and instance variable should use the most restrictive access modifier possible.

Exposing Object Functionality

Once all of your internal implementation details are hidden, the class must have a set of `public` methods that expose its functionality to other objects. In most classes, all of the instance variables will use the `private` access modifier. The `public` methods should be the only required methods that other classes need to use this class. Any method used internally and not required by external classes should not be `public`.

Methods that are `public` can be compared to buttons on the outside of a radio. Only a few exist but they allow the radio to be controlled. However, inside the radio are many wires and controls that should not be altered, and do not need to be altered to control the radio. The outside buttons are like `public` methods, while the inside components are like `private` methods and instance variables.

Earlier in this chapter, interfaces were discussed. If a class implements an interface, it is required to implement each method in the interface as a `public` method. They are called interfaces because they represent the interface that other classes must use to work with this class. The `public` methods of any class can be thought of as an interface for the class. External objects have no knowledge of the underlying details of the class. They can only see and use the public interface that an object presents them.

Setters and Getters

Setters and getters are the final concept of information hiding and encapsulation. As was discussed previously, it is good design to make all instance variables `private`. This means external classes have no way to access these variables. Sometimes an external object may need to read one of these variables to determine its state, or it may have to set it. To achieve this, a `public` method is created for the variable to both get and set the value. These are called getters and setters. They can be as simple as one line that only sets or returns a value. The following example is a class that has one instance variable and a setter and getter:

```
public class ScoreBoard {
  private int score;

  public int getScore() {
    return this.score;
  }

  public void setScore(int score) {
    this.score = score;
  }
}
```

Notice in this example that there is a `private` instance variable named `score`. The two methods that are present are a getter and setter for the variable `score`. In this case, the class is giving read and write access to the variable via the methods. In some cases, a class may only have one or the other. The getter and setter in the example are simple and only set or return the value. However, if the class had to perform an action every time the `score` variable was changed, it could be done from the setter. For example, each time the score is changed, the class must record it to a log. This can be done right in the setter. This is the benefit of keeping instance variables private. It gives control to the class as to how its instance variables are accessed.

Getters and setters are the standard way of creating access to a class's instance variables. When developers are working with a class, they expect to find getters and setters. They also expect a JavaBeans naming convention to be followed. When creating a getter, the name should start with a lowercase 'get', followed by the variable name with no spaces and the first letter capitalized. The one exception to this is when a `boolean` value is returned. In this case, instead of using 'get', 'is' is used with the same rules being applied to the variable name. When creating a setter, a similar convention should be followed. A setter should start with the word 'set', followed by the variable name with the first letter capitalized.

Variable Type and Name	Getter and Setter Name
`int boatNumber`	`public int getBoatNumber()` `public void setBoatNumber(int boatNumber)`

`boolean boatRunning`	`public boolean isBoatRunning()`
	`public void setBoatRunning(boolean`
	`    boatRunning)`

`Object position`	`public Object getPosition()` `public void setPosition(Object position)`

CERTIFICATION OBJECTIVE

Advanced Examples of Classes with Inheritance and Encapsulation

Exam Objective 3.2   Develop code that declares concrete classes, abstract classes, and interfaces, code that supports implementation and interface inheritance, code that declares instance attributes and methods, and code that uses the Java access modifiers: private and public.

This section will conclude the chapter by revisiting all of the concepts that have been discussed and demonstrating them with code examples. Each example will be followed by a detailed explanation of what is being highlighted and how it works. Pay close attention to the examples. They should help reinforce all of the concepts already covered.

Examples of Java Access Modifiers

The following example is a class implemented with its implementation details hidden. It uses public methods to expose an interface, as well as getters and setters to allow access to its instance variables.

```java
public class PhoneBookEntry {
  private String name = "";
  private int phoneNumber = 0;
  private long lastUpdate = 0;

  public String getName() {
    return name;
  }

  public void setNameNumber(String name, int phoneNumber) {
    this.name = name;
    this.phoneNumber = phoneNumber;
    lastUpdate = System.currentTimeMillis();
  }

  public int getPhoneNumber() {
    return phoneNumber;
  }

  public void setPhoneNumber(int phoneNumber) {
    this.phoneNumber = phoneNumber;
    lastUpdate = System.currentTimeMillis();
  }
}
```

The preceding example is a well-encapsulated class. It is a class that represents a basic phone book entry. It can store a name and a phone number. It also uses an instance variable to track the last time it was updated. All of the instance variables use the `private` access modifier. This means external classes are unable to read or modify them. It then uses getters and setters to modify the instance variables. In the preceding example, there is no setter to set the name instance variable. To set the name instance variable, the object must also set the phoneNumber variable. This ensures there is never a name without a phone number. If the instance variables were public, this class could not prevent another class from only setting a name without a number.

This example also uses its setters to update the `lastUpdate` variable. This variable is used to track the last time this class had its information updated. By using the getters and setters, the class can guarantee that any time an external object updates a field via a setter, the `lastUpdate` variable will also be updated. The details of how `lastUpdate` becomes updated are invisible to external objects.

Examples of Inheritance with Concrete Classes

A concrete class is the standard Java class. All of its methods are implemented and it can be instantiated. The following example is of a `Bicycle` class. The base class represents a basic bicycle. Another class represents a ten-speed bicycle. It is called `TenSpeedBicycle` and extends the `Bicycle` class. The `TenSpeedBicycle` class is able to inherit some of its functionality while overriding the parts of the base class that need to behave differently. The `TenSpeedBicycle` class has the ability to change its gear ratio in addition to what the `Bicycle` class can do.

```java
public class Bicycle {
  private float wheelRPM;
  private int degreeOfTurn;

  public void pedalRPM(float pedalRPM){
    float gearRatio = 2f;
    this.wheelRPM = pedalRPM * gearRatio;
  }

  public void setDegreeOfTurn(int degreeOfTurn){
    this.degreeOfTurn = degreeOfTurn;
  }

  public float getWheelRPM() {
    return this.wheelRPM;
  }

  public int getDegreeOfTurn() {
    return this.degreeOfTurn;
  }
}
```

The preceding is the `Bicycle` class. This is a concrete class and therefore can be instantiated. This class represents a basic bicycle. It has two instance variables, wheelRPM, which is used to store the RPM of the wheels, and degreeOfTurn, which is used to store the degree the handlebars are turned. Each variable has a getter, and degreeOfTurn has a setter. The wheelRPM variable is set with the method pedalRPM(float pedalRPM). This accepts an argument that contains the RPM of the pedals, and then multiplies that by a set gear ratio to find and set the wheelRPM variable.

```java
public class TenSpeedBicycle extends Bicycle {
  private float gearRatio = 2f;
  private float wheelRPM;

  public void setGearRatio(float gearRatio) {
    this.gearRatio = gearRatio;
  }

  public void pedalRPM(float pedalRPM) {
    this.wheelRPM = pedalRPM * gearRatio;
  }

  public float getWheelRPM() {
    return this.wheelRPM;
  }
}
```

The TenSpeedBicycle class, listed in the preceding example, extends the Bicycle class. This class represents a bicycle that has ten different possible gear ratios. The regular Bicycle class cannot be used because it has a fixed gear ratio. The TenSpeedBicycle class adds a method and instance variable so a gear ratio can be set. It also overrides the wheelRPM variable. This must be done because the Bicycle class has no setter to set that variable directly. The TenSpeedBicycle class also overrides the pedalRPM(float pedalRPM) method. In the Bicycle class version of this method, the gear ratio was fixed. In the newer version, it uses the gear ratio that can be set. To retrieve the wheelRPM variable, the getter must also be overridden. This is because the original version of this method can only return the instance variable that is in its same class.

```java
public class Main {
  public static void main(String[] args) {
    System.out.println("Starting...");
    System.out.println("Creating a bicycle...");
    Bicycle b = new Bicycle();
    b.setDegreeOfTurn(0);
```

```
        b.pedalRPM(50);
        System.out.println("Turning: " + b.getDegreeOfTurn());
        System.out.println("Wheel RPM: " + b.getWheelRPM());
        System.out.println("Creating a 10 speed bicycle...");
        TenSpeedBicycle tb = new TenSpeedBicycle();
        tb.setDegreeOfTurn(10);
        tb.setGearRatio(3f);
        tb.pedalRPM(40);
        System.out.println("Turning: " + tb.getDegreeOfTurn());
        System.out.println("Wheel RPM: " + tb.getWheelRPM());
    }
}
```

The preceding segment of code is the code that uses both classes. This code prints information to standard out for each step it takes. First, it creates a `Bicycle` object. It then sets the degree of turn to 0 and the pedal RPM to 50. The code then prints out the degree of turn, which will be 0, and the wheel RPM, which will be 100, since the gear ratio is 2 (2 * 50).

Next, a `TenSpeedBicycle` object is created. This object has its degree of turn set to 10, its gear ratio set to 3 and its pedal RPM set to 40. Finally, this object prints out its degree of turn, which is 10, and its wheel RPM, which is 120 (3 * 40). Notice that the `TenSpeedBicycle` object's `getDegreeOfTurn()` and `setDegreeOfTurn()` were inherited from the base class `Bicycle`.

```
Starting...
Creating a bicycle...
Turning: 0
Wheel RPM: 100.0
Creating a 10 speed bicycle...
Turning: 10
Wheel RPM: 120.0
```

This is the output of the program if it was compiled and run. This example shows most of the basic concepts of inheritance, as can be seen in Figure 7-3.

As preparation for the SCJA exam, this should be reviewed until it is understood how the preceding output was generated.

Examples of Inheritance with Abstract Classes

This example will demonstrate an abstract class. An abstract class is a class in Java that cannot be instantiated. Another class must extend it. An abstract class may contain both concrete methods that have implementations, and abstract methods

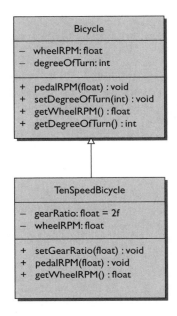

that must be implemented by the subclass. This example creates a plant simulator. It has a `Plant` abstract class that is extended by a `MapleTree` class and `Tulip` class. The `Plant` class is a good abstract class because a plant is an abstract, or general, thing. Plants all share some characteristic that can be placed in this class. Each specific class can then contain the implementation details. The following code segment is the abstract `Plant` class:

```java
public abstract class Plant {
  private int age=0;
  private int height=0;

  public int getAge() {
    return age;
  }

  public void addYearToAge() {
    age++;
  }

  public int getHeight() {
    return height;
  }
```

```
      public void setHeight(int height) {
        this.height = height;
      }

      abstract public void doSpring();
      abstract public void doSummer();
      abstract public void doFall();
      abstract public void doWinter();
    }
```

The preceding abstract class is a very simplistic view of what represents a plant. It contains two instance variables that every type of plant would use: age and height. There is both a getter and setter for height, and a getter for age. The age instance variable has a method that is used to increment it each year.

The Plant class has four abstract methods. Each of these methods represents the actions that a plant must take during the specified season. These actions are specific to the type of plant and therefore cannot be generalized. Having them declared in the abstract Plant class guarantees that they must be implemented by any class that extends the Plant class.

```
public class MapleTree extends Plant {
  private static final int AMOUNT_TO_GROW_IN_ONE_GROWING_SEASON = 2;

  // A tree grows upwards a certain number of feet a year.
  // A tree does not die down to ground level during the winter.
  private void grow() {
    int currentHeight = getHeight();
    setHeight(currentHeight + AMOUNT_TO_GROW_IN_ONE_GROWING_SEASON);
  }

  public void doSpring() {
    grow();
    addYearToAge();
    System.out.println("Spring: The maple tree is starting to grow " +
        "leaves and new branches");
    System.out.println("\tCurrent Age: " + getAge() + " " +
        "Current Height: " + getHeight());
  }

  public void doSummer() {
    grow();
    System.out.println("Summer: The maple tree is continuing to grow");
```

```
      System.out.println("\tCurrent Age: " + getAge() + " " +
         "Current Height: " + getHeight());
   }

   public void doFall() {
      System.out.println("Fall:    The maple tree has stopped growing" +
         " and is losing its leaves");
      System.out.println("\tCurrent Age: " + getAge() + " " +
         "Current Height: " + getHeight());
   }

   public void doWinter() {
      System.out.println("Winter: The maple tree is dormant");
      System.out.println("\tCurrent Age: " + getAge() + " " +
         "Current Height: " + getHeight());
   }
}
```

The preceding class is the `MapleTree` class. It extends the `Plant` class and is used as a simple representation of a maple tree. Since the `Plant` class is abstract, the `MapleTree` class must implement all of its abstract methods. The `MapleTree` class contains one variable named `AMOUNT_TO_GROW_IN_ONE_GROWING_SEASON`. This variable is marked as `private static final int`. This is how Java declares a constant. These details are beyond the scope of the SCJA exam. Just consider this a constant that is a primitive `int` and is `private`. This variable is used to set the amount of growth that a maple tree completes during a growing season.

The `MapleTree` class contains a method to grow, called `grow()`. This method is used to add the new height to the current height. The next four methods are all methods required to be implemented. These abstract methods are declared in the `Plant` class, with each one representing a different season. When they are invoked, they perform any required action that is needed for that season and then print two lines to standard out. The first line of text states what season it is and what the maple tree is doing. The next line displays the values of the `age` and `height` variables.

```
public class Tulip extends Plant {
   private static final int AMOUNT_TO_GROW_IN_ONE_GROWING_SEASON = 1;

   //A tulip grows each year to the same height. During
   //the winter they die down to ground level.
   private void grow() {
      int currentHeight = getHeight();
```

```java
    setHeight(currentHeight + AMOUNT_TO_GROW_IN_ONE_GROWING_SEASON);
  }

  private void dieDownForWinter(){
    setHeight(0);
  }

  public void doSpring() {
    grow();
    addYearToAge();
    System.out.println("Spring: The tulip is starting to grow " +
        "up from the ground");
    System.out.println("\tCurrent Age: " + getAge() + " " +
        "Current Height: " + getHeight());
  }

  public void doSummer() {
    System.out.println("Summer: The tulip has stopped growing " +
        "and is flowering");
    System.out.println("\tCurrent Age: " + getAge() + " " +
        "Current Height: " + getHeight());
  }

  public void doFall() {
    System.out.println("Fall:   The tulip begins to wilt");
    System.out.println("\tCurrent Age: " + getAge() + " " +
        "Current Height: " + getHeight());
  }

  public void doWinter() {
    dieDownForWinter();
    System.out.println("Winter: The tulip is dormant underground");
    System.out.println("\tCurrent Age: " + getAge() + " " +
        "Current Height: " + getHeight());
  }
}
```

The preceding class is the `Tulip` class. It is intended to represent a tulip. It extends the `Plant` class and therefore must also implement all its abstract methods. Like the `MapleTree` class, the `Tulip` class also has a constant that is used to store the amount of growth per growing season.

The `Tulip` class has two private methods. A `grow()` method that is like the one present in the `MapleTree` class. It also has a method named `dieDownForWinter()`.

This method is used to reset the `height` to zero when the tulip loses all of its leaves during the winter.

The last four methods in the class are the abstract methods from the `Plant` class. Each season method performs the needed actions first, such as grow, die down, or age. It then prints to standard out a message about what it is doing, and what season it is. The second line of text contains the values of the `age` and `height` variables.

```java
public class Simulator{
  public static void main(String[] args) {
    System.out.println("Creating a maple tree and tulip...");
    MapleTree mapleTree = new MapleTree();
    Tulip tulip = new Tulip();
    System.out.println("Entering a loop to simulate 3 years");
    for (int i = 0; i < 3; i++) {
      mapleTree.doSpring();
      tulip.doSpring();
      mapleTree.doSummer();
      tulip.doSummer();
      mapleTree.doFall();
      tulip.doFall();
      mapleTree.doWinter();
      tulip.doWinter();
    }
  }
}
```

This final code segment is the `main()` method that uses both the `Tulip` and `MapleTree` classes. First, an object of each type is created. Then there is a `for` loop that invokes the methods for all four seasons for each object. This loop represents a simple simulation program. Each time through the loop represents one year. Both objects age and grow from year to year. When the preceding code is executed, it will produce the output shown next.

```
Creating a maple tree and tulip...
Entering a loop to simulate 3 years
Spring: The maple tree is starting to grow leaves and new branches
        Current Age: 1 Current Height: 2
Spring: The tulip is starting to grow up from the ground
        Current Age: 1 Current Height: 1
Summer: The maple tree is continuing to grow
        Current Age: 1 Current Height: 4
Summer: The tulip has stopped growing and is flowering
```

```
             Current Age: 1 Current Height: 1
Fall:    The maple tree has stopped growing and is losing its leaves
             Current Age: 1 Current Height: 4
Fall:    The tulip begins to wilt
             Current Age: 1 Current Height: 1
Winter: The maple tree is dormant
             Current Age: 1 Current Height: 4
Winter: The tulip is dormant underground
             Current Age: 1 Current Height: 0
Spring: The maple tree is starting to grow leaves and new branches
             Current Age: 2 Current Height: 6
Spring: The tulip is starting to grow up from the ground
             Current Age: 2 Current Height: 1
Summer: The maple tree is continuing to grow
             Current Age: 2 Current Height: 8
Summer: The tulip has stopped growing and is flowering
             Current Age: 2 Current Height: 1
Fall:    The maple tree has stopped growing and is losing its leaves
             Current Age: 2 Current Height: 8
Fall:    The tulip begins to wilt
             Current Age: 2 Current Height: 1
Winter: The maple tree is dormant
             Current Age: 2 Current Height: 8
Winter: The tulip is dormant underground
             Current Age: 2 Current Height: 0
Spring: The maple tree is starting to grow leaves and new branches
             Current Age: 3 Current Height: 10
Spring: The tulip is starting to grow up from the ground
             Current Age: 3 Current Height: 1
Summer: The maple tree is continuing to grow
             Current Age: 3 Current Height: 12
Summer: The tulip has stopped growing and is flowering
             Current Age: 3 Current Height: 1
Fall:    The maple tree has stopped growing and is losing its leaves
             Current Age: 3 Current Height: 12
Fall:    The tulip begins to wilt
             Current Age: 3 Current Height: 1
Winter: The maple tree is dormant
             Current Age: 3 Current Height: 12
Winter: The tulip is dormant underground
             Current Age: 3 Current Height: 0
```

Notice in the preceding output how the maple tree continues to grow each year. The tulip, however, must re-grow each year. Both the `Tulip` and the `MapleTree` objects have access to the `getAge()` and `getHeight()` methods that were implemented in the abstract Plant class. Review the code and the output thoroughly. A good understanding of the examples in this section will better prepare you for the SCJA exam.

Add Functionality to the Plant Simulator

This exercise will use the previous plant simulator and add new functionality to it.

1. Copy the plant simulator into the text editor or IDE of your choice.
2. Compile and run the example to ensure the code has been copied correctly.
3. Add a new class called Rose that will represent a rose. Use the Plant base class and implement all of the required methods.
4. Add your new class into the simulator and run the application.

Examples of Interfaces

This final example involves interfaces. An interface is a public set of methods that must be implemented by the class that uses the interface. By using an interface, a class is saying it implements the functionality defined by the interface. This example has two interfaces. One is called Printer and provides a public interface that printers should implement. Any class that implements Printer can be said to have the ability to print. The other interface in this example is Fax. It provides the public interface for a faxing capability. Finally, this example has a class that implements both interfaces. This class represents an all-in-one printer/fax machine. The class is called PrinterFaxCombo. The following are the two interfaces:

```
public interface Printer {
   public void printFile(File f);
   public int getInkLevel();
}
```

The preceding interface is for a printer. It provides a basic public interface that all printers should have. In this simple example, the printer can do two things. It can print a file with the printFile(File f) method, or check the ink levels with the getInkLevel() method.

```
public interface Fax {
  public void sendFax(File f,int number);
  public Object getReceivedFaxes();
}
```

This interface is for a fax machine. This simple fax machine can send a file with the sendFax(File f,int number) method, or return a fax as an Object with the getReceivedFaxes() method. The following is the PrinterFaxCombo class. This class implements both interfaces.

```
public class PrinterFaxCombo implements Fax, Printer{
  private Object incomingFax;
  private int inkLevel;

  public void sendFax(File f, int number) {
    dialNumber(number);
    faxFile(f);
  }

  public Object getReceivedFaxes() {
    return incomingFax;
  }

  public void printFile(File f) {
    sendFileToPrinter(f);
  }

  public int getInkLevel() {
    return inkLevel;
  }

  private boolean dialNumber(int number){
    boolean success = true;
    /* Dial number set success to false if it is not successful */
    return success;
  }

  private void faxFile(File f){
    /* Send the File f as a fax */
  }

  private void sendFileToPrinter(File f){
    /* Print the File f */
  }
```

```
/*
 * This class would contain many more methods to
 * implement all of this functionality.
 */
}
```

The preceding `PrinterFaxCombo` class is a simplistic version of a printer that can also fax. The class is not fully implemented, but the comments in the empty methods should explain the purpose of each method. The important point of this example is that this class implements both the `Printer` and `Fax` interfaces. By implementing the interfaces, the `PrinterFaxCombo` class is obligated to implement each method they contain. The advantage of implementing interfaces is that it allows an external object to know that this class provides the functionality of a printer and fax machine. Every class that implements the `Printer` interface provides printing functionality and has the same public interface. This creates modular code and allows easy swapping in and out of different classes based on the needs of the application. Interfaces also allow for polymorphism. This will be discussed in detail in Chapter 8.

CERTIFICATION SUMMARY

This chapter has been about class inheritance and encapsulation. Inheritance is an important concept in Java. It is the term used to describe one class gaining the methods and instance variables of a parent class. This concept allows a developer to find commonality between classes and create a general parent class that each specific class can extend, or inherit, to then gain common functionality. This promotes code reuse.

Concrete classes and abstract classes are both able to be extended to create subclasses. The class that is extended is then considered the superclass, or base class. A class may only extend one class. Concrete classes are a traditional class with each method implemented. A class that extends a concrete class gains all of its visible methods. Abstract classes must be extended and cannot be instantiated in code. They contain a mixture of implemented and abstract, or unimplemented, methods. When an abstract class is extended, all of its abstract methods must be implemented by the subclass.

Interfaces are a set of unimplemented methods. When a class implements an interface, that class must then implement each method that is in the interface. Interfaces are used to define a predetermined set of exposed methods. Classes may implement as many interfaces as they need as long as all methods are then implemented in that class.

Next, Java access modifiers were discussed. The `public` and `private` access modifiers are used to prefix a method or instance variable. The `public` access modifier allows any code to access that method or instance variable. The `private` access modifier only allows code within its own class to access the method or instance variable.

Another major concept covered in this chapter was encapsulation. Encapsulation is the design concept of allowing access to a class only through a public interface while hiding the rest of the implementation details. A public interface is created by the methods that have the `public` access modifier. Implementation details should be hidden by using the `private` access modifier. The code that uses this class can only access data through public methods and never accesses data directly since `private` is used. Getters and setters are normally used to access the hidden data. A getter is a simple method that returns an instance variable, while a setter is a method that sets an instance variable to the value passed to it as an argument.

This chapter concluded with code examples. These examples are important to understand since the SCJA exam will have questions based on a given code segment.

TWO-MINUTE DRILL

- ❑ Inheritance is used to place common code in a base class.
- ❑ Inheritance makes code more modular and easier to maintain.
- ❑ The extends keyword is used to extend or inherit a class.
- ❑ When a class inherits another class, it gains access to all of its visible methods and instance variables.
- ❑ The class that is being inherited is referred to as the base class or superclass.
- ❑ The class that gains the functionality is called the subclass.
- ❑ A method in a superclass can be overridden by the subclass having a method with an identical signature.
- ❑ The super keyword can be used to access the overridden method.
- ❑ A class can only extend one other class.
- ❑ A concrete class is a class that can be instantiated; all of its methods have been implemented.
- ❑ An abstract class cannot be instantiated. It must be extended and may or may not contain abstract methods.
- ❑ When a class extends an abstract class, all of the abstract methods must be implemented.
- ❑ An interface is used to define a public interface that a class must have.
- ❑ The keyword implements is used to implement an interface.
- ❑ A class may implement multiple interfaces by using a comma-delimited list.
- ❑ A class that implements an interface must implement all of the methods contained in the interface.
- ❑ Encapsulation is the concept of storing related data and code together.
- ❑ Access modifiers can be used to restrict access to methods and instance variables.
- ❑ The public access modifier allows any class to access the public method or instance variable.
- ❑ The private access modifier allows only methods in the same class to access the private method or instance variable.

❑ Information hiding is the concept of using restrictive access modifiers to hide the implementation details of a class.

❑ When creating methods or instance variables, the most restrictive access modifier possible should be used.

❑ A getter is used to access private instance variables.

❑ A setter is used to set private instance variables.

❑ Both getters and setters should follow the JavaBeans naming convention. They should start with 'get', 'set', or 'is', followed by the variable name, starting with a capital letter.

SELF TEST

Inheritance and Class Type

1. What contains methods and instance variables and can be instantiated?
   A. Concrete class
   B. Abstract class
   C. Java class
   D. Interface

2. What is used to define a public interface?
   A. Concrete class
   B. Abstract class
   C. Java class
   D. Interface

3. What can contain unimplemented methods and instance variables and cannot be instantiated?
   A. Concrete class
   B. Abstract class
   C. Java class

4. Inheritance provides which of the following? (Choose all that apply.)
   A. Faster execution times since methods can inherit processor time from superclasses
   B. Allows developers to place general code in a class that more specific classes can gain through inheritance
   C. Promotes code reuse
   D. Is an automated process to transfer old code to the latest Java version

5. What is a class being inherited referred to as? (Choose all that apply.)
   A. Subclass
   B. Superclass
   C. Base class
   D. Super duper class

Encapsulation

Refer to this class for the following two questions.

```java
public class Account {
  private int money;

  public int getMoney() {
    return this.money;
  }

  public void setMoney(int money) {
    this.money = money;
  }
}
```

6. In the code segment, what is the method `getMoney()` considered?

  A. Get method

  B. Access method

  C. Getter method

  D. Instance variable method

7. In the code segment, what is the method `setMoney(int money)` considered?

  A. Set method

  B. Access method

  C. Setter method

  D. Instance variable method

8. Which of the following defines information hiding?

  A.   Informationhiding is hiding as much detail about your class as possible so others can't steal it.

  B.   Information hiding is about hiding implementation details and protecting variables from being used the wrong way.

  C.   Information hiding is used to obscure the interworking of your class so external classes must use the public interface.

9. What access modifier is used to make the instance variable or method only available to the class it is defined in?

  A. `public`

  B. `private`

  C. `protected`

  D. *package-private* (default)

10. What access modifier is used to create an interface for other objects regardless of their package or their base classes?

    A. `public`

    B. `private`

    C. `protected`

    D. *package-private* (default)

Advanced Examples of Classes with Inheritance and Encapsulation

11. What is the proper signature for class X if it inherits class Z?

    A. `public class X inherits Z{ … }`

    B. `public class X extends Z{ … }`

    C. `public class X implements Z{ … }`

12. How many classes can a class extend directly?

    A. Zero

    B. One

    C. Two

    D. As many as it needs

13. How many interfaces can a class implement directly?

    A. Zero

    B. One

    C. Two

    D. As many as it needs

14. Consider the following UML illustration for assistance with this question:

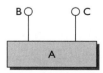

What is the proper signature for class A if it implements interfaces B and C?

A. `public class A implements B, implements C{ … }`

B. `public class A implements B, C{ … }`

C. `public class A interface B, interface C{ … }`

D. `public class A interface B, C{ … }`

E. `public class A extends B, C{ … }`

15. Consider the following UML illustration for assistance with this question:

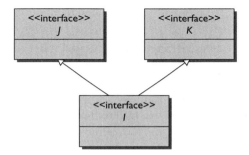

What is the proper signature for interface I to inherit interfaces J and K?

A. `public interface I extends J, K{ … }`

B. `public interface I implements J, K{ … }`

C. `public interface I implements J, implements K{ … }`

D. `public interface I interface J, K{ … }`

SELF TEST ANSWERS

Inheritance and Class Type

1. What contains methods and instance variables and can be instantiated?

    A. Concrete class

    B. Abstract class

    C. Java class

    D. Interface

    Answer:

    ☑ **A.** A concrete class is the standard Java class that is used to create objects.

    ☒ **B, C,** and **D** are incorrect. **B** is incorrect because an abstract class cannot be instantiated. **C** is incorrect because a Java class is a made-up term. **D** is incorrect because an interface does not contain methods and cannot be instantiated.

2. What is used to define a public interface?

    A. Concrete class

    B. Abstract class

    C. Java class

    D. Interface

    Answer:

    ☑ **D.** An interface is used to define a public list of methods that must be implemented by the class. This represents a public interface.

    ☒ **A, B,** and **C** are incorrect. **A** is incorrect because a concrete class is used to build objects. **B** is incorrect because abstract classes are used to define abstract methods for other classes to override. **C** is incorrect because a Java class is a made-up term.

3. What can contain unimplemented methods and instance variables and cannot be instantiated?

    A. Concrete class

    B. Abstract class

    C. Java class

Answer:

☑ **B.** An abstract class must always be extended; it cannot be instantiated to create an object. It can contain implemented and unimplemented methods.

☒ **A** and **C** are incorrect. **A** is incorrect because a concrete class is not able to have any unimplemented methods. **C** is incorrect because a Java class is a made-up term.

4. Inheritance provides which of the following? (Choose all that apply.)

   A. Faster execution times since methods can inherit processor time from superclasses

   B. Allows developers to place general code in a class that more specific classes can gain through inheritance

   C. Promotes code reuse

   D. Is an automated process to transfer old code to the latest Java version

Answer:

☑ **B** and **C.** Both statements are true about inheritance.

☒ **A** and **D** are incorrect. **A** is incorrect because inheritance has no effect on processor scheduling. **D** is incorrect because inheritance has no relationship to the Java version.

5. What is a class being inherited referred to as? (Choose all that apply.)

   A. Subclass

   B. Superclass

   C. Base class

   D. Super duper class

Answer:

☑ **B** and **C.** The class that is inherited is the base class or superclass in reference to the class that extends it.

☒ **A** and **D** are incorrect. **A** is incorrect because the subclass is the class that inherits from another. **D** is incorrect because this is a made-up term.

Encapsulation

Refer to this class for the following two questions.

```java
public class Account {
  private int money;

  public int getMoney() {
    return this.money;
  }

  public void setMoney(int money) {
    this.money = money;
  }
}
```

6. In the code segment, what is the method `getMoney()` considered?

   A. Get method

   B. Access method

   C. Getter method

   D. Instance variable method

   Answer:

   ☑ **C.** This is a getter. Getters are used to retrieve a `private` instance variable. The name of a getter method is always 'get' followed by the variable name with a capital letter. If the variable is a boolean, the 'get' is replaced with 'is'.

   ☒ **A, B,** and **D** are all incorrect terms.

7. In the code segment, what is the method `setMoney(int money)` considered?

   A. Set method

   B. Access method

   C. Setter method

   D. Instance variable method

   Answer:

   ☑ **C.** This is a setter. Setters are used to set a `private` instance variable. The name of a setter method is always 'set', followed by the variable name with a capital letter. They take one argument and use this to set the variable.

   ☒ **A, B,** and **D** are all incorrect terms.

8. Which of the following defines information hiding?

    A. Information hiding is hiding as much detail about your class as possible so others can't steal it.

    B. Information hiding is about hiding implementation details and protecting variables from being used the wrong way.

    C. Information hiding is used to obscure the interworking of your class so external classes must use the public interface.

Answer:

    ☑ **B.** Good class design hides as many methods and instance variables as possible. This is done by using the `private` access modifier. This is so external objects do not try to interact with the object in ways the developer has not intended. Hiding information makes code easier to maintain and more modular.

    ☒ **A and C** are incorrect. **A** is incorrect because information hiding has nothing to do with protecting your code from others. **C** is incorrect because access modifiers should be used to force external classes to use the proper public interface.

9. What access modifier is used to make the instance variable or method only available to the class it is defined in?

    A. `public`

    B. `private`

    C. `protected`

    D. *package-private* (default)

Answer:

    ☑ **B.** The `private` access modifier is used to allow only the methods in the class to access the method or instance variable.

    ☒ **A, C,** and **D** are incorrect. **A** is incorrect because `public` would make the instance variable available to every class. **C** is incorrect because `protected` would make the instance variable available to any subclass or class in the same package. **D** is incorrect because *package-private*, or the default access level, would make the instance variable available to any other class in the same package.

10. What access modifier is used to create an interface for other objects regardless of their package or their base classes?

    A. `public`

    B. `private`

    C. `protected`

    D. *package-private* (default)

    Answer:

    ☑ **A.** The `public` access modifier allows any object in the application to access the instance variable or method.

    ☒ **B, C,** and **D** are incorrect. **B** is incorrect because `private` would make the method only available to the class it is defined in. **C** is incorrect because `protected` would make the method only available to subclasses and classes defined in the same package. **D** is incorrect because *package-private*, or the default access level, would make the method only available to classes defined in the same package.

Advanced Examples of Classes with Inheritance and Encapsulation

11. What is the proper signature for class X if it inherits class Z?

    A. `public class X inherits Z{ ... }`

    B. `public class X extends Z{ ... }`

    C. `public class X implements Z{ ... }`

    Answer:

    ☑ **B.** The `extends` keyword is used to inherit a class.

    ☒ **A** and **C** are incorrect. **A** is incorrect because inherits is not a valid Java keyword. **C** is incorrect because the `implements` keyword is used for interfaces, not classes.

12. How many classes can a class extend directly?

    A. Zero

    B. One

    C. Two

    D. As many as it needs

Answer:

☑ **B.** A class can only extend one other class. However, it is possible to have one class extend a class that extends another class, and so on.

☒ **A, C,** and **D** are incorrect.

13. How many interfaces can a class implement directly?

A. Zero

B. One

C. Two

D. As many as it needs

Answer:

☑ **D.** Unlike extending other classes, a class can implement as many interfaces as it needs.

☒ **A, B,** and **C** are incorrect.

14. Consider the following UML illustration for assistance with this question:

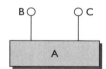

What is the proper signature for class A if it implements interfaces B and C?

A. `public class A implements B, implements C{ … }`

B. `public class A implements B, C{ … }`

C. `public class A interface B, interface C{ … }`

D. `public class A interface B, C{ … }`

E. `public class A extends B, C{ … }`

Answer:

☑ **B.** A class uses the keyword `implements` to implement an interface. To implement multiple interfaces, they are shown in a comma-delimited list after the keyword `implements`.

☒ **A, C, D,** and **E** are incorrect. **A** is incorrect because the `implements` keyword should not be listed more than once. **C** is incorrect because the `implements` keyword should be used instead of interface, and it should be listed only once. **D** is incorrect because `implements` should be used instead of interface. **E** is incorrect because `extends` is used for classes not interfaces; `implements` should be used instead.

15. Consider the following UML illustration for assistance with this question:

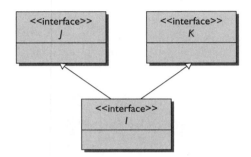

What is the proper signature for interface I to inherit interfaces J and K?

A. `public interface I extends J, K{ … }`

B. `public interface I implements J, K{ … }`

C. `public interface I implements J, implements K{ … }`

D. `public interface I interface J, K{ … }`

Answer:

☑ **A.** An interface can also inherit other interfaces. Unlike classes, they can inherit or extend as many other interfaces as needed. An interface uses the keyword `extends`, followed by a comma-delimited list of all the other interfaces it wants to extend.

☒ **B, C,** and **D** are incorrect. **B** is incorrect because only classes implement interfaces. An interface `extends` other interfaces. **C** is incorrect because `extends` should be used and only listed once. **D** is incorrect because the `interface` keyword is not used correctly.

8

Understanding Polymorphism

CERTIFICATION OBJECTIVES

- Polymorphism

- Practical Examples
  of Polymorphism

✓ Two-Minute Drill

Q&A Self Test

Polymorphism

Exam Objective 1.5   Describe polymorphism as it applies to classes and interfaces, and describe and apply the "program to an interface" principle.

Polymorphism is a fundamental aspect of object-oriented programming languages. Java is no exception to this. Polymorphism allows the developer to write code that is more generic. The generic code is more flexible and allows for easier code reuse, another fundamental object-oriented principle. The concept of programming to an interface is a manifestation of polymorphism. When a developer programs to an interface, polymorphism is used. The developer specifies the interface they are expecting instead of the actual objects. This allows any object to be used with the code as long as it implements the expected interface.

This section will explore how polymorphism works, and what it allows a developer to do. The chapter will also examine the concept of programming to an interface. On the surface polymorphism can look like a complex subject. But don't be deceived. Polymorphism is just an extension of the concepts of inheritance that have already been covered.

Polymorphism

The word *polymorphism* comes from the Greeks and roughly means "many forms." In Java, polymorphism means that one object can take the form, or place of, an object of a different type. Polymorphism can exist when one class inherits another. It can also exist when a class implements an interface. This section will describe how polymorphism can apply in both cases. Finally, this section will demonstrate what polymorphism looks like in Java code. The following topics will be discussed:

- Polymorphism via class inheritance
- Polymorphism via implementing interfaces
- Polymorphism in code

Polymorphism via Class Inheritance

Polymorphism happens when a certain object type is needed and an object of that type or another more specific object is accepted in its place. Remember, an object is a more specific type of another object when it extends that object. For example, a method may require a Human object. When the Child and Adult classes extend the Human class they would each possess all of the functionality of a Human, plus all the more specific functionality of their age. The Child and Adult objects are guaranteed to have all of the methods that a Human object has because they gain them through inheritance. Therefore both the Child and Adult objects would satisfy any operation that required a Human object. This could be continued further with the Shannon and Colleen classes, which each extend the Adult class. Each of the objects created from the Shannon and Colleen classes would have the functionality of the more general Adult and Human classes, and can be used anywhere a Human or Adult object is required.

Polymorphism utilizes the is-a relationship. In Figure 8-1 the Child object is-a Human object, and the Adult object is-a Human object. Both Child and Adult are just specific types of a Human object. Furthermore, the Shannon object is-an Adult object and is-a Human object. This is also true for the Colleen object. The Shannon object is not only a more specific type of Adult object, but also a more specific type of Human object. Any object is a more specific type of an object that it is a subclass of. The is-a relationship is created when an object inherits, or extends, another. Any object that extends another object can be said to have an is-a relationship to the object that it extends. Any object that has an is-a relationship with another can polymorphically be used as that object.

When an object is polymorphically acting as another object, the more specific object is restricted to only using the public interface of the more general object.

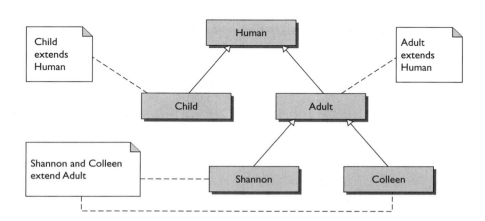

FIGURE 8-1

Polymorphic objects

In the above example, when the `Adult` object is used as a `Human` object, only the methods that are available in the `Human` class can be used. This is because the Java code that is using the `Adult` object as a `Human` object has no knowledge that this `Human` object is really an `Adult` object. This is the benefit of polymorphism. The Java code does not always have to be aware of the specifics of an object. If a general object meets the needs of a method, then that method does not care if it is a general object or more specific object. The only requirement is that the object has an is-a relationship with the object that the method requires.

This relationship is unidirectional. Only the more specific object can take the place of a general object. For example, if an `Adult` object were needed, a more general `Human` object would not be able to provide all of the functionality of an `Adult` object.

Abstract classes and concrete classes behave the same way with polymorphism. Since an abstract class cannot be instantiated, the only way to assign an object to an abstract data type is by using polymorphism. Pay close attention to how abstract classes are initialized.

Polymorphism via Implementing Interfaces

The application of polymorphism is not limited to class inheritance. Polymorphism can also be applied to the objects of classes that implement interfaces. When a class implements an interface, it is then required to implement all of the methods that the interface contains. By doing this, the class is guaranteed to have the functionality that the interface defines. This allows the objects created from these classes to polymorphically behave as the data type of the interface.

An interface called `Display` can be used for classes that have the ability to display text on a screen. This interface contains two methods. One method is used to display text, and the second is used to get the text that is currently being displayed. Any class that implements this interface is declaring to other objects that it has the functionality of a `Display`. By implementing this interface the class is required to then implement every method that the interface contains.

Since the object was created from a class that implements the `Display` interface, it is guaranteed to have the functionality of a display. The object has an is-a relationship with `Display`. This object can now masquerade as an object of the `Display` type. An object can polymorphically act as any interface that its class or any superclass implements.

on the *job*

Polymorphism and interfaces are very powerful tools. They are used extensively on large projects. As a professional developer, it is a good idea to study design patterns. This will provide common reusable software designs that make use of the concepts in this chapter. A good developer not only understands all of the basic concepts, but also knows how to best use them.

Polymorphism in Code

When one specific object can be used as another general object polymorphically, the specific object can be used in place of the more general one without being cast. For example (see Figure 8-2), if class `TypeC` extends `TypeB`, and `TypeB` extends

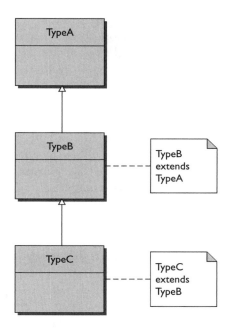

FIGURE 8-2

TypeA, TypeB, and TypeC

TypeA, anytime an object type of TypeA or TypeB is needed, TypeC can be used. The following code segment shows an example of this:

```
TypeA var1 = new TypeA();
TypeA var2 = new TypeB();
TypeA var3 = new TypeC();

TypeB var4 = new TypeB();
TypeB var5 = new TypeC();

TypeC var6 = new TypeC();
```

In this example any subclass can be used interchangeably with its superclass. The variable var3 is declared as a TypeA object but is initialized with a new TypeC object. Even though var3 is really a TypeC object, it will be treated as a TypeA object anywhere var3 is referenced. This is okay because the TypeC object has inherited all of the functionality of the TypeA and TypeB objects. However, since var3 was declared as TypeA, it can now only be treated as an object of this type. If TypeC objects have additional methods that are not part of the TypeA class, these methods would be unavailable.

More commonly, polymorphism will be used for method arguments. This allows a method to be written more abstractly and therefore be more flexible. For instance, a method may be required to accept a type of animal object as its argument and use it to determine if the animal is hungry. In this scenario, there is no benefit in creating a method that would accept a Penguin object and another that accepts a PolarBear object. Instead, it would be a better design to create one single method that accepts an Animal class. The state of hunger is general to the Animal class. The Animal class is a superclass for both the Penguin class and PolarBear class.

These are basic examples to help give more meaning to the concepts of polymorphism. Keep in mind that they are described at a very high level. This chapter will conclude with examples that show polymorphism in greater depth.

Programming to an Interface

Programming to an interface is the concept that code should interact based on a defined set of functionality instead of an explicitly defined object type. In other words, it is better for the public interfaces of objects to use data types that are defined as interfaces as opposed to a particular class when possible. When an object is implementing an interface, it is declaring that it has a certain set of functionalities. Many different classes can implement the same interface and provide its functionality.

By a method using an interface as its argument type, it allows any object, regardless of its type, to be used as long as it implements the interface. This allows the code to be more abstract and flexible. It also promotes code reuse.

w a t c h

This chapter goes deeper into polymorphism than is required for the SCJA exam. This should better help you understand the test questions. Most of the questions on the test either will be a theory question regarding the definition of polymorphism, or will be a simple scenario that will require the SCJA candidate to choose a code segment that is correct.

CERTIFICATION OBJECTIVE

Practical Examples of Polymorphism

Exam Objective 3.4   Develop code that uses polymorphism for both classes and interfaces, and recognize code that uses the "program to an interface" principle.

This section will continue examining polymorphism. While the first section in this chapter approached the topic from a theoretical viewpoint, this section will look at coding examples. These examples are important to understand, and if reviewed carefully, they should provide a clear understanding of the concepts presented in the earlier section.

Examples of Polymorphism

This section will provide examples of polymorphism. The first example will demonstrate how polymorphism can be applied when a class extends another. There is no difference between the use of concrete or abstract classes. The next example demonstrates the use of polymorphism when interfaces are used. These examples will help reinforce the concepts covered in this chapter. The SCJA exam will require knowledge of how to use polymorphism. Understanding these examples will better prepare you for the polymorphism questions on the test.

Examples of Polymorphism via Class Inheritance

The following example is intended to demonstrate the use of polymorphism with class inheritance. This example has three classes. Two classes are used to represent phones. The Phone class is intended to be a simple representation of a standard phone. This class has a method to dial a number, and return the state of whether the phone is ringing or not. The second class represents a smart phone, and is appropriately named SmartPhone. The SmartPhone class extends the Phone class. This class adds the additional functionality of being able to send and receive e-mails. The final class is named Tester and is used as a driver to test both phone classes and demonstrate polymorphism in action. The phone classes are simple representations, and most of their functionality is not implemented. Instead, it is noted as comments regarding its intended purposes. The following is the Phone class:

```
public class Phone {

    public void callNumber(long number) {
        System.out.println("Phone: Calling number " + number);
        /* Logic to dial number and maintain connection. */
    }

    public boolean isRinging() {
        System.out.println("Phone: Checking if phone is ringing");
        boolean ringing = false;
        /* Check if the phone is ringing and set the ringing variable */
        return ringing;
    }
}
```

The Phone class is a simple class used for a normal phone with basic features. The class has a callNumber() method that is used to call the number that is passed as an argument. The isRinging() method is used to determine if the phone is currently ringing. This class prints to standard out its class name and what action it is performing as it enters each method. The Phone class is the base class for the SmartPhone class. The SmartPhone class is listed next.

```
public class SmartPhone extends Phone {

    public void sendEmail(String message, String address) {
        System.out.println("SmartPhone: Sending Email");
```

```
  /* logic to send email message */
}

public String retrieveEmail() {
  System.out.println("SmartPhone: Retrieving Email");
  String messages = new String();
  /* Return a String containing all of the messages*/
  return messages;
}

public boolean isRinging() {
  System.out.println("SmartPhone: Checking if phone is ringing");
  boolean ringing = false;
  /* Check for email activity and only continue when their is none. */
  /* Check if the phone is ringing and set the ringing variable */
  return ringing;
}
}
```

The SmartPhone class represents a smart phone. This class extends the Phone class and therefore inherits its functionality. The SmartPhone class has a sendEmail() method that is used to send an e-mail message. It has a retrieveEmail() method that will return as a String any messages that have not been retrieved yet. This class also has an isRinging() method that overrides the isRinging() method from the superclass Phone. Similar to the Phone class, the SmartPhone class prints to standard out the class name and function it will perform each time it enters a method.

The final class is named Tester. The class has the main() method for the demonstration program. This class exercises all of the methods in the Phone and SmartPhone classes.

```
public class Tester {
  public static void main(String[] args) {
    new Tester();
  }

  public Tester() {
    Phone landLinePhone = new Phone();
    SmartPhone smartPhone = new SmartPhone();
    System.out.println("About to test a land line phone " +
      "as a phone...");
    testPhone(landLinePhone);
    System.out.println("\nAbout to test a smart phone " +
      "as a phone...");
```

```
      testPhone(smartPhone);
      System.out.println("\nAbout to test a smart phone " +
        "as a smart phone...");
      testSmartPhone(smartPhone);
    }

    private void testPhone(Phone phone) {
      phone.callNumber(5559869447);
      phone.isRinging();
    }

    private void testSmartPhone(SmartPhone phone) {
      phone.sendEmail("Hi","edward@scjaexam.com");
      phone.retrieveEmail();
    }
  }
```

The main() method kicks off the program by creating a Tester object and therefore calling Tester() the constructor. The constructor is used to call each test method. In between each method call, it prints a line to standard out that indicates what the programming is doing. The testPhone() method is used to test each method of the Phone class. It accepts a Phone object as an argument. The final method is the testSmartPhone() method. This method tests each method of the SmartPhone class.

The Tester() constructor starts by creating two local variables. The first is called landLinePhone and is a Phone object. The second is called smartPhone and is a SmartPhone object. The constructor then displays a message and calls the testPhone() method with the landLinePhone variable as an argument.

Next, the constructor displays another message and again calls the testPhone() method. The smartPhone variable is used as the argument. The testPhone() method requires a Phone object as its argument, but the example has used a SmartPhone object instead. This is polymorphism. A smart phone is a more specific type of phone. A smart phone can do everything a landline phone can and more. This is represented in the SmartPhone class by it extending Phone. It is important to notice that the testPhone() method is expecting a Phone object as an argument. It is perfectly acceptable if it gets a more specific type of phone. However, any additional method of the more specific class cannot be utilized. Since this method is designed for a Phone object as an argument, it can only use methods declared in the Phone class.

Finally the constructor displays another status message and calls the `testSmartPhone()` method. This method exercises the methods declared in the `SmartPhone` object. Since polymorphism is unidirectional, the `testSmartPhone()` method cannot be called with a `Phone` object as its argument. The following is the output that would be generated by this program:

```
About to test a land line phone as a phone...
Phone: Calling number 5559869447
Phone: Checking if phone is ringing

About to test a smart phone as a phone...
Phone: Calling number 5559869447
SmartPhone: Checking if phone is ringing

About to test a smart phone as a smart phone...
SmartPhone: Sending Email
SmartPhone: Retrieving Email
```

When the `landLinePhone` variable is used with the `testPhone()` method, the output is simply generated from the `Phone` class since it is a `Phone` object. When the `smartPhone` variable is used with the `testPhone()` method, the flow of execution is more complex. Since the `SmartPhone` class extends the `Phone` class, the `SmartPhone` class inherits both the `callNumber()` and `isRinging()` methods. However, the `SmartPhone` class overrides the `isRinging()` method with its own. When the `callNumber()` method is invoked on a `SmartPhone` object, the method in the `Phone` class is used since it is not overridden. However, when the `isRinging()` method is called, the method in the `SmartPhone` class is used. This follows the basic rule of inheritance and overriding methods.

Examples of Polymorphism via Implementing Interfaces

This example will focus on an object's ability to behave polymorphically as an interface that its class implements. This allows objects that may be radically different, but share some common functionality, to be treated similarly. The common functionality is defined in an interface that each class must implement.

This example is composed of three classes and one interface. There is a `Tester` class to test the program. The other two classes are objects representing a goat and a box. Both in this program and conceptually, the objects are very different. A goat is a living animal and a box is an inanimate object. However, they both share a common ability. Both the `Goat` class and the `Box` class can describe themselves. This functionality

INSIDE THE EXAM

Unidirectional Polymorphism

The SCJA exam may try to present the test taker with a polymorphism question where the more general object behaves as the more specific one. Remember, polymorphism only works in one direction. Only specific objects can behave as more general ones.

has been reflected in the fact that they both implement the Describable interface. Classes that implement this interface are required to then implement the getDescription() method. Below is the Describable interface:

```
public interface Describable {
   public String getDescription();
}
```

This interface only has one method. The getDescription() method is used to return a description about the object. Any class that implements this interface is stating it has a method that can be used to get its description. The Goat class is shown next.

```
public class Goat implements Describable {

   private String description;

   public Goat(String name){
      description = "A goat named " + name;
   }

   public String getDescription() {
      return description;
   }
   /*
    * Implement other methods for a goat
    */
}
```

The Goat class is a simple class that can be used to represent a goat. This class implements the Describable interface and therefore is required to implement the getDescription() method. The constructor of the Goat class has one parameter that it uses to place the name of the goat in the description string. The next class in this example is the Box class. It is listed below:

```java
public class Box implements Describable {

    private String description;
    private int height;
    private int width;
    private int length;

    public Box(int height, int width, int length) {
        this.height = height;
        this.width = width;
        this.length = length;
        this.description = "A box that is " + height + " high, "
            + length + " long and " + width + " wide ";
    }

    public String getDescription() {
        return description;
    }
    /*
     * Implement other methods for a box
     */
}
```

The Box class is designed to model a box. Its constructor requires that the dimensions of the box be used as arguments. The constructor also creates the description text that is returned in the getDescription() method. Similar to the Goat class, this class also implements the Describable interface. The final class is the Tester class. This class is used to demonstrate the concept of polymorphism with interfaces.

```java
public class Tester {

    public static void main(String[] args) {
        new Tester();
    }
```

```
public Tester() {
  Goat goat = new Goat("Bob");
  Box box = new Box(3, 5, 3);
  System.out.println(description(goat));
  System.out.println(description(box));
}

private String description(Describable d){
  return d.getDescription();
}
}
```

The `Tester` class contains the `main()` method that starts the execution of the program. This calls the `Tester()` constructor where a `Goat` object and `Box` object are both created. The `description()` method is then used to print to standard out the description of each object. The `description()` method requires a `Describable` object. It is impossible to have a true `Describable` object since it is an interface. However, classes that implement this interface are declaring that they have the functionality of `Describable`. These objects can then polymorphically act as if they were of type `Describable`. Below is the output of this program:

```
A goat named Bob
A box that is 3 high, 3 long and 5 wide
```

EXERCISE 8-1

Add Functionality to the `Describable` Example

This exercise will use the preceding example. The goal of the exercise is to compile and run the above example and add a class that implements the `Describable` interface.

1. Copy the example into the text editor or IDE of your choice.
2. Compile and run the example to ensure the code has been copied correctly.
   Add a new class that implements the `Describable` interface.
3. Compile and run the application.

Examples of Programming to an Interface

This example will demonstrate the concept of programming to an interface. This concept allows a developer to define the functionality that is required instead of defining an actual object type. This creates more flexible code that adheres to the object-oriented design principle of creating reusable code.

A developer may create a class that is used for creating log files. This class is responsible for creating and managing the log file on the file system, and then appending the log messages to it. This class can be called `Logger`. The `Logger` class has a method called `appendToLog()` that accepts one object as an argument and then appends a message about it in the log. The developer could overload this method with every possible data type that the program uses. While this would work, it would be very inefficient. If the program to an interface concept is used, the developer would instead create an interface that defines the required method for a logable class. This interface could be called `Logable`. The `appendToLog()` method would then use the `Logable` interface as its argument. Any class that required logging could implement this interface and then be used polymorphically with the `appendToLog()` method. The following is the `Logable` interface:

```
public interface Logable {
  public String getInitInfo();
  public String getLogableEvent();
}
```

The `Logable` interface is a basic interface that defines the methods required to work with the `appendToLog()` method in the `Logger` class. The `appendToLog()` method is not concerned with the details of an object other than what pertains to logging. By using this interface the developer has defined a functionality requirement as opposed to a strict object data type. This is what is meant when the term programming to an interface is used. The `Logger` class is displayed next.

```
import java.io.BufferedWriter;
import java.io.FileWriter;
import java.io.IOException;

public class Logger {

  private BufferedWriter out;

  public Logger() throws IOException {
    out = new BufferedWriter(new FileWriter("logfile.txt"));
  }
```

```
    public void appendToLog(Logable logable) throws IOException {
      out.write("Object history: " + logable.getInitInfo());
      out.newLine();
      out.write("Object log event: " + logable.getLogableEvent());
      out.newLine();
    }

    public void close() throws IOException {
      out.flush();
      out.close();
    }
  }
```

This is the `Logger` class. This class creates a `BufferedWriter`, which is a means to write to a file. This is beyond the scope of this chapter, and therefore will not be discussed. The `appendToLog()` method is used to write to the log file. This class uses the `Logable` interface to remain flexible. This method will work with any other class that implements this interface and will follow the "program to an interface" concept. The next class is the `NetworkConnection` class. This is a class that implements the `Logable` interface.

```
  public class NetworkConnection implements Logable {

    private long createdTimestamp;
    private String currentLogMessage;

    public NetworkConnection() {
      createdTimestamp = System.currentTimeMillis();
      currentLogMessage = "Initialized";
    }

    public void connect(){
      /*
       * Established connection
       */
      currentLogMessage = "Connected at " + System.currentTimeMillis();
    }

    public String getInitInfo() {
      return "NetworkConnection object created " + createdTimestamp;
    }
```

```
    public String getLogableEvent() {
      return currentLogMessage;
    }
  }
```

This class implements the Logable interface and all of the methods required for it. When this class is polymorphically behaving as the Logable data type, the code being used does not care about the implementation details of the class. As long as the class implements the Logable interface, it is free to choose how the methods are implemented. The SystemStatus class is the other class that uses the Logable interface. It is listed next.

```
  public class SystemStatus implements Logable {

    private long createdTimestamp;

    public SystemStatus() {
      createdTimestamp = System.currentTimeMillis();
    }

    private int getStatus(){
      if(System.currentTimeMillis() - createdTimestamp > 1000){
        return 1;
      }
      else{
        return -1;
      }
    }

    public String getInitInfo() {
      return "SystemStatus object created " + createdTimestamp;
    }

    public String getLogableEvent() {
      return String.valueOf("Status: "+getStatus());
    }
  }
```

The SystemStatus class's only similarity to the NetworkConnection class is that they both implement the Logable interface. This class chooses to implement the required getInitInfo() and getLogableEvent() methods in a different manner than the NetworkConnection class. The final class is the Tester class.

This is a simple class that demonstrates all of the preceding classes and interface in action.

```
public class Tester {

  public static void main(String[] args) throws Exception {
    new Tester();
  }

  public Tester() throws Exception {
    Logger logger = new Logger();
    SystemStatus systemStatus = new SystemStatus();
    NetworkConnection networkConnection = new NetworkConnection();
    logger.appendToLog(systemStatus);
    logger.appendToLog(networkConnection);
    networkConnection.connect();
    Thread.sleep(2000);
    logger.appendToLog(systemStatus);
    logger.appendToLog(networkConnection);
    logger.close();
  }
}
```

The `Tester` class does all of its work in its constructor. The class creates a new `Logger` object called `logger`. It then creates a `SystemStatus` object named `systemStatus` and a `NetworkConnection` object named `networkConnection`. It then uses the `appendToLog()` method from the `Logger` object. This method uses the `Logable` object as a parameter. Since both the `SystemStatus` and `NetworkConnection` classes implement this interface, their objects can be used polymorphically with this method.

```
Object history: SystemStatus object created 1238811437373
Object log event: Status: -1
Object history: NetworkConnection object created 1238811437374
Object log event: Initialized
Object history: SystemStatus object created 1238811437373
Object log event: Status: 1
Object history: NetworkConnection object created 1238811437374
Object log event: Connected at 1238811437374
```

The preceding text is written to the log file.

CERTIFICATION SUMMARY

Polymorphism is a fundamental concept of any object-oriented programming language. This chapter has discussed the fundamental concepts of polymorphism and then demonstrated these concepts through examples. Polymorphism is a tool that can be used to create more reliable code, and produce it faster.

The first part of this chapter defined polymorphism. Polymorphism is the ability to treat an object as if it were a more general object. In other words, a class's object can masquerade as any object that the class uses to derive itself. The benefit is that applications can be written more abstractly. A common form of polymorphism is between classes that extend other classes. A class's object can be treated as any object that it extends, this includes both concrete and abstract classes. Polymorphism also allows an object to be treated as any interface that it implements.

Polymorphism is most commonly used for method arguments. Oftentimes, a method will only require a general object. A more specific object can be used since it will provide all of the functionality of the general object. The is-a relationship can be used to help understand polymorphism. One example is a specific object like `Blue` is-a `Color`. `Blue` is a specific object and extends the `Color` object.

This chapter then covered the benefits of programming to an interface. Programming to an interface allows the developer to specify the capabilities or behaviors that are expected, instead of strictly defining an expected object type. This allows the code to be more abstract and flexible.

The chapter then concluded with examples of polymorphism, and programming to an interface. These examples highlighted all of the important concepts discussed in theory previously in this chapter.

✓ TWO-MINUTE DRILL

Polymorphism

❑ Polymorphism is a fundamental concept of object-oriented languages, including Java.

❑ Polymorphism stimulates code reuse.

❑ Polymorphism allows one object to act as either one of its superclasses, or as an interface that it implements.

❑ A subclass (more specific) "is-a" superclass (more general) object.

❑ Polymorphism is unidirectional. More specific objects can only polymorphically act as more general objects.

❑ By implementing an interface, an object is declaring it has the functionality defined in the interface. This allows that object to polymorphically act as the interface.

❑ Programming to an interface is the concept where the developer defines the required functionality instead of defining strict object data types. This allows other developers to interact with the code using any object they choose as long as it implements the required interfaces.

Practical Examples of Polymorphism

❑ An object can be used interchangeably with any of its superclasses without the need to be cast.

❑ An object can be used interchangeably with any interface that it implements without the need to be cast.

❑ When a more specific object is polymorphically used as a general object, the more specific functionality is not available.

❑ Polymorphism is commonly used for method arguments.

SELF TEST

Polymorphism

I. Which statement is true about the term polymorphism?

    A. It is a Latin word that roughly means "changeable."

    B. It is a Greek word that roughly means "many forms."

    C. It is an Old English word that roughly means "insectlike."

    D. It is a new technical term that means "Java object."

2. What type of object can polymorphically behave as another?

    A. An object can act as any subclass of the class it was created from.

    B. An object can act as any superclass of the class it was created from.

    C. An object can act as any other abstract class.

3. Polymorphism helps to facilitate which of the following? (Choose all that apply.)

    A. Highly optimized code

    B. Code reuse

    C. Code obfuscation

    D. Code that is generic and flexible

4. What is a correct "is-a" relationship?

    A. A specific object "is-a" more generic one.

    B. A generic object "is-a" more specific one.

    C. A null object "is-an" object.

5. Which of the following statements explain why an object can polymorphically behave as an interface?

    A. By implementing the interface, the object is required to have all of the functionality that the interface represents.

    B. By implementing the interface, the object inherits all the required methods it defines.

    C. An object can behave as an interface because interfaces do not have a strict expected behavior and therefore any object can act as an interface.

6. What does it mean if a developer is programming to an interface?

   A. They are implementing an interface for the class they are working on

   B. They were given a set of interfaces they must implement.

   C. They are defining the functionality instead of strict object types as much as possible.

Practical Examples of Polymorphism

The following code example will be referenced in questions 7 through 12. Afterward, see Figure 8-3.

The Drivable interface:

```
public interface Drivable {
/*
 * Drivable definitions
 */
}
```

The Tractor class:

```
public class Tractor implements Drivable{
/*
 * Tractor functionality
 */
}
```

The Vehicle class:

```
public class Vehicle {
/*
 * Vehicle functionality
 */
}
```

The Car class:

```
public class Car extends Vehicle implements Drivable{
/*
 * Car functionality
 */
}
```

The Truck class:

```
public class Truck extends Vehicle implements Drivable{
/*
 * Truck functionality
 */
}
```

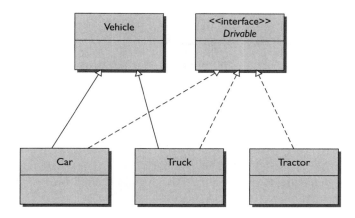

FIGURE 8-3

UML for
questions 7–12

7. Given the preceding classes and interface, would the following code segment produce errors
when compiled?

```
Car car = new Car();
Vehicle vehicle = car;
```

A. No errors would be produced.

B. This code would result in compile errors.

8. Given the preceding classes and interface, would the following code segment produce errors
when compiled?

```
Truck truck = new Truck();
Drivable drivable = truck;
```

A. No errors would be produced.

B. This code would result in compile errors.

9. Given the preceding classes and interface, would the following code segment produce errors
when compiled?

```
Tractor tractor = new Tractor();
Vehicle vehicle = tractor;
```

A. No errors would be produced.

B. This code would result in compile errors.

10. Given the preceding classes and interface, would the following code segment produce errors
when compiled?

```
Drivable drivable = new Drivable();
Truck truck = drivable;
```

    A. No errors would be produced.

    B. This code would result in compile errors.

11. Given the preceding classes and interface, would the following code segment produce errors when compiled?

```
Vehicle vehicle = new Vehicle();
Object o = vehicle;
```

    A. No errors would be produced.

    B. This code would result in compile errors.

12. Given the preceding classes and interface, would the following code segment produce errors when compiled?

```
Truck truck = new Truck();
Object o = truck;
```

    A. No errors would be produced.

    B. This code would result in compile errors.

SELF TEST ANSWERS

Polymorphism

1. Which statement is true about the term polymorphism?

　　A. It is a Latin word that roughly means "changeable."

　　B. It is a Greek word that roughly means "many forms."

　　C. It is an Old English word that roughly means "insectlike."

　　D. It is a new technical term that means "Java object."

> Answer:
>
> ☑ **B.** The word polymorphism comes from the Greeks and means "many forms."
>
> ☒ 　 **A, C,** and **D** are incorrect.

2. What type of object can polymorphically behave as another?

　　A. An object can act as any subclass of the class it was created from.

　　B. An object can act as any superclass of the class it was created from.

　　C. An object can act as any other abstract class.

> Answer:
>
> ☑ **B.** An object inherits all of the functionality of its superclasses, and therefore can polymorphically behave as they do.
>
> ☒ 　 **A** and **C** are incorrect. **A** is incorrect because an object cannot behave as its subclass since this class is more specific and contains functionality that is not present in the superclass. **C** is incorrect because there needs to be an "is-a" relationship between the classes. This answer does not mention what the relationship is.

3. Polymorphism helps to facilitate which of the following? (Choose all that apply.)

　　A. Highly optimized code

　　B. Code reuse

　　C. Code obfuscation

　　D. Code that is generic and flexible

Chapter 8: Understanding Polymorphism

Answer:

☑ **B** and **D.** Polymorphism aids in creating reusable code because it allows the code to be written more abstractly, thus **B** is correct. Similar to B, polymorphism allows the code to be generic by using generic data types that any more specific object can fulfill. Thus, **D** is also correct.

☒ **A** and **C** are incorrect. **A** is incorrect because polymorphism has no effect on the level of optimization of the code. **C** is incorrect because obfuscated code (code that is intentionally hard to read) is not related to polymorphism.

4. What is a correct "is-a" relationship?

A. A specific object "is-a" more generic one.

B. A generic object "is-a" more specific one.

C. A null object "is-an" object.

Answer:

☑ **A.** A more specific object can be considered to be a more generic one. This is the fundamental principle of polymorphism.

☒ **B** and **C** are incorrect. **B** is incorrect because generic objects do not have all of the functionality of more specific ones and therefore do not possess an "is-a" relationship with the specific objects. **C** is incorrect because a null object has no effect on its relationship with other objects.

5. Which of the following statements explain why an object can polymorphically behave as an interface?

A. By implementing the interface, the object is required to have all of the functionality that the interface represents.

B. By implementing the interface, the object inherits all the required methods it defines.

C. An object can behave as an interface because interfaces do not have a strict expected behavior and therefore any object can act as an interface.

Answer:

☑ **A.** When a class implements an interface it is then required to implement all the methods the interface contains. This gives the class the functionality defined in the interface and therefore allows this class to behave as the interface.

☒ **B** and **C** are incorrect. **B** is incorrect because nothing is inherited when an interface is implemented. **C** is incorrect because each interface has a strict behavior expected of it. This is represented by the methods that must be implemented.

6. What does it mean if a developer is programming to an interface?

    A. They are implementing an interface for the class they are working on.

    B. They were given a set of interfaces they must implement.

    C. They are defining the functionality instead of strict object types as much as possible.

Answer:

    ☑ **C.** Programming to an interface means that a developer is defining functionality instead of object data types. This allows any objects to be used with this code as long as they implement the interface.

    ☒ **A** and **B** are incorrect. **A** is incorrect because programming to an interface is a larger concept than just implementing one interface in one class. **B** is incorrect because, in this situation, the developer is just implementing a group of interfaces that have been predetermined.

Practical Examples of Polymorphism

The following code example will be referenced in questions 7 through 12.

The `Drivable` interface:

```
public interface Drivable {
/*
 * Drivable definitions
 */
}
```

The `Tractor` class:

```
public class Tractor implements Drivable{
/*
 * Tractor functionality
 */
}
```

The `Vehicle` class:

```
public class Vehicle {
/*
 * Vehicle functionality
 */
}
```

The Car class:

```
public class Car extends Vehicle implements Drivable{
/*
 * Car functionality
 */
}
```

The Truck class:

```
public class Truck extends Vehicle implements Drivable{
/*
 * Truck functionality
 */
}
```

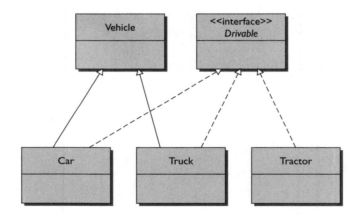

FIGURE 8-3

UML for
questions 7–12

7. Given the preceding classes and interface, would the following code segment produce errors when compiled?

```
Car car = new Car();
Vehicle vehicle = car;
```

A. No errors would be produced.

B. This code would result in compile errors.

Answer:

☑ **A.** No errors would be produced because the Car class extends the Vehicle class and therefore can be used as a Vehicle object.

8. Given the preceding classes and interface, would the following code segment produce errors when compiled?

   ```
   Truck truck = new Truck();
   Drivable drivable = truck;
   ```

   A. No errors would be produced.

   B. This code would result in compile errors.

   Answer:

   ☑ **A.** No errors would be produced because the `Truck` class implements the `Drivable` interface and therefore can be used as a `Drivable` object.

9. Given the preceding classes and interface, would the following code segment produce errors when compiled?

   ```
   Tractor tractor = new Tractor();
   Vehicle vehicle = tractor;
   ```

   A. No errors would be produced.

   B. This code would result in compile errors.

   Answer:

   ☑ **B.** This code would result in compile errors because the `Vehicle` class is not a superclass for the `Tractor` class.

10. Given the preceding classes and interface, would the following code segment produce errors when compiled?

    ```
    Drivable drivable = new Drivable();
    Truck truck = drivable;
    ```

    A. No errors would be produced.

    B. This code would result in compile errors.

    Answer:

    ☑ **B.** This code would result in compile errors because the `Drivable` interface cannot be instantiated since it is an interface.

11. Given the preceding classes and interface, would the following code segment produce errors when compiled?

```
Vehicle vehicle = new Vehicle();
Object o = vehicle;
```

A. No errors would be produced.

B. This code would result in compile errors.

Answer:

☑ **A.** No errors would be produced because the `Vehicle` class is concrete, and the `Object` class is the superclass for every Java object.

12. Given the preceding classes and interface, would the following code segment produce errors when compiled?

```
Truck truck = new Truck();
Object o = truck;
```

A. No errors would be produced.

B. This code would result in compile errors.

Answer:

☑ **A.** No errors would be produced because the `Object` class is the superclass for all Java objects.

9

Representing Object-Oriented Concepts with UML

CERTIFICATION OBJECTIVES

- Recognizing Representations of Significant UML Elements

- Recognizing Representations of UML Associations

✓   Two-Minute Drill

Q&A   Self Test

The Unified Modeling Language (UML) is a specification that defines a modeling language for the specification, presentation, construction, and documentation of object-oriented system elements. The UML standard is the culmination of the works from James Rumbaugh's object-modeling technique, Grady Booch's "Booch method," and Ivar Jacobson's object-oriented software engineering method. The collaborative effort of this trio has crowned them with the name, "The Three Amigos." The origins of their efforts leading to the UML standard are detailed in Table 9-1.

The modern UML specification, maintained by the Object Management Group (OMG), has gone through several revisions as represented in Table 9-2. The current UML 2.X.X specification is comprised of two parts: the OMG UML Infrastructure Specification version 2.X.X and the OMG UML Superstructure Specification version 2.X.X. The Infrastructure specification has a tighter focus based around class-based structures and houses all of the basic information needed for the exam. The Superstructure specification details user-level constructs and cross-references the Infrastructure specification in such a manner that the two parts may be integrated into one volume in the future. The current versions of the specifications are obtainable from the OMG at www.omg.org/spec/UML/Current. In short, this chapter will teach you how to recognize the main diagram elements and relationships used by UML, fulfilling the needs of the two UML "recognition" objectives. And while the formal OMG UML specification may be useful, it is not required reading material for the exam.

| TABLE 9-1 | Object Methodologies Preceding the Unified Modeling Language |

Methodologists	Method(s)	Emphasis	Circa
James Rumbaugh, Michael Blaha, William Premerlani, Frederick Eddy, William Lorensen	Object Modeling Technique (OMT)	Object-oriented analysis (OOA)	1991
Ivar Jacobson	Objectory, object-oriented software engineering (OOSE) method	Object-oriented software engineering (OOSE)	1992
Grady Booch	Booch method	Object-oriented design (OOD)	1993

TABLE 9-2   Evolving UML Specifications

OMG Formal UML Specifications	Official Release Date	Significant Release Changes
UML 2.2	February 2009	Adoption of the profile diagram, various revisions.
UML 2.1.2	November 2007	Various minor revisions and bug fixes have been resolved.
UML 2.1.1	August 2007	Minor updates including implementation of redefinition and bidirectional association.
UML 2.0	July 2005	For this major release, several changes, enhancements, and additions have been made, including enhanced support for structural and behavior models.
UML 1.3, UML 1.4.X, UML 1.5	Various	Various minor revisions and bug fixes have been resolved.
UML 1.1	November 1997	The OMG formally adopted UML.

on the **job**

The SCJA exam requires minimum knowledge of the UML Infrastructure and Superstructure specifications. Of the 14 UML diagram types, the class diagram is the only diagram type on the exam. There is value in understanding UML diagrams and features that are outside the scope of this exam. So in your independent research on UML, don't ignore the other diagram types since this knowledge will surely come in handy later for you at work.

The complete set of 14 UML diagrams from the UML 2.2 standard is shown in Table 9-3.

TABLE 9-3   Types of UML Diagrams

Structure Diagram	Behavior Diagram	Interaction Diagram
Class diagram (on the exam)	Activity diagram	Communication diagram
Component diagram	State machine diagram	Interaction overview diagram
Composite structure diagram	Use case diagram	Sequence diagram
Deployment diagram		Timing diagram
Object diagram		
Package diagram		
Profile diagram		

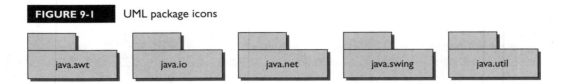

FIGURE 9-1   UML package icons

Two closely related UML objectives are on the SCJA exam. One objective relates to the recognitions of simple class structure artifacts and basic OO principles. The other relates to depicting UML features related to class relationships. To start with your first UML element, or in this case let's call it an icon, we'll take a look at the exam-related package icons represented in Figure 9-1. The package icons are typically represented by a folder with the package name located in the top-left compartment (also known as the tab). The package name may also be optionally placed into the larger compartment (as shown in Figure 9-1), as is commonly done when no other UML elements are enclosed in the package icon. Note that the package icon is not on the test, but we include it in many of the diagrams to show packages that enclose depicted classes.

It's now a good time to look at the core UML information that will be on the exam. This chapter is filled with details on the representation of these UML elements. When you have completed the chapter, you will be able to recognize all of the core UML elements, as well as relationships between elements.

CERTIFICATION OBJECTIVE

Recognizing Representations of Significant UML Elements

Exam Objective 2.1   Recognize the UML representation of classes, (including attributes and operations, abstract classes, and interfaces), the UML representation of inheritance (both implementation and interface), and the UML representation of class member visibility modifiers (-/private and +/public).

Getting acquainted with the different UML elements can actually be quite fun, and the sense of accomplishment when mastering the art of reading and writing class relationship diagrams with UML is equally rewarding.

Sun's first UML-related certification objective is geared toward the class diagrams themselves. Attributes and operations compartments and visibility modifiers are also covered. Once you work though this section, you will know how to recognize the basic class elements of UML. To a strong fundamental extent, you will also be able to create UML diagrams from code and vice versa. The topics listed next will be covered in the following subsections:

- Classes, abstract classes, and interface diagrams
- Attributes and operations
- Visibility modifiers

Classes, Abstract Classes, and Interface Diagrams

One of the simplest ways to represent classes and interfaces in UML is to show the class diagrams with only their name compartments. This holds true as well with representing interface implementations and class inheritances. Figure 9-2 depicts two interfaces, two classes, one abstract class, and their generalization and realization relationships. Abstract classes, concrete classes, and interfaces are all represented in a rectangle with their names in boldface. Abstract classes are italicized. Interfaces are prefaced by the word interface between guillemet characters (for example, <<interface>>). An interface can be optionally depicted with its name aside the lollipop element.

on the **Items contained between guillemet characters are considered to be**
job **stereotypes. Stereotypes are extensibility mechanisms that allow designers to extend the vocabulary of UML by creating new model elements.**

The generalization and realization relationships between the classes in Figure 9-2 are further explained in the following sections.

FIGURE 9-2

Class diagram

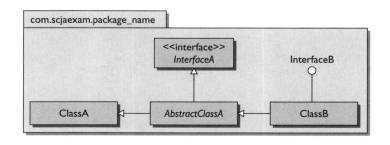

Generalization

Generalization is expressed as an is-a relationship where a class allows its more general attributes and operations to be inherited. In Figure 9-2, `ClassB` inherits from `AbstractClassA` and also from `ClassA`. `AbstractClassA` inherits from `ClassA`. We can also say `ClassB` is-an `AbstractClassA`, `ClassB` is-a `ClassA`, and `AbstractClassA` is-a `ClassA`. We could also say that `ClassA` and `AbstractClassA` are superclasses to `ClassB`, and appropriately, `ClassB` would be their subclass. The generalization class relationship is depicted with a solid line and a closed arrowhead.

Realization

Realization is the general principle of implementing an interface. `AbstractClassA` implements the `InterfaceA` interface. `ClassB` implements the `InterfaceB` interface. The realization class relationship is depicted with a dotted line and a closed solid arrowhead or the lollipop element.

Code Engineering from UML Diagrams

UML provides many benefits; it is not limited to just explaining existing code. When a system architect or system designer models the classes for a particular application, someone will need to develop code to those models. Many UML modeling tools can automatically generate the code structure for these models. However, most coders will use UML as a guide and choose to begin their coding from scratch. Let's examine what the code would look like for each of the elements in Figure 9-2 with the following Scenario & Solution.

SCENARIO & SOLUTION

You need to write the code for the `ClassA` class. What will it look like?	`public ClassA {}`
You need to write the code for the `ClassB` class. What will it look like?	`public ClassB extends AbstractClassA implements InterfaceB {}`
You need to write the code for the `AbstractClassA` class. What will it look like?	`public AbstractClassA extends ClassA implements InterfaceA {}`
You need to write the code for the `InterfaceA` interface. What will it look like?	`public interface InterfaceA {}`
You need to write the code for the `InterfaceB` interface. What will it look like?	`public interface InterfaceB {}`

UML features are commonly integrated into many tools such as Computer-Aided Software Engineering (CASE) tools and Integrated Development Environments (IDEs) such as Sparx Systems Enterprise Architect and Sun Java Studio Enterprise IDE, respectively. An added benefit of UML integration with these tools is forward and reverse code engineering. As such, generating UML from code can be beneficial when taking over an existing project. This is because you will be able to clearly see a class relationship in the UML diagrams.

Attributes and Operations

Attributes, also known as member variables, define the state of a class. Operations, sometimes called member functions, detail the methods of a class. Let's take a look at adding attributes and operations to a class UML diagram. The following is a code listing for an arbitrary `PrimeNumber` class. We will depict this class with UML.

```java
import java.util.ArrayList;
import java.util.List;
public class PrimeNumber {
  private Boolean isPrime = true;
  private Double primeSquareRoot = null;
  private List<String> divisorList = new ArrayList<String>();
  public PrimeNumber(long candidate) {
    validatePrime(candidate);
  }
  public void validatePrime(Long c) {
    primeSquareRoot = Math.sqrt(c);
    isPrime = true;
    for (long j = 2; j <= primeSquareRoot.longValue(); j++) {
      if ((c % j) == 0) {
        divisorList.add(j + "x" + c / j);
        isPrime = false;
      }
    }
  }
  public List getDivisorList() {
    return divisorList;
  }
  public Double getPrimeSquareRoot() {
    return primeSquareRoot;
  }
  public Boolean getIsPrime() {
```

```
      return isPrime;
    }
    public void setIsPrime(Boolean b) {
      isPrime = b;
    }
}
```

Before we actually look at the associated UML diagram(s), let's examine the scope and required format for the information within the attributes and operations compartments.

Attributes Compartment

The attributes compartment houses the classes' attributes, also known as member variables. The attributes compartment is optionally present under the name compartment of the class diagram. The UML usage for each variable of the attributes compartment is detailed, but for the scope of the test you will only need to be concerned with the following optionally condensed attributes format:

```
[<visibility>] <variable_name> [: <type>] [= default_value]
```

Here, visibility defines the optionally displayed visibility modifier. The name would be the variable's name, and the type would be the type of the variable.

Operations Compartment

The operations compartment houses the classes' operations, also known as member functions or methods. The operations compartment is optionally present under the attributes compartment of the class diagram. If the attributes compartment is excluded, then the operations compartment may reside under the name compartment of the class diagram. The UML usage for each method of the operations compartment is detailed, but for the scope of the test, you will only need to be concerned with the following optionally condensed operations format:

```
[<visibility>] <method_name> [<parameter-list>] [: <return-type>]
```

Here, visibility defines the optionally displayed visibility modifier. The name would be the method's name, the optionally displayed parameter-list is just as it says, and this is the same for the return-type.

Displaying the Attributes and Operations Compartments

The display of level-of-detail information in regards to most UML elements is optional. This is true for the member variables and methods in the attributes and operations compartments as well. Figure 9-3 shows a more complete usage as defined in the compartment sections.

In Figure 9-4, a more condensed representation of attributes and operations usages is shown with the following:

For attributes: `<variable_name> [: <type>]`

For operations: `<method_name> [<parameter-list>]`

Both representations are valid, and by taking the time to completely understand this, it will lessen your confusion when taking the exam.

on the

ⓘob *Know your audience when creating UML diagrams. Sometimes class diagrams without representations of the attributes and operations compartments may be more appropriate for a given presentation or document. If you took the time to create these compartments or generated them from the code, you won't necessarily have to discard your work. Many UML tools allow you to hide the attributes and operations compartments in the diagrams via checkbox selections in configuration dialog boxes.*

FIGURE 9-3

Detailed
attributes and
operations
compartments

PrimeNumber
− divisorList: List<String> = new ArrayList<S…   − isPrime: Boolean = true   − primeSquareRoot: Double = null
+ getDivisorList() : List   + getIsPrime() : Boolean   + getPrimeSquareRoot() : Double   + PrimeNumber(candidate : long)   + setIsPrime(b : Boolean) : void   + validatePrime(c : Long) : void

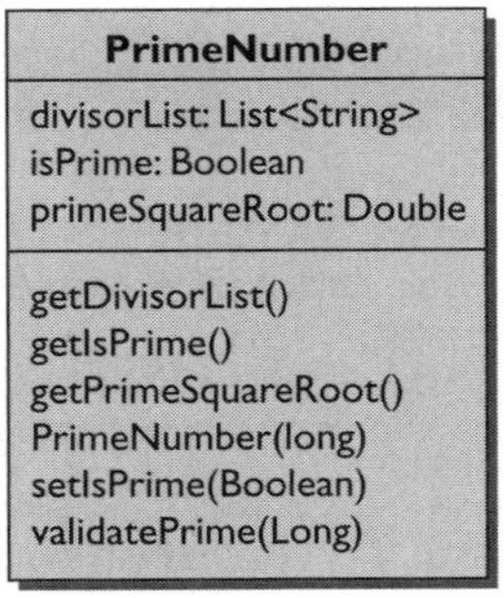

FIGURE 9-4

Abbreviated
attributes and
operations
compartments

PrimeNumber
divisorList: List<String> isPrime: Boolean primeSquareRoot: Double
getDivisorList() getIsPrime() getPrimeSquareRoot() PrimeNumber(long) setIsPrime(Boolean) validatePrime(Long)

Visibility Modifiers

As you are aware, there are four access modifiers: public, private, protected, and *package-private*. These modifiers are depicted with symbols in UML and are used as shorthand in the attributes and operations compartments of a class diagram. These symbols are known as visibility modifiers or visibility indicators. The visibility indicator for the public access modifier is the plus sign (+). The visibility indicator for the private access modifier is the minus sign (−), while the visibility indicator for the protected access modifier is the pound sign (#), and the visibility indicator for the *package-private* modifier is the tilde (~) modifier. The protected and *package-private* visibility indicators are not on the exam. All four visibility modifiers are depicted in Figure 9-5 within the attributes and operations compartments. Visibility indicators are also optional and need not be displayed.

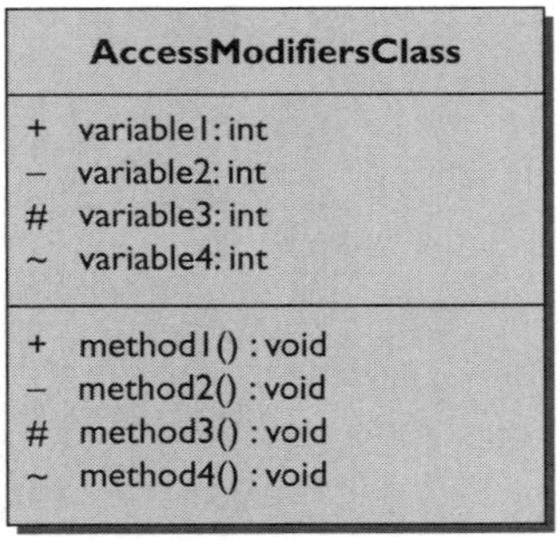

FIGURE 9-5

Visibility
modifiers

AccessModifiersClass
+   variable1: int −   variable2: int #   variable3: int ~   variable4: int
+   method1() : void −   method2() : void #   method3() : void ~   method4() : void

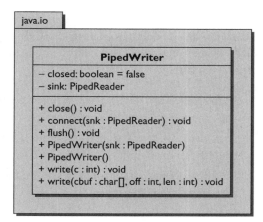

FIGURE 9-6

Tight
encapsulation

You may need to know when a class is tightly encapsulated. You can look for the presence of "only" `private (-)` *visibility indicators in the attributes compartment. When all of the instance variables have* `private` *access modifiers, you will know that there is no state of the object that can be directly accessed from outside of the class, thus tight encapsulation is achieved. An example is represented in Figure 9-6.*

Several UML modeling tools are both freely and commercially available in the marketplace. Being familiar with these tools will make you more productive in the workplace, will assist in collaboration, and will ultimately give you a more professional edge.

EXERCISE 9-1

Creating a Basic UML Diagram with a UML Tool

This exercise will have you creating a UML diagram with a UML modeling tool. At a minimum, UML modeling tools allow for the quick creation of professional-quality diagrams. We have chosen the evaluation version of Enterprise Architect (EA) for you to use to build a basic UML Class relationship diagram. For the exercise, you may choose a different modeling tool instead of EA—just do a web search on a string similar to "UML modeling tools." This exercise does include the initial installation steps of Enterprise Architect.

1. Using a web browser, go to the Sparx Systems main web site since they are the commercial vendor for Enterprise Architect: www.sparxsystems.com/.

2. Provided that the web site's main page has not changed, click the "Test drive the 30-day trial" link.

3. Find the download button, click it, and follow all the necessary instructions to a complete installation. Make sure you create a desktop shortcut to the EA application.

4. Double-click the Enterprise Architect icon on your desktop. The application will launch.

5. Click the menu buttons File | New Project.

6. In the File Name: edit box, type in the name of the exercise project: **SCJA EA Exercise.eap**.

7. When the Select model(s) dialog box opens, select Common from the Select From: combo box and choose the Class checkbox. Click OK.

8. Click the menu buttons Project | Add Package. The Create New View dialog box will be displayed. In the Name edit box, type the name of the diagram, **Class Diagram Exercise**. Select the Class View radio button. Click OK.

9. In the Project Browser pane, click Class Diagram Exercise.

10. Click the menu buttons Project | Add Diagram. The New Diagram dialog box will open. Select UML Structural and Class from the list boxes. Click OK. Congratulations, you are now ready to create your first UML diagram with a CASE tool.

11. Drag the Class icon from the toolbox into the diagram area. The Class1 dialog box will be displayed. Click OK.

12. Drag another Class icon from the toolbox into the diagram area and release the mouse. The Class2 dialog box will be displayed. Click OK.

13. Single-click the generalization association element. Click Class2 in the diagram, hold the mouse button and drag up to Class1, and then release. The generalization element will connect the two class diagrams. The end result should look like the image in the following Illustration:

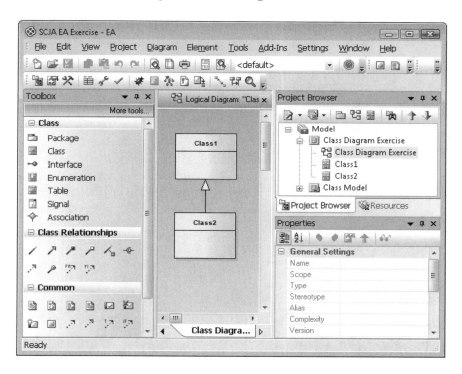

CERTIFICATION OBJECTIVE

Recognizing Representations of UML Associations

Exam Objective 2.2   Recognize the UML representation of class associations, compositions, association multiplicity indicators, and association navigation indicators.

The previous section solidified your knowledge of basic class diagrams and their main components. This next objective focuses on the relationships between classes in regards to their associations and compositions. Multiplicity indicators and role names are detailed as well to assist in specifying the relationships between classes. When you have completed this chapter, you will know how to recognize connectors used between classes and how to interpret any specified multiplicity indicators and role names. The following topics will be covered:

- Graphic paths
- Relationship specifiers

Graphic Paths

The structure diagram graphic paths, also defined as class relationships, that are included on the SCJA exam include notations for aggregation, association, composition, and dependency, as depicted in Figure 9-7. Generalization and realization graphic paths are also on the exam, but these were covered in the previous objective.

FIGURE 9-7

Graphic path notations

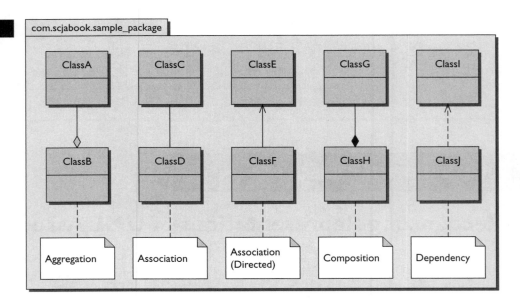

Aggregation Association   Aggregation association depicts one class as the owner of one or more classes. Aggregation is depicted with a solid line and an unfilled diamond. The diamond is on the side of the classifier. In Figure 9-7, you could say that a `ClassA` object is part of a `ClassB` object.

Association   An association that is not marked by navigability arrows is implied to be navigable in both directions; therefore, each association end is owned by the opposite classifier. Association is depicted with a solid line. In Figure 9-7, you could say there is an association between `ClassC` and `ClassD` objects.

Directed Association   An association has (directed) navigation when it is marked with a navigability arrow, also described as a stick arrow. This directed association's arrow denotes navigation in the direction of that end, the classifier has ownership of the marked association end, and the unmarked association's end is owned by the association. In addition to the navigability arrow, directed association is depicted with a solid line. In Figure 9-7, you could say that a `ClassE` object has a `ClassF` object.

Composition   Composition association depicts a class being composed of one or more classes. The component parts/classes only live as long as the composite class. Composition is depicted with a solid line and a filled diamond. The diamond is on the side of the classifier. In Figure 9-7, you could say that a `ClassH` object is composed of one or more `ClassG` objects.

Dependency   Dependency association depicts one class having a temporary association with another class. Dependency associations occur when a class needs another class to exist or when an object is used as a return value, local variable, or method argument. Dependency is depicted with a dotted line and a stick arrow. In Figure 9-7, you could say that a `ClassJ` object depends on a `ClassI` object.

As you probably noticed upon reading through the explanations of the relationships, class relationships can be written out using catchphrases between the objects. Common relationship catchphrases include "has-a", "is-a", "is composed of", "is part of", and "uses-a".

Notes   Notes are represented in UML as a rectangle with an upper-right folded corner. Comments are placed into the notes element and a dotted line is drawn from the notes element to the artifact being commented on.

SCENARIO & SOLUTION

You wish to textually represent a direct association. Fill in the blank: ClassA _____ ClassB	ClassA has a ClassB
You wish to textually represent generalization. Fill in the blank: ClassA _____ ClassB	ClassA is a ClassB, ClassA is derived from ClassB
You wish to textually represent a temporary association. Fill in the blank: ClassA _____ ClassB	ClassA uses a ClassB, ClassA depends on ClassB
You wish to textually represent an aggregate association. Fill in the blank: ClassA _____ ClassB	ClassA is part of ClassB, ClassB aggregates ClassA
You wish to textually represent a composition association. Fill in the blank: ClassA _____ ClassB	ClassA is composed of ClassB

on the
Job

Design patterns are commonly used when developing and refactoring Java applications. Using UML to depict class relationships (during design or reverse-code engineering) can help in determining the appropriate use and/or need of existing design patterns. A valuable resource for design patterns is Design Patterns: Elements of Reusable Object-Oriented Software *by Erich Gamma, Richard Helm, Ralph Johnson, and John M. Vlissides (Addison-Wesley, November 1994). For Java EE design patterns, reference* Core J2EE Patterns: Best Practices and Design Strategies (2nd Edition) *by Deepak Alur, Dan Malks, and John Crupi (May 2003).*

EXERCISE 9-2

Hand-Drawing UML Diagrams from the Java API Specification

In this exercise, you will use your UML skills to hand-draw UML diagrams for classes and interfaces of your own selection from the Java Platform, Standard Edition online API Specification.

1. With a web browser, go to the online Java Platform, Standard Edition API Specification. Optionally you can view API documentation at JDocs. JDocs (www.jdocs.com/) provides a more comprehensive approach to viewing the API information, including viewing options of the source code.

2. Select a package from the online API. You will see summary listings of interfaces, classes, and exceptions. Note: To stay within the scope of this exam, you may wish to work with packages specified in Objective 5.3. These packages are `java.awt`, `java.swing`, `java.io`, `java.net`, and `java.util`.

3. Click a link to the documentation of a concrete class, abstract class, or interface. The documentation will show you the known superclasses, subclasses, superinterfaces, and subinterfaces of your selection, as well as detailed state and operations information.

4. You now have in front of you all the input criteria necessary to hand-draw UML diagrams of classes and/or interfaces. For the element you have selected, depict in UML the name, attributes, and operations compartments. Optionally, you can draw out the relationships it has with other classes and interfaces.

5. To validate your work, reference the sections within this chapter.

If you feel really adventurous, you can reverse-code engineer some of the Java SE API classes with a UML modeling tool. You'll need to download the source code for the desired Java SE API first. Once you have reverse-engineered the code, you will be able to directly validate/compare your hand-drawn UML diagrams with the diagrams produced by the UML modeling tool.

Relationship Specifiers

Sometimes depicting class relationships with the basic UML elements such as class diagrams and connectors is not enough to convey the true relationship between classes. A reader may clearly see there is a relationship, but may wish to know more in regards to the constraints and high-level interaction. Multiplicity indicators and role names are specifiers used to further define and clarify these relationships.

Multiplicity Indicators

Multiplicity indicators are numerical representations used to depict the number of objects that may or must be used in an association. Table 9-4 defines the meanings of the different multiplicity indicators. If an association end does not show a multiplicity indicator, then the value is assumed to be 1. Multiplicity indicators can take the form of a single value or can be represented as a bounded relationship (`<lowerbound>..<upperbound>`).

TABLE 9-4	Multiplicity Indicators and Their Meanings	
Multiplicity Indicator	**Example**	**Meaning of the Multiplicity Indicator**
*	*	Object(s) of the source class may be aware of many objects of the destination class.
0	0	Object(s) of the source class are not aware of any objects of the destination class. This notation is not typically used.
1	1	Objects(s) of the source class must be aware of exactly one object of the destination class.
[x]	10	Object(s) of the source class must be aware of the specified number of objects of the destination class.
0..*	0..*	Object(s) of the source class may be aware of zero or more objects of the destination class.
0..1	0..1	Object(s) of the source class may be aware of zero or one object of the destination class.
0..[x]	0..5	Object(s) of the source class may be aware of zero or more objects of the destination class.
1..*	1..*	Objects(s) of the source class must be aware of one or more objects of the destination class.
1..[x]	1..7	Object(s) of the source class must be aware of one or up to the specified number of objects of the destination class.
[x]..[y]	3..9	Object(s) of the source class must be aware of the objects of the destination class within the specified range.
[x]..[y],[z]	4..7,10	Object(s) of the source class must be aware of the objects of the destination class within the specified range or the specified number.

Multiplicity indicators in use are represented in Figure 9-8. Here you see the following: ResearchStation objects must be aware of twenty or more ResearchBuoy objects. ResearchBuoy objects must be aware of at least one ResearchStation. Each ResearchBuoy must be composed of 0 or more GpsDevice objects.

FIGURE 9-8

Multiplicity indicators

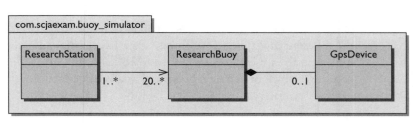

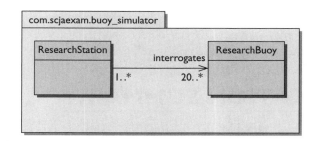

FIGURE 9-9

Association
role name

Association Role Names

Role names are commonly used to clarify the usage of the associated objects and their multiplicities. In Figure 9-9, we see that the `ResearchStation` interrogates the `ResearchBuoy`. Without this descriptive role name, the relationship may have

INSIDE THE EXAM

Object-Oriented Principles and UML

In order to perform well against the more advanced UML questions you may find on the exam, you'll need to understand object-oriented principles thoroughly. These areas include multiple inheritance, polymorphism, tight encapsulation, and so forth. This chapter only touches on the conceptual UML representation of these concepts. For a more in-depth review of the concepts themselves, go back and revisit the object-oriented chapters of this book.

You may find some questions on the exam where more than one object-oriented principle is represented. You'll need to be able to clearly discern these principles. If there is the slightest bit of confusion on your part, the UML elements will only add to the complexity of the situation. Take the extra effort to know your object-oriented principles.

been unclear. We can also deduce that the `ResearchStation` object is aware of twenty `ResearchBuoy` objects, and each `ResearchBuoy` object is associated with one or more `ResearchStation` objects.

CERTIFICATION SUMMARY

The Unified Modeling Language (UML) is a specification that defines a modeling language for the specification, presentation, construction, and documentation of object-oriented system elements. Even though the UML specification defines the model for several diagrams, the class diagram is the sole focus of the exam. UML depictions of concrete classes, abstract classes, and interfaces are represented on the exam, along with their class relationship principles of generalization and realization. It was reviewed that generalization is the principle of class inheritance, and realization is the principle of interface implementation. We learned in this chapter how to depict these associations with UML. We also used structure diagram graphic paths, known as class relationships, which included notations for association, directed association, aggregation, composition, and dependency. Multiplicity indicators, the numerical representations used to depict the number of objects that may or must be used in an association, were covered as well. Finally, visibility indicators were discussed in regards to UML representation of access modifiers.

TWO-MINUTE DRILL

Recognizing Representations of Significant UML Elements

- ❏ Concrete classes are modeled as a boldface name in a rectangular box.
- ❏ Abstract classes are modeled as a boldface italicized name in a rectangular box.
- ❏ Interfaces are modeled as a boldface name, prefaced by the stereotype word interface enclosed in guillemet characters (<<interface>>).
- ❏ Generalization is the concept of inheriting a class.
- ❏ Generalization can be represented as ClassB extends ClassA.
- ❏ Generalization can be represented as ClassB is-a ClassA.
- ❏ Generalization's graphic path is a solid line and a closed arrowhead.
- ❏ Realization is the concept of implementing an interface.
- ❏ Realization can be represented as ClassB implements InterfaceA.
- ❏ Realization's graphic path is depicted with a dotted line and a closed arrowhead.
- ❏ Realization can be represented with the lollipop element and interface name.
- ❏ The attributes compartment is optional and extends off of the name compartment of the class diagram.
- ❏ The attributes compartment houses the member variables, also known as the state of the system.
- ❏ The SCJA condensed usage for individual member variables within the attributes compartment is:

  `[<visibility>] <name> [: <type>]`

- ❏ The operations compartment is optional and extends off of the bottom of the class box and is below the attributes compartment if it is present.
- ❏ The operations compartment houses the member functions, also known as the methods.
- ❏ The SCJA condensed usage for individual member functions within the operations compartment is:

  `[<visibility>] <name> [<parameter-list>] [: <return-type>]`

❑ Four visibility indicators are used to represent access modifiers in UML.

❑ The plus sign (+) is used to represent the `public` access modifier.

❑ The minus sign (-) is used to represent the `private` access modifier.

❑ The pound sign (#) is used to represent the `protected` access modifier.

❑ The tilde sign (~) is used to represent the *package-private* default modifier.

❑ Only the `public` and `private` visibility indicators are on the test.

Recognizing Representations of UML Associations

❑ The association class relationship depicts the knowledge or services of another class.

❑ The directed association class relationship depicts the services of another class, as well as defining its destination class.

❑ The composition association class relationship depicts a class that is composed of one or more classes. The component parts/classes only live as long as the composite class.

❑ Composition association is represented with a solid line and a filled diamond.

❑ The aggregation association class relationship depicts one class as the owner over one or more classes.

❑ Aggregation association is represented with a solid line and an unfilled diamond.

❑ The dependency association class relationship depicts one class having a temporary association with another class.

❑ The navigation indicator is denoted by a stick arrowhead attached to the end of the association.

❑ Multiplicity indicators are used to represent the number of objects that can be present in an association.

❑ Multiplicity indicator representations include *, 0, 0..*, 0..1, 0..[x], 1, 1..*, 1..[x], [x]..[y], and [x].

❑ Association role names are used to provide further clarification of class relationships.

SELF TEST

Recognizing Representations of Significant UML Elements

1. What does the abbreviation UML stand for?

A. Unified Modeling Languages

B. Unification Modeling Language

C. Unified Modeling Language

D. Unifying Model Language

2. Which are correct representations of visibility modifiers? (Select all that apply.)

A. "+" public

B. "!" private

C. "#" protected

D. "~" *package-private*

3. In the name compartment of a class diagram, which of the following is a defined stereotype used for an interface?

A. <<class>>

B. <<interface>>

C. <<interfaced>>

D. <<interfacing>>

4. In a class diagram, which compartments are optional?

A. The name compartment

B. Only the operations compartment

C. The attributes compartment, but only when the operations compartment is also excluded

D. The attributes compartment and/or operations compartment

5. The operations compartment is used for what type of Java elements?

A. Member functions

B. Member variables

C. Member functions and member variables

6. Member functions (methods) are displayed in the operations compartment of UML class diagrams. In relationship to the following code segment, which UML representation for the method is represented incorrectly?

```
private void setIsPrime (Boolean b) {
   isPrime = b;
}
```

A. `setIsPrime(Boolean) : void`

B. `- setIsPrime(b) : void`

C. `setIsPrime(b : Boolean) :: void`

D. `setIsPrime(b : Boolean)`

7. Consider the following illustration. How would you describe what is represented?

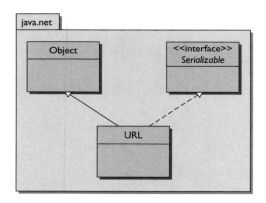

A. Class implementation and interface implementation

B. Class inheritance and interface implementation

C. Class implementation and interface inheritance

D. Class inheritance and interface inheritance

8. Consider the following illustration. Which object-oriented principle is represented?

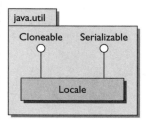

A. Generalization

B. Aggregation association

C. Multiple "class" inheritance

D. Multiple "interface" implementation

Recognizing Representations of UML Associations

9. What is the class-relationship term for an is-a relationship?

A. Synchronization

B. Association

C. Participation

D. Generalization

10. Which of the following is an invalid multiplicity indicator?

A. 0..*

B. 0..1

C. 5

D. 7..6

11. Consider the following illustration. Which class relationships are represented? (Select all that apply.)

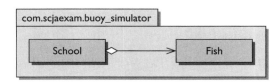

A. Directed association

B. Composition association

C. Aggregation association

D. Generalization

12. What are commonly used with multiplicity indicators for clarification of associations?

A. Visibility modifiers

B. Additional compartments

C. Role names

D. Notes

SELF TEST ANSWERS

Recognizing Representations of Significant UML Elements

1. What does the abbreviation UML stand for?

A. Unified Modeling Languages

B. Unification Modeling Language

C. Unified Modeling Language

D. Unifying Model Language

> Answer:
>
> ☑ **C.** UML stands for the Unified Modeling Language.
>
> ☒ **A, B,** and **D** are incorrect because the meanings are wrong.

2. Which are correct representations of visibility modifiers? (Select all that apply.)

A. "+"   public

B. "!"   private

C. "#"   protected

D. "~"   *package-private*

> Answer:
>
> ☑ **A, C,** and **D.** The visibility modifiers depicted for the public (+), protected (#), and *package-private* access modifiers are all correct.
>
> ☒ **B** is incorrect because the UML specification denotes a minus sign for the private access modifier, not an exclamation point.

3. In the name compartment of a class diagram, which of the following is a defined stereotype used for an interface?

A. <<class>>

B. <<interface>>

C. <<interfaced>>

D. <<interfacing>>

Answer:

☑ **C.** <<interface>> is the stereotype used for interfaces. The word "interface" is shown between guillemet characters in the name compartment to clearly specify that the class diagram is being used for an interface. The interface name is always shown below the interface stereotype.

☒ **A, B,** and **D** are incorrect because <<class>>, <<interfaced>>, and <<interfacing>> are not defined stereotypes used for interfaces.

4. In a class diagram, which compartments are optional?

   A. The name compartment

   B. Only the operations compartment

   C. The attributes compartment, but only when the operations compartment is also excluded

   D. The attributes compartment and/or operations compartment

Answer:

☑ **D.** The attributes and/or operations compartments are optional.

☒ **A, B,** and **C** are incorrect. **A** is an incorrect answer because the name compartment is required. **B** is incorrect because the attributes compartment is optional. **C** is incorrect because the attributes compartment, being optional, is not dependent on the operations compartment.

5. The operations compartment is used for what type of Java elements?

   A. Member functions

   B. Member variables

   C. Member functions and member variables

Answer:

☑ **A.** The operations compartment is used for member functions.

☒ **B** and **C** are incorrect. **B** is incorrect because the attributes compartment is used for member variables. **C** is incorrect because the operations compartment is used exclusively for member functions.

6. Member functions (methods) are displayed in the operations compartment of UML class diagrams. In relationship to the following code segment, which UML representation for the method is represented incorrectly?

```
private void setIsPrime (Boolean b) {
   isPrime = b;
}
```

A. setIsPrime(Boolean) : void

B. - setIsPrime(b) : void

C. setIsPrime(b : Boolean) :: void

D. setIsPrime(b : Boolean)

Answer:

☑   **C.** There is an extra colon represented (: :). This is not allowed.

☒   **A, B,** and **D** are incorrect. The answers are all valid representations of the setIsPrime() method.

7. Consider the following illustration. How would you describe what is represented?

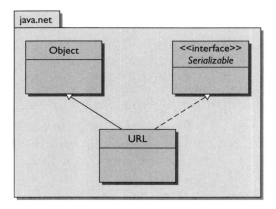

A. Class implementation and interface implementation

B. Class inheritance and interface implementation

C. Class implementation and interface inheritance

D. Class inheritance and interface inheritance

Answer:

☑ **B.** The URL class inherits from the object class, and the URL class implements the Serializable interface.

☒ **A, B,** and **D** are incorrect. **A** is incorrect because classes are inherited. **C** is incorrect because classes are considered to be inherited (as we just mentioned), and interfaces are considered to be implemented. **D** is incorrect because interfaces are implemented.

8. Consider the following illustration. Which object-oriented principle is represented?

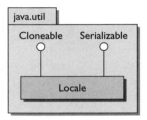

A. Generalization

B. Aggregation association

C. Multiple "class" inheritance

D. Multiple "interface" implementation

Answer:

☑ **D.** The diagram represents multiple interface implementations. The Locale class implements the Cloneable and Serializable interfaces.

☒ **A, B,** and **C** are incorrect. **A** is incorrect because generalization is not represented in the diagram. **B** is incorrect because aggregation association is not represented in the diagram. **C** is incorrect because multiple class inheritance is not represented in the diagram.

Recognizing Representations of UML Associations

9. What is the class-relationship term for an is-a relationship?

A. Synchronization

B. Association

C. Participation

D. Generalization

> **Answer:**
>
> ☑ **D.** Generalization is used to describe inheritance and the is-a relationship.
>
> ☒ **A, B,** and **C** are incorrect. **A** is incorrect because "synchronization" is not a term used for class relationships. **B** is incorrect because association uses the term has-a to describe its relationships. **C** is incorrect because "participation" is not a term used for class relationships.

10. Which of the following is an invalid multiplicity indicator?

A. 0..*

B. 0..1

C. 5

D. 7..6

> **Answer:**
>
> ☑ **D.** The range cannot decrease. [6 . . 7] would have been an acceptable multiplicity indicator.
>
> ☒ **A, B,** and **C** are incorrect. [0 . . *], [0 . . 1], and [5] all represent valid multiplicity indicators.

11. Consider the following illustration. Which class relationships are represented? (Select all that apply.)

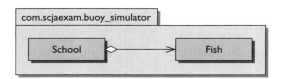

A. Directed association

B. Composition association

C. Aggregation association

D. Generalization

> Answer:
>
> ☑ **A and C.** Aggregation and directed association are both represented in the diagram. Aggregation is represented with a clear diamond. Directed association is represented with an arrow.
>
> ☒ **B and D** are incorrect. **B** is incorrect because composition association is not represented in the diagram. **D** is incorrect because generalization is not represented in the diagram.

12. What are commonly used with multiplicity indicators for clarification of associations?

A. Visibility modifiers

B. Additional compartments

C. Role names

D. Notes

> Answer:
>
> ☑ **C.** Role names are commonly used with multiplicity indicators for clarification purposes.
>
> ☒ **A, B,** and **D** are incorrect. Visibility modifiers, additional compartments, and notes are not directly used with multiplicity indicators.

Part III

Java-Related Platforms and Technologies

CHAPTERS

10   Understanding Java-Related Platforms and
Integration Technologies

11   Understanding Client-Side Technologies

12   Understanding Server-Side Technologies

10

Understanding Java-Related Platforms and Integration Technologies

CERTIFICATION OBJECTIVES

- Understanding Java Platforms

- Working with the Java Remote Method Invocation API

- Working with Database Technologies

- Working with Additional Java Integration APIs

✓ Two-Minute Drill

Q&A Self Test

J ava-based technologies provide the components and means necessary for creating client, client-server, enterprise, and mobile applications. Figure 10-1 represents a good portion of these technologies. The figure also includes other important technologies that are not Java-based (for example, SQL). Review this figure because all of the technologies represented are on the exam. These technologies are also covered in Chapters 11 and 12, as well as this chapter. The technologies are needed to be understood only from a high level. For example, you'll need to know what JavaServer Pages is, why it's used, and its key benefits. You will not be asked to create a JavaServer Pages web page or describe its low-level details, however. When you are ready to dive in deeper, you can find lower-level types of questions in Sun's specialty exams, such as the Sun Certified Web Component Developer. High-level knowledge, as obtained from this study guide, will help you lead yourself—and/or your team—in selecting the most appropriate and optimal Java-based solution, as well as pass the SCJA exam.

This chapter will provide you with the high-level platform information needed for the exam, discussing the general layout of Java SE, Java ME, and Java EE. The RMI, JDBC, and JNDI integration technologies will also be discussed as needed for the exam. A few thoughts may cross your mind when reading through these sections such as, "Specifically, how do I develop with these technologies? Why isn't this book showing me any sample code for the APIs?" For the SCJA exam, Coding against the technology APIs, Java ME, and Java EE platforms is beyond the scope of the SCJA exam. You simply need to know what the technologies are, their benefits, and when to use them.

---

e x a m
ⓦatch

You may see the original shorthand for Java platforms in the exam referenced as J2SE, J2ME, and J2EE. Currently, the platforms are known as Java SE, Java ME, and Java EE, respectively.

FIGURE 10-1   Java technologies

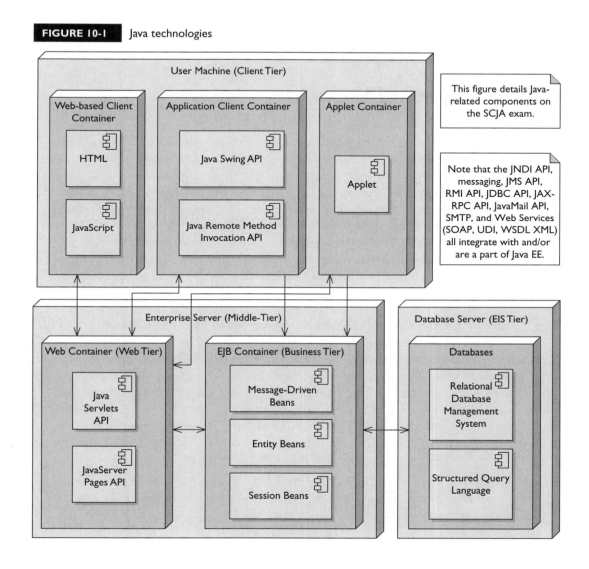

CERTIFICATION OBJECTIVE

Understanding Java Platforms

Exam Objective 6.1   Distinguish the basic characteristics of the three Java platforms: J2SE, J2ME, and J2EE, and given a high-level architectural goal, select the appropriate Java platform or platforms.

The Java SE platform is designed primarily for client-side solutions; the Java ME platform is designed for embedded solutions; and the Java EE platform is designed for enterprise solutions. To pass the SCJA exam, you'll need to understand what each platform offers and when you will need to select a particular platform to help you accomplish a specific goal.

Let's do a brief case study. You've spent several years working with teams of people on several projects. However, you've recently started a new job being the IT director for a small firm. You show up on the first day to find out that not only are you the IT director but you will be playing the role of senior architect, designer, and developer over a small group of junior programmers. The owner of the firm comes to you and says, "There are a few improvements that I've wanted to add to our Java-based security system for a while now. There have been a lot of break-ins in the area in the last couple of months so I need a system that is more informative. So here are the requirements. See if you guys can have the improved system up and running in 30 days." He hands you a small piece of paper with the following information:

- Requirements for alarm system improvements:
  - Must be able to record all security events into a database.
  - Must be able to administer the system with a local application.
  - Must automatically receive alarm notification via e-mail.
  - Must be able to disable or enable the security system from my cell phone.
  - Must be able to view the audit log from my home computer.
  - Must be able to authenticate remote logins from a preexisting naming and directory service.

Being new to the computer and maybe even Java technologies, you may look at this list and think there is no way this can be done in such a small amount of time. However, if you were Java-technology savvy, you would be able to quickly associate a technology with each requirement. You would then be able to work up a quick architecture and task out the pieces of the assignment to the different task members. Let's take a look at breaking things up:

- Alarm system improvements, forward plan:
  - Task programmer A to build a SQL database and interface code with the JNDI API of the Java SE platform.
  - Task programmer B to build a client application administration tool using the Swing API of the Java SE platform.
  - Task programmer C to write a notification module using the JavaMail API of the Java EE platform.
  - Task programmer D to build a cell phone application to enable or disable the alarm system using the Java ME platform.
  - Task programmer E to build a web-based application to log in and view the audit log using JSP and servlets of the Java EE platform.
  - Task programmer F to authenticate remote logins from a preexisting naming and directory service using the JNDI API of the Java SE platform.
  - Task yourself to integrate all of the components together as the developers return them to you.

So now that you know the concept of selecting Java-based technologies for real-world solutions, what you need to know is exactly what the technologies are and when and where you would use them. This section details the platforms that house the technologies; the following sections and chapters detail the technologies themselves:

- Java Platform, Standard Edition
- Java Platform, Micro Edition
- Java Platform, Enterprise Edition

Java Platform, Standard Edition

The Java Platform, Standard Edition is composed of the rich Java SE API, the Java Runtime Environment, the Java Development Kit, and the underlying operating system, as shown in Figure 10-2. Each of these elements serves its own specific purpose. Collectively, these components provide the means to develop, deploy, and run client and/or client-server based systems.

FIGURE 10-2

The Java SE
platform

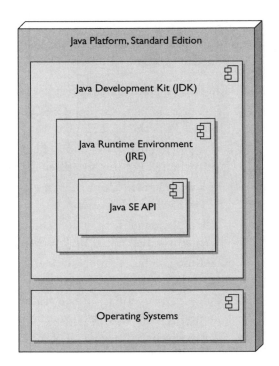

The Java SE platform

The Java SE API

The Java SE API is a collection of software packages. Each package houses
a related set of classes and interfaces. All the packages you will need to have
general knowledge of are represented in Table 10-1. Many of these packages have
subpackages that are not listed since the subpackages won't likely be on the exam.

The Java Runtime Environment

The Java Runtime Environment (JRE) is the set of software that allows Java
applications to run. The JRE includes the following items:

- Java Virtual Machines (JVMs)
    - Java Hotspot Client Virtual Machine
    - Java Hotspot Server Virtual Machine

TABLE 10-1	Name	Description	Package Name
	Java Abstract Window Toolkit API	Provides native GUI functionality and an event handling model	`java.awt`
Java Packages Covered in the SCJA Exam	Java Basic I/O API	Provides general input/output functionality	`java.io`
	Java Database Connectivity API	Provides universal data access	`java.sql,` `javax.sql`
	Java Core Language	Provides core Java language classes and interfaces	`java.lang`
	Java Naming and Directory Interface API	Provides naming and directories services access	`javax.naming`
	Java Networking API	Provides general networking functionality	`java.net,` `javax.net`
	Java RMI API	Provides Remote Method Invocation functionality	`java.rmi`
	Java Swing API	Provides GUI building functionality	`javax.swing`
	Java Utilities API	Provides general utilities including the collections framework, event models, and time facilities	`java.util`

- Deployment Technologies
  - Java Plug-in
  - Java Web Start Technology
  - Java Control Panel
  - Java Update Mechanism

Java is compiled into byte code, and each operating system has its own Java Virtual Machine that will run that byte code. This is what gives Java the "WORA" capability. WORA is the acronym for Sun Microsystems' slogan, "Write once, run anywhere."

The Java Development Kit

The Java Development Kit is, in essence, a developer's toolbox. Not only does it contain the JRE and the Java SE API, but it also contains all of the utilities you will need to compile, test, and debug your applications. Table 10-2 lists the common

TABLE 10-2	JDK Tool	Description
	jar	The Java archiving tool
Common	java	The Java interpreter
Development	javac	The Java compiler
Tools Used as	javadoc	The API documentation generator
Part of the JDK	javap	The class file disassemble
	jconsole	The monitoring and management utility released with Java 5.0
	jdb	The Java debugger
	JPDA	The Java Platform Debugger Architecture
	rmic	The RMI stub and skeleton generator

tools in the JDK that you will be using as a developer. For more information on the Java compiler and interpreter, see Chapter 1.

When you install a version of the JDK to your computer, you will want to take note of its location. This is important since you may need to specify its location in your system's path or point to it with your IDE.

Supported Operating Systems

Sun directly supports the Solaris, Linux, and Microsoft Windows operating systems with fully compliant JVMs, JDKs, and JREs. You can get the latest JRE and JDK here: http://java.sun.com/javase/downloads/. Legacy versions are kept in Sun's

SCENARIO & SOLUTION

You wish to compile Java source code. Exactly where will you find the compiler?	The Java compiler (javac) resides in the bin folder of the Java Development Kit.
You wish to interpret Java bytecode. Exactly where will you find the interpreter?	The Java interpreter (java) resides in the bin folders of both the Java Runtime Environment and the Java Development Kit.
You wish to find various Java demonstration applications provided by Sun. Where can you find them?	The Java Development Kit has a demo folder that contains various Java demonstration applications. The corresponding source code is also included.

archives here: http://java.sun.com/products/archive/. Third-party sources also make JREs and JDKs available for other operating systems. Many of these third-party solutions are listed and linked here: http://java-virtual-machine.net/other.html.

Java 2 Platform, Micro Edition

The Java 2 Platform, Micro Edition is designed for embedded devices such as high-end PDAs and mobile phones. Java ME's architecture is based on configurations, profiles, and optional packages, as shown in Figure 10-3. For additional detailed information, outside of the following sections, on Java ME and MIDlets see the "Java ME MIDlets" section in Chapter 11.

The J2ME 1.4
platform

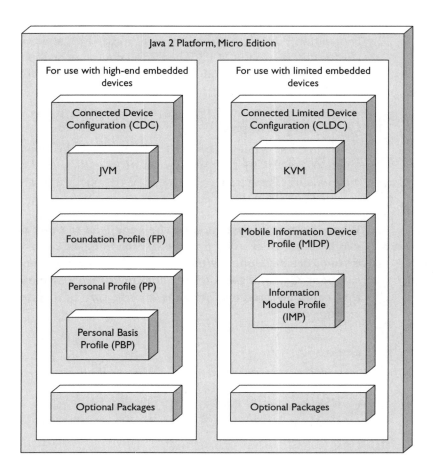

Configurations

Java ME has two configurations: the Connected Device Configuration (CDC) and the Connected Limited Device Configuration (CLDC). These configurations contain a virtual machine containing a small but focused set of libraries making up the runtime environment. CDC is supplied with the standard Java Virtual Machine and is utilized for devices that do not have extreme constraints of resources. CLDC has a small compact virtual machine known as Sun's K Virtual machine (KVM) and a reduced set of class libraries.

Profiles

Profiles are necessary to work in conjunction with configurations as part of the necessary runtime environment. Profiles are APIs that define the application's life-cycle model, user interface, and device properties access. CDC contains the Foundation Profile (FP), the Personal Profile (PP), and the Personal Basis Profile (PBP). PBP is a subset of PP. The CLDC contains the Mobile Information Device Profile (MIDP) and the Information Module Profile (IMP). IMP is a subset of MIDP.

Optional Packages

As discussed in detail in Chapter 1, packages are collections of related classes and functionality. Additional packages can be added as needed to expand on Java ME functionality. These packages that can be optionally used are initially excluded (not included by default) in order to keep the Java ME footprint as small as possible.

on the
job

When designing a system, it can be beneficial to think outside of the box. For example, consider using peripheral technologies. Unfortunately, many business systems are developed without even considering technologies such as mobile solutions. Can you think of any handheld device or mobile phone application that could be integrated into the architecture of a system you are currently working on?

Squawk

Squawk is a Java-compliant and CLDC-compatible virtual machine implementation, making it a piece of the Java ME architecture. Where most JVMs are written in C and C++, the majority of the Squawk JVM is pure Java. Squawk was designed to be as light as possible and is used with Sun's wireless Small Object Programmable Technology kits (Sun SPOTs). These "hobby" kits which include a 3D accelerometer, temperature and light sensors, LCDs, and push buttons are designed to encourage research and development of mobile technologies. The Squawk JVM is not on the exam, but you can find out more about the Sun SPOT project at www.sunspotworld.com.

Java Platform, Enterprise Edition

The Java Platform, Enterprise Edition provides a means to create true enterprise systems that are flexible, scalable, and secure. A major benefit of enterprise systems is the separation of software components. Java EE follows the Model-View-Controller (MVC) architecture where servlets work as the controller, JavaServer Pages handle the view or presentation logic, and the business logic is represented as the model, typically the Enterprise JavaBeans (EJBs). Servlets, JSPs, and EJBs are covered in Chapter 12. The Java Enterprise Edition requires a collection of optional packages that support each of these areas, as well as complementary technologies. The packages are actually implementations of specifications. Table 10-3 depicts the specifications of the Java EE 5 platform.

A Java Specification Request (JSR) is the description of Java platform–related specifications—proposed and final. For more information on JSRs, visit the Java Community Process (JCP) home page: http://jcp.org/en/home/index. The JCP maintains the JSRs.

Remember that the SCJA exam is currently geared towards the J2EE 1.4 specification. Therefore, J2EE 1.4 APIs are described in this and the following two chapters, which include:

- Enterprise Java Beans 2.1
- Servlet 2.4
- JavaServer Pages 2.0
- Java Message Service 1.1
- JavaMail 1.3
- Web Services 1.1
- JAX RPC 1.1

When developing Java EE systems, you will always need a Java Development Kit. Since the JDK is the main piece of the Java SE platform, you could essentially say that Java SE is part of Java EE. You will often have the option of using newer

| TABLE 10-3 | Java EE 5 Technology JSRs |

JSR	Specification Name	Abbreviation	Version
Web Services Technologies			
JSR-67	Java APIs for XML Messaging 1.0	SAAJ	1.3
JSR-101	Java API for XML-Based RPC	JAX-RPC	1.1
JSR-109	Implementing Enterprise Web Services	N/A	1.2
JSR-173	Streaming API for XML	StAX	1.0
JSR-181	Web Service Metadata for the Java Platform	N/A	2.0
JSR-222	Java Architecture for XML Binding (JAXB) 2.0	JAXB	2.0
JSR-224	Java API for XML-Based Web Services (JAX-WS) 2.0	JAX-WS	2.0
Web Application Technologies			
JSR-52	A Standard Tag Library for JavaServer Pages	JSTL	1.2
JSR-154	Java Servlet 2.4 Specification	Servlets	2.5
JSR-252	JavaServer Faces 1.2	JSF	1.2
JSR-245	JavaServer Pages 2.1	JSP	2.1
Enterprise Application Technologies			
JSR-112	J2EE Connector Architecture 1.5	N/A	1.5
JSR-220	Java Persistence API	N/A	1.0
JSR-220	Enterprise JavaBeans 3.0	EJB	3.0
JSR-250	Common Annotations for the Java Platform	N/A	1.0
JSR-907	Java Transaction API (JTA)	JTA	1.0
JSR-914	Java Message Service (JMS) API	JMS	1.1
JSR-919	JavaMail	N/A	1.4.1
JSR-925	JavaBeans Activation Framework 1.1	JAF	1.1
Management and Security Technologies			
JSR-77	J2EE Management	N/A	1.0
JSR-88	Java EE Application Deployment	N/A	1.2
JSR-115	Java Authorization Contract for Containers	JACC	1.1

versions of the JDK with the Java EE implementation of your choice. Be aware that there is no direct correlation between the Java SE and Java EE version numbers. So you must check the documentation to see which versions of the JDK will work with your Java EE implementation. For a specific example of a case that would work, you could use Sun's JDK 1.5 with Oracle's Application Server 10gR3, which is a J2EE 1.4 implementation.

e x a m
w a t c h

The exam will give you scenarios where you will need to determine which Java platforms are necessary to build a specific application. Understanding which APIs are included in each platform is critical in answering these questions.

The following Scenario & Solution section exercises your knowledge of which platforms contain specific APIs. However, we do not explicitly supply the names of the APIs used—you'll have to figure that out yourself. Review this Scenario & Solution section again after you have completed the chapter.

SCENARIO & SOLUTION

You wish to automate a business process using online forms and a relational database. Which Java editions would you use?	You would need to use the Java Platform, Standard Edition and the Java Platform, Enterprise Edition.
You wish to develop an application to convert database records into XML files. Which Java edition would you use?	You would need to use the Java Platform, Standard Edition.
You wish to develop a simple client-side text editor. Which Java edition would you use?	You would need to use the Java Platform, Standard Edition.
You wish to develop a prize-fighting boxing game for use on a cell phone. Which Java edition would you use?	You would need to use the Java Platform, Micro Edition.
You wish to develop a web-accessible application that also accesses a naming and directory service. Which Java editions would you use?	You would need to use the Java Platform, Standard Edition and the Java Platform, Enterprise Edition.

Getting and staying involved in the Java community is an excellent way to keep up to date with the latest Java Technologies. Consider joining a Java User Group (JUG) to share people's experiences and expertise. You can find out more about JUGs here: http://java.sun.com/community/usergroups/. Online technology forums also offer a rich opportunity for acquiring Java knowledge. Consider frequenting Sun Java forums or the Java Ranch.

EXERCISE 10-1

Embracing Java Technology Forums as Valuable Information Resources

Many individuals are familiar with forums, especially technology forums. We are not going to make the assumption that you have this familiarity, since many entry-level programmers will be studying for this exam who may have never visited a technology forum. Forums provide an excellent place to ask questions and find answers about technologies, hard-to-solve problems, bugs, certifications, and the like. Newbies to technology forums need to understand that a certain etiquette is followed when posting messages. Always search the forum for your question before asking it, since it may have already been asked and even answered. Don't ask the same question across multiple forums of the same web site and make sure your questions are in the right place. Let's take a look at using a very popular Java forum, the JavaRanch.

1. Sit back and think of a Java-related question you may have, preferably Java technology–related since we are in the Java technologies chapter.

2. Head off to the JavaRanch—www.javaranch.com—to start the process of getting your answer.

3. Click the link to the Big Moose Saloon or the animated image of the one-eyed moose. This will bring you to the JavaRanch's message forum. You will see several forums, each specializing in a specific area such as the Java Micro Edition, JDBC, and the SCJA exam forums.

4. At the top of the web page, find the Search link and click it. You'll be brought to the search form. Remember that question you came up with? Derive from that question some keywords, place them into the search form, and click the Search button. You will be presented with a list of links showing the topics of related questions posted to the forum.

5. Browse through the list, clicking the topics you feel may have your answer.

6. If you can't find your answer, consider registering (for posting rights) in the forum (it's free). Then, post your question. Since you were to come up with a specific Java technology–based question, make sure you place it in the appropriate forum. Remember the etiquette: If it is a real basic question, you may wish to post it to the "Java in General (beginner)" forum.

7. Check back to the forum regularly to see if an answer to your question has been posted. Note that this and many other forums can send you e-mail notifications when your questions have been responded to.

CERTIFICATION OBJECTIVE

Working with the Java Remote Method Invocation API

Exam Objective 6.2   Describe at a high level the benefits and basic characteristics of RMI.

Wouldn't it be great if you could invoke a method from an object on another machine? Remote Method Invocation (RMI) technology does just that since it is Java's basic remote procedure call mechanism. This section discusses RMI's main goal, which is to allow for the sharing of Java objects between Java Virtual Machines.

The Java Remote Method Invocation API

The Java Remote Method Invocation API resides in the `java.rmi` package. This API provides the means in which Java applications perform distributed computing. In a classic client-server scenario, the RMI server maintains the remote objects, while the RMI client maintains the client objects that invoke the remote methods. This is done by implementing a remote interface through a client stub. You must understand that all of this work is not performed auto-*magic*-ally. The developer needs to solicit the creation of the stubs in order for the distributed communications to occur, as shown in Figure 10-4.

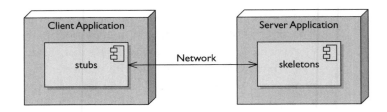

Stubs (client stubs) and skeletons (remote stubs) are created with the command-line utility 'rmic'. Stubs and skeletons have their own key points:

- Client stubs
    - The 'rmic'-created stub for the client side is called a "stub."
    - When using JDK 1.4 and earlier versions (prior to JDK 5.0), you are required to use the 'rmic' utility to generate stub classes.
    - In JDK 5.0 and later, the RMI runtime generates the stub classes automatically (by constructing a proxy).
    - The client stub's marshal method calls the name and arguments and sends them to the skeleton on the server side. After they receive the results from the sender, they return the result back to the method call invoker.
- Server stubs (skeletons)
    - The 'rmic'-created stub for the server side is called a "skeleton."
    - As of JDK 1.2 and later, skeletons are no longer needed.
    - The server stub's receive marshal method calls the name and arguments from the client stubs, performs the necessary operations, and returns the result back to the client stub.

The underlying protocol for the Java-only implementation of RMI is Java Remote Method Protocol (JRMP). RMI is not the only Java technology available for remote procedure calls. Java Remote Method Invocation over Internet Inter-Orb Protocol (RMI-IIOP) is used for Java to non-Java distributed computing solutions. Java-IDL is used by Common Object Request Broker Architecture (CORBA) developers to provide a CORBA to Java distributed computing solutions. You should not see RMI-IIOP or Java-IDL on the exam.

exam

ⓦatch
The term "marshal" is the technique of passing method parameters and results for a remote procedure call. "Demarshal" is the reverse technique. The action form of these terms is marshalling and demarshalling.

A few benefits of RMI technologies include the heavy usage with Enterprise Java Beans; RMI is lightweight, allowing for servers to be initialized with minimum effort; and RMI hides the fine details of network communication and object serialization. Serialization is the process of flattening and restoring objects, thereby allowing the application to save the object's state as a series of bytes. This flattened object can therefore be saved to disk and/or sent across a network, where it is then reconstituted on the other side, as in the case of RMI.

exam

ⓦatch
RMI's competing technology is simple sockets. Sockets are not on the exam per se—that is, you may see socket-related information referenced in answer choices.

INSIDE THE EXAM

Refining Your RMI Skills Through the SCJD Assignment

You only need to know RMI from a very high level for the SCJA exam. However, you will have the opportunity to master RMI through Sun's certification path if you decide to take the Sun Certified Java Developer (SCJD) assignment/exam. The various assignments that are part of the SCJD certification process require that a choice be made between implementation of an RMI or a "serialized objects over simple socket connection" solution. If you choose RMI for your given assignment, which many candidates do, you'll have the full opportunity to work with RMI. Be aware, though, that you must pass the SCJP exam before signing up for the SCJD.

When you finally get to the SCJD exam, you'll want to consider reviewing the following book: *SCJD Exam with J2SE 5, Second Edition* by Andrew Monkhouse and Terry Camerlengo (Apress, December 2005).

CERTIFICATION OBJECTIVE

Working with Database Technologies

Exam Objective 6.3   Describe at a high level the benefits and basic characteristics of JDBC, SQL, and RDBMS technologies.

Database Management Systems (DBMS) are designed to organize and maintain valuable information. Relational Database Management Systems (RDBMS) provide advanced flexible features that are directly related to their table-based design. The Structured Query Language (SQL) is an industry standard programming language used to work with these relational databases. SQL is supported by the Java Database Connectivity API. The following subsections will acquaint you with everything you'll need to know about database technologies as represented on the exam.

Relational Database Management Systems

A Relational Database Management System (RDBMS) is a type of database management system that organizes its data in the form of interrelated tables. Benefits of an RDMBS include the following:

- Provides a persistent data store
- Processes SQL queries
- Manages users
- Performs backups and restores

A list of popular RDBMS programs is shown in Table 10-4. All of these databases can be interfaced via the Structured Query Language.

TABLE 10-4 RDBMS Programs	RDBMS Program	Web Site Link
	Java DB	http://developers.sun.com/javadb/
	MySQL Enterprise Server	www.mysql.com/products/enterprise/server.html
	Oracle Database	www.oracle.com/database/
	PostgreSQL	www.postgresql.org/
	Microsoft SQL Server	www.microsoft.com/sqlserver/2008/en/us/
	IBM DB2	www-01.ibm.com/software/data/db2/9/

Structured Query Language

The Structured Query Language (SQL), pronounced "ess-kew-ell," is a software language designed for retrieval and management of information in RDBMS systems. More specifically, SQL provides the following features:

- Operations to support querying/retrieval of information from relational databases.

- Operations to support modification—for example, insertion, updating, and deletion of information in relational databases.

- Operations to support the management of relational databases.

- Operations to support execution plans. An execution plan is generated by the RDBMS to specify how it will execute a piece of application code.

- Operations to support stored procedures. A stored procedure is a piece of application code that is stored and executed within the database. You will get an execution plan as a result of compiling a stored procedure.

SQL is an ANSI and ISO standard and has several implementations with comprehensive extensions to the language.

The Java Database Connectivity API

The Java Database Connectivity (JDBC) API provides for a Java application to connect to an RDBMS server and take advantage of SQL. JDBC allows for the invocation of SQL commands and stored procedures, as well as the processing of such queries. In order to use JDBC, you'll need to import the necessary JDBC packages from the Java SE platform, as well as implement the service provider interface and make use of the RDMBS-specific JDBC driver.

on the
ΰ o b

Sun maintains a resource of over 200 JDBC drivers via their JDBC Data Access API, allowing you to get JDBC drivers from various vendors. You can access the API at http://developers.sun.com/product/jdbc/drivers.

e x a m
ⓦ a t c h

For the novice, JDBC and JNDI technologies may be easily confused since both are integration technologies that perform connection and access capabilities. Remember that the JDBC API is used to connect to and interface with databases, while the JNDI API is used to connect to and interface with naming and directory services. You will probably see these technologies in the same group of answers on the exam.

CERTIFICATION OBJECTIVE

Working with Additional Java Integration APIs

Exam Objective 6.4   Describe at a high level the benefits and basic characteristics of JNDI, messaging, and JMS technologies.

Several Java integration APIs exist. We already discussed RMI and JDBC. Let's now take a look at JNDI and JMS. The JNDI API allows for integration with naming and directory services. The JMS API allows for access to point-to-point and publish/subscribe messaging systems. JNDI and JMS objectives are grouped together under the presumed reason that JMS, as well as other APIs, uses JNDI to interface with necessary resources. These topics will be covered in the following subsections.

The Java Naming and Directory Interface API

The Java Naming and Directory Interface (JNDI) API provides general client-side querying features against directory and naming services by both attributes and a hierarchy of names. Examples of supported directory and naming services include the Lightweight Directory Access Protocol (LDAP), the Novell Directory Services (NDS), the Domain Name Service (DNS), the Network Information Systems (NIS), File Systems, EJB naming services, and Common Object Request Broker Architecture (CORBA), as shown in Figure 10-5. Naming and directory services are designed as database structures that are typically laid out as hierarchal directories, not relational table-based databases.

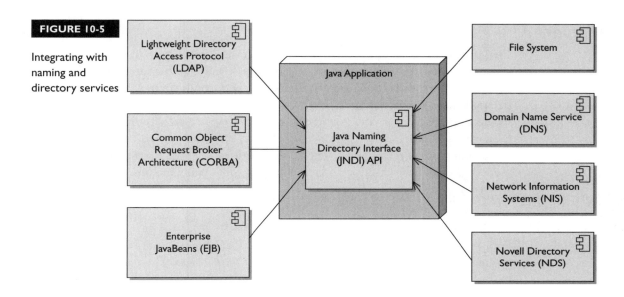

FIGURE 10-5

Integrating with naming and directory services

JNDI methods include connection capabilities, as well as searching, retrieval, and storage of naming and directory service objects. JNDI operations support the association of attributes with objects to assist in the management and retrieval of information related to those objects. JNDI provides an event interface that allows the client application to be notified when directory information has been changed.

JNDI lays out its elements as a tree structure of directories and objects. When creating a connection, you need to establish an initial base context. Think of the context as the directory starting point in the tree. You may change the context whenever you like. However, when the context is set, you can only traverse the downward portion of the tree when performing querying operations.

on the job

Several LDAP browsers are freely available, such as JXplorer and the Softerra LDAP Browser. These utilities let the user remotely access LDAP servers. Their viewing and filtering capabilities are extremely beneficial in understanding the full layout of an LDAP server. These structural details are important to have before you start developing your client code. Many LDAP browser vendors have a full LDAP administrator version available that is often provided in a commercial fashion.

The Java Message Service API

The Java Message Service (JMS) API resides in the `javax.jms` package. This API is used to access the common features of enterprise messaging systems. The JMS API allows for the creation, sending, receiving, and reading of messages with Java EE application components. All of this distributed-computing communications of separate applications is done asynchronously; this is essentially the definition of a messaging system.

Several types of messaging systems can be utilized. JMS supports two common models: the publish/subscribe and point-to-point messaging models. Look for this on your exam.

The Publish/Subscribe Messaging Model

Publish/subscribe messaging is based on events. Consumers subscribe to events of interest by specifying a topic that is part of a set of messages. The producers of these messages will route these messages to the consumers who register for them. The consumers will then consume the events when they arrive.

The Point-to-Point Messaging Model

Point-to-point (PTP) messaging involves applications routing messages to consumers while using a shared queue. The consumer maintains this queue of awaiting messages, and the messaging application sends messages to that queue.

on the Job

Apache ActiveMQ is an open-source message broker that fully supports JMS 1.1 as part of the J2EE 1.4 specification. Consider researching ActiveMQ for a more practical understanding of the Java Message Service API; http://activemq.apache.org/.

CERTIFICATION SUMMARY

This chapter discussed the differences between the Java platforms, as well as their practical applicability. All three platforms were covered in detail: Java SE, Java ME, and Java EE. SCJA-related Java integration technologies, including the Java RMI API, JDBC API, JNDI API, and the JMS API, were also explored. Let's take a minute to summarize the high-level points of what we've learned.

The Java Platform, Standard Edition comprises the JDK, JRE, and Java SE APIs. The Java Development Kit includes all of the tools necessary to develop, debug, and test Java applications. The JDK includes the JRE. The Java Runtime Environment contains the deployment technologies and Java Virtual Machines necessary to execute bytecode. The JRE includes the Java SE API, which in turn contains software packages encompassing related classes and interfaces.

The Java Platform, Micro Edition is a configurations-based architecture designed for embedded devices such as high-end PDAs and mobile phones.

The Java Platform, Enterprise Edition is used to build flexible, scalable, and secure enterprise systems. In Java enterprise systems, there is a clear separation between business and presentation logic.

The Remote Method Invocation API allows for distributed computing through remote procedure calls. Client-side stubs and server-side stubs (skeletons) provide the stubs necessary for marshaling system references and values.

The Java Database Connectivity API provides database support, allowing you to execute SQL queries and process the results of the queries.

The Java Naming and Directory Interface API lets you access naming and directory services. JNDI methods include the searching, retrieval, and storage capabilities of naming and directory service objects.

The Java Message Service API is used to access the features of messaging systems, specifically systems that use the publish/subscribe and point-to-point messaging models.

You will not need to retain all of the finer details discussed in this chapter in regards to the core topics of platforms and integration technologies. However, the more information you can retain, the easier the high-level questions will be for you come exam time.

✓ TWO-MINUTE DRILL

Understanding Java Platforms

❑ The Java SE platform is used to build client and/or client-server systems.

❑ The Java SE platform contains the Java SE API, which includes JDBC, JNDI, RMI, AWT, I/O, Swing, networking, language, and utilities APIs.

❑ The Java SE platform contains the Java Runtime Environment, which houses the Java SE API, JVMs, and deployment APIs.

❑ The Java SE platform contains the Java Development Kit, which includes all necessary compilation and debugging tools.

❑ The Java SE platform is considered to contain the underlying operating system—for example, Solaris, Linux, or Windows.

❑ The Java ME platform is used to build applications for embedded and mobile devices.

❑ Java ME includes the CDC and CLDC configurations.

❑ Java ME includes the CDC Personal Profile (PP), Personal Basis Profile (PBP), and Foundation Profile (FP).

❑ Java ME includes the CLDC Mobile Information Device Profile (MIDP) and the Information Module Profile (IMP).

❑ The Java EE platform is used to build enterprise systems.

❑ The Java EE platform includes an MVC design pattern that cleanly separates the controlling tier, presentation tier, and business tier, providing a scalable, flexible, and secure development and deployment environment.

❑ Java EE includes the EJB, JMS, Web Services, JAX-RPC, Servlets, JSP, and JavaMail APIs.

Working with the Java Remote Method Invocation API

❑ The Remote Method Invocation API provides a means for Java applications to perform distributed computing.

❑ RMI technologies are heavily used with Enterprise JavaBeans.

❑ RMI allows for servers to be initialized with minimum effort.

❑ Java Remote Method Protocol (JRMP) is the Java-only implementation of RMI.

❑ The command-line tool 'rmic' is used to create RMI stubs and skeletons. This tool is not required for J2SE 5.0 and later.

Working with Database Technologies

❑ An RDBMS is a type of database management system that organizes its data in the form of interrelated tables.

❑ SQL is a software language designed for retrieval and management of information in RDBMS systems.

❑ A group of SQL statements is considered a stored procedure. A stored procedure is compiled into a single execution plan and is executed within the database.

❑ The JDBC API establishes connections with relational databases.

❑ The JDBC API sends SQL queries to relational databases.

❑ The JDBC API receives and processes the results of SQL queries from relational databases.

Working with Additional Java Integration APIs

❑ JNDI allows for interaction with naming and directory services.

❑ JNDI methods include connection capabilities of naming and directory service objects.

❑ JNDI methods include searching, retrieval, and storage capabilities of naming and directory service objects.

❑ JNDI operations support the association of attributes with objects to assist in the management and retrieval of information related to those objects.

❑ JNDI provides an event interface that allows the client application to be notified when directory information has been changed.

❑ JNDI essentially lays things out in a tree structure of directories and objects.

❑ JMS messages include asynchronous requests, reports, and events.

❑ JMS supports the publish/subscribe messaging system model.

❑ JMS supports the point-to-point messaging system model.

SELF TEST

Understanding Java Platforms

1. Which Java platform contains the specifications for servlets, JavaServer Pages, and JavaServer Faces?

   A. Java ME

   B. Java SE

   C. Java EE

   D. Java EA

2. Which two Java ME profile statements are correct?

   A. The Personal Profile (PP) is a CDC profile.

   B. The Personal Basis Profile (PBP) is a CLDC profile.

   C. The Foundation Profile (FP) is a CLDC profile.

   D. The Mobile Information Device Profile (MIDP) is a CLDC profile.

3. Which Java platform contains the JNDI and JDBC integration APIs?

   A. Java ME

   B. Java SE

   C. Java EE

   D. Java SE and Java EE

4. Consider the following illustration. Cascading Style Sheets (CSS) is a stylesheet language used to support the rendering of presentation logic. Which container does CSS belong in?

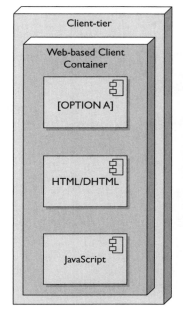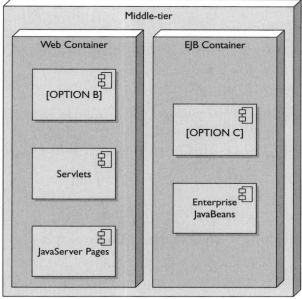

A. Option A—the web-based client container

B. Option B—the web container

C. Option C—the EJB container

D. None of the above.

Working with the Java Remote Method Invocation API

5. Which is not an advantage of RMI?

A. Creating an RMI solution would involve creating a custom protocol.

B. RMI technologies are heavily used with Enterprise JavaBeans.

C. RMI allows for servers to be initialized with minimum effort.

D. RMI hides the fine details of network communication and object serialization.

6. What is the underlying protocol for the Java-only implementation of RMI?

A. Jini

B. Java Remote Method Protocol (JRMP)

C. RMI-IIOP

D. CORBA

7. What is the command-line tool used to create RMI stubs?

A. `rmi_create`

B. `stub_create`

C. `rmi -c`

D. `rmic`

Working with Database Technologies

8. What is a group of SQL statements called that is compiled into a single execution plan?

A. RMI

B. JNDI

C. A stored procedure

D. JDBC

9. What are the three main capabilities of the JDBC API?

A. Sending of SQL queries

B. Establishment of a connection with a database

C. Processing the results from SQL queries

D. Establishment of a connection with a naming server

10. Do you need to have a JDBC technology–enabled driver for a given database, in addition to using the JDBC API?

A. Yes

B. No

Working with Additional Java Integration APIs

11. JNDI allows for interaction with which of the following naming and directory services?

    A. LDAP, NDS, DNS, NIS(YP)

    B. LADP, NDS, DNS, NIS(YP)

    C. LDAP, SDN, DNS, NIS(YP)

    D. LDAP, NDS, DNS, NIIS(XP)

12. JMS messages consumed by enterprise applications include which asynchronous items?

    A. requests

    B. listeners

    C. reports

    D. events

13. Which model does JMS support?

    A. Publish/subscribe

    B. Transmit/receive

    C. Dictate/annotate

    D. Publish/render/subscribe

SELF TEST ANSWERS

Understanding Java Platforms

1. Which Java platform contains the specifications for servlets, JavaServer Pages, and JavaServer Faces?

A. Java ME

B. Java SE

C. Java EE

D. Java EA

Answer:

☑ **C.** The Java EE platform contains the specifications related to dynamic web content solutions, including servlets, JavaServer Pages, and JavaServer Faces.

☒ **A, B,** and **D** are incorrect. **A** is incorrect because Java ME is the Java Micro Edition used for embedded solutions. **B** is incorrect because Java SE is the Java 2 Standard Edition used for basic application development. **D** is incorrect because Java EA is fictitious.

2. Which two Java ME profile statements are correct?

A. The Personal Profile (PP) is a CDC profile.

B. The Personal Basis Profile (PBP) is a CLDC profile.

C. The Foundation Profile (FP) is a CLDC profile.

D. The Mobile Information Device Profile (MIDP) is a CLDC profile.

Answer:

☑ **A** and **D. A** is correct because the Personal Profile (PP) is a CDC profile. **D** is correct because the Mobile Information Device Profile (MIDP) is a CLDC profile.

☒ **B** and **C** are incorrect because the Personal Basis Profile (PBP) and Foundation Profile (FP) are actually CDC profiles.

3. Which Java platform contains the JNDI and JDBC integration APIs?

A. Java ME

B. Java SE

C. Java EE

D. Java SE and Java EE

Answer:

☑ **B.** The Java Platform, Standard Edition houses the implementations of the APIs for JNDI and JDBC.

☒ **A, C,** and **D** are incorrect because Java ME and Java EE do not house the APIs.

4. Consider the following illustration. Cascading Style Sheets (CSS) is a stylesheet language used to support the rendering of presentation logic. Which container does CSS belong in?

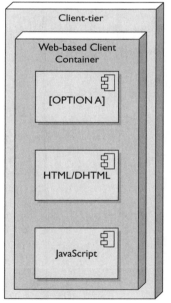 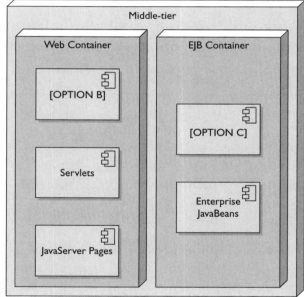

A. Option A—the web-based client container

B. Option B—the web container

C. Option C—the EJB container

D. None of the above.

Answer:

☑ **A.** Cascading Style Sheets (CSS) are used within web-based client containers such as web browsers. CSS is commonly used to style web pages written in HTML. Note that CSS is not on the exam, this was a simply a critical-thinking question in relationship to the Java EE platform.

☒ **B, C,** and **D** are incorrect. JSPs and servlets can produce inline CSS code in relationship to HTML content, but the code is ultimately sent to and used by web browsers. Therefore, **B** is incorrect because CSS does not directly relate to the web container. **C** is incorrect because CSS has no relationship to the EJB container.

Working with the Java Remote Method Invocation API

5. Which is not an advantage of RMI?

   A. Creating an RMI solution would involve creating a custom protocol.

   B. RMI technologies are heavily used with Enterprise JavaBeans.

   C. RMI allows for servers to be initialized with minimum effort.

   D. RMI hides the fine details of network communication and object serialization.

Answer:

☑ **A.** Creating an RMI solution does not involve creating a custom protocol.

☒ **B, C,** and **D** are incorrect. These answers represent advantages of RMI. **B** is incorrect because RMI is utilized with EJBs. **C** is incorrect because servers that initialize using RMI do so with minimum effort. **D** is incorrect because network communications and object serialization is handled behind the scenes with RMI.

6. What is the underlying protocol for the Java-only implementation of RMI?

   A. Jini

   B. Java Remote Method Protocol (JRMP)

   C. RMI-IIOP

   D. CORBA

Answer:

☑ **B.** JRMP is the underlying protocol for Java-based implementations of RMI.

☒ **A, C,** and **D** are incorrect. These answers are not underlying Java-based implementations of RMI. Jini is a dynamic networking architecture. Java Remote Method Invocation over Internet Inter-Orb Protocol (RMI-IIOP) provides Common Object Request Broker Architecture (CORBA) distributed computing support.

7. What is the command-line tool used to create RMI stubs?

   A. `rmi_create`

   B. `stub_create`

   C. `rmi -c`

   D. `rmic`

Answer:

   ☑ **D.** The `rmic` command is used to create RMI client-side stubs.

   ☒ **A, B,** and **C** are incorrect. These answers do not represent valid tools because the commands `rmi_create`, `stub_create`, and `rmi` do not exist.

Working with Database Technologies

8. What is a group of SQL statements called that is compiled into a single execution plan?

   A. RMI

   B. JNDI

   C. A stored procedure

   D. JDBC

Answer:

   ☑ **C** is the correct answer because a set of SQL statements is known as a stored procedure.

   ☒ **A, B,** and **D** are incorrect answers. RMI, JNDI, and JDBC are all integration technologies and are not directly related to a single execution plan.

9. What are the three main capabilities of the JDBC API?

   A. Sending of SQL queries

   B. Establishment of a connection with a database

   C. Processing the results from SQL queries

   D. Establishment of a connection with a naming server

Answer:

   ☑ **A, B,** and **C.** The JDBC API allows for the establishment of database connections, the sending of SQL queries, and the processing of results from those queries.

   ☒ **D** is incorrect. The best way to connect to a naming server is through the JNDI API.

10. Do you need to have a JDBC technology–enabled driver for a given database, in addition to using the JDBC API?

A. Yes

B. No

Answer:

☑ **A.** Yes, the JDBC API is designed to use different drivers, but you must obtain the driver you will need to use.

Working with Additional Java Integration APIs

11. JNDI allows for interaction with which of the following naming and directory services?

A. LDAP, NDS, DNS, NIS(YP)

B. LADP, NDS, DNS, NIS(YP)

C. LDAP, SDN, DNS, NIS(YP)

D. LDAP, NDS, DNS, NIIS(XP)

Answer:

☑ **A.** The list represents existing naming and directory services supported by JNDI. The services listed are more formally known as the Lightweight Directory Access Protocol (LDAP), the Novell Directory Services (NDS), the Domain Name Service (DNS), and the Network Information Systems (NIS). In the case of NIS, YP represents the original name of Yellow Pages that had to be changed due to trademark issues.

☒ **B, C,** and **D** are incorrect. LADP, SDN, and NIIS (XP) are not naming and directory interfaces that actually exist.

12. JMS messages consumed by enterprise applications include which asynchronous items?

A. requests

B. listeners

C. reports

D. events

Answer:

☑ **A, C,** and **D.** Asynchronous requests, reports, and events are consumed by enterprise applications.

☒ **B** is incorrect. "Listeners" makes no logical sense to this question.

13. Which model does JMS support?

    A. Publish/subscribe

    B. Transmit/receive

    C. Dictate/annotate

    D. Publish/render/subscribe

Answer:

☑ **A.** JMS supports the publish/subscribe model also known as an asynchronous messaging paradigm.

☒ **B, C,** and **D** are incorrect.

11

Understanding Client-Side Technologies

CERTIFICATION OBJECTIVES

- Using Thin Clients with HTML and the JavaScript API

- Using J2ME MIDlets

- Using Java Applets as Fat Clients

- Using the Java Swing API as a Fat Client

✓ Two-Minute Drill

Q&A Self Test

This chapter examines the different options developers have for allowing users to access their applications. This is a very critical area of planning that is often underestimated. An application could have a very thoroughly planned out and optimized backend, but if the client-side interface is poorly designed, the user may have a poor experience with the software. The SCJA exam contains questions about the four different technologies used to create the client side of an application, as shown in Figure 11-1. This section of the test has more breadth than depth. After studying this chapter, it is important to be familiar with the advantages and disadvantages of each technology. A common exam question will address which technology is best suited for a given device or situation.

Using Thin Clients with HTML and the JavaScript API

Exam Objective 7.1   Describe at a high level the basic characteristics, benefits, and drawbacks of creating thin-clients using HTML and JavaScript and the related deployment issues and solutions.

This section discusses the use of web pages with HTML and JavaScript as a client-side user interface. This technology is best suited for applications that require

FIGURE 11-1   Java-based client-side technologies

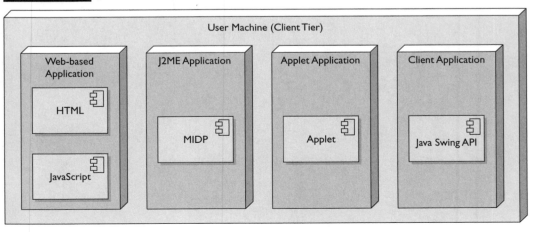

many users to have access to the same data. Oftentimes, an enterprise server will work in conjunction with an enterprise database to provide this solution. The users can access the database via the web interface. The majority of the data processing is done remotely on the enterprise server. The topics listed next will be covered in the following subsections.

- HyperText Markup Language
- JavaScript API
- Thin clients with HTML and JavaScript
- Thin-client disadvantages
- Thin-client deployment

HyperText Markup Language

HyperText Markup Language (HTML) is the markup language used to create web pages. HTML provides a way of describing how a page should be displayed to the remote web browser. HTML was used as early as 1990. At that time, it was designed to be a very simple markup language that would be used to display static content. The first formal standard was HTML 2.0 (1.0 was never formally standardized) and was published in 1995. As of this publication, the current version of the HTML specification is HTML 4.01 (www.w3.org/TR/REC-html40/) and is maintained by the W3C (World Wide Web Consortium).

HTML has the ability to display forms to the user and then send them back to the server. On the server side, this form can be processed and a response sent back to the user as a new HTML web page. This was the first web application.

Over time, HTML matured into the rich language it is today. Modern HTML can display and format a page in almost any way conceivable. The best thing about HTML is that the user only needs a web browser to view the web pages. HTML is platform independent and will look almost identical and work nearly identically on any operating system. Modern web applications have also made great advances. HTML can now be dynamically created on the server and sent to a user. This allows you to change the content you send to different users.

Dynamic creation of HTML can be used to create a client-side interface to your Java server application. This is a great way to show reports generated from a database or to enter new data. This allows an application to be used on any system that has a web browser and a network connection to your enterprise server.

JavaScript API

The JavaScript API, despite its name, has practically no connection to Java. In fact, JavaScript was originally named LiveScript and only through a marketing agreement between Sun Microsystems and Netscape was the name later changed. It was first developed in 1995 by Netscape to provide a means of creating dynamic web pages. JavaScript was intended to be a scripting language that could be used to modify and update static HTML content.

It was designed to be a simple and easy to use scripting language, and shares the same C style syntax and many of the same naming conventions as Java. JavaScript differs from Java by having weakly typed variables and is interpreted by the web browser instead of being compiled. This allows the target audience of web designers to not have to learn the details of compilers and object-oriented software design. When JavaScript was developed, its sole purpose was to provide interactivity to otherwise static HTML web pages. Since then, JavaScript has become a general-purpose scripting language. While it is still most commonly used together with HTML to create interactive web pages, JavaScript can be found doing many other tasks.

on the
Óob
Consider taking advantage of the jQuery JavaScript Library when building your web applications; http://jquery.com. jQuery is an optimized JavaScript library used for fast HTML document traversing, event handling, animation, and AJAX interactions.

The JavaScript code is included with the HTML when it is sent to a client. The remote web browser executes the JavaScript. All of the processing of the JavaScript is done on the client's system. It is most commonly used for input validation and interacting with users as they view the web page.

e**x**a m
ⓦatch
JavaScript is a general-purpose scripting language. Look for JavaScript and HTML to be paired together on the exam. Both technologies complement each other when creating web pages.

Thin Clients

HTML and JavaScript are a well-suited pair of technologies for creating thin-client user interfaces. A user can open their web browser and access the application just as they would for any other web page. When the application is first accessed, a web server can send the HTML and JavaScript code to the user. The HTML may be dynamically created if a more advanced application is needed. This can be accomplished using servlets and/or JavaServer Pages. See Chapter 12 for more information on servlets and JavaServer Pages.

on the **job**

The HTML and JavaScript combination has become a very popular method of creating web applications. In the past, JavaScript was limited in usefulness by having buggy implementations across different browsers. Recently this has changed. Web browsers from different vendors, on different platforms, have standardized how they interpret JavaScript code. This has allowed web programmers to use many advanced features in the language that were either too buggy to use before, or have only recently been added to the language. These advancements have allowed for the creation of very complex and rich interfaces that have never been seen before in a web application. These rich graphical user interfaces have greatly narrowed the gap between native applications and web applications.

AJAX is a term for asynchronous JavaScript and XML. This is the primary technology behind these new advanced web applications. At its core, AJAX is just a fancy word for HTML modified by JavaScript that uses XML and its asynchronous communication between client and server. XML stands for Extensible Markup Language. In short, it is used as a general-purpose specification for designing application-specific markup languages. The asynchronous communication allows for data to be validated and updated without the entire page reloading. The term AJAX is not used on the SCJA.

Thin-Client Disadvantages

HTML used with JavaScript can create a very rich and dynamic web site. This site can be used as the front-end of an enterprise application. However, this application will not have the same feel as a native application designed for a target environment. It will be constrained to run inside a web browser and will have some limitations as to what can be done with the user interface. An advanced or very custom interface may be impossible or buggy to implement across different web browsers.

Users must always have a network connection to the enterprise server that is hosting the web application. There is no possibility of deploying the application locally on a user's system. If the client system has a slow network connection, the responsiveness of the web application will suffer.

Thin-Client Deployment

HTML and JavaScript are deployed to a system that runs on a web server. HTML and JavaScript are not compiled, they are interpreted. There is no need to deploy anything directly to the clients. When a client runs the application, they will use a web browser to connect to the web server. The web server will send the clients the current version of the HTML and JavaScript.

CERTIFICATION OBJECTIVE

Using J2ME MIDlets

Exam Objective 7.2   Describe at a high level the basic characteristics, benefits, drawbacks, and deployment issues related to creating clients using J2ME midlets.

This section covers the SCJA requirements for J2ME MIDlets. A MIDlet is an application for a MIDP device. Common MIDP devices are mobile phones. These applications belong to the J2ME branch of Java. The SCJA exam will only have questions about MIDlets, but for clarity this section will discuss general aspects of J2ME along with more specific details of MIDlets. The following topics will be covered.

- J2ME and MIDlets
- Configurations and profiles
- J2ME disadvantages
- J2ME deployment

J2ME and MIDlets

The Java 2 Platform Micro Edition (J2ME) is a Java variant intended to be used on resource-constrained devices. This edition of Java is important because it extends the already familiar Java language to mobile and embedded devices. Any developer that has experience with standard Java, J2SE, will not find it difficult to work with J2ME. Prior to J2ME, mobile devices often required developers to learn a unique set of libraries, build environments, and use specialized deployment strategies. J2ME simplified this and created a much more unified development environment. Best of all, since J2ME is just a branch of Java, developers have the ability to test their applications on a standard desktop computer.

J2ME is a subset of the standard Java APIs. The exact subset is dependent on the profile and configuration of the devices. The configuration is a general description of the device. A profile is used to define the features of a device and may contain more or less of the Java class libraries based on the resources of the device. A profile may also be different based on available hardware components. For example, an embedded device with no screen would have no use for the user interface Java class libraries.

on the
(j)ob

Most IDEs provide an easy way to create and test MIDlets. For example, the NetBeans IDE provides the ability to automatically create a J2ME development environment and includes Sun's mobile phone emulator. The emulator allows the developer to test their application on an emulated phone on their desktop PC, instead of requiring it be deployed to a real mobile phone for testing. Figure 11-2 is an example of this emulator.

Mobile phones and PDAs are the most common places to use J2ME. These devices use the Mobile Information Device Profile (MIDP). Applications created with this profile are often called MIDlets. MIDlets allow for the creation of a limited user interface on these portable devices. This profile also contains libraries for playing audio and has basic 2-D and 3-D capabilities. J2ME has become a very popular technology to create simple games for mobile phones. MIDlets can also be used for enterprise applications that connect to a backend enterprise server. These applications can make it easy to have portable access to your enterprise data, but care must be taken to keep data synchronized across all devices and the server. The MIDP is the only profile on the SCJA exam. However, it is useful to understand the following section about other configurations and profiles. This section will provide a good view of how J2ME works and utilizes different configurations and profiles in order to work with different device types.

FIGURE 11-2

FIGURE 11-2

Mobile phone
emulator

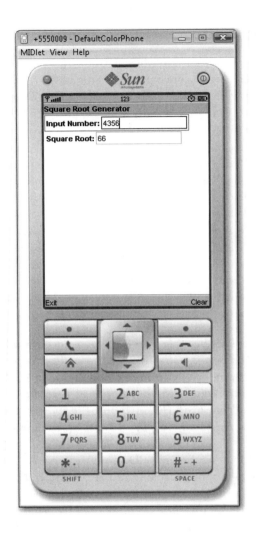

exam
ⓦatch
A MIDlet is a name given to an application that uses the Mobile Information Device Profile or MIDP. The SCJA exam will focus on this profile and on mobile devices.

Configurations and Profiles

J2ME makes use of configurations and profiles to classify a nearly infinite number of devices into a few groups that share common features. These groups then give developers well-defined targets to create their applications against. A configuration is the most basic and general description of the minimum required Java class libraries and includes features that the Java Virtual Machine must support. A device is allowed to supersede the minimum requirements of the configuration, but must be able to successfully execute any application designed for the configuration it supports. Currently there are two J2ME configurations: Connected Limited Device Configuration and Connected Device Configuration.

The Connected Limited Device Configuration (CLDC) is a configuration used for resource-limited devices. It dictates a minimum level of features that the Java Virtual Machine must provide and contains the most basic Java class libraries. CLDC contains profiles that further define the target device. The profiles define Java class libraries in addition to the Java class libraries defined in the CLDC. The Mobile Information Device Profile or MIDP is a CLDC profile. It is the profile nearly all mobile phones implement. This is the most common J2ME profile and the applications are often referred to as MIDlets. It provides the Java class libraries to create user interfaces for devices with small screens. It also provides many other phone-specific Java class libraries that are very useful when working on mobile phones.

Another common CLDC profile is the Information Module Profile (IMP). IMP is designed for headless systems. Embedded control units and vending machines are two examples of where this profile may be found. In general, it is a small subset of MIDP, with its most notable exclusion being the Java class libraries for creating graphical user interfaces.

The second J2ME configuration is the Connected Device Configuration (CDC). This configuration has a more complete set of Java class libraries than the CLDC. It contains nearly the entire set of Java class libraries from the standard edition of Java, with the exception of the user interface libraries. This configuration is intended for use with hardware that contains more resources than the standard embedded device, but it is not a full computer.

Like the CLDC, the CDC has profiles that further define the target device. The Foundation Profile defines a full implementation of the Java Virtual Machine and most of the Java class libraries, excluding the user interface classes. The Personal Basis Profile adds the AWT class libraries, in addition to what the Foundation Profile defines. Finally, the Personal Profile includes everything contained in the previously mentioned profiles, with the addition of support for applets.

Configurations and profiles are beneficial from a development perspective because they allow you to group similar, but still different, devices together and share common code between them. A developer is not required to learn the details of every device they work with, just its configuration and profile. Since the configuration and profile are used across many devices, the time spent learning this can then be applied to many devices.

J2ME Disadvantages

J2ME attempts to create a much more unified development environment for developers to work with. No longer does a developer have to learn different languages and libraries to work with different devices. However, J2ME does not completely follow the Java motto of "write once, run anywhere." Mobile and embedded devices vary too much for this to be true. Configurations and profiles address this problem to a degree, but the experienced J2ME developer will still find many nuances that exist between devices, especially in areas dealing with user interfaces.

J2ME is not intended for very complex applications. This has more to do with the intended targeted devices than with this edition of Java. Since the targeted devices are resource limited, the user interface libraries only contain basic interface elements. While this keeps the application smaller and more efficient, it also limits how complex an interface a developer can create. J2ME is ideal for creating applications to look up or record simple information. Creating complex software such as a word processor would quickly push up against the limitations of the device and J2ME libraries.

J2ME Deployment

J2ME MIDlets are generally deployed over a network. They can be manually loaded onto a device, but that isn't very useful for a large install base. Typically, they will be loaded by a web server, serving them to clients upon their request. A MIDlet on a web server will consist of at least two files: a Java Application Descriptor, or JAD, and the Java Archive, or JAR file. The JAD file is used to describe the MIDlet. It is a text file that contains information such as the MIDlet's version, the location of the JAR, the location of the icon (if it exists), and many other attributes. The exact specification of creating a JAD is beyond the scope of the SCJA. It is important, however, to remember that the JAD is used to describe what the MIDlet is to the target devices. The JAR file is the same as a standard Java JAR file. It is a collection of all the binary files and resources that make up the MIDlet.

on the job *The current SCJA exam uses the term J2ME for the mobile addition of Java. Since the test has been published, Sun Microsystems has changed its official name to Java ME. Both J2ME and Java ME refer to the same thing and can be used interchangeably. However, if you want to stay up-to-date, you should use Java ME. To avoid confusion, this book will use the same terms as the exam.*

CERTIFICATION OBJECTIVE

Using Java Applets as Fat Clients

Exam Objective 7.3   Describe at a high level the basic characteristics, benefits, drawbacks, and deployment issues related to creating fat-clients using Applets.

Applets are one of the two fat-client technologies that the SCJA exam will cover. A fat-client technology is one where most or all of the processing for the application is done on the client side. Applets, as the name implies, are mini-applications. They are useful when creating an application with a complex interface, but would still like to tightly couple it with a web page. The SCJA exam will have questions that require you to choose when using an applet would be appropriate and determine their advantages and disadvantages. The following topics will be covered in the next few subsections.

- Java applets
- Java applet disadvantages
- Java applet deployment

Java Applets

Applets are simple and effective tools that have existed in Java since 1995. They were created to add an interactive element to an HTML web page. Applets can be embedded in more than just HTML; they may be used in full applications or even as a standalone application. However, their primary function is to provide interactive qualities to a web site that cannot be produced in HTML alone. Since applets are really just a special Java application, they can be executed regardless of the platform the user is running. Applets are executed entirely on the client side. Their only requirement is that the remote system has the Java browser plug-in and Java Virtual Machine installed.

From a programming perspective, there is very little difference between a Java desktop application and a Java applet. An applet can easily be modified into a standard desktop application. With some exceptions, a simple desktop application can be changed into an applet. The main difference between the two is the way the code is invoked. The programming difference will not be on the SCJA exam.

An applet's advantage is its ability to be embedded in a web page but still retain powerful features that would normally be found in a standard desktop application. An applet will allow the client to access backend enterprise servers such as web servers, web services, and databases. It also can make use of advanced Java user interface elements such as Swing and multimedia libraries for media playback.

Java Applet Disadvantages

Despite the simplicity of a Java applet, there are some disadvantages to using them. As stated earlier, to execute the applet the Java Virtual Machine must be used. It also must be a current version. If an applet is executed on an out-of-date Virtual Machine, the applet will attempt to download the latest version. This may create a substantial delay in the startup time of the applet.

Applets have much tighter runtime restrictions than a standard Java application. By default, they are not permitted to create network connections to arbitrary servers on the Internet. They also are executed in a sandbox that gives them limited access to the client-side system. And even if more than one applet is embedded in the same page, intercommunication is impossible. These restrictions may be relaxed but the user must agree to it via a prompt from the Java Virtual Machine.

Since applets are often located inside web pages, they are not able to be executed offline. The user must have a network connection to the server that contains the applet. If the user does have a network connection but limited bandwidth, the user may suffer from very slow load times since the applet is reloaded each time it is run. Some cache is available to help speed up this process, but this is unreliable since it can easily be cleared.

on the *Applets were Sun Microsystems' attempt to create dynamic web pages.*
Job *When Sun first introduced them in 1995, web pages were not able to do much except serve static content. Applets allowed fully functioning "mini" applications to be embedded in web pages, but were plagued with problems from the start. Applets were resource hungry and had compatibility problems between Sun's Virtual Machine and Microsoft's. By the time these problems had been addressed, new technologies such as JavaScript provided similar functionality. Currently, applets are rarely used outside of special cases.*

Java Applet Deployment

Applets are easy to deploy. They reside on the web server and are embedded in the web page. When the user accesses the web page, as long as the user has the Java Virtual Machine installed with the Java browser plug-in, the applet will load. The advantage of this system of deployment is that the user never needs to install an application. From the user's perspective, they are just visiting a web page. This also allows the programmer to control the deployed version of the applet. When a new version is released, it can be loaded on the web server and the next time the user visits the site and loads the applet, the newer version will be used.

CERTIFICATION OBJECTIVE

Using the Java Swing API as a Fat Client

Exam Objective 7.4   Describe at a high level the basic characteristics, benefits, drawbacks, and deployment issues related to creating fat-clients using Swing.

Swing is the second fat-client technology present on the SCJA exam. Swing is a graphical user interface toolkit for creating an application's interface. It is responsible for drawing and maintaining all the components on screen, such as buttons, text boxes, scroll bars, and so on. The SCJA exam will ask questions about when it is appropriate to use Swing over other competing technologies and the benefits it provides. The following topics will be covered in the next few subsections.

- Java Swing API
- Java Swing API disadvantages
- Java Swing API deployment

e x a m
watch

On the SCJA, when they refer to Swing, they are normally using it in the context of a desktop application. It is important to remember that Swing is a library for creating user interfaces. It is normally used in desktop applications but can also be used to build the interfaces of applets.

Java Swing API

Swing is Sun Microsystems' second version of a graphical user interface toolkit for Java. It is used to create the user interfaces for applets and desktop applications. The Abstract Window Toolkit (AWT) is the predecessor of this toolkit. At a low level, Swing extends some of the classes of AWT. However, there is a vast difference on how they render their components. AWT is considered heavyweight. This means that they rely on the native system's windowing components. An AWT component will utilize the native system to render and control each component used. This guarantees the interface will look like the interface of a native application. Since all native toolkits do not work the same way, AWT had to make some assumptions to work across platforms. While AWT managed to work fairly well, the assumptions it made created some minor bugs and strange behaviors that depended on which native toolkit was being used.

To solve the problems of AWT, Sun created the Swing API. Unlike AWT, Swing is a lightweight toolkit. This means that Swing does not rely on the native toolkit but instead draws and manages all of its own components. This makes the interface more portable because it does not depend on different native components behaving similarly. However, since Swing does draw its own components, the look and feel may be slightly different from a native or AWT application. Swing does have the advantage of being skin-able. Skin-able is a term that means the developer can change the look and feel of Swing without having to modify its components. The source code of a component does not require modification to change its look and feel. It is distributed with different skins that give it the appearance of a native application on different platforms.

Swing is a standard part of J2SE. It allows for the creation of fully featured desktop applications. These applications are often designed to run on a client's system just like they run on any other native program—oftentimes being indistinguishable. Swing offers the richest set of user interface components. The applications have full access to the system they are executed on, and can feature a complex interface for performing more demanding tasks. The only requirement to run a Swing application is to have the Java Virtual Machine installed. It does not require a network connection unless it is required to connect to a server during runtime.

on the
job

In modern applications, AWT is rarely used for components. Swing has proven to be more efficient and consistent across different platforms. AWT can create an application that looks more native than Swing, but the difference is normally insignificant.

Currently, a total of 16 related Swing API packages (that is, subpackages) are available. It is important to be aware of them for development purposes, but this knowledge is not directly required for the exam.

Java Swing API Disadvantages

Swing has default skins that resemble the native look of many platforms. However, users still may notice subtle differences between a Swing application and a native or AWT one. Since Swing is a full-blown toolkit for creating user interfaces, it may not run as well on older hardware or systems that have limited resources. If your application is simple, sometimes a full Swing application introduces more complexity to a project than needed. It may be easier for the developer, and user, to create a simple web application with an HTML interface.

Java Swing API Deployment

A desktop Swing application can be deployed in two ways. The first method, and the traditional method, is to release your software as a package distributed by CD or for download over the network. The user will then run some form of installer to load the software onto their system. This is good if the software rarely changes. The user will have the software on their computer and will not have to worry about having a good network connection or reloading it from the enterprise server every time. However, if your software will be updated often, then the user will have to install the updates themselves.

The second way to deploy a Swing application is to use Java Web Start. Java Web Start is a technology developed by Sun Microsystems to deploy Java applications like a Java applet. It allows a full desktop application to be launched from a web browser. Like an applet, it downloads all of the required files from a remote server. However, unlike an applet, it does not run inside the browser. It runs on the system similar to a native application. By default, a Web Start application is restricted from accessing the local file system and is limited as to which remote servers it can connect to. These restrictions can be overcome if the user allows it.

CERTIFICATION SUMMARY

This chapter focused on client-side Java technologies. End-users will typically access your data via a client-side application. No matter how well designed the software is on the backend, or server side, if the client-side application is poorly designed or inaccessible when needed, your user will find limited value in your software solution. In this chapter, we discussed a few different Java technologies used on the client side. On the SCJA, you will need to understand from a high level the advantage and disadvantage of each technology. It is also important to understand when it is appropriate to use one of the technologies over the other. Finally, you must understand how each technology is deployed and how this will affect the maintainability of the software.

We started the chapter by discussing thin clients that use HTML and JavaScript. This type of client is a web-based front-end to your backend enterprise server. HTML alone allows for only a limited interactive user interface. JavaScript can be used to add more, but still limited, interactivity. JavaScript can also be used for input validation. This client type does nearly all of its processing on the server side. Maintenance is simplified since the software is located on your web server. The web server is also used to send that data to the user.

Next, we covered J2ME. J2ME is aimed squarely at mobile and embedded devices. While its syntax is the same as J2SE and J2EE, since it is targeted at lower-power and resource-limited devices, it does not have access to all of the same libraries. J2ME only allows for a simple user interface, but on small devices it tends to provide all the functionality needed. Despite the drawbacks of J2ME, it does allow you to create client-side applications that can then connect to your backend enterprise servers. The tradeoff of limited functionality is quickly compensated with portability when a mobile phone is used as the target environment.

Finally, we looked at two fat-client technologies: Java applets and Swing. Java applets allow for the creation of very dynamic and advanced user interfaces using Java, but then embed them in a web page. Applets are easy to maintain and deploy since they reside on your server and are transferred by a web server each time they are started. However, applets do come with restrictions. They are limited as to how they can interact with the client system and whom they can communicate with over the network.

Swing is a technology in Java for building user interfaces. Swing is a standard part of J2SE. Normally, it is used to create full standalone Java applications. These applications can be created to look and feel like a native application for the target platform. A Swing application can connect to a backend database, or server. It tends to require more resources than the other technologies we discussed, but it can also provide the user with the most advanced user interface. Swing applications can utilize Java Web Start for deployment to simplify maintenance issues.

TWO-MINUTE DRILL

Using Thin Clients with HTML and the JavaScript API

- ❏ HTML is a markup language used to present static content in the form of web pages.
- ❏ JavaScript is different than Java; it is a scripting language used to provide interactivity in web pages.
- ❏ A thin client is an application that is not much more than a user interface that connects to an enterprise server for its data and processing.
- ❏ HTML and JavaScript are useful for creating user interfaces.
- ❏ All the user needs to access an HTML application is a web browser.
- ❏ HTML and JavaScript provide only limited user interface components.

Using J2ME MIDlets

- ❏ J2ME is a branch of Java.
- ❏ J2ME is for resource-limited devices.
- ❏ MIDlets are applications written in J2ME for a MIDP device.
- ❏ Profiles and configurations are used to define a device.
- ❏ MIDlets can be developed and tested on desktop computers.
- ❏ MIDlets can only display basic user interfaces.

Using Java Applets as Fat Clients

- ❏ Applets are Java programs that are normally embedded in web pages.
- ❏ Applets can contain simple or complex interfaces.
- ❏ Applets are normally launched from a web page and downloaded before they start.
- ❏ Applets can download updates to the Java Virtual Machine if needed.
- ❏ Each time an applet is started, they are reloaded, ensuring that users will always have the latest version.
- ❏ Applets may be slow to start since they are loaded from the network.

Using the Java Swing API as a Fat Client

❑ Swing is a graphical user interface toolkit.

❑ Swing is lightweight, meaning it draws and manages its own components.

❑ AWT is a heavyweight graphical user interface toolkit, meaning it relies on native components to render its interface.

❑ Swing can be used to create the richest and most complex interfaces.

❑ Using Swing can add complexity to a project and increase the needed resources for it to run.

SELF TEST

Using Thin Clients with HTML and the JavaScript API

1. What technology is used to create interactive web pages?
    A. HTML
    B. Java
    C. Enterprise servers
    D. JavaScript

2. What is true of HTML and JavaScript user interfaces? (Choose all that apply.)
    A. The user must have a network connection to your web server.
    B. There is limited access to the client system.
    C. The JavaScript processing is done on the client-side system.
    D. Complex and rich interfaces can be created.

3. What displays and executes HTML and JavaScript user interfaces?
    A. Applets
    B. Mobile devices
    C. Web browsers
    D. Swing

Using J2ME MIDlets

4. Which devices would most likely use J2ME? (Choose two.)
    A. A candy vending machine
    B. A desktop computer
    C. A PDA (personal digital assistant)
    D. A web server

5. What are used to define the features that a J2ME device has? (Choose all that apply.)
    A. Profiles
    B. Configurations
    C. XML
    D. A properties file
    E. UML

6. Which of the following are true about J2ME applications? (Choose all that apply.)

   A. They are deployed via Java Web Start.

   B. They can have complex user interfaces.

   C. They can play back multimedia files.

   D. They are written in JavaScript.

7. Which of the follow is NOT true about J2ME applications?

   A. They can be developed and debugged on most desktop computers.

   B. They are designed for resource limited devices.

   C. They can have complex and rich user interfaces.

   D. Applications for mobile phones are often called MIDlets.

Using Java Applets as Fat Clients

8. Finish the sentence: Applets are normally embedded in _____.

   A. Mobile devices

   B. Enterprise servers

   C. Web pages

   D. MIDlets

   E. User interfaces

9. Which of the following are advantages of applets? (Choose all that apply.)

   A. When a new version is released, users will automatically receive it.

   B. They start up very quickly.

   C. They look and work like native applications.

   D. They don't need to be installed on the user's system.

10. Which of the following is NOT true about applets?

   A. Applets have full access to the user's computer.

   B. Applets will download the latest Java Virtual Machine if the remote system is not up to date.

   C. Applets will always be the latest deployed version of the application because they are reloaded from the remote server every time they are launched.

11. Applets can use Swing to create complex graphical user interfaces?

    A. True

    B. False

Using the Java Swing API as a Fat Client

12. Which of the following is true?

    A. Swing and AWT are both heavyweight toolkits.

    B. Swing and AWT are both lightweight toolkits.

    C. Swing is a heavyweight toolkit and AWT is a lightweight toolkit.

    D. Swing is a lightweight toolkit and AWT is a heavyweight toolkit.

13. Swing can be used to do the following. (Choose all that apply.)

    A. Create relatively native looking applications

    B. Create complex and rich user interfaces

    C. Play an audio file

    D. Be used inside of an applet

    E. Be used inside of a MIDlet

14. Which of the following can Java Web Start do? (Choose all that apply.)

    A. Execute JavaScript code

    B. Deploy the latest versions of a Java application

    C. Display HTML web pages

    D. Load and start a Java application

15. Which of the following will produce the most native looking application for a desktop system?

    A. Swing

    B. MIDlet

    C. Applet

    D. XML

    E. AWT

SELF TEST ANSWERS

Using Thin Clients with HTML and the JavaScript API

1. What technology is used to create interactive web pages?

   A. HTML

   B. Java

   C. Enterprise Servers

   D. JavaScript

> Answer:
>
> ☑ **A and D.** HTML and JavaScript can be used together to validate user input and interact with the user as they browse a web page.
>
> ☒ **B and C** are incorrect. **B** is incorrect because Java is a broad programming language. Java can be used to create HTML dynamically on the server side, but not actually create interactive web pages. **C** is incorrect because an enterprise server is used to host the web content.

2. What is true of HTML and JavaScript user interfaces? (Choose all that apply.)

   A. The user must have a network connection to your web server.

   B. There is limited access to the client system.

   C. The JavaScript processing is done on the client-side system.

   D. Complex and rich interfaces can be created.

> Answer:
>
> ☑ **A, B,** and **C. A** is correct since a network connection is required because an HTML and JavaScript interface can only be run via a web page and cannot be installed locally. **B** is correct because HTML and JavaScript web pages cannot access resources on the client's system. **C** is correct because all of the JavaScript is processed on the client's system.
>
> ☒ **D** is incorrect. HTML and JavaScript do not provide a means for very complex interfaces.

3. What displays and executes HTML and JavaScript interfaces?

   A. Applets

   B. Mobile devices

C. Web browsers

D. Swing

Answer:

☑ **C.** Web browsers render the HTML and process the JavaScript.

☒ **A, B,** and **D** are incorrect. **A** is incorrect because applets are programs; they do not display and execute HTML unless they are programmed to do so. **B** is incorrect because mobile devices may have a web browser installed that can handle HTML and JavaScript, but otherwise they cannot. **D** is incorrect because Swing is a user interface toolkit. While some of its components may be able to handle HTML or JavaScript, it is only at a basic level.

Using J2ME MIDlets

4. What devices would most likely use J2ME? (Choose two.)

A. Candy vending machine

B. Desktop computer

C. PDA (personal digital assistant)

D. Web server

Answer:

☑ **A** and **C. A** is correct because a vending machine would most likely use an embedded system. J2ME is designed for limited-resource devices, like an embedded system. **C** is correct because a PDA is a limited-resource device that J2ME would be suitable for.

☒ **B** and **D** are incorrect. **B** is incorrect because a desktop computer would use the full version of Java J2SE. **D** is incorrect because a web server would be a likely candidate for J2EE.

5. What are used to define the features that a J2ME device has? (Choose all that apply.)

A. Profiles

B. Configurations

C. XML

D. A properties file

E. UML

Answer:

☑ **A** and **B**. **A** is correct because profiles are used to define the features of a J2ME device. **B** is correct because configurations are used to define a general class of devices.

☒ **C, D,** and **E** are incorrect.

6. Which of the following are true of J2ME applications? (Choose all that apply.)

A. They are deployed via Java Web Start.

B. They can have complex user interfaces.

C. They can play back multimedia files.

D. They are written in JavaScript.

Answer:

☑ **C**. J2ME has many class libraries for handling multimedia files.

☒ **A, B,** and **D** are incorrect. **A** is incorrect because Java Web Start is used to deploy standard desktop applications. **B** is incorrect because J2ME can only create simple interfaces. **D** is incorrect because JavaScript is a scripting language that is used mainly for web pages.

7. Which of the following is NOT true of J2ME applications?

A. They can be developed and debugged on most desktop computers.

B. They are designed for resource limited devices.

C. They can have complex and rich user interfaces.

D. Applications for mobile phones are often called MIDlets.

Answer:

☑ **C**. Most J2ME devices that run J2ME cannot handle a very complex user interface.

☒ **A, B,** and **D** are incorrect. **A** is incorrect because it is a true statement. Since they are written in Java most of the time, they can be tested on standard desktop systems first. **B** is incorrect because it is also a true statement. J2ME was created to handle limited-resource devices. **D** is incorrect because this is a true statement as well. MIDlets get their name from the fact that they are written for the MIDP profile.

Using Java Applets as Fat Clients

8. Finish the sentence: Applets are normally embedded in _____.

    A. Mobile devices

    B. Enterprise servers

    C. Web pages

    D. MIDlets

    E. User interfaces

> Answer:
>
> ☑ **C.** Applets are embedded in web pages.
>
> ☒ **A, B, D**, and **E** are incorrect. **A** is incorrect because mobile devices normally run J2ME. **B** is incorrect because enterprise servers typically use J2EE. **D** is incorrect because MIDlets are J2ME applications. **E** is incorrect because user interfaces have nothing to do with applets and where they are embedded.

9. Which of the following are advantages of applets? (Choose all that apply.)

    A. When a new version is released, users will automatically receive it.

    B. They start up very quickly.

    C. They look and work like native applications.

    D. They don't need to be installed on the user's system.

> Answer:
>
> ☑ **A** and **D. A** is correct because applets download to the user every time they are started. When a new version is deployed to the web server, your user will get it the next time they start the applet. **D** is correct because applets are always launched from a web browser. They are never installed on the remote system.
>
> ☒ **B** and **C** are incorrect. **B** is incorrect because applets may be slow starting up since they need to download to the user. **C** is incorrect because applets are embedded in web pages and they tend to look and act differently than most native applications.

10. Which of the following is not true about applets?

    A. Applets have full access to the user's computer.

    B. Applets will download the latest Java Virtual Machine if the remote system is not up to date.

    C. Applets will always be the latest deployed version of the application because they are reloaded from the remote server every time they are launched.

> **Answer:**
>
> ☑ **A.** Applets, by default, run in a strict sandbox for security reasons.
>
> ☒ **B** and **C** are incorrect. Both statements are true.

11. Applets can use Swing to create complex graphical user interfaces?

    A. True

    B. False

> **Answer:**
>
> ☑ **A.** This is true because applets can use Swing to create the graphical user interface. Swing is Java's richest toolkit for developing interfaces.

Using the Java Swing API as a Fat Client

12. Which of the following is true?

    A. Swing and AWT are both heavyweight toolkits.

    B. Swing and AWT are both lightweight toolkits.

    C. Swing is a heavyweight toolkit and AWT is a lightweight toolkit.

    D. Swing is a lightweight toolkit and AWT is a heavyweight toolkit.

> **Answer:**
>
> ☑ **D.** Swing is considered lightweight because it renders its own components. AWT relies on the native widgets of the operation system to render its components.
>
> ☒ **A, B,** and **C** are incorrect.

13. Swing can be used to do the following. (Choose all that apply.)

    A. Create relatively native looking applications

    B. Create complex and rich user interfaces

    C. Play an audio file

    D. Be used inside of an applet

    E. Be used inside of a MIDlet

Answer:

☑ **A, B,** and **C.**

☒ **C** and **E** are incorrect. **C** is incorrect because Swing applications can play audio files but the sound functionality is done outside of the Swing package. It is only for creating user interfaces. **E** is incorrect because Swing cannot be used to create the interface of a MIDlet. MIDlets use J2ME, which uses its own user interface toolkit.

14. Which of the following can Java Web Start do? (Choose all that apply.)

A. Execute JavaScript code

B. Deploy the latest versions of a Java application

C. Display HTML web pages

D. Load and start a Java application

Answer:

☑ **B** and **D. B** is correct because Java Web Start will deploy the latest version of the application each time it is started up. It will even download updates to the Java Virtual Machine if needed. **D** is correct because Java Web Start is also used to launch and deploy a Java application from within a web browser. Unlike an applet, it runs outside of the browser once it is launched.

☒ **A** and **C** are incorrect. **A** is incorrect because JavaScript is a scripting language used with HTML to create web pages. **C** is incorrect because Java Web Start has nothing to do with displaying HTML.

15. Which of follow will produce the most native looking application for a desktop system?

A. Swing

B. MIDlet

C. Applet

D. XML

E. AWT

Answer:

☑ **E.** AWT is a heavyweight toolkit that uses native components and therefore most closely resembles native applications.

☒ **A, B, C,** and **D** are incorrect. **A** is incorrect because Swing is a lightweight toolkit. It draws its own components that resemble native components. **B** is incorrect because MIDlets are J2ME applications. **C** is incorrect because an applet runs within a web browser. **D** is incorrect because XML is a markup language.

12

Understanding
Server-Side
Technologies

CERTIFICATION OBJECTIVES

- Understanding Java EE–Related
  Tiers and Technologies

- Understanding Server-Side Solutions

- Understanding Dynamic Web
  Content Solutions

- Understanding Enterprise Business
  Logic Solutions

✓ Two-Minute Drill

Q&A Self Test

T he server side includes all of the Java EE technologies, such as business logic APIs and dynamic web content solutions. Many of these technologies are defined as optional packages. The complete set of optional packages that must be made available by the Java EE 5 platform is detailed in Table 10-3. A subset of these APIs (from the J2EE 1.4 JSR-151) is on the exam. These J2EE 1.4 exam-related packages are listed in Table 12-1. The packages are separated into web services, web application, and enterprise application sections. You can find the Java Specifications Requests (JSRs) online to review detailed information about each technology at http://jcp.org/en/jsr/overview/.

By the end of this chapter, you will have a high-level understanding of the exam-related server-side technologies, as well as how they fit into the different architecture tiers.

TABLE 12-1	JSR	Specification Name	Abbreviation	Version
J2EE 1.4 Optional Package Technologies Covered on the SCJA Exam	Web Services Technologies			
	JSR-101	Java API for XML-Based RPC	JAX-RPC	1.1
	JSR-109	Implementing Enterprise Web Services	Web Services	1.1
	JSR-110	Java APIs for WSDL	* External to Java EE	
	Web Application Technologies			
	JSR-152	JavaServer Pages 2.0 Specification	JSP	2.0
	JSR-154	Java Servlet 2.4 Specification	Servlets	2.4
	Enterprise Application Technologies			
	JSR-153	Enterprise JavaBeans 2.1	EJB	2.1
	JSR-904	JavaMail Specification	JavaMail	1.2
	JSR-914	Java Message Service (JMS) API	JMS	1.1

CERTIFICATION OBJECTIVE

Understanding Java EE–Related Tiers and Technologies

Exam Objective 8.4   Describe at a high level the fundamental benefits and drawbacks of using J2EE server-side technologies, and describe and compare the basic characteristics of the web-tier, business-tier, and EIS tier.

Java EE server-side technologies make up the heart and soul of many of today's e-commerce and e-business solutions, providing for fast, flexible, and secure functionality. The following subsections explore the advantages and disadvantages of these server-side solutions and the logical separation of enterprise functionality into their own domains (tiers). Topics covered include:

- Pros and cons of Java EE server-side technologies
- Enterprise tiers

For real-world discussions, whitepapers, tutorials, and more related to server-side solutions, consider visiting the following web sites: DZone's Javalobby (http://java.dzone.com/), TheServerSide (www.theserverside.com/), and the JavaRanch (www.javaranch.com/). Since JavaServer Faces is a leading user interface technology for server-side solutions, you may also want to explore JSFtutorials.net (www.jsftutorials.net/).

Pros and Cons of the Server Side

Java EE architecture and technologies have numerous capabilities and qualities that make Java EE ideal for building e-commerce and e-business systems. The *Sun Certified Enterprise Architect for Java EE Study Guide* by Paul R. Allen and Joseph J. Bambara (McGraw-Hill Professional 2007) details eleven Java architecture capabilities and qualities. These all represent pros of the server side.

The competitive solution to Java EE is Microsoft's .NET framework. Googling for articles that compare and contrast their features is a great way to determine the platform and architecture that best fits your needs. In your search, you may find some entertaining articles along the way.

TABLE 12-2	Java EE System Qualities	

System Quality	Definition	Real-World Example
Availability	The ability of a system to be accessible, having limited downtime.	System is available 24/7.
Capacity	The ability of a system to efficiently multitask within a period of time.	System can maintain five million concurrent users.
Extensibility	The ability for functionality to be extended.	System can easily add a PDF generation library and functionality.
Flexibility	The ability to address configuration changes while maintaining the system's integrity.	System can move a database to a new server with minor configuration changes.
Manageability	The ability to manage system resources.	System can modify access rights of registered users while the system is operational.
Performance	The ability to perform functionality within specified goals.	System must retrieve database queries within three seconds.
Reliability	The ability to ensure the integrity and consistency of a system and its transactions.	System sends e-mails that are not corrupted.
Reusability	The ability to reuse a component.	System uses the same login component for various applications.
Scalability	The ability to support functionality when load increases.	System querying services respond in the required time goal, regardless of the number of users.
Security	The ability to ensure information assurance.	System encrypts and decrypts data traveling over a network.
Validity	The ability to validate results of a system or user input.	System disallows input fields that are not in the necessary format.

The main disadvantage to the Java EE architecture is its complexity. To be able to program with the Java EE APIs as a software maintainer you must know the fundamentals of Java very well. To be able to effectively develop code in the Java EE environment, you should understand the more advanced object-oriented features of the language, including the various design patterns; see *Core J2EE Patterns: Best Practices and Design Strategies* (2nd Edition) by Deepak Alur, Dan Malks, and John Crupi, Prentice Hall (May 2003). Because of the complexity and size of Java EE applications, teams of individuals are typically needed to assist in all phases of the traditional Software Development Lifecycle (SDLC) process. Even though a handful of people could wear the hats of requirement engineer, system architect, designer, developer, tester, and deployer, it is more effective to have individuals specializing in their given area.

Enterprise Tiers

Enterprise systems can be broken into multiple tiers. A common Java-based architecture design is the separation of application functionality into three distinct tiers. Unfortunately, various terms are used to describe each tier, which can lead to some mild confusion. Table 12-3 details some of the common terms you will see in references to the different tiers related to Java EE architecture. The webtier and the business tier are parts of the middle tier. The database tier is the most common component of the EIS tier. The client tier includes web browsers and client-based applications.

Understanding the Web Tier

The web tier is the tier within an enterprise system that contains the presentation layer. Servlets and JavaServer Pages are part of the web tier. These are web application technologies used for creating dynamic web content. JavaServer Pages deliver web pages from the web tier. Servlets handle HTTP web requests from the web tier. There are many web containers that implement the JSP and servlets specifications such as Apache Tomcat, Jetty, and the Sun Java System Web Server. Web containers such as Apache Tomcat can run alone or on top of an application server such as Geronimo Application Server or Sun's Glassfish. Alone, Apache Tomcat must run with a JRE or JDK, shown in Figure 12-1. The Sun Java System Web Server has extended functionality to support specifications outside of Java's domain, such as Microsoft's Active Server Pages, Adobe Coldfusion, PHP: Hypertext Preprocessor (PHP), and the Common Gateway Interface (CGI).

TABLE 12-3   Common Nomenclature of Enterprise Tier Components

Client Tier (Client Layer)	Middle Tier (Service Layer)		EIS Tier (Backend Layer)
Commonly known as the client layer (includes web browsers and client-based applications)	Web tier (a.k.a.) front-end server tier presentation tier GUI layer client tier (too) *Includes web container	Business tier (a.k.a.) backend server tier middleware * Includes EJB container	(a.k.a.) backend tier database tier data tier

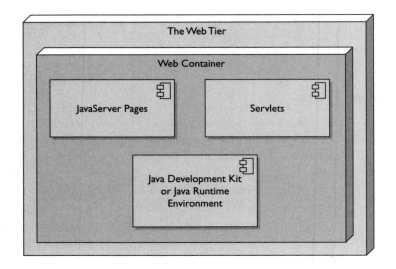

The JavaServer Faces (JSF) API and JavaServer Pages Standard Tag Library (JSTL) provide additional web contents solutions. JSF is a user-interface component framework that lets you easily build components, add validators and converters to the values of those components, and provides page navigation and state management support. JSTL is a tag library that is built off of the JSP framework.

Understanding the Business Tier

The business tier is the tier within an enterprise system that contains the business logic. Enterprise JavaBeans is one of the major components of the business tier. The other major components are the JAX-WS web service endpoints and the Java Persistence API entities, as shown in Figure 12-2. The Java Persistence API supersedes EJB entity beans. The exam focuses on Enterprise JavaBeans, which is covered in the section "Enterprise JavaBeans API."

Understanding the EIS Tier

The Enterprise Information System (EIS) tier is the tier within an enterprise system that contains the data layer. Common activities are persistence support through database management systems. The EIS tier includes databases, relational databases, legacy applications, enterprise resource planning systems, CRM systems, and legacy data stores. The EIS tier is typically on its own machine. For example, an enterprise-scale Oracle database can reside on its own server and is interfaced with remotely.

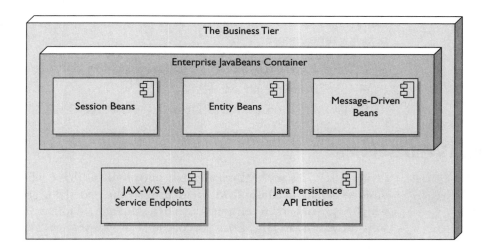

FIGURE 12-2

The business tier

Java EE technologies that can be used to access EIS tier data include the Java Database Connectivity API (JDBC), the Java Persistence API, the J2EE Connector Architecture, and the Java Transaction API (JTA). The exam focuses on JDBC, as detailed in Chapter 10.

CERTIFICATION OBJECTIVE

Understanding Server-Side Solutions

Exam Objective 8.1   Describe at a high level the basic characteristics of: EJB, servlets, JSP, JMS, JNDI, SMTP, JAX-RPC, Web Services (including SOAP, UDDI, WSDL, and XML), and JavaMail.

This section discusses the details of the interrelated mail technologies SMTP and the JavaMail API, JAX-RPC, and web services. When completed, you will have a very good high-level understanding of these server-side technologies.

Servlets and JSPs are covered in a later section of this chapter, "Understanding Dynamic Web Content Solutions." EJBs, meanwhile, are also covered later in this chapter, "Understanding Enterprise Business Logic Solutions." The Java Message Service (JMS) API and Java Naming and Directory Interface (JNDI) API are technologies discussed in Chapter 10. The following topics will be covered in the next few subsections:

- Java web services
- SMTP and the JavaMail API
- Java API for the Java XML-based Remote Procedure Call

Java Web Services

Java web services are XML-based messaging protocols that enable business-to-business communications. XML helps achieve the underlying goal of web services, which is to send and receive messages in a standardized format. Java web services were introduced in J2EE 1.4 as part of the Java Web Services Development Pack (JWSDP). The current pack, JWSDP 2.0, can be downloaded and integrated with a web container such as Tomcat, Glassfish Application Server, or the Sun Java System Application Server Platform. JWSDP 2.0 includes the following features:

- JAX-WS Version 2.0 EA (Java API for XML Web Services)
- Fast Infoset Version 1.0.1
- Sun Java Streaming XML Parser Version 1.0 EA
- XML Digital Signature Version 1.0.1
- XML and Web Services Security Version 2.0 EA2
- JAXB Version 2.0 EA (Java Architecture for XML Binding)
- JAXP Version 1.3.1_01 (Java API for XML Processing)
- JAXR Version 1.0.8_01 EA (Java API for XML Registries)
- JAX-RPC Version 1.1.3_01 EA (Java API for XML-based RPC)
- SAAJ Version 1.3 EA (SOAP with Attachments API for Java)

Web services technologies which do not require a web container to run include JAXB, JAXP, JAXR, SAAJ, and the XML Digital Signature. For the SCJA exam, the only related web services technologies you will need to know are XML, JAX-RPC (covered in the next section), and the three foundational standards of web services (SOAP, UDDI, and WSDL).

XML

The Extensible Markup Language (XML) is a general-purpose specification used for creating markup languages with the design purposes of transporting and storing data.

The XML specification allows for the creation of custom tags in structured text files. Web-based solutions make common use of XML files such as configuration, deployment descriptor, and tag libraries files. Again, XML was designed to structure, store, and/or carry data, not to display data.

XML is based on tags that the user must define. When creating tags, the user should name the tags descriptively. The following is an XML example that uses tags from the JavaServer Faces configuration file. When this XML is read with the JSF framework, it associates the tag elements with the code in its framework and performs the necessary functionality. In this example, when the loginSuccess value is returned, the web browser will display the welcome page.

```
<navigation-rule>
 <navigation-case>
  <from-outcome>loginSuccess</from-outcome>
  <to-view-id>/pages/welcome.jsp</to-view-id>
 </navigation-case>
</navigation-rule>
```

Simple Object Access Protocol

The Simple Object Access Protocol (SOAP) is a simple XML-based communication protocol used for information exchange within a decentralized and distributed environment. SOAP is used in various situations such as messaging and remote procedure calls.

SOAP is made up of three main parts: the envelope, the encoding rules, and the RPC. The envelope is the root XML element that contains the message recipient, message content, and processing information of the message. The encoding rules specify how the data-type instances will be exchanged. The RPCs defines the convention for representing the remote calls and responses. The following listing shows an example of a SOAP message:

```
<SOAP-ENV:Envelope xmlns:SOAP-ENV="http://schemas.xmlsoap.org/
soap/envelope/"
   SOAP-ENV:encodingStyle="http://schemas.xmlsoap.org/soap/
   encoding/">
 <SOAP-ENV:Header/>
 <SOAP-ENV:Body>
 <s:GetDinnerSpecial xmlns:m="Specified-URI">
   <Dish>Shrimp Scampi with Linguini</Dish>
 </s:GetDinnerSpecial>
 </SOAP-ENV:Body>
</SOAP-ENV:Envelope>
```

on the
🛈ob *The SOAP with Attachment API for JAVA (SAAJ) allows developers to send SOAP messages without having to construct the XML that is required when using SOAP by itself.*

WSDL

The Web Service Definition Language (WSDL) is an XML standard for businesses and individuals to access available services that each provide. The WSDL XML documents include a set of definitions. These definitions describe network services as a set of endpoints operating on messages containing either document or procedure-oriented information. These elements are described and bound to network protocols and message formats to define an endpoint. More specifically, an endpoint is a WSDL port that represents the contact point of the service. This endpoint consists of the protocol and location information.

UDDI

The Universal Description, Discovery, and Integration (UDDI) specification is an XML-based registry that is used by businesses to make their services and general business descriptions available through the Internet. UDDI can communicate via CORBA, SOAP, or the Java RMI protocols. UDDI makes use of WSDL in describing interfaces to web services. As such, the UDDI specification includes a set of WSDL definitions for modifying and searching its registry, and the registry itself includes the web service's metadata and a pointer to the WSDL service description.

SMTP and the JavaMail API

The Simple Mail Transfer Protocol (SMTP) and the JavaMail API are often used together to provide e-mailing solutions. An example of a secure way to send e-mail from a web application is to have a user fill out a contact form, have that data moved into the business logic upon a submit button, then use the JavaMail API to send the e-mail to the desired recipient by connecting and sending the e-mail from an SMTP server. Let's explore the SMTP and JavaMail technologies a little closer.

Simple Mail Transfer Protocol

The Simple Mail Transfer Protocol is exactly what its name describes: a protocol for sending mail. More specifically, SMTP is an Internet standard used for e-mail transmission over Internet Protocol (IP) networks with the main objective of transferring that mail reliably and efficiently. The SMTP server and protocol work well with Java since the JavaMail API was designed to connect to the SMTP server

FIGURE 12-3

The SMTP server

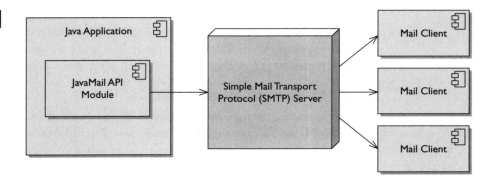

to transfer its mail. Take a look at Figure 12-3 to see how the SMTP server falls into system architecture.

A quick way to test the connection to your SMTP server is with the telnet utility. Type telnet <mailserver.com> 25 where mailserver.com is the name of your SMTP mail server. Note that the standard SMTP port is 25. A positive response may include the following "...`Connected to mailserver.com`*..."* *While telnet is a commonly used utility, it is not part of the Java toolset and isn't available on all operating systems by default. If the tool is not resident on your system, you may have to download it off the Internet.*

The JavaMail API

The JavaMail API is a standardized framework that provides electronic mail functionality. The JavaMail API is available in the `javax.mail` package and is part of the Java EE platform. Figure 12-4 shows commonly used JavaMail API classes from the JavaMail API package.

FIGURE 12-4

Commonly used JavaMail API classes

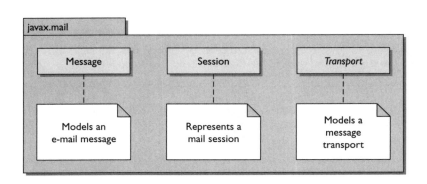

The Java Mail API is also available for download outside of the Java EE platform, for direct integration into Java SE. JavaMail has an application interface as well as a service provider interface. The application interface allows you to create code to send e-mail messages to specified recipients with subject and body content and a specified sender address. The service provider interface allows the user to specify the service that will be used, such as SMTP.

The JavaMail API supports various protocols and standards such as the discussed SMTP protocol, the POP and IMAP protocols, and the MIME standard.

Java API for XML-Based Remote Procedure Call

The Java API for XML-based Remote Procedure Call (JAX-RPC) is an API used to generate remote procedure calls in order to build web services and clients. The Java EE JAX-RPC API is available in the `javax.xml.rpc` package and subpackages. Figure 12-5 shows the various JAX-RPC packages.

JAX-RPC uses various web services discussed in this chapter to support remote procedure calls—that is, JAX-RPC uses the HTTP transport protocol and the SOAP standard to support building these remote calls for use over the Internet. The API also supports the importing and exporting of WSDL documents.

SCENARIO & SOLUTION

You need to use a protocol that will support the delivery of your e-mail. Which protocol would you use that is supported by the JavaMail API?	You would make use of the Simple Mail Transfer Protocol (SMTP).
You need to use a simple protocol to receive e-mail. Which protocol would you use that is supported by the JavaMail API?	You would make use of the Post Office Protocol (POP).
You need to use an advanced protocol to receive e-mail that has more options than POP. Which protocol would you use that is supported by the JavaMail API?	You would make use of the Internet Message Access Protocol (IMAP).
You need to make use of a standard that defines the structure of the mail content to be transferred. Which standard would you use that is supported by the JavaMail API?	You would make use of the Multipurpose Internet Mail Extensions (MIME).

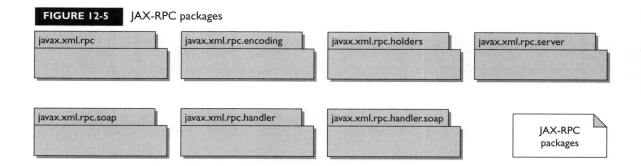

FIGURE 12-5   JAX-RPC packages

    The current version of the JAX-RPC specification has been renamed from JAX-RPC to JAX-WS. This Java API for XML Web Services (JAX-WS) specification is being developed under JSR 224.

CERTIFICATION OBJECTIVE

Understanding Dynamic Web Content Solutions

Exam Objective 8.2   Describe at a high level the basic characteristics of servlet and JSP support for HTML thin-clients.

Servlets and JavaServer Pages provide dynamic web content support. Servlets and JavaServer Pages (JSP) are specifications that are tied to Java EE releases. Various commercial and non-commercial vendors implement those specifications. The implementations are designed within either a web container, application server, or both. Noncommercial web containers include, but are not limited to, Apache Tomcat, Jetty, and Winstone. A current list of commercial web containers can be found on Wikipedia (the free online encyclopedia) at http://en.wikipedia.org/wiki/List_of_Servlet_containers. Table 12-4 details commonly used web containers and their versions. This table is presented to help you conceptualize the implementations of web containers in the real world.

TABLE 12-4	Various Servlet and JSP Web Containers and Their Versions				
Servlet/JSP Specification	**Java EE/SE Implementation**	**Apache Tomcat Version**	**Jetty Version**	**Winstone Version**	**Sun Java System Web Server**
Servlet 3.0 JSP 2.1	Java EE 6 w/ Java SE 6.0	Tomcat 7.0.x	Jetty-7.0	Pending	Pending
Servlet 2.5 JSP 2.1	Java EE 5 w/ J2SE 5.0	Tomcat 6.0.x	Jetty-6.1	Winstone 0.9	JSWS 7.0
Servlet 2.4 JSP 2.0	J2EE 1.4 w/ J2SE 1.3	Tomcat 5.5.x	Jetty-5.1	Winstone 0.6	JSWS 7.0
Servlet 2.3 JSP 1.2	J2EE 1.3 w/ J2SE 1.2	Tomcat 4.1.x	Jetty-4.2		JSWS 6.1

The following sections detail the purpose of servlets and JSPs and their capabilities, and cover the topics listed next.

- Java Servlet API
- JavaServer Pages API

Java Servlet API

The Java Servlet API allows a pure-Java program to execute in response to a web-based HTTP request. This Servlet API is made available in the `javax.servlet` package and subpackages. Servlets allow for web interfacing functionality so Java developers can add dynamic web content to their software. This web content is normally generated HTML, but may be XML. Servlets play an important "dynamic" role since the developer can programmatically decide what HTML is rendered. This is an advantage over deploying web pages by themselves since (again) servlets let HTML content be rendered based on conditions.

A big disadvantage of servlets is the lack of ease and cleanliness of writing HTML code, because creating syntactical errors is common and conceptualizing the presentation is hard. As you can see in the following servlet, writing HTML code can be tedious and error-prone. Fortunately, JavaServer Pages was designed to expedite and ease the creating of web content.

```
import java.io.IOException;
import java.io.PrintWriter;
import javax.servlet.ServletException;
```

```
import javax.servlet.http.HttpServlet;
import javax.servlet.http.HttpServletRequest;
import javax.servlet.http.HttpServletResponse;
public class SampleServlet extends HttpServlet {
  // Called from web browser
  public void doGet(HttpServletRequest request,
      HttpServletResponse response)
      throws ServletException, IOException {
    PrintWriter out = response.getWriter();
    out.println("<p>HTML page message from doGet method.</p>");
  }
  // Called via standard input stream
  public void doPost(HttpServletRequest request,
      HttpServletResponse response)
      throws ServletException, IOException {
    PrintWriter out = response.getWriter();
    out.println("<p>HTML page message from doPost method.</p>");
  }
}
```

Servlets work on the basic principle of overriding the `doGet` and `doPost` methods as they relate to web browsers' requests and response interactions. In the previous example, the `doGet` and `doPost` methods are overridden. For the former method, the user would access this servlet (and the `doGet` method) by typing in the class name in the web browser's address bar (for example, www.scjaexam. com/SampleServlet). After pressing the ENTER key, the browser will send a request message to execute the `doGet` method. In response, the associated HTML content will be sent to, and rendered by, the web browser.

exam
ⓦatch
JavaServer Pages and servlets are used for dynamic web content solutions. Remember that servlets act as the controller and that JSPs are converted into servlets before the pages are rendered for deployment. Servlets are loaded into memory the first time they are called, causing a slight delay. However, subsequent calls are handled very quickly, allowing JSP/servlet pages to run faster than competing technologies like PHP and Perl.

JavaServer Pages API

JavaServer Pages (JSP) provide a dynamic web content solution by using template data and custom elements to expedite and ease the development of the presentation layer. This combination of a scripting and tag-based approach allows for the easy creation of interactive web pages. The tags let embedded Java code dynamically control what is rendered in the HTML pages. JSP also allows for Java libraries integration. This means Java EE services such as JNDI, JDBC, JavaMail, and JMS can be embedded into JSP code. Beware though—just because you can embed plenty of Java code into JSP pages, this does not make it a good practice. Good design is to have the servlet (that is, the controller) manage the conditional logic and have the JSP pages render the presentation code.

on the
()ob

JavaServer Pages are commonly used with larger frameworks such as Seam, Shale, Struts, Spring and JavaServer Faces.

Many competing technologies place all of the application code on the page level. JSP provides a clean separation of front-end presentation logic and business logic. This separation of logic and coding responsibilities, coupled with the ease of creating pages, provides for code maintainability and a Rapid Application Development (RAD) approach to building web applications.

JSP technology has a feature known as extensible tags that allows for the creation of custom tags, extending the JSP pages tag syntax. Custom tag developers ease the development of web pages by making the complexity of the added functionality transparent to the page authors. Sun provides the JavaServer Pages Standard Tag Library that supports common iteration and conditional tasks, as well as internationalization (i18n), SQL, and XML features.

on the
()ob

Session objects live on the client machine in cookies. Cookies are data files written to a web client's computer when a web application is run through a web browser. JSP provides session tracking support allowing access to the data inside these cookies.

EXERCISE 12-1

Creating Servlets, JSP Pages, and JSF Pages

The best way to adequately familiarize yourself with technology specifics is to actually work with the APIs. This exercise will have you creating code that will render web pages with Java technologies, including servlets, JavaServer Pages, and

JavaServer Faces. The small number of steps that follow make the exercise appear small. However, the endeavor may end up taking you several hours since major tools and components may need to be installed and/or configured (if you don't have them set up already).

1. Set up an application server and/or web container to which you plan to deploy. Open-source candidates that can be set up quickly and integrated with common IDEs include Geronimo Application Server and Sun's Glassfish Server.

2. Set up an integrated development environment that supports Java. Open-source IDE candidates include Eclipse and NetBeans. Note that you must ensure that the IDE can deploy to the application server you set up. If it doesn't, you may simply need to install a plug-in, as is the case with Eclipse and Geronimo. The plug-in installation process only takes a couple of minutes.

3. In the IDE, create a web application project. Go through the IDE's menus and find the feature that will allow you to automatically import the basic structure of servlets, JSPs, and JSF in web files.

4. With the file generation option you have found, create a servlet. Add content to the servlet that will define text to be displayed in a web page. Note that overriding the doGet method will allow you to directly get to the page from your web browser.

5. With the file generation option, create a JSP page. Add content to the JSP page that will define text to be displayed in a web page.

6. With the file generation option, create a JSF page. Add content to the JSF page that will define text to be displayed in a web page.

7. Build your web project with the IDE.

8. Deploy your web project to the application server you installed with your IDE.

9. Use your web browser to access the three deployed web pages.

10. Smile. You can be very proud of yourself; this was no easy exercise. But it did set you up with the basic foundation of web development. More importantly, you now have direct experience with servlets, JSP pages, and JSF pages.

Understanding Enterprise Business Logic Solutions

Exam Objective 8.3   Describe at a high level the use and basic characteristics of EJB session, entity, and message-driven beans.

The Enterprise JavaBeans API came about in the early days of Java. Back in 1998, the first EJB specification was released: EJB 1.0. Its focus was on providing a framework for how Java-based enterprise business logic would be implemented in the business tier. Because of the critical nature of this tier, the EJB specification has and continues to evolve, adding and refining functionality along the way. The exam targets EJB 2.1 (JSR-153), which is part of Java EE 1.4. The current development release of Enterprise JavaBeans is EJB 3.1.

Enterprise JavaBeans API

At its simplest, the Enterprise JavaBeans API allows for the creation of enterprise beans. Three different types of enterprise beans are shown in Table 12-5. They are session, entity, and message-driven beans. These enterprise beans are components in the business tier that are responsible for executing the business logic of an application. The beans are managed by the EJB container that handles responsibilities such as security authorization and transaction management. The EJB container handles these tasks behind the scenes, allowing the software developers to stay focused on creating their business logic. Unlike languages such as Coldfusion, which contains the business logic at the page level, EJBs are designed to separate the business logic from the presentation logic. This separation of logic allows the business tier developers to focus on creating the business logic and lets the page authors focus on creating the presentation logic. In producing their separate code, the different domain developers can collaborate, or they can work off of defined interfaces that they can glue together once they are completed.

The Enterprise JavaBeans API resides in the `javax.ejb` package. The interfaces for session, entity, and message-driven beans are `SessionBean`, `EntityBean`, and `MessageDrivenBean` (respectively), as shown in Figure 12-6. These interfaces

TABLE 12-5	Enterprise JavaBeans	Definition
Enterprise JavaBeans	Session Bean	A type of EJB that performs tasks (methods) for a client. There are stateful and stateless session beans. A stateful bean maintains a conversation state for the client, while a stateless bean does not.
	Entity Bean	A persistent type of EJB, representing a business entity object, that is typically associated with a table in a relational database.
	Message-Driven Bean	A type of EJB that processes messages asynchronously, acting as a Java Message Service listener.

all implement the interface `EnterpriseBean`, allowing for polymorphism. See Chapter 8 for more on polymorphism. The `EnterpriseBean` class also exists for serialization purposes (that is, saving and restoring objects) since the only thing it does explicitly is extend the `Serializable` interface. As is the nature of interfaces, each EJB has several methods that must be implemented.

FIGURE 12-6

Enterprise JavaBeans

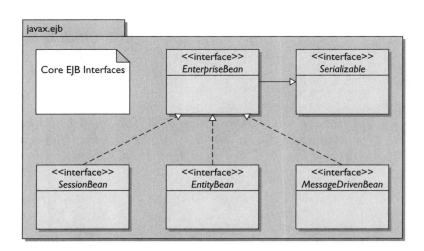

CERTIFICATION SUMMARY

You must understand the differences in regards to enterprise tiers and the basic purpose of the server-side technologies. This chapter discussed various server-side technologies and solutions, as well as where they belong in different tiers.

The web tier was discussed. This tier is responsible for the presentation layer, supporting dynamic web content. The web tier contains a web container where the JSP and servlet APIs are implemented. The JSP API specification is for a scripting and tag library used for rendering web content. The servlet API is designed to render web content as well, but servlets generally produce the HTML from JSP pages. Actually, JSP pages are converted into servlets. Servlets, also known as controllers, interface with the external web browsers, displaying the web pages and controlling the logic.

The business tier was discussed. This tier is responsible for the business logic and is supported by Enterprise JavaBeans. Separating the business logic from the presentation logic allows the code to be more maintainable. Three main types of Enterprise JavaBeans support the business tier: session beans, message-driven beans, and entity beans. EJB session beans perform methods for the client. Stateful and stateless session beans also exist. Stateful session beans maintain the state of the client's session. EJB message-driven beans handle messages asynchronously. EJB entity beans provide database mapping support. The Java Persistent API provides an alternative to the EJB entity beans.

The Enterprise Information System (EIS) tier was discussed. This tier includes databases, relational databases, legacy applications, and enterprise resource planning systems. The most common use of the EIS tier is the execution of a relational database on an external server.

Additional server-side solutions that were discussed include JMS, SMTP, JavaMail, JAX-RPC, and the web services APIs. SMTP and the JavaMail API work together to provide mail solutions. JAX-RPC is an API designed for remote procedure calls. Web Services include SOAP, UDDI, and WSDL, which are all web-based solutions based on XML.

✓ TWO-MINUTE DRILL

Understanding Java EE–Related Tiers and Technologies

❏ The web tier is the tier within an enterprise system that contains the presentation layer.

❏ Web tier components include servlets, JavaServer Pages, and JavaServer Faces.

❏ The business tier is the tier within an enterprise system that contains the business logic.

❏ Business tier components include Enterprise JavaBeans.

❏ The EIS tier is the tier within an enterprise system that contains the data layer.

❏ EIS tier activities include persistence support through database management systems.

Understanding Server-Side Solutions

❏ The Simple Object Access Protocol (SOAP) is a protocol used for information exchange within a decentralized and distributed environment.

❏ The Universal Description, Discovery, and Integration (UDDI) specification is an XML-based registry that is used by businesses to make their services and general business descriptions available through the Internet.

❏ The Web Service Definition Language is an XML standard for businesses and individuals to access available services that each provides.

❏ The Extensible Markup Language is a general-purpose specification used for creating markup languages.

❏ The Simple Mail Transfer Protocol (SMTP) is a protocol for sending mail.

❏ The JavaMail API is a framework that provides electronic mail functionality.

❏ The Java API for XML-based Remote Procedure Call (JAX-RPC) is an API used to build remote procedure calls in order to build web services and clients.

Understanding Dynamic Web Content Solutions

❑ Servlets provide a pure-Java program that functions in response to an HTTP request.

❑ JavaServer Pages (JSPs) provide a dynamic web content solution that uses template data and custom elements to expedite and ease the development of the presentation layer.

Understanding Enterprise Business Logic Solutions

❑ The session bean is a type of EJB that performs methods for a client.

❑ There are *stateful* and *stateless* session beans.

❑ A stateful bean maintains a conversation state for the client, while a stateless bean does not.

❑ The entity bean is a persistent type of EJB that is typically associated with a table in a relational database.

❑ The message-driven bean is a type of EJB that processes messages asynchronously, acting as a JMS listener.

SELF TEST

Understanding Java EE–Related Tiers and Technologies

1. Which attributes are representative of the Java EE architecture?

    A. Secretiveness, security, and manageability

    B. Extensibility, morphability, and availability

    C. Reliability, availability, and marketability

    D. Scalability, flexibility, and security

2. Which two are responsibilities of the business tier?

    A. The business tier may manage the execution of EJBs.

    B. The business tier may include message-server beans.

    C. The business tier may include legacy systems.

    D. The business tier may include stateless session beans.

3. Which two are responsibilities of the web tier?

    A. The web tier may include mainframe transaction processing systems.

    B. The web tier may include presentation logic.

    C. The web tier may include controller logic.

    D. The web tier may include entity beans.

4. Which two are responsibilities of the EIS tier?

    A. The EIS tier may include relational databases.

    B. The EIS tier may include EJBs.

    C. The EIS tier may include enterprise-resource planning systems.

    D. The EIS tier may include JavaBeans components.

Understanding Server-Side Solutions

5. Which API uses remote procedure calls to build web services and clients?

    A. JNDI

    B. JMS

    C. JAX-RPC

    D. SMTP

6. The DTD Schema is used to validate the structure of which type of documents?

    A. HTML

    B. XML

    C. JavaScript

    D. JavaServer Pages

7. Which technology provides a standardized format for describing a web service?

    A. SOAP

    B. UDDI

    C. JSTL

    D. WSDL

Understanding Dynamic Web Content Solutions

8. Which Java EE technologies provide dynamic web content solutions?

    A. Servlets

    B. Adobe Coldfusion

    C. Perl

    D. JavaServer Pages

    E. Microsoft Active Server Pages

9. Which of the following are JavaServer Pages translated into?

    A. JavaScript

    B. XML

    C. JavaBeans

    D. Servlets

10. Which are some of the benefits of JavaServer Pages?

    A. JSP technology is open source.

    B. JSP pages are platform-independent.

    C. JSP allows for the separation of presentation logic from business logic.

    D. JSP technology provides a fast development approach for building web applications.

    E. All of the above.

Understanding Enterprise Business Logic Solutions

11. Which statement is false about session beans?

A. Session beans act as JMS message listeners.

B. Session beans can only have one client.

C. Session beans are not persistent.

D. Session beans exist as two types: stateless and stateful.

12. Which statement is false about entity beans?

A. Entity beans are persistent.

B. Entity beans have primary keys.

C. Entity beans allow shared access.

D. Entity beans cannot interact with other entity beans.

13. Which statement is false about message-driven beans?

A. Message-driven beans are short-lived.

B. Message-driven beans have state.

C. Message-driven beans act as JMS message listeners.

D. Message-driven beans are used to receive messages asynchronously.

SELF TEST ANSWERS

Understanding Java EE–Related Tiers and Technologies

1. Which attributes are representative of the Java EE architecture?

    A. Secretiveness, security, and manageability

    B. Extensibility, morphability, and availability

    C. Reliability, availability, and marketability

    D. Scalability, flexibility, and security

    Answer:

    ☑ **D.** Scalability, flexibility, and security are all strong attributes of a Java EE system.

    ☒ **A, B,** and **C** are incorrect. Secretiveness, morphability, and marketability are not attributes of a Java EE system.

2. Which two are responsibilities of the business tier?

    A. The business tier may manage the execution of EJBs.

    B. The business tier may include message-server beans.

    C. The business tier may include legacy systems.

    D. The business tier may include stateless session beans.

    Answer:

    ☑ **A** and **D.** The business tier manages the execution of EJBs, including stateless (and stateful) session beans.

    ☒ **B** and **C** are incorrect. **B** is incorrect because there is no such thing as message-server beans, but there are message-driven beans. **C** is incorrect because legacy systems typically reside in the EIS tier, not the business tier.

3. Which two are responsibilities of the web tier?

    A. The web tier may include mainframe transaction processing systems.

    B. The web tier may include presentation logic.

    C. The web tier may include controller logic.

    D. The web tier may include entity beans.

Answer:

☑ **B** and **C.** Servlets act as controllers in the web tier. Both servlets and JSPs are responsible for presentation logic.

☒ **A** and **D** are incorrect. **A** is incorrect because mainframe transaction processing systems are in the EIS tier. Entity beans are part of EJBs in the business tier.

4. Which two are responsibilities of the EIS tier?

   A. The EIS tier may include relational databases.

   B. The EIS tier may include EJBs.

   C. The EIS tier may include enterprise-resource planning systems.

   D. The EIS tier may include JavaBeans components.

Answer:

☑ **A** and **C.** The EIS tier may include relational databases and enterprise-resource planning systems.

☒ **B** and **D** are incorrect. **B** is incorrect because EJBs are found in the business tier. **D** is incorrect because JavaBeans components are found in the web tier.

Working with Miscellaneous Server-Side Technologies

5. Which API uses remote procedure calls to build web services and clients?

   A. JNDI

   B. JMS

   C. JAX-RPC

   D. SMTP

Answer:

☑ **C.** JAX-RPC uses remote procedure calls to build web services and clients.

☒ **A, B,** and **D** are incorrect. **A** is incorrect because JNDI is used as a unified interface to naming and directory services. **B** is incorrect because JMS is used to allow distributed communications. **D** is incorrect because SMTP is a standard for distributed e-mail transmissions.

6. The DTD Schema is used to validate the structure of which type of documents?

A. HTML

B. XML

C. JavaScript

D. JavaServer Pages

Answer:

☑ **B.** DTD Schemas are used to validate the structure of XML documents.

☒ **A, C,** and **D** are incorrect. HTML, JavaScript, and JavaServer Pages do not have any direct relationship to DTD Schemas.

7. Which technology provides a standardized format for describing a web service?

A. SOAP

B. UDDI

C. JSTL

D. WSDL

Answer:

☑ **D.** WSDL provides a standardized format for describing a web service.

☒ **A, B,** and **C** are incorrect. **A** is incorrect because SOAP is used as a standardized way of invoking methods of objects in distributed systems. **B** is incorrect because UDDI is an XML-based registry for businesses to list themselves worldwide on the Internet. **C** is incorrect because JSTL is a JSP standard tag library.

Working with Dynamic Web Content

8. Which Java EE technologies provide dynamic web content solutions?

A. Servlets

B. Adobe Coldfusion

C. Perl

D. JavaServer Pages

E. Microsoft Active Server Pages

Answer:

☑ **A and D.** Servlets and JavaServer Pages provide dynamic web content solutions as part of the Java Enterprise Edition.

☒ **B, C,**and **E** are incorrect. **B** is incorrect because Adobe Coldfusion provides web content solutions but is not part of Java EE. **C** is incorrect because Perl provides web content solutions but is not part of Java EE. **E** is incorrect because Microsoft Active Server Pages provides web content solutions but is not part of Java EE.

9. Which of the following are JavaServer Pages translated into?

    A. JavaScript

    B. XML

    C. JavaBeans

    D. Servlets

Answer:

☑ **D.** JavaServer Pages are translated into servlets.

☒ **A, B,**and **C** are incorrect. JSPs are only translated into servlets.

10. Which are some of the benefits of JavaServer Pages?

    A. JSP technology is open source.

    B. JSP pages are platform-independent.

    C. JSP allows for the separation of presentation logic from business logic

    D. JSP technology provides a fast development approach for building web applications.

    E. All of the above.

Answer:

☑ **E.** *All of the above* is correct. JSP is open source, platform-independent, separates out business logic, and provides a fast development approach for web applications.

☒ Any answer(s) except **E** would be technically incorrect since **E** represents "All of the above."

Working with Enterprise Business Logic

11. Which statement is false about session beans?

    A. Session beans act as JMS message listeners.

    B. Session beans can only have one client.

    C. Session beans are not persistent.

    D. Session beans exist as two types: stateless and stateful.

Answer:

    ☑ **A.** Session beans do *not* act as JMS message listeners.

    ☒ **B, C,** and **D** are incorrect. **B** is incorrect because we were looking for a false answer and this answer is true. As stated, session beans can only have one client. **C** is incorrect because we were looking for a false answer and this answer is true. As stated, session beans are not persistent. **D** is incorrect because we were looking for a false answer and this answer is true. As stated, session beans exist as two types: stateless and stateful.

12. Which statement is false about entity beans?

    A. Entity beans are persistent.

    B. Entity beans have primary keys.

    C. Entity beans allow shared access.

    D. Entity beans cannot interact with other entity beans.

Answer:

    ☑ **D.** Entity beans *can* interact with other entity beans.

    ☒ **A, B,** and **C** are incorrect. **A** is incorrect because entity beans are persistent. **B** is incorrect because entity beans have primary keys. **C** is incorrect because entity beans allow shared access.

13. Which statement is false about message-driven beans?

    A. Message-driven beans are short-lived.

    B. Message-driven beans have state.

    C. Message-driven beans act as JMS message listeners.

    D. Message-driven beans are used to receive messages asynchronously.

Answer:

☑ **B.** Message-driven beans do *not* have state.

☒ **A, C,** and **D** are incorrect. **A** is incorrect because message-driven beans are typically short-lived. **C** is incorrect because message-driven beans do act as JMS message listeners. **D** is incorrect because message-driven beans are used to receive messages asynchronously.

Part IV

Appendixes

A

About the CD

T he CD-ROM included with this book comes complete with MasterExam and the electronic version of the book. The software is easy to install on any Windows 2000/ XP/Vista computer and must be installed to access the MasterExam feature. You may, however, browse the electronic book directly from the CD without installation. To register for the bonus MasterExam, simply click the Bonus MasterExam link on the main launch page and follow the directions to the free online registration.

System Requirements

Software requires Windows 2000 or higher and Internet Explorer 6.0 or above and 20MB of hard disk space for full installation. The electronic book requires Adobe Acrobat Reader.

Installing and Running MasterExam

If your computer CD-ROM drive is configured to auto run, the CD-ROM will automatically start up upon inserting the disk. From the opening screen you may install MasterExam by clicking the MasterExam link. This will begin the installation process and create a program group named LearnKey. To run MasterExam use Start | All Programs | LearnKey | MasterExam. If the auto run feature did not launch your CD, browse to the CD and click on the LaunchTraining.exe icon.

MasterExam

MasterExam provides you with a simulation of the actual exam. The number of questions, the type of questions, and the time allowed are intended to be an accurate representation of the exam environment. You have the option to take an open book exam, including hints, references, and answers; a closed book exam; or the timed MasterExam simulation.

When you launch MasterExam, a digital clock display will appear in the bottom right-hand corner of your screen. The clock will continue to count down to zero unless you choose to end the exam before the time expires.

Electronic Book

The entire contents of the Study Guide are provided in PDF. Adobe's Acrobat Reader has been included on the CD.

Enterprise Architect Project File

Enterprise Architect (EA) is a CASE tool that supports UML modeling and reverse source code engineering. EA was used to create the draft UML diagrams for this book. Since knowing UML is a requirement for the exam, the authors have included the project file for these diagrams on the CD to assist you in your learning.

To open up the project file you must have a version of EA. You can download a 30-day trial version of the application from the Sparx Systems web site, http:// www.sparxsystems.com/. Once installed, you will be able to view and modify each of the UML diagrams. You will find the diagrams to be organized in the EA project as they are presented in each chapter. You can reference Chapter 9 for detailed information on UML.

Help

A help file is provided through the help button on the main page in the lower left-hand corner. An individual help feature is also available through MasterExam.

Removing Installation(s)

MasterExam is installed to your hard drive. For best results removing programs, use the Start | All Programs | LearnKey | Uninstall option to remove MasterExam.

Technical Support

For questions regarding the content of the electronic book, Enterprise Architect project file, or MasterExam, please visit www.mhprofessional.com or email customer .service@mcgraw-hill.com. For customers outside the 50 United States, email international_cs@mcgraw-hill.com.

LearnKey Technical Support

For technical problems with the software (installation, operation, removing installations), please visit www.learnkey.com, email techsupport@learnkey.com, or call toll free at 1-800-482-8244.

B

Exam-Related Packages and Classes

Packages and Classes Covered on the SCJA

Since Java is a programming language, the SCJA exam focuses on many of the packages and classes within the core Java SE and Java EE platform distributions. Table B-1 details the Java SE packages and classes covered on the exam. Table B-2 details the Java EE packages and classes covered on the exam.

Java SE Packages and Classes

Learning the low-level details of all the common Java packages is not needed to perform well on the SCJA exam. To a large extent, just knowing what the packages are designed for and what type of functionality they contain will help you achieve a high score. However, you only need to know a limited number of Java SE classes. These are accompanied by asterisks in Table B-1.

TABLE B-1   SCJA Exam: Java SE Packages and Classes

Name	Package Name	Commonly Used Classes and Interfaces	Chapter
Java Applet API	`java.applet`	`Applet`	11
Java AWT API	`java.awt`	`Button`, `CheckBox`, `Component`, `Label`, `Frame`, `Panel`, `TextArea`, `TextField`, and so on	1
Java Basic I/O API	`java.io`	`File`, `FileDescriptor`, `FilenameFilter`, `RandomAccessFile`, as well as `Reader`, `Writer`, and their subclasses	1
Java Database Connectivity (JDBC) API	`java.sql` and `javax.sql`	`Connection`, `Statement`, `SQLException`	10
Java Language API	`java.lang`	`Byte`, `*Boolean`, `*Character`, `Double`, `*Float`, `*Integer`, `Short`	4
		`CharSequence`, `*String`, `StringBuffer`, `StringBuilder`	3
Java Naming and Directory Interface (JNDI) API	`javax.naming`	`Context`, `InitialContext`, `NamingException`	10
Java Networking API	`java.net` and `javax.net`	`Socket`, `ServerSocket`, `URL`, `Inet4Address`	1

TABLE B-1		SCJA Exam: Java SE Packages and Classes (Continued)	

Name	Package Name	Commonly Used Classes and Interfaces	Chapter
Java Utilities API	`java.util`	`Date, Calendar, TimeZone, Locale, Currency, Random, StringTokenizer, Timer`	1
Java Remote Method Invocation (RMI) API	`java.rmi and javax.rmi`	`Remote, RemoteException, RemoteObject, RemoteServer, UnicastRemoteObject, Naming`	10
Java Swing API	`javax.swing`	`JButton, JCheckBox, JComponent, JLabel, JFrame, JPanel, JTextArea, JTextField`, and so on	1

Java EE Packages and Classes

Java EE exam coverage emphasizes the formal names of the packages and what functionality they contain. You may not see references to the package names and/or class names at all. There is value added in conceptualizing how the technologies are organized within specified packages. Table B-2 provides this information. Be aware that many of the technologies have subpackages related to the listed packages. These subpackages are not listed in the table.

TABLE B-2 SCJA Exam: Java EE Packages and Classes	Name	Package Name	Chapter
	Enterprise JavaBeans (EJB) API	`javax.ejb`	12
	Java API for XML-Based RPC (JAX-RPC) API	`javax.xml.rpc`	12
	Java Message Service (JMS) API	`javax.jms`	10
	Java Servlet API	`javax.servlet`	12
	Java Web Services	`Web Services Developer Pack (WSDL)`	10
	JavaMail API	`javax.mail`	12
	JavaServer Pages (JSP) API	`javax.servlet.jsp`	12

C

Unicode Standard

Unicode Standard Compliancy

The Unicode Standard is a character coding system designed to form a universal character set. This standard is maintained by the Unicode Consortium standards organization. The characters in this set are technically known as Unicode scalar values (in other words, hex numbers). Commonly known as Unicode characters, the characters are primarily organized into symbol and punctuation characters, as well as by script characters (for example, spoken language characters).

Code charts are maintained by the consortium for easy reference. The "Code Charts for Symbols and Punctuation" can be accessed at the following web site address: http://unicode.org/charts/symbols.html. "The Unicode Character Code Charts by Script" can be accessed from http://unicode.org/charts/index.html.

The Java SE 6 and J2SE 5.0 API's character information is based on the Unicode standard, version 4.0. The J2SE 1.4 API's character information is based on the Unicode standard, version 3.0. This Unicode compliancy information is found in the documentation of the Character class.

Many Unicode standard groupings of characters exist, such as language characters, currency symbols, Braille patterns, arrows, and mathematical operators. The most commonly used characters are the ASCII punctuation characters.

ASCII Punctuation Characters

The first 128 characters are the same as those in the American Standard Code for Information Exchange (ASCII) character set. The Unicode Consortium references them as ASCII punctuation characters. Table C-1 represents these characters. The values \u0000–\u001F, and 0007F represent nonprintable ASCII characters. The values \u0020–\u007E represent printable ASCII characters. The character \u0020 represents a blank space. As an example, the space could also be referenced by its decimal equivalent value (that is, 32), its octal equivalent value (040), its HTML equivalent value ( ), or directly by its printable character, as in char c = ' ';.

TABLE C-1	Printable and Nonprintable ASCII Characters

	000	**001**	**002**	**003**	**004**	**005**	**006**	**007**
0	NUL	DLE	SP	0	@	P	`	p
1	SOH	DC1	!	1	A	Q	a	q
2	STX	DC2	"	2	B	R	b	r
3	ETX	DC3	#	3	C	S	c	s
4	EOT	DC4	$	4	D	T	d	t
5	ENQ	NAK	%	5	E	U	e	u
6	ACK	SYN	&	6	F	V	f	v
7	BEL	ETB	'	7	G	W	g	w
8	BS	CAN	(	8	H	X	h	x
9	HT	EM	)	9	I	Y	i	y
A	LF	SUB	*	:	J	Z	j	z
B	VT	ESC	+	;	K	[	k	{
C	FF	FS	,	<	L	\	l	|
D	CR	GS	-	=	M	]	m	}
E	SO	RS	.	>	N	^	n	~
F	SI	US	/	?	O	_	o	DEL

D

Bracket Conventions

Java Bracket Conventions

The Java programming language, like many programming languages, makes strong use of brackets. The SCJA exam requires familiarization with the different types of brackets. Table D-1 contains each type of bracket seen throughout this book and the exam. This table details the bracket names as they are used in the Java Language Specification as well as common alternative names.

TABLE D-1 Bracket Conventions

Brackets	Typical Java Language Specification Nomenclature	Alternative Brackets Nomenclature	Common Brackets Usage in Java
( )	Parentheses	Round brackets, curved brackets, oval brackets	Surrounds set of method arguments
{ }	Braces	Curly brackets	Surrounds blocks of code
[ ]	Box brackets	Square brackets	Used with arrays
< >	Angle brackets	Diamond brackets, chevrons	Encloses generics
« »	Guillemet characters	Angle quotes	Specifies UML Stereotypes

Glossary

abstract   A modifier that indicates that either a class or method has some behavior that must be implemented by its subclasses.

access modifiers   Modifiers that define the access privileges of interfaces, classes, methods, constructors, and data members.

AJAX   An acronym for *Asynchronous JavaScript and XML*. A web application model where the client layer interfaces with the server without the need for the associated HTML pages to be reloaded.

applet   An application that executes within applications, devices, and most commonly web browsers. It must support the applet programming model.

application server   A server that hosts various applications and their environments.

arithmetic operator   Java programming language operator that performs addition (+), subtraction (-), multiplication (*), division (/), or remainder production (%) operations.

array   A fixed-length group of same type variables or references that are accessed with an index.

assignment statement   A statement that allows for the definition or redefinition of a variable by assigning it a value. It is represented by '=' in Java code.

association   A relationship between classes.

attributes   A system's state consisting of its instance variables.

base class   *See* superclass.

bean   A reusable software component conforming to design and naming conventions.

block   Code between matching braces—for example, { int x; }.

boolean   A Java keyword that is used to define a primitive variable as having a Boolean type with a value of either `true` or `false`. The corresponding wrapper class is `Boolean`.

business logic   The code that implements the functional algorithms of an application. In the EJB tier, this code is implemented by Enterprise JavaBeans.

business tier   The tier within an enterprise system that contains the business logic. Enterprise JavaBeans are one of the major components of the business tier.

byte   A Java keyword that is used to define a primitive variable as an integer having a storage of one byte. The corresponding wrapper class is `Byte`.

CASE   The acronym for *Computer Aided Software Engineering*. The scientific application of computer-based tools, utilities, and methods to enhance the end result of a software application or project.

CDC   An acronym for *Connected Device Configuration*. A Java ME configuration that is supplied with the standard Java Virtual Machine and is utilized for devices that do not have extreme constraints of resources.

char   A Java keyword that is used to define a variable as having two bytes of storage normally used to store a specified Unicode character. The corresponding wrapper class is `Character`.

child class   *See* subclass.

class   A file that contains valid Java code. A class is a blueprint for creating objects at runtime.

classpath   An argument set that tells the Java Virtual Machine where to look for user-defined classes and packages. The classpath is used by various command-line tools.

class variable   *See* static variable.

CLDC The acronym for *Connected Limited Device Configuration*. A common Java ME configuration that has a small compact virtual machine known as Sun's K Virtual Machine (KVM) and a reduced set of class libraries.

comment Text within source files that provides explanations of associated code. In Java, comments are delimited with //, /*...*/, or /**...*/, the latter being used with the Javadoc documentation API.

composition association A whole-part relationship between classes where the whole is responsible for the lifetime of its parts. Composition is also known as containment and is a strong relationship.

concatenation operator An operator (+) that is used to concatenate (that is, join) two strings.

concrete class A class that has all of its methods implemented.

conditional statement A decision-making control flow used to execute statements and blocks of statements conditionally. Examples are `if`, `if else`, `if else if`, and `switch`.

configuration A term used with Java ME to describe a general JVM target. A configuration may change based on whether the targeted hardware contains different features.

container Software that provides life-cycle support to Java EE components—for example, web and EJB containers.

cookie Mechanism where information is set and retrieved on the client side by the resources of web applications.

declaration A statement that establishes an identifier with associated attributes.

design pattern A proven, familiar pattern that is recurrent in the process of implementing software solutions. Several general software design patterns, as well as specific Java EE design patterns, are commonly used today.

double   A Java keyword that is used to define a primitive variable as a floating point number having storage of eight bytes. The corresponding wrapper class is `Double`.

EJB   An acronym for *Enterprise JavaBean*. An enterprise component supporting business logic. The three types of EJBs are session beans, entity beans, and message-driven beans. EJBs provide significant behind-the-scenes security, concurrency, transaction handling, and persistence support so that software programmers can concentrate most of their work on the business logic of the bean.

encapsulation   The principle of bundling classes that expose a concise public interface used to interact with the class while hiding their implementation details with private methods and instance variables.

Enterprise Information System tier (EIS tier)   The tier within an enterprise system that contains the data layer. Common activities are persistence support through database management systems.

entity bean   A persistent type of EJB that is typically associated with a table in a relational database.

enumeration type   A type with a fixed set of constants as fields.

expression statement   A statement that changes part of the application's state. Expression statements include method calls, assignments, object creation, pre/post increments and pre/post decrements. An expression statement can be evaluated to a single value.

fat client   A Java-based client as part of a client-server application. This style of client will do most of its data processing and manipulation on the client side.

float   A Java keyword that is used to define a primitive variable as a floating point number having a storage of four bytes. The corresponding wrapper class is `Float`.

getter   A simple public method used to return a private instance variable.

heap   A memory area where objects are stored.

heavyweight component   An AWT component that is characterized as being heavier than its Swing equivalent. AWT components are considered heavyweight because they use the native operating system component libraries. Unlike Swing, they are not a pure-Java implementation.

HTML   An acronym for *HyperText Markup Language*. A collection of tags used to create hypertext documents (for instance, web pages).

IDE   An acronym for *Integrated Development Environment*. A development suite that allows developers to edit, compile, debug, connect to version control systems, collaborate, and do much more depending on the specific tool. Most modern IDEs have add-in capabilities for various software modules to enhance the IDE's capabilities.

IMAP   An acronym for *Internet Message Access Protocol*. A client/server protocol allowing for the retrieval and management of e-mail messages on a remote server. It is similar to the POP protocol but has more features.

IMP   An abbreviation for *Information Module Profile*. This is a Java ME profile commonly found on headless systems.

import statement   A statement used in the beginning of a class that allows for external packages to be made available within the class.

inheritance   A term for the ability of one Java class to extend another and gain its functionality.

instance variable   A variable that is declared in the class instead of in a particular method. This variable has a life cycle that lasts for the duration of the object's existence. This variable is in scope for all methods.

int   A Java keyword that is used to define a primitive variable as an integer having a storage of four bytes. The corresponding wrapper class is `Integer`.

interface   A definition of public methods that must be implemented by a class.

iteration statement   A control flow where a statement or block of statements is iterated through, based on a maintained state of a variable or expression. The `for` loop, enhanced `for` loop, and the `while` and `do-while` statements are used for iterating.

J2EE   An acronym for *Java 2 Platform, Enterprise Edition*. A software development platform that includes a collection of enterprise API specifications for EJBs, servlets, and JSPs. J2EE compliance is reached when an application server (full compliance) or web container (partial compliance) implements the necessary J2EE specifications. J2EE is currently known as Java EE.

J2ME   An acronym for *Java 2 Platform, Micro Edition*. A software development platform including a collection of APIs designed for embedded devices. J2ME is currently known as Java ME.

J2SE   An acronym for *Java 2 Platform, Standard Edition*. A software development platform including a collection of APIs designed for client application development. J2SE is currently known as Java SE.

JAD   An acronym for *Java Application Descriptor*. A file used with MIDlets to deploy to the target device.

JAR   An acronym for *Java Archive*. A JAR file is used to store a collection of Java class files. It is represented by one file with the `.jar` extension in the file system. It may be executable.

JavaBean   A reusable Java component based on a platform-independent reusable component model in which there is a standardized means to access and modify the object state of the bean.

Javadoc   A tool that produces HTML documentation from extracted comments of Java source code.

JavaMail API   A standardized framework that provides electronic mail functionality.

JavaScript   A scripting language that is most often used in conjunction with HTML. JavaScript has no connection to Java other than sharing a name.

JAX-RPC   An acronym for *Java API for XML-Based RPC*. An API used to build remote procedure calls in order to generate web services and clients.

JDBC   An acronym for *Java Database Connectivity*. A database-connectivity API providing independent connectivity between the Java programming language and various data sources—for example, databases.

JDK   An acronym for *Java Development Kit*. A bundled set of development utilities for compiling, debugging, and interpreting Java applications. The Java Runtime Environment is included in the JDK.

JMS   An acronym for the *Java Message Service API*. The messaging-support API is used to access the common features of enterprise messaging systems, allowing for the creation, sending, receiving, and reading of messages with Java EE application components.

JNDI   An acronym for *Java Naming and Directory Interface API*. A support API that provides general client-side querying features against directory and naming services by both attributes and a hierarchy of names.

JRE   An acronym for *Java Runtime Environment*. An environment that is used to run Java applications. It contains basic client and server JVMs, core classes, and supporting files.

JSF   An acronym for *JavaServer Faces API*. A presentation layer web technology for the Java platform, designed as a component framework for building web user interfaces. Page navigation and state management are also supported.

JSP   An acronym for *JavaServer Pages API*. A dynamic web content solution that uses template data, and custom elements to expedite and ease the development of the presentation layer. JavaServer Pages are converted to servlets before the pages are rendered for deployment.

JSR   An acronym for *Java Specification Request*. A recommendation that is put forward to the Java Community Process (JCP) organization for review. Approved requests are adopted for fulfillment.

JSTL   An acronym for *JavaServer Pages Standard Tag Library*. An extended library of JavaServer Pages tag functions.

JTA   An acronym for *Java Transaction API*. A technology that allows applications and Java EE servers to access transactions.

JVM   An acronym for *Java Virtual Machine*. The platform-independent environment where the Java interpreter executes.

keyword   A word in the Java programming language that cannot be used as an identifier (in other words, a variable or method name). Java SE 6 maintains 50 keywords, each designed to be used for a specific purpose.

lightweight component   A Swing component characterized as being lighter than its legacy AWT equivalent. Lightweight components are a pure-Java component library. Unlike AWT, they have no direct connection to the native operating system's components.

literal   A value represented as an integer, floating point, or character value that can be stored in a variable. For example, 1115 is an integer literal, 12.5 is a floating point literal, and 'A' is a character literal.

local variable   A variable that is only in scope for a single method, constructor, or block.

logical operator   Java programming language operators that perform logical operations such as the Boolean NOT (!), conditional AND (&&), and conditional OR (| |) operators.

long   A Java keyword used to define a primitive variable as an integer having a storage of 8 bytes. The corresponding wrapper class is Long.

message-driven bean   A type of EJB that processes messages asynchronously, acting as a JMS listener.

method argument   A variable that is passed to a method. A method may have multiple arguments, or none.

method parameter   A variable that is in scope for the entire method. It is declared in the method signature and is initialized from the method arguments.

method   A procedure that contains the code for performing operations in a class.

MIDlet   An abbreviation for *Mobile Information Device Applet*. A small Java program designed to run in an embedded device such as a cell phone.

MIDP   An acronym for *Mobile Information Device Profile*. A common Java ME profile found on mobile phones and PDAs.

MIME   An acronym for *Multipurpose Internet Mail Extensions*. A standard that defines the structure of mail content (for example, messages and files) that is to be transferred between servers.

modulus   The remainder production operator (%).

multiplicity   The value or range of how many participating objects are in an association between objects.

multiplicity indicators   Numerical representations used in UML to depict the number of objects that may or must be used in an association.

MVC   An acronym for *Model-View-Controller Architecture*. A design pattern separating business and presentation logic into model, view, and controller functional areas. The model represents the state of components. The view represents the components on the screen. The controller represents the functionality that ties the user-interface components to events.

null   A null type has a null reference represented by the literal `null`.

object   An instance of a class created at runtime from a class file.

object-oriented   The design principle that uses objects and their interactions to design applications.

operator   A Java element that performs operations on up to three operands and returns a result.

overloading   The process of implementing more than one method with the same return type and name, while using various numbers and/or types of parameters to distinguish between them.

overriding   The process of overriding a superclass's method by using the same method signature.

package   A statement at the beginning of a class that indicates the package name it is associated with.

package-private modifier   The default modifier that allows package-only access to the associated class, interface, constructor, method, or data member.

parent class   *See* superclass.

pass by reference   The action of passing an argument to a method where the JVM gives the method a reference to the same object that was passed to it. This is how objects are passed.

pass by value   The action of passing an argument to a method where the JVM copies the value for the method. This is how primitives are passed.

polymorphism   This is a concept that allows data of one type to be handled and referred to by a type that is more general. Generalities can be created by using inheritance and extending classes, or by implementing interfaces.

POP   An acronym for *Post Office Protocol*. A protocol allowing for the retrieval of e-mail messages on a remote server.

presentation logic   The code that implements the display algorithms of an application. In the Java web-tier environment, the implemented code of the presentation layer is supported by servlets, JavaServer Pages, and JavaServer Faces.

primitive   A fundamental data type that is not an object. Examples include, but are not limited to: `int`, `float`, `boolean`.

primitive cast   A technique in Java of changing the primitive data type of a variable to another primitive type.

private access modifier   A Java keyword that allows class-only access to the associated constructor, method, or data member.

profile   A term used in Java ME to describe more specific features that a JVM target implements.

protected access modifier   A Java keyword that allows package-external subclass access and package-only access to the associated constructor, method, or data member.

public access modifier   A Java keyword that allows unrestricted access to the associated class, interface, constructor, method, or data member.

publish/subscribe messaging model   A messaging model based on events. Consumers subscribe to events by specifying a topic that is part of a set of messages. The producers of these messages will route these messages to registered consumers. The consumers will consume the events when they arrive.

RDBMS   An acronym for *Relational Database Management System*. A type of database management system that organizes its data in the form of interrelated tables.

relational operator   A Java programming language operator that performs relational operations such as less than ($<$), less than or equal to ($<=$), greater than ($>$), greater than or equal to ($>=$), value equality ($==$), and value inequality ($=!$).

RMI   An acronym for *Remote Method Invocation API*. A distributed-computing API that allows Java applications to carry out distributed computing by performing remote procedure calls.

RMI-IIOP   An acronym for *Java Remote Method Invocation over Internet Inter-Orb Protocol*. A protocol used for Java to non-Java distributed computing solutions.

scope   The block of code where a variable is in existence.

servlet   A pure-Java program that functions in response to an HTTP request.

session bean   A type of EJB that performs methods for a client. There are *stateful* and *stateless* session beans. A stateful bean maintains a conversational state for the client, while a stateless bean does not.

setter   A simple public method that accepts one argument and is used to set the value of an instance variable.

short   A Java keyword that is used to define a primitive variable as an integer having a storage of two bytes. The corresponding wrapper class is Short.

SMTP   An acronym for *Simple Mail Transfer Protocol.* A TCP/IP protocol used by mail servers for sending mail messages.

SOAP   An acronym for *Simple Object Access Protocol.* A protocol used for information exchange within a decentralized and distributed environment.

SQL   An acronym for *Structured Query Language.* A software language designed for retrieval and management of information in RDBMS systems.

statement   A command that performs an activity when executed by the Java interpreter. Common Java statements include expression, conditional, iteration, and transfer of control statements.

static variable   A variable that is declared in the class like an instance variable. However, this variable is common to all objects of the same type. Only one instance of this variable exists for all objects of a particular type. Each instance of the class shares the same variable.

String class   A class representing an immutable character string.

subclass   A term for a class that is derived from another class through inheritance. This may also be called a child class.

superclass   A term that describes a class used to derive other classes through inheritance. This may also be called a parent class or base class.

Swing API   A rich GUI API complete with an event model that is used for creating and managing user interfaces.

thin client A non-Java-based client that is part of a client-server application. In this client-server architecture, Java only runs on the server, and most of the processing and manipulation of data is done on the server side.

transfer of control statement A statement used to change the controlled flow in an application. Transfer of control statements include the `break`, `continue`, and `return` statements.

UDDI An acronym for *Universal Description, Discovery and Integration*. An XML-based registry used by businesses to make their services and general business descriptions available through the Internet.

UML An acronym for *Unified Modeling Language*. A specification that defines a modeling language for the specification, presentation, construction, and documentation of object-oriented system elements.

Unicode character A 16-bit set of characters.

variable A term for a symbolic reference to data in Java code.

web server Software that hosts web sites, supports various protocols, and executes server-side applications such as servlets.

web services Web-based applications designed to exchange data with clients while making use of XML-based standards and transport protocols.

web tier The tier within an enterprise system that contains the presentation layer. Servlets, JavaServer Pages, and JavaServer Faces are all part of the web tier.

WSDL An acronym for *Web Service Definition Language*. An XML standard for businesses and individuals to access available services that each provide.

XML An acronym for *Extensible Markup Language*. A general-purpose specification used for creating markup languages. This specification allows for the creation of custom tags in structured text files. Web-based solutions make common use of XML files as configuration, deployment descriptor, and tag library files.

INDEX

! (logical negation) operator, 93–95
! (not equal to) operator, 91–92
(pound sign), 298
% (modulus) operator, 87
& (ampersand), 23, 92–95
&& (logical AND) operator, 92–95
( ) parenthesis, 99, 104, 434
* (multiplication) operator, 87
+ (addition) operator, 87
+ (concatenation) operator, 44
+ (plus sign), 298
+ (String concatenation) operator, 97–101
+= (assignment by addition) operator, 84
- (subtraction) operator, 87
-= (assignment by subtraction) operator, 84
. (period), 22
/ (division) operator, 87
/ (forward slash), 22
: (colon), 22
:= (pseudo-code assignment) operator, 85
; (semicolon), 22, 44
= (equal sign), 84
== (equal to) operator, 91
?: (conditional ternary) operator, 82
< (less than) operator, 89–90
< > (angle brackets), 434
<= (less than or equal to) operator, 89–90
> (greater than) operator, 89–90
>= (greater than or equal to) operator, 89–90
[ ] (box brackets), 434
\ (backward slash), 22
{ } (braces), 46, 59, 162, 434
~ (tilde), 298
| | (logical OR operator), 92–95
« » (Guillemet characters), 434

A

abstract classes, 221–222, 235–242, 293
abstract keyword, 63, 222
Abstract Window Toolkit (AWT) API, 15, 329, 372
access modifiers, 227–233
addition (+) operator, 87
aggregation association, 192, 194, 196–199, 303
AJAX (asynchronous JavaScript and XML), 363
algorithms, pseudo-code, 61–67
ampersand (&), 23, 92–95
AND operator (&&), 92–95
angle brackets (< >), 434
Apache ActiveMQ, 344
APIs
    AWT, 15, 329, 372
    Basic Input/Output, 14, 329
    Collections, 12–13
    Database Connectivity, 329
    EJB, 404–405
    Java SE, 328
    Java Servlet, 400–401
    Java Swing, 15–17, 329, 371–373
    Java Utilities, 12–13, 17–19, 329
    JavaMail, 396–398
    JavaScript, 360–364
    JAX-RPC, 398–399
    JAX-WS, 399
    JDBC, 329, 341–342
    JMS, 344
    JNDI, 342–343
    JSF, 389, 392, 395, 402–403
    Naming and Directory Interface, 329
    Networking, 14–15, 329
    New I/O, 14

APIs (*Cont.*)
    RMI, 329, 337–339
    SAAJ, 396
applets, Java, 369–371
applications. *See* Java applications
arguments
    method, 168–169, 264, 265
    polymorphism and, 264, 265
    primitives as, 169–170
arithmetic operators, 87–89
`ArrayList`, 58–60
arrays, 104, 138–139
ASCII characters, 430–431
`assert` keyword, 63
`assert` statement, 42
assignment by addition operator (+=), 84
assignment by subtraction operator (–=), 84
assignment operators, 84–87
assignment statements, 44–46
association navigation, 195, 200–201
associations, 188–190
    aggregation, 192, 194, 196–199, 303
    composition, 191–192, 194–195, 303
    dependency, 303
    direct, 191, 194
    examples, 194, 196–199
    overview, 188–190
    role names, 307–308
    temporary, 192–193, 194
    types of, 191–193
    UML, 301–308
asynchronous JavaScript and XML (AJAX), 363
autoboxing, 133
availability, 390
AWT (Abstract Window Toolkit) API, 15, 329, 372
AWT Focus subsystem, 15

B

backward slash (\), 22
`bin` directory, 26

binary values, 92
bitwise AND operator, 94
bitwise OR operator, 94
Blaha, Michael, 290
blocks, 46, 162–164
Booch, Grady, 290
Boolean AND operator, 94
`boolean` keyword, 63
`boolean` primitive, 132, 133, 135
Boolean values, 46, 48, 49, 89–92
`Boolean` wrapper class object, 50
box brackets [ ], 434
braces { }, 46, 59, 162, 434
bracket conventions, 433–434
`break` keyword, 63
`break` statements, 42, 52, 53, 54–55
bugs, 100–101, 220, 226
business tier, 391, 392, 393
button containers, 16
`byte` keyword, 63
`byte` primitive, 134, 135
bytecode, 20–25, 330. *See also* code
bytecode files, 20, 21
byte-stream subclasses, 14

C

capacity, 390
`case` keyword, 52, 63
`case` statements, 42, 52, 54
`catch` keyword, 63
CD, included with book, 421–423
CDC (Connected Device Configuration), 332, 367–368
cell phones, 223, 331–333, 335, 364–369
chaining, 107
`char` keyword, 63
`char` primitives, 90, 132, 133, 135
character-stream subclasses, 14
`charAt` method, 102
class associations. *See* associations

class compositions
    examples of, 199–200
    overview, 188–190
class coupling, 5
class keyword, 63
class relationships, 190–193
classes. *See also specific classes*
    abstract, 221–222, 235–242, 293
    compiling, 20
    concrete, 221, 233–235, 262, 265
    covered in exam, 426–427
    data stream, 14
    encapsulation, 225–231
    importing, 9
    information hiding, 226, 228–229
    inheritance. *See* inheritance
    interfaces. *See* interfaces
    naming, 141
    package-derived, 11–19
    packaging. *See* packages
    relationships, 188–193
    subclasses, 220, 222, 227, 229, 264
    superclasses, 218, 220, 221, 228, 264
    UML, 293–295
    user-defined, 21–22
    version, 25
    vs. objects, 135–136
classes directory, 21
classpath, 25
classpath directories, 22
CLASSPATH environment variable, 22
-classpath option, 21–22
CLDC (Connected Limited Device Configuration), 332, 367–368
client layer, 325, 360, 391
client tier, 325, 360, 391
client-side technologies, 359–385
    fat clients, 369–373
    J2ME MIDlets, 369–371
    Java applets, 369–371
    Java Swing API, 371–373
    thin clients, 360–364

code. *See also* programming; source files
    bytecode, 20–25, 330
    compiling with -classpath option, 21–22
    compiling with -d option, 21
    compiling with javac, 19–22
    duplicated, 217
    HTML. *See* HTML
    interpreting with -classpath option, 23
    interpreting with -D option, 23
    polymorphism in, 263–264
    refactoring, 60–61
code blocks, 46, 162–164
code charts, 430
Collections API, 12–13
colon (:), 22
command-line tools, 21
Comparator interface, 12
compiler, 19–22
compiler switches, 22
compiling
    with -classpath option, 21–22
    with -d option, 21
    java classes, 20
    with javac, 19–22
    packaged software, 26–27
composition association, 191–195, 303
compositions. *See* class compositions
compound assignment operators, 84–85
com.scjaexam.tutorial package, 26–27
concatenation operator (+), 44
concrete classes, 221, 233–235, 262, 265
conditional operators, 94
conditional statements, 44, 46–54
conditional ternary operator (?:), 82
Connected Device Configuration (CDC), 332, 367–368
Connected Limited Device Configuration (CLDC), 332, 367–368
const keyword, 63
continue keyword, 63
continue statement, 42, 55

cookies, 402
curly brackets { }, 46, 59, 162, 434
Currency class, 13

D

-D option, 24–25
-d option, 21
data stream classes, 14
Database Management Systems (DBMS), 340
database tier, 391
databases, 340–342
DBMS (Database Management Systems), 340
default keyword, 63
demarshalling, 339
demo folder, 330
dependency association, 303
direct association, 191, 194
directed association, 303
directories
    bin, 26
    classpath, 22
    hierarchical, 342
    home, 25
    Java, 25
    JNDI, 342–343
    source, 100
    working, 22, 25
division (/) operator, 87
do keyword, 63
doGet method, 401
doPost method, 401
double keyword, 63
double primitive, 92, 134, 135
do-while statement, 42, 55, 60
dynamic web content, 399–403

E

EA (Enterprise Architect), 299–301, 423
Eclipse SDK, 57

Eddy, Frederick, 290
EE (Enterprise Edition). *See* J2EE
EIS (Enterprise Information System) tier, 392–393
EJB API, 404–405
EJB containers, 404
EJBs (Enterprise JavaBeans), 333, 392, 404–405
electronic book, 422
else branch, 47
else clause, 46
else if branch, 47
else keyword, 63
e-mail solutions, 396–398
empty statement, 42
encapsulation, 225–231, 299
endpoints, 396
endsWith method, 105
enhanced for loop statement, 42, 55, 58
enterprise application technologies, 334, 388
Enterprise Architect (EA), 299–301, 423
enterprise business solutions, 404–405
Enterprise Edition. *See* J2EE
Enterprise Information System (EIS) tier, 392–393
Enterprise JavaBeans. *See* EJBs
enterprise tiers, 391–393
EnterpriseBean class, 405
Entity Bean, 405
enum keyword, 63, 139–140
enumerations, 139–140, 144
equal sign (=), 84
equal to (==) operator, 91–92
equality operators, 91–92
.exe extension, 20
explicit statements, 9–11
expression statements, 42, 44–46. *See also* assignment statements
expressions, regular, 13
extending classes. *See* inheritance
extends keyword, 63, 218
extensibility, 390
Extensible Markup Language. *See* XML
extensible tags, 402

F

`false` conditions, 48, 50
false literal, 63
fat clients, 369–373
`File` class, 14
`FileDescriptor` class, 14
`FilenameFilter` class, 14
files
    bytecode, 20, 21
    interpreting, 22–26
    JAD, 368
    JAR, 368
    log, 273–276
    source, 6, 106
    XML, 335
`file.separator` property, 25
`final` keyword, 63
`finally` keyword, 63
FindBugs tool, 100–101
flexibility, 390
`float` keyword, 63
`float` primitive, 92, 131–132, 133, 135
floating points, 89, 90, 131, 134, 137
`for` keyword, 63
`for` loop statement, 42, 55, 56–58
`for` statement, 64
forward slash (/), 22
Foundation Profile (FP), 332, 367
FP (Foundation Profile), 332, 367

G

generalization class relationship, 294
getters/setters, 195, 230–231
`goto` keyword, 63
graphic paths, 302–305
greater than (>) operator, 89–90
greater than or equal to (>=) operator, 89–90
GreetingsUniverse.java source file, 19–27
Guillemet characters « », 434

H

help file, 423
HTML (HyperText Markup Language)
    dynamic web content, 399–403
    Java applets, 369–371
    JavaServer Pages, 333, 400–403
    overview, 361
    using thin clients with, 360–364
HTML standards, 361
HTTP requests, 400
HTTP transport protocol, 398
HTTP web requests, 391
HyperText Markup Language. *See* HTML

I

IDEs (Integrated Development Environments), 21,
    59, 145–146, 403
`if` keyword, 63
`if` statement, 42, 46–50, 64
`if-then` statement, 42, 46, 47, 48–50
`if-then-else` statement, 43, 46, 47, 51–52
IMAP (Internet Message Access Protocol), 398
IMP (Information Module Profile), 332, 367
`implements` keyword, 63
implicit statements, 9–11
`import` keyword, 63
`import` statements, 6, 7–11
importing
    classes, 9
    packages, 6, 7–11
    static imports, 9
`indexOf` method, 103
information hiding, 226, 228–229
Information Module Profile (IMP), 332, 367
inheritance
    abstract classes, 221–222, 235–242
    advanced concepts, 224–225
    concrete classes, 233–235
    interfaces. *See* interfaces

inheritance (*Cont.*)
overriding methods, 220–221
overview, 216–220
polymorphism and, 217, 260–262, 266–269
InputStream class, 14
instance variables, 165–167
instanceof keyword, 63
int keyword, 63
int primitives, 90, 92, 131, 133, 135
Integrated Development Environments (IDEs), 21, 59, 145–146, 403
interface keyword, 63, 222–223
interfaces. *See also specific interfaces*
examples of, 242–244
implementing polymorphism via, 262–263, 269–272
overview, 222–224
programming to, 264–265, 273–276
Internet Message Access Protocol (IMAP), 398
Internet Protocol (IP) networks, 396–398
interpreter, 22–26, 330
interpreter switches, 22
IP (Internet Protocol) networks, 396–398
is-a relationship, 261–263, 294
iteration statements, 44, 54–60

J

J2EE (Java 2 Enterprise Edition), 326, 333–335, 389–393
J2ME (Java 2 Micro Edition), 326, 331–333, 365–369
J2ME MIDlets, 364–369
J2SE (Java 2 Standard Edition), 106, 326, 327–331
J2SE 1.4.2 API specification, 17
J2SE 5.0 API specification, 18
J2SE 6 API specification, 18–19
J2SE source files, 106
Jacobson, Ivar, 290
JAD (Java Application Descriptor), 368
Jalopy tool, 59

JAR files, 368
jar tool, 330
Java Abstract Window Toolkit (AWT) API, 15, 329, 372
Java API for XML Web Services (JAX-WS), 399
Java API for XML-based Remote Procedure Call (JAX-RPC), 398–399
Java applets, 369–371
Java Application Descriptor (JAD), 368
Java applications
naming conventions, 141–142
vs. Java applets, 370
web, 334, 362, 363, 402, 403
Web Start, 373
Java Basic Input/Output (I/O) API, 14, 329
Java classes. *See* classes
Java Collections Framework, 12–13
Java Community Process (JCP) homepage, 333
Java compiler (javac), 19–22, 330
Java Core Language, 329
Java Database Connectivity (JDBC) API, 329, 341–342
Java Development Kit. *See* JDK
Java EE. *See* J2EE
Java Enterprise Edition. *See* J2EE
Java forums, 336–337
Java interpreter (java), 22–26, 330
Java language
compiling source files, 20–21
strongly typed, 140–141
Java ME (Micro Edition). *See* J2ME
Java Message Service (JMS) API, 344
Java Micro Edition (ME). *See* J2ME
Java Naming and Directory Interface. *See* JNDI
Java Networking API, 14–15, 329
Java objects. *See* objects
Java packages. *See* packages
Java platforms, 326–337
J2EE (Enterprise Edition), 326, 333–335, 389–393
J2ME (Micro Edition), 326, 331–333, 365–369

J2SE (Standard Edition), 106, 326, 327–331
  overview, 326–327
`java` prefix, 17
Java Remote Method Protocol (JRMP), 338
Java RMI API, 329, 337–339
Java Runtime Environment (JRE), 328–329, 330
Java SE. *See* J2SE
Java Servlet API, 400–401
Java Specification Requests (JSRs), 333–334
Java Standard Edition. *See* J2SE
Java statements. *See* statements
Java Swing API, 15–17, 329, 371–373
Java technologies, 323–357
`java` tool, 330
Java User Group (JUG), 336
Java Utilities API, 12–13, 17–19, 329
Java Virtual Machines. *See* JVMs
Java web services, 334, 388, 394–396
Java Web Services Development Pack (JWSDP), 394
Java Web Start, 373
`javac` (Java compiler), 19–22, 330
`java.class.path` property, 25
`java.class.version` property, 25
`javadoc` tool, 330
`java.home` property, 25
Java-IDL, 338
`java.io` package, 14, 329
`java.lang` package, 12
Javalobby site, 389
JavaMail API, 396–398
`java.naming` package, 329
`java.net` package, 14–15, 329
`java.nio` package, 14
`javap` tool, 330
JavaRanch site, 336–337, 389
`java.rmi` package, 329, 337
JavaScript API, 360–364
JavaServer Faces (JSF) API, 389, 392, 395, 402–403
JavaServer Pages (JSP), 333, 400–403
JavaServer Pages Standard Tag Library (JSTL), 392
`java.sql`, 329
`java.swing` package, 15–17

`java.util` package, 12–13, 17–19
`java.vendor` property, 25
`java.vendor.url` property, 25
`java.version` property, 25
`javaw` command, 23
`javax` prefix, 17
`javax.awt` package, 15, 329
`javax.ejb` package, 404
`javax.io` package, 329
`javax.jms` package, 344
`javax.lang` package, 329
`javax.mail` package, 397
`javax.net` package, 14, 329
`javax.servlet` package, 400
`javax.sql`, 329
`javax.xml.rpc` package, 398
JAX-RPC (Java API for XML-based Remote
  Procedure Call), 398–399
JAX-WS (Java API for XML Web Services), 399
`jconsole` tool, 26, 330
JCP (Java Community Process) homepage, 333
`jdb` tool, 330
JDBC (Java Database Connectivity) API, 329,
  341–342
JDBC drivers, 341
JDK (Java Development Kit)
  contents of, 19, 20, 26, 329–330
  described, 329
  obtaining, 330–331
  third-party sources, 331
JDK bin folder, 20
JDocs, 106
JMS (Java Message Service) API, 344
JNDI (Java Naming and Directory Interface),
  342–343
JNDI API, 342–343
`JPDA` tool, 330
jQuery JavaScript Library, 362
JRE (Java Runtime Environment), 328–329,
  330–331
JRMP (Java Remote Method Protocol), 338
JSF (JavaServer Faces) API, 389, 392, 395, 402–403

JSFtutorials.net site, 389
JSP (JavaServer Pages), 333, 400–403
JSRs (Java Specification Requests), 333–334
JSTL (JavaServer Pages Standard Tag Library), 392
JUG (Java User Group), 336
JVMs (Java Virtual Machines)
    contents of, 328
    Java applets and, 369–371
    new operator and, 135–136
    sharing via RMI API, 336–337
    Squawk, 332–333
JWSDP (Java Web Services Development Pack), 394
JXplorer browser, 343

K

K Virtual machine (KVM), 332
keystrokes, 85
keywords, 46, 55, 63–65. *See also specific keywords*
KVM (K Virtual machine), 332

labeled statement, 43
language code, 25
LDAP browsers, 343
LearnKey technical support, 423
length method, 103–104
less than (<) operator, 89–90
less than or equal to (<=) operator, 89–90
line.separator property, 25
Linux operating system, 330
literals, 142–143
LiveScript, 362
local variables, 162–165, 167
log files, 273–276
logical AND operator (&&), 92–95
logical conditional operators, 94
logical negation (!) operator, 93–95
logical operators, 92–95

logical OR operator (||), 92–95
long keyword, 63
long primitive, 92, 134, 135
loops, 55, 56–58, 139
Lorensen, William, 290

M

manageability, 390
management and security technologies, 334
marshalling, 339
MasterExam, 422–423
ME (Micro Edition). *See* J2ME
Message-Driven Bean, 405
method inputs, 168–171
method outputs, 172–173
method parameters, 165, 167, 339
methods. *See also specific methods*
    arguments, 168–169, 264, 265
    chaining, 107
    constructing, 168–173
    overriding, 220–221
    passing objects by reference, 170–171
    passing primitives by value, 169–170, 171
    returning variables via, 173
Micro Edition (ME). *See* J2ME
MIDlets, J2ME, 364–369
MIDP (Mobile Information Device Profile), 332,
    365–366
MIME (Multipurpose Internet Mail Extensions), 398
minus sign (-), 298
mobile devices, 223, 331–333, 335, 364–369
Mobile Information Device Profile (MIDP), 332,
    365–366
model-view-controller (MVC), 17, 333
modulus (%) operator, 87
multiplication (*) operator, 87
multiplicities, 193–200
multiplicity indicators, 305–307
Multipurpose Internet Mail Extensions (MIME), 398
MVC (model-view-controller), 17, 333

N

naming conventions, 141–142
native keyword, 63
New I/O API, 14
new keyword, 63
new operator, 135–136
non-logical expressions, 94
not equal to (!) operator, 91–92
null literal, 63

O

Object class, 224
object functionality, 229–230
Object Management Group. *See* OMG
Object Modeling Technique (OMT), 290
object-oriented analysis (OOA), 290
object-oriented design (OOD), 290
object-oriented software engineering (OOSE), 290
objects, 134–138
    compiling/running, 137–138
    examples of, 145
    getters/setters, 195, 230–231
    multiplicity, 193–200
    overview, 134–135
    passing to methods, 170–171
    polymorphic, 261–262
    using, 136–138
    vs. classes, 135–136
OMG (Object Management Group), 290–291
OMG UML specifications, 290, 291
OMT (Object Modeling Technique), 290
OOA (object-oriented analysis), 290
OOD (object-oriented design), 290
OOSE (object-oriented software engineering), 290
operands, 82, 83
operating systems, 25, 330–331
operators. *See also specific operators*
    arithmetic, 87–89
    assignment, 84–87
    association, 82, 83
    equality, 91–92
    fundamental, 82–95
    logical, 92–95
    overview, 82–83
    precedence, 82, 83
    relational, 89–92
OR operator (| |), 92–93, 95
os.arch property, 25
os.name property, 25
os.version property, 25
OutputStream class, 14

P

package attributes, 5
package design, 5–6
package keyword, 63
package statements, 6–7
packaged software, 26–27
package-derived classes, 11–19
package-private modifier, 227–228, 230, 298
packages. *See also specific packages*
    covered on exam, 388, 426–427
    examples of, 7, 11–19
    importing, 6, 7–11
    Java SE, 106, 326, 327–331
    maintaining, 5, 6
    names, 5, 7
    overview, 4–11
    placing source files into, 6
    size, 5
    subpackages, 13
    user-defined, 21–22
packaging, 4
parenthesis ( ), 99, 104, 434
path separator, 25
path.separator property, 25
PBP (Personal Basis Profile), 332, 367
PDAs (personal digital assistants), 331–333, 365
performance, 390

period (.), 22
Personal Basis Profile (PBP), 332, 367
personal digital assistants (PDAs), 331–333, 365
Personal Profile (PP), 332
plus sign (+), 298
point-to-point (PTP) messaging, 344
polymorphic objects, 261–262
polymorphism, 259–288
    abstract classes, 262, 265
    in code, 263–264
    examples of, 265–276
    inheritance and, 217, 260–262, 266–269
    method arguments, 264, 265
    overview, 260
    unidirectional, 270
    via implementing interfaces, 262–263, 269–272
POP (Post Office Protocol), 398
Post Office Protocol (POP), 398
postfix decrement operator (x--), 88, 89
pound sign (#), 298
PP (Personal Profile), 332
prefix decrement operator (--x), 88, 90
prefix increment operator (++x), 88
Premerlani, William, 290
primitives, 130–134. *See also specific primitives*
    as arguments, 169–170
    arrays of, 138–139
    examples of, 143–144
    overview, 130–131
    passing to methods by value, 169–170, 171
    types of, 131–133, 134, 135
    vs. wrapper class, 133
    wrapper class, 144
`private` keyword, 63, 227–231
`private` modifiers, 227–230, 298, 299
profiles, 332, 365–368
programming. *See also* code
    fundamental statements, 43–61
    to interfaces, 264–265, 273–276
    pseudo-code, 61–67
`Properties` class, 24

`PropertiesManager` class, 24
`protected` keyword, 63, 227–229
`protected` modifiers, 227–230, 298
pseudo-code algorithms, 61–67
pseudo-code assignment operator (:=), 85
pseudo-code conventions, 64
pseudo-code exercises, 65–67
PTP (point-to-point) messaging, 344
`public` keyword, 63, 227–229
`public` modifiers, 227–230, 298
publish/subscribe messaging, 344

R

RAD (Rapid Application Development), 402
`Random` class, 13
`RandomAccessFile` class, 14
Rapid Application Development (RAD), 402
RDBMS (Relational Database Management
    System), 340
`Reader` class, 14
realization class relationship, 294
refactoring code, 60–61
reference variables, 91–92
regular expressions, 13
Relational Database Management System
    (RDBMS), 340
relational operators, 89–92
relationship specifiers, 305–308
reliability, 390
Remote Method Invocation. *See* RMI
Remote Method Invocation over Internet Inter-Orb
    Protocol (RMI-IIOP), 338
`replace` method, 104, 107
reserved literals, 63
`return` keyword, 63
return statement, 43, 172
return type, 172
reusability, 390
RMI (Remote Method Invocation) API, 329,
    337–339

RMI client, 337–338
RMI server, 337–338
rmic tool, 330
RMI-IIOP (Remote Method Invocation over
    Internet Inter-Orb Protocol), 338
role names, 307–308
Rumbaugh, James, 290

S

SAAJ (SOAP with Attachment API
    for JAVA), 396
scalability, 390
SCJD (Sun Certified Java Developer) exam, 339
scope, 162–167
SE (Standard Edition). *See* J2SE
security, 390
semicolon (;), 22, 44
Serializable interface, 405
server-side technologies, 387–417
    dynamic web content, 399–403
    enterprise business solutions, 404–405
    Enterprise JavaBeans (EJBs), 404–405
    J2EE, 389–393
    Java Servlet, 400–401
    JavaMail API, 396–398
    JavaServer Faces, 389, 392, 395, 402–403
    JavaServer Pages, 400–403
    JAX-RPC, 398–399
    overview, 388
    SMTP, 396–398
    SOAP, 395–396
    solutions, 393–405
    UDDI, 396
    WSDL, 396
    XML, 394–396
servlets, 400–401, 403
Session Bean, 405
session tracking, 402
setProperty method, 24
setters/getters, 195, 230–231
short keyword, 63

short primitive, 134
Simple Mail Transfer Protocol (SMTP), 396–398
Simple Object Access Protocol (SOAP), 395–396
skeletons, 338
"skin-able" capability, 372
SMTP (Simple Mail Transfer Protocol), 396–398
SMTP servers, 396–397
SOAP (Simple Object Access Protocol), 395–396
SOAP with Attachment API for JAVA (SAAJ), 396
sockets, 339
Softerra LDAP browser, 343
Solaris operating system, 330
source code. *See* code
source files, 6, 20–21, 106. *See also* code
SQL (Structured Query Language), 340, 341
Squawk, 332–333
Standard Edition. *See* J2SE
startWith method, 105
statement-related keywords, 63–65
statements, 41–80. *See also specific statements*
    assignment, 44–46
    combined, 45
    conditional, 44, 46–54
    expression, 42, 44–46
    fundamental, 43–61
    iteration, 44, 54–60
    overview, 42–44
    transfer of control, 44
static imports, 9
static keyword, 63
strictfp keyword, 63
String class, 97, 101–107
String concatenation operator (+), 97–101
string objects, 95–107
StringBuffer class, 97
StringBuilder class, 97
strings
    bugs in, 100–101
    creating, 96–97
    overview, 95–97
StringTokenizer, 13
Structured Query Language. *See* SQL

stubs, 337–338
subclasses, 220, 222, 227, 229, 264
subpackages, 13
substring method, 106, 107
subtraction (–) operator, 87
Sun Certified Java Developer (SCJD) exam, 339
Sun JDK compiler, 57
Sun Small Object Programmable Technology (Sun
    SPOTs), 332–333
super keyword, 63, 221
superclasses, 218, 220, 221, 228, 264
switch keyword, 63
switch statement, 43, 46, 52–54, 64
switches, 22
synchronized keyword, 63
synchronized statement, 43
system coupling, 5
system properties, 25
system requirements, 422

T

tag libraries, 392, 402
technical support, 423
telnet utility, 397
temporary association, 192–193, 194
TheServerSide site, 389
thin clients, 360–364
this keyword, 166
throw keyword, 63
throw statement, 43
throws keyword, 63
tilde (~), 298
time zone, 25
toString method, 98–99
transfer of control statements, 44
transient keyword, 63
trim method, 106, 107
true conditions, 50
true literal, 63
try keyword, 63
try-catch-finally statement, 43

U

UDDI (Universal Description, Discovery, and
    Integration), 396
UML (Unified Modeling Language), 289–320
    associations, 301–308
    attributes, 295–298
    classes, 293–295
    code engineering from, 294–295
    comments/notes, 303
    graphic paths, 302–305
    interfaces, 291, 293–295
    multiplicity indicators, 305–307
    object-oriented principles, 307
    operations, 295–298
    overview, 290–292
    relationships, 195, 305–308
    role names, 307–308
    visibility modifiers, 298–301
UML diagrams
    code engineering from, 294
    considerations, 297, 303
    creating basic, 299–301
    drawing from Java API specification,
        304–305
    types of, 291
UML elements, 292–301, 307
UML package icons, 292
UML tools, 299–301
unboxing, 133
Unicode character strings, 95
Unicode Standard, 96, 429–431
unidirectional polymorphism, 270
Unified Modeling Language. *See* UML
Universal Description, Discovery, and Integration
    (UDDI), 396
user.dir property, 25
user.home property, 25
user.language property, 25
username, 25
user.name property, 25
user.timezone property, 25

validity, 390
variable scope, 162–167
variables
    assigning values to, 84–85
    casting, 140–141
    declaring, 165
    instance, 165–167
    local, 162–165, 167
    naming, 141–142
    passing by reference, 170–171
    passing by value, 169–170, 171
    primitive vs. object, 142
    reference, 91–92
    returning via methods, 173
    strongly typed, 140–141
vendor, Java platform, 25
-version option, 25–26
visibility modifiers, 298–301
void keyword, 63
volatile keyword, 63

web applications, 334, 362, 363, 388, 402, 403
web containers, 399–400
web content, 399–403

Web Service Definition Language (WSDL), 396
web services, 334, 388, 394–396
Web Start applications, 373
web tier, 391–392
while keyword, 63
while statement, 42, 55, 58–59, 64
Wikipedia, 399
Windows operating system, 330
WORA (write once, run anywhere), 329
wrapper class, 133, 144
write once, run anywhere (WORA), 329
Writer class, 14
WSDL (Web Service Definition Language), 396

x-- (postfix decrement operator), 88, 89
x++ (postfix increment operator), 88
--x (prefix decrement operator), 88, 89
++x (prefix increment operator), 88
XML (Extensible Markup Language), 363,
    394–396
XML files, 335
XML specification, 395
XML tags, 395
XML-based messaging protocols, 394
XML-based Remote Procedure Call, 397